Also by Robert Palmer

Baby, That Was Rock and Roll:
The Legendary Leiber and Stoller (1978)

A Tale of Two Cities: Memphis Rock and New Orleans Roll (1979)

Jerry Lee Lewis Rocks! (1981)

Deep Blues: A Musical and Cultural History
of the Mississippi Delta (1981)

The Rolling Stones (1983)

Rock & Roll: An Unruly History (1995)

BLUES&
CHAOS

The Music Writing of
ROBERT PALMER

Robert Palmer

Edited by Anthony DeCurtis

Scribner
New York   London   Toronto   Sydney

Scribner
A Division of Simon & Schuster, Inc.
1230 Avenue of the Americas
New York, NY 10020

First Scribner hardcover edition November 2009

SCRIBNER and design are registered trademarks of The Gale Group, Inc., used under license by Simon & Schuster, Inc., the publisher of this work.

For information about special discounts for bulk purchases, please contact Simon & Schuster Special Sales at 1-866-506-1949 or business@simonandschuster.com.

The Simon & Schuster Speakers Bureau can bring authors to your live event. For more information or to book an event contact the Simon & Schuster Speakers Bureau at 1-866-248-3049 or visit our website at www.simonspeakers.com.

Designed by Carla Jayne Jones

Manufactured in the United States of America

10   9   8   7   6   5   4   3   2   1

Library of Congress Control Number: 2009014346

ISBN 978-1-4165-9974-6
ISBN 978-1-4391-0963-2 (ebook)

Contents

Flirtations with Chaos:
The Life and Work of Robert Palmer

"Don't worry, I know everything": That's the way music critic Ira Robbins once described the tone of Bob Palmer's writing to me. We both laughed when he said that, because his statement perfectly got at Palmer's ability to mix erudition with ease, to reassure his readers with his confidence and command. But, despite the arrogance that remark might imply, Bob was never showy about his knowledge. In a style that blended elegance and hipster enthusiasm, he would travel deeper and deeper into his subject, bringing his readers along with him in the interest of turning them on to something he loved.

Bob is best known as the author of *Deep Blues: A Musical and Cultural History of the Mississippi Delta*, which was published in 1981 and is still in print. It remains essential reading for anyone interested in the indelible music that, drawing on its African roots, originated in the Delta, moved to Chicago, and made an inestimable contribution to the creation of rock & roll. In his conclusion to that book, Bob writes of the blues, "A literary and musical form . . . a fusion of music and poetry accomplished at a very high emotional temperature . . . these are different ways of describing the same thing. A gigantic field of feeling . . . that's a way of describing something enduring, something that could be limitless. How much thought . . . can be hidden in a few short lines of poetry? How much history can be transmitted by pressure on a guitar string? The thought of generations, the history of every human being who's ever felt the blues come down like showers of rain."

The notion that "pressure on a guitar string," the singular tone of a musician's playing, could convey all that is important in human history lies at the center of Bob's thinking, writing, and playing—at the center of his being, really. He was not a religious person in any traditional sense; he was probably closer to a pagan. But music was one of the means through which he sought transcendence. "For Bob, music was a religion," says Robbie Robertson, the former guitarist and main songwriter in the Band, who knew Palmer for many years. "It would stream out of him in the same way that somebody would be trying to impress you with their knowledge of God."

Anyone who read Bob's work, and certainly anyone who knew him, was aware of the stunning range and depth of his musical passion. It wasn't until I began working on this anthology, however, that I truly began to understand the extent of his achievement. Everyone I mentioned Bob to, of course, knew about his writing on the blues—but nearly everyone also had a recommendation from well beyond that world. As with so many great writers and thinkers, each person I spoke to seemed to have his or her own version of Bob Palmer and stories about the impact his work made on them.

Jazz devotees discussed his writing with the greatest respect. Fans of classic rock raved about his pieces on the Rolling Stones and Led Zeppelin. Veterans of New York's punk scene expressed deep gratitude for his vital support of that music in *The New York Times* and elsewhere. Avant-gardists talked about his pieces on Philip Glass, LaMonte Young, and Steve Reich. His writing about the Master Musicians of Jajouka excited interest in Moroccan music, and world music in general, nearly four decades ago, long before it became fashionable.

But more extraordinary than even how many different types of music

Bob could write about compellingly was how multifaceted his knowledge was. No aspect of his understanding seemed to cancel out any other; in fact, in the rarest of gifts, each element of his comprehension enhanced the others. He was a musician himself, of course, but his writing about music was never insiderish or unnecessarily technical. The sheer physical *sound* of music was his great subject, but when he discussed lyrics, he did so with the sensitivity of a literary critic. He loved and believed in music's mythic qualities, but that faith never compromised his grasp of the social and compositional components of musical creation.

Bob viewed music as a vehicle of transcendence but wrote and spoke colorfully about the nitty-gritty, down-to-earth contexts and larger-than-life personalities that gave it birth. It's almost as if, if you read Bob, you didn't need to read anyone else—his vision of music was so complete. Reviewing *Deep Blues* in *The Nation*, David A. Lusterman concluded that "at heart, it's a book for anyone who ever wonders where music, any music, really comes from." That understanding of music's origins in the human spirit suffuses every word that Bob wrote.

This collection, then, attempts to convey the character and breadth of Bob's achievement, a daunting task. It would be a foolish one as well, were it not for the ability of Bob's writing to communicate in whatever context it appears. This could have been a rock collection or a punk collection or a blues collection, and, hopefully, such anthologies and others will follow. But to fully comprehend Bob's magnificent gifts, I believe, you need to see them all on display. The array of musical subjects in this book is part of its very point.

As the scale of this book would suggest, Bob was extremely prolific. In addition to *Deep Blues*, he wrote a number of other books: *Baby, That Was Rock and Roll: The Legendary Leiber and Stoller* (1978); *A Tale of Two Cities: Memphis Rock and New Orleans Roll* (1979); *Jerry Lee Lewis Rocks!* (1981); *The Rolling Stones* (1983); and *Rock & Roll: An Unruly History* (1995). From 1981 until 1988, he was the chief pop music critic at *The New York Times*, the first person to hold that title, and he wrote for the *Times* for a number of years before and after that. He began writing for *Rolling Stone* in the early seventies—about jazz, blues, Moroccan music, soul, R&B, and, of course, rock & roll—and continued to do so as a contributing editor until his death. He wrote liner notes for dozens of releases, and his work appeared in virtually every music magazine—*Down Beat*, *Crawdaddy*, *Guitar World*, *Musician*, to cite just a few—that published while he was alive.

And he wasn't exclusively a writer. After he left the *Times* and moved back to the South in 1987, he inspired Matthew Johnson, a blues obsessive, to launch Fat Possum Records in Oxford, Mississippi, where Bob was teaching at the University of Mississippi. Bob produced raw, unvarnished, and influential albums by Junior Kimbrough and R. L. Burnside for the label and wrote liner notes to accompany them. He had previously brought national exposure to those two artists and a number of others from the north Mississippi hill country in the riveting 1993 documentary *Deep Blues: A Musical Pilgrimage to the Crossroads*, which he wrote and hosted and which Robert Mugge directed. He also wrote and codirected the documentary *The World According to John Coltrane* (1990).

Impressive as it is, that list does little to capture the texture or importance—the sheer impact—of Bob's work. That's because, whether in his books or in an overnight review, Bob had a way of getting readers to be as passionate about music as he was. He felt the music deeply and personally, and he made his readers feel it that way too.

Musician and music writer Ted Drozdowski said it best in the obituary he wrote for *The Boston Phoenix* when Bob died in 1997. "He was instantly funny, engaging, incisive, and inclusive," Drozdowski wrote about his first meeting with Bob in 1992. "And thanks to his introductions, I was soon able to travel through the dusty backroads of Mississippi, learning about the blues in its birthland firsthand. In a way, he'd set me on that journey nearly a decade earlier when I'd found his book *Deep Blues* (Penguin). I was so charmed by his writing, his knowledge, and his obvious love for the music that I treated it as a Bible, reading each chapter and then buying every record it mentioned. It was a post-grad-level course. But it was nothing like the firsthand encounters with the music I've had in places like Holly Springs, Clarksdale, Greenville, and Rolling Fork. Those have been experiences that have changed my life and broadened my understanding of humanity and myself.

"How do you pay someone back for that? Especially when he's gone."

Many of Bob's friends and family, and many of his readers, wondered about that, too, when Bob died. They all would agree, I hope, that a collection like this is one way to start repaying the debt, while making it possible for many more people to accept the invaluable gifts that Bob had to give.

The one quality that runs through every aspect of Bob's relationship to music is his conviction that music provided a route of transcendence. I believe that, for him, that process began when music enabled him to transcend the enclosed, segregated white world of his upbringing in Little Rock, Arkansas, in the 1950s.

"I personally integrated in reverse all the black rhythm and blues shows that came to the auditorium in Little Rock starting when I was fifteen years old, and that was in 1960," Bob told National Public Radio in 1995. "There were no integrated shows in Arkansas. I was the first white kid to start showing up at all the black shows. It was such a novelty that nobody thought to stop me, even though I was only fifteen years old and I was going into these places where people were drinking and pulling knives and all sorts of things, you know.

"But I was able to go in and to hear people like Sam Cooke and Otis Redding, Solomon Burke, all these great, great people," he continued. "That really was what got me started in the music was going to those shows. I rarely missed one. By the time I was college age, there were several more local white kids going to these shows, but there was only me to begin with. And then when I was in college I was the only white musician in an otherwise all-black band that played around almost entirely in black joints. I had a real sort of involvement in black music and black culture that I really think was possible because I grew up in Arkansas at that particular time."

No question, Bob was an undeniable product of the South of that era. The segregation that was meant to "protect" young white people like him from being infected by black culture—and the language of the early reporting on rock & roll and racial mixing was just that charged, if not worse—made it and the secret world surrounding it all the more alluring to him. Just as rock & roll itself was exploding on the national scene, Little Rock was the site of some of the most bitter integration battles in the South. To a bookish young man with a flair for rebellion, the hardness of the lines that were drawn must have made them all the more desirable to cross.

Writing decades later about the experiences crossing the racial divide that music made possible for him, Bob explained, "Basically a suburban kid, a music freak, and a loner, I now felt that I had penetrated some underground cult or secret society, one that somehow thrived in the shadows, out beyond the neat suburban plots and well-lit streets of familiar white-bread reality. Penetrated, but not like an anthropologist braving some primitive backwater. I had been accepted; whatever this new world signified, I was somehow part of it."

There were even specific points of initiation. In his 1995 NPR interview, Bob declared that "everybody has that magic moment when the music rocked them for the first time." That was typical of his belief that music could, indeed must, change lives. He was a rock & roll Paul on the road to boogie-woogie Damascus, and hearing the Coasters sing "Searchin'" and "Young Blood" transformed him forever. "I remember that coming on when I was about eleven or twelve years old," he recalled of those songs. "I had been hearing pre–rock & roll popular music on the radio for a few years prior to that. I was very interested in music but I wasn't that crazy about what was passing for pop music at the time.

"Then I heard 'Searchin'' by the Coasters and a little after that I heard Ray Charles, and that was the music that really turned me around. . . . I think it was really the quality of the voices. It was the fact that these black singers—there was all this grit in their voices, and these kinds of sounds like they were maybe ripping their vocal cords a little bit when they were singing. It seemed to convey so much emotion and energy and excitement, you know. Just the sound of the voices and the texture of the voices and the way that the voices blended together had a kind of harmony that was not conventional harmony—it was something else. Having heard very conventional harmony, you know, all my life, having never heard blues or even any really down-home country and western music, but just having heard that fifties white-bread pop, the first time I heard black voices and black rhythms, I was just floored. I probably never got over it."

From those years on, Bob would view music through an uncompromising African-American lens. Having grown up where he grew up, having seen what he had seen, having visited the forbidden realms he visited, he would never be guilty of downplaying the contributions of black musicians in any genre of music he listened to, played, or covered. That would be the ultimate betrayal for him—one he was surrounded by in so much of the music press, just as he was surrounded by segregation in the South. In his view, it was just plain wrong. He knew the unruly history of rock & roll as well as anyone, and from that vantage figures like Ike Turner, Howlin' Wolf, and Muddy Waters were as important, if not more so, than the likes of Elvis Presley, the Beatles, and Bob Dylan.

Some white musicians could earn his respect, but only if they shared his faith—and were willing to pay the price. This exchange between Bob and fellow white Southerner Jerry Lee Lewis says it all.

> "I read awhile back that you believe you're a sinner and going to hell for playing rock & roll," I said. "Is that true?" Lewis looked me right in the eye. "Yep," he said. "I *know* the right way. I was raised a good Christian. But I couldn't make it. . . . Too weak, I guess." But, I argued, why would playing rock & roll damn you to hell? Lewis looked at me as if I'd just asked an impossibly stupid question. "I can't picture Jesus Christ," he said evenly, "doin' a whole lotta shakin'."

Bob and I were close, but we rarely saw each other. Even though he had already well established his reputation, I hadn't met or spoken with him until I became the editor of *Rolling Stone*'s record-review section in 1990. He hadn't been doing much writing for the magazine, and he was among the first writers I sought to bring back into its pages.

The frequent and riveting telephone conversations I had with Bob in the editorial—and strangely intimate—relationship we struck up once prompted writer Daisann McLane to suggest that I write a story called "Calling Robert Palmer." Bob had a great voice, a slow Arkansas drawl that he used as an effective counterbalance to his lambent intelligence. He would render the wildest ideas, the most impossible experiences, as if he were just whiling away the minutes until something genuinely interesting came to mind. You got the sense that, just as in his writing, he knew what he was doing with his cadences and enjoyed their lulling effect. Once we got the business at hand out of the way, Bob would, at my prompting, entertain me with stories about evenings spent at the Dakota with John Lennon and Yoko Ono, recording sessions with Keith Richards and Bono, juke-joint nights with menacing blues guitarist Junior Kimbrough, tours of New Orleans with Robert Plant and Jimmy Page.

There's no question that, along with his command of music history and the passion that suffused his tastes, Bob won the respect of musicians because he was a musician himself. He played clarinet and saxophone in bands in Arkansas and Memphis, and later, after he moved north in 1967, in the Insect Trust, the eclectic quintet (plus innumerable sidemen) that released two prized albums, *The Insect Trust* (1969) and *Hoboken Saturday Night* (1970). In addition, he played with the visionary Ornette Coleman (on Coleman's 1973 album *Dancing in Your Head*, among other times), and he wasn't loathe to jam with some of his more famous subjects either. "He was one of those writers who had a very broad knowledge of all kinds of music, and he understood about the backgrounds of music. He understood about all the different strands that make up the popular music of America," Mick Jagger said when I interviewed him for Bob's obituary in *Rolling Stone*. "He respected it all, and was enthusiastic about it. And he wasn't snobbish. He had a very good and interesting take on it all. His background and his love of blues and folk music was a great bond as far as musicians were concerned. That's how I remember him. He would introduce you to all kinds of new things and old things—he was just very in touch with it."

Jagger paused for a moment. "And he loved to come and jam and play the clarinet!" he continued. "That's what he used to do. I remember him coming to the studio and listening to our new tracks or something, and then he'd go out and jam on a blues."

Of course, Bob loved the Rolling Stones and wrote about them frequently, including in his book *The Rolling Stones*, excerpted here. He had also signed on to work with Jagger on his autobiography, a project that Jagger eventually decided he did not want to complete.

Bob also played clarinet on a track called "Silver and Gold" that Bono, Keith Richards, and Ron Wood recorded for Little Steven Van Zandt's 1988 *Artists United Against Apartheid* album. In addition, he served as something of a consultant for the roots sound that Bono was seeking for the song. "When we were doing 'Silver and Gold' with Keith and Ronnie, it was a big weekend," Bono recalled. "I'd just gotten back from Africa and ended up at this Artists Against Apartheid session in New York. This is before *The Joshua Tree*; actually, we were just getting into that.

"We kind of wrote ['Silver and Gold'], recorded it, and did everything in about forty-eight hours. I got him to play clarinet on it. He's on the track. It's pretty free-form, so in the mix he's not in it as much as he was on the day, but when he's there, he's there. He was kind of embarrassed about it all—'Oh, you don't really want me to play on this—take me out! Take me out!'

"I knew that I didn't know much. I had to kind of go, 'Is this the kind of thing you mean?' I really was a student. I still am, but back then, I knew fuck-all about American music, but I was just naïve enough for that not to stop me. He'd go, 'Yep, yep, yeah, you got it.' I'm glad of that—he was the insurance policy! If he thought it was okay, we could put it out."

Later, when U2 began to explore American music in earnest, Bob took the singer and U2 bassist Adam Clayton to guitarist Junior Kimbrough's juke joint near Holly Springs, Mississippi, on a kind of educational road trip. "*Deep Blues*—that was it," Bono recalled about the book that first developed his understanding of the blues. "Around about the time that we were starting our naïve journey into American roots music, Adam and I met up with him in Memphis, and we went out on a trip into the backwoods, where there was an illegal Sunday juke joint.

"We traveled way, way out," Bono continued, "and everybody was drinking that moonshine stuff. It was like peach schnapps. Everybody was drinking moonshine, and it was extraordinary—like an IV introduction to the blues. He was like this übertutor. Hanging around with him was like doing a PhD in whatever subject he was interested in. I guess some people saw him as a kind of boho, but I saw him as this gentleman of the South. This academic kind of guy, who was the greatest introduction to the blues you could meet. And the more I got to know him, as eclectic as his taste in music was, he had this way of making it very accessible. I thought it was great that he was in *The New York Times*, because he could open up this world not just to music fans but to regular folks. He made me laugh. It was, like, from Sonic Youth to Rod Stewart! I just thought, this is great. He just didn't see the world with the same kind of eyes. It was like, Is there a voice? Is there a tune? Is there a spirit here I hadn't come across before?"

Robbie Robertson first met Palmer in Arkansas, where he spent considerable time in the early sixties as the teenage guitarist in Ronnie Hawkins and the Hawks. As a teenage sax player in Arkansas, Palmer had worked some of the same venues as the Hawks, and he recalled that they "were especially admired for their tough takes on the most intense black R&B of the day. . . . The Hawks also had a reputation for pill popping, whoring, and brawling that was second to none." Bob later wrote about Robertson and the Band, once for a 1991 *Rolling Stone* interview, when he got together with Robertson in New Orleans, where Bob was living at the time.

"When we were in New Orleans talking, we would go out and drive around and go through some different neighborhoods, and it was great with him," Robertson recalled. "How colorful his musical knowledge was from one ward to the next. You'd be driving and you'd go through the Thirteenth Ward or something, and he'd say, 'Oh, this is the area where Chief Jolie taught the songs to the Meters, and eventually they hooked up and became the Wild Tchoupitoulas . . .'—it was just such rich knowledge. When you're in New Orleans and you're driving around doing that, it really hits you deeply, because it's so colorful and right in front of your eyes."

Bob's breadth of tastes should not be misinterpreted as a lack of standards, or as a willingness to embrace whatever trend was making its way down the pike. And he did have certain blind spots—blind spots, that is, if you disagreed with him. Bob was a believer in authenticity, and, as a result, manufactured pop artists like Madonna, for example, were essentially meaningless to him. He viewed them as if he were an anthropologist who had discovered a ritual of some vague familiarity, but whose significance was not merely unknowable but not worth knowing.

Here is Bob's response to Madonna's first concert tour, in 1985, which he reviewed when it stopped at Radio City Music Hall in New York for three nights. "The Music Hall crowd, primed by the records and videos, shrieked delightedly when they first caught sight of Madonna, before she had sung a note," Bob wrote. "They kept shrieking for every song, their Pavlovian responses suggesting the results of an experiment set up by behavioral psychologists in order to prove that Skinner was right after all.

"Because the fact of the matter," he continued, "was that Madonna—

backed by a competent but rather ordinary touring band—simply didn't sing very well. Her intonation was atrocious; she sang sharp and she sang flat, and the combination of her unsure pitch and thin, quavery vocal timbre made the held notes at the end of her phrases sound like they were crawling off somewhere to die. In her higher range, she had a more attractive sound, with just a smattering of street-corner edginess to it. But this woman needs to see a good vocal coach before she attempts another tour. And one hopes that the next time she performs here, she will have learned not to toss tambourines into the air unless she's going to be able to catch them."

And much as he was an ardent supporter of punk, particularly its noisiest, most intellectually challenging, and most aesthetically brash manifestations, he disdained the Ramones as a one-joke band. Reviewing them in 1978, he wrote, "It is difficult to believe that people have formed serious intellectual attachments to the Ramones and consider their music great or even good rock & roll. Rock & roll music has always had room for passionate performers who intentionally circumscribed their range of expression in order to make a point; it has often been best when it was simplest. But the Ramones do not project passion, they play dumb in order to look cool. And they have circumscribed their music to such an extent that the only thing it effectively satirizes is itself. They are the kind of joke one tires of very rapidly."

And even his Southern-bred modesty concealed a deep confidence. Bob never felt the need to assert his views aggressively because he was so certain they were true. Asked about his rigorously understated portrayal of Don Corleone in *The Godfather*, Marlon Brando observed that when you have real power you don't have to shout. Bob must have believed that too.

"There was no doubt in my mind that Robert did feel like he had the best musical taste of anybody in the world," Robbie Robertson said, laughing, "and that he was ninety percent right and everybody else was ninety percent wrong. He really felt like, 'Listen, I've devoted more time and more love to this than anybody on the planet possibly can, so I have no competition here.'

"I think that everybody had a very unanimous feeling about him in his writing," Robertson continued. "A love of music was more evident in him than in anybody I ever met. It was so obvious. It was a kind of god to him. And the fact that he had nineteen stories to go with every person or every piece of music that you could bring up was all the evidence you needed."

In addition to sharpening his critical acumen, Bob's understanding of musicians enabled him to assume an intimacy with them in interview situations that few journalists can muster. I recall being floored by this exchange with Eric Clapton in a 1985 *Rolling Stone* interview. Bob's "question" about the sessions for *Layla and Other Assorted Love Songs* (1970)—really more of an extended reverie—has to rank among the greatest interview gambits ever:

> Palmer: The first time I ran into you was during those ses-
> sions at Criteria Recording Studios. There was a lot of dope
> around, especially heroin, and when I showed up, everyone
> was just spread out on the carpet, nodded out. Then you
> appeared in the doorway in an old brown leather jacket,
> with your hair slicked back like a greaser's, looking like you
> hadn't slept in days. You just looked around at the wreck-
> age and said, to nobody in particular, "The boy stood on
> the burning deck/Whence all but he had fled." And then
> you split.
>
> Clapton: Yeah. We were staying in this hotel on the beach, and
> whatever drug you wanted, you could get it at the news-
> stand; the girl would just take your orders. We were on
> the up and the down, the girl and the boy, and the drink
> was usually Ripple or Gallo. Very heavy stuff. I remember
> Ahmet [Ertegun, chairman of Atlantic Records] arriving at
> some point, taking me aside and crying, saying he'd been
> through this shit with Ray [Charles], and he knew where
> this was gonna end, and could I stop now. I said, "I don't
> know what you're talking about, man. This is no problem."
> And, of course, he was dead right.

Of course that conversation introduces another subject that, while damaging his life, likely enhanced Bob's interactions with at least some musicians: his drug use. Bob believed in the ability of psychedelics to provide transcendent experiences, and it's impossible to read his mesmerizing descriptions of his days among the Master Musicians of Jajouka in Morocco without realizing that such experiences were the very point of music for him.

But Bob also used heroin and cocaine, and somewhere along the way contracted the hepatitis C virus that eventually led to liver failure and his death in 1997. While it did not affect the quality of the work he produced, Bob's drug use did sometimes affect his ability to meet deadlines. When he left his job at *The New York Times* and moved back down South in 1988, it was partly in the belief that, as Robbie Robertson put it, "in that part of the country there just wouldn't be as many demons lurking around, tempting him." Needless to say, that did not prove to be true. When people move, their demons tend to travel with them.

Eventually, Bob moved to New Orleans. When I once mentioned that he was living in New Orleans to his friend Townes Van Zandt, the singer shook his head and dropped his face in his hands. "Louisiana would kill a healthy man," he said, finally. Singer-songwriter Eric Andersen once described to me a late-night scene of Bob and Townes embracing each other outside the New York club Tramps, each expressing the wish that they would live to see each other another day.

By the time I began editing Bob in 1990, the rap on him in the publishing world was that he was brilliant but "unreliable." He never missed an important deadline for me, but he would disappear without notice for weeks at a time. He never discussed his drug use with me either—partly because I was a source of good work and income, and partly, I genuinely believe, out of a kind of respect. Still, there were some unmistakable hints. We were discussing his having hepatitis C one time when Bob was living in Little Rock. I asked if he was getting decent health care, and he explained that his physician was Dr. Nick—the infamous Dr. George Nichopoulos, who had supplied Elvis Presley with endless amounts of drugs.

"Dr. Nick is your doctor?" I asked, incredulous. "Well," Bob said in his slowest drawl, "you can talk to Dr. Nick about a lot of things that you can't talk to other doctors about."

Robbie Robertson had a revealing—and darkly funny—exchange with Bob during their 1991 interview in New Orleans. "I remember when we were doing that interview, he really looked unhealthy to me," Robertson recalled about Palmer. "And he behaved unhealthy as well. I was comparing him to the last time I had seen him, and there was something wrong. I thought it was drugs, which probably wasn't far off.

"I remember kidding with him," he continued. "We'd spent some time together and we were hanging out, and he was acting kind of strange and having physical problems. I remember saying to him, 'You know something, Bob? You don't look the part. You'll always look like a bookworm to me. You don't look like a junkie.' And he kind of sniffled and blew his nose, and said, 'Well, I'm from the William Burroughs school of junkies.' And I thought, 'Oh, that's right, there are some like that.'"

When Bob became seriously ill in 1997, many of the people who cared about and respected him—musicians, writers, editors, record-company executives, friends, loved ones—rallied to try to save his life. He didn't have insurance and needed a liver transplant. He was deteriorating rapidly, and before he could even qualify for a transplant, his condition needed to be stabilized. He was flown from New Orleans to New York on a private plane, courtesy of one of his benefactors, and entered Westchester County Medical Center in Valhalla, New York. Then he waited.

In the meantime, friends organized fund-raisers and benefit concerts and tried to solicit donations for his operation. I called a number of artists' managers myself and, in general, got surprisingly generous responses—surprising only because it's typically so easy for such people to say no. In fairness, I came to understand how often they must get approached for help in situations like this, particularly in the U.S., which shamefully lacks a national health-care system.

I spoke to Bob a number of times while he was in the hospital. Initially his mood was upbeat and he seemed genuinely touched by the intense efforts being made on his behalf. Because he'd been relatively isolated from the music community since leaving the *Times* and moving South a decade earlier, he seemed to have grown unaware of the regard and affection people held for him.

When I visited Bob in the hospital, I was shocked at how much he'd deteriorated physically. It seemed unlikely to me that he could survive a transplant, even if a suitable liver became available. He did not last long afterward. He died while listening to Yoko Ono's *Rising*.

A memorial service for Bob was hastily organized—to use the term loosely—in New York. It took place at Tramps, a Chelsea club that has since closed down, on the Sunday after his death. It's always a bit strange to be in a club during off-hours. The daylight coming in from outside drains the room of its magic, the ordinariness of the environment—the tables, chairs, stained floor, lingering smells of detergent and alcohol— undeniably communicating a fall from the Eden of showtime into the dreariness of everyday. A late-November Sunday afternoon at Tramps epitomized such a moment. As a musician and a writer, Bob, I'm sure, experienced many of them.

The room was not nearly as full as it should have been, or as it surely would have been had more time been taken to plan the service and get the word out. But in its own shambling way the event captured something about Bob, who loved flirtations with chaos, both in music and in his life. I wrote something about him and read it, then somehow was drafted as the day's emcee. That was difficult given that I had no idea who was there to speak, read, or play. Again, though, something about feeling so rudderless felt right.

"Bob showed me that writing about music and playing music could be the same thing," said guitarist Lenny Kaye when he came to the stage. Then Kaye, Patti Smith, and guitarist Oliver Ray tore into a visceral musical tribute to Bob. "However fucked-up, transcendent, or humorous the next few minutes may be," Smith said before she began to wail on clarinet and improvise verses based on Palmer's writing, "Bob, it's all for you." Smith also expressed smiling gratitude to Bob as the only critic ever to praise her clarinet playing. A clarinetist himself, Bob was partial to anyone who attempted that instrument. Velvet Underground drummer Maureen Tucker and her band the Kropotkins also performed, as did New York guitarist Gary Lucas.

Everyone's heart was in the right place, and the various appearances occasionally evoked this or that aspect of Bob and his writing. We were all in a daze and, essentially orderless, the event veered wildly in mood.

The person who struck deepest, understandably, was Bob's widow, JoBeth Briton, who bravely rose to speak. The room, of course, fell silent when she took the stage. She sat down in a chair, adjusted the microphone, and simply started talking. She spoke for a long time, at least as I remember it, and was utterly riveting. At once out of control and entirely in command, she careened through an associative reminiscence of their life together that was unlike anything I've ever heard. Intermittently she collapsed into tears. Her voice was ghostly, as if she were reporting from another harrowing world where she was searching, futilely, for her lost love. I've never heard anyone be so wracked by grief and able to remain articulate. The effect was devastating.

The headline on Bob's obituary in *Rolling Stone* read AMERICA'S PRE-EMINENT MUSIC WRITER DEAD AT 52. He deserved that status, and deserves it still. Now what we have left of Bob is his incomparable work. That may well be where he created the best, most gripping version of himself. Without ever overwhelming his subjects, Bob inhabits these pieces fully. As he was dying, Bob came to understand how much his writing had meant to so many and was deeply moved by that knowledge. In gathering this collection, and having many conversations about Bob in the course of doing so, I was struck by how many people in so many different musical worlds revered him and all that he had done, all that he stood for. No doubt, reading any of these pieces will deliver a similar understanding to you.

Anthony DeCurtis
New York City
May 2009

THE BIG PICTURE: "THE OPINIONS EXPRESSED ARE DANGEROUSLY SUBJECTIVE."

What Is American Music?

DOWN BEAT | FEBRUARY 27, 1975

Michael Tilson Thomas is the young American conductor who directs the Buffalo Philharmonic and the New York Philharmonic's Young People's Concerts. I was interviewing him last summer and the conversation naturally turned to what it is that makes American music . . . American. Thomas suggested that "we have a musical culture forming now in this country which is made up like our social culture, of all these different elements." Then he thought some more and added, "And there's this interesting sense of non-proprietariness.

"Well," he said, "somebody asked me the other day what's really important to me about Charles Ives. There are a lot of things, of course. He used quarter-tones and polyrhythms before any other Western composer. But there's something else about Ives, and Carl Ruggles, that whole New England crowd. Not only were they far out ahead of everybody else, doing these various things, but the European composers who did the same things instantly transformed them into systems, into schools, into methods. Ives and those people just did these things to get across what they had to get across at a particular moment; then they went on to something else. Ives must have said something like, 'The next thing I want to get across is this, and it seems to call for quarter-tones.' So he wrote these quarter-tone pieces which are among the best ever written. Then he said, 'I need polyrhythms here,' and he *just did it*. That's a very American way of doing."

American music is nonproprietary, then, in that American composers (and performers) innovate and then move on. They don't, as Thomas later remarked, "ask themselves how much more mileage they can get" out of their creations. Certainly Ives's successors in the so-called American Experimental Tradition were as suspicious of schools and methods as the grand old man of modernism himself. This quite untraditional tradition is not, wrote Peter Yates in his *Twentieth Century Music*, "a concerted tradition like the Germanic but a widely dispersed and weedlike growth of fresh ideas in new soil. One country's weeds may in another country become hothouse or ornamental plants, being cultivated there to greater or more prolific beauty, though they are not natural to the climate." Thus, during the first half of this century, Edgar Varèse and Stefan Wolpe became "American" composers and contributed to the nonproprietary experimental climate with their own innovations.

In at least one sense, however, American music *is* proprietary. Despite the generally open-minded attitudes of composers and musicians, our concepts of musical worth remain essentially European. "Serious" composition is the only accepted, accredited kind of composition, a proprietary attitude which leaves many of our most vital musical traditions out in the cold. It can be argued, of course, that distinctions between "jazz" and "classical" music have been breaking down at an ever-accelerating pace during the past decade; that a number of governmental and private funding agencies are recognizing composers in a variety of non-European idioms through continuing programs of grants and fellowships; that in some of our more enlightened musical arenas—lower Manhattan, certain universities—musicians educated in Afro-American and European traditions are composing and performing each other's music.

Nevertheless, the gap is far from closed. There is not yet a coherent program for funding such cultural institutions as the late Duke Ellington's orchestra, while most of our metropolitan philharmonic orchestras would be foundering without just such subsidies. Dr. Donald Byrd, former chairman of the Jazz Studies Department at Howard University, and renowned trumpeter and composer, remarked not long ago that "I want to document black music on the same level as they establish Stravinsky. In other words, I want to deal with James Brown like you would deal with, like, Prokofiev." Educational programs all over the country are beginning to "deal" with the major figures of jazz history in this manner, but in terms of academic prestige and impact in the larger cultural sphere they are, as yet, relatively negligible.

The interests of young American musicians on the "serious" or "classical" side indicate a change. Steve Reich, the composer whose *Drumming* was recently recorded by Deutsche Grammophon, has studied with Ghanaian master drummers and brought West African rhythmic usages into the concert hall. Michael Tilson Thomas is also interested in rhythmic aspects of black music. "I was influenced," he says, "by Chuck Berry and James Brown and the whole black music experience, in the sense of total steadiness and total drive and *the smallest rhythmic unit being what drives the music,* the pulse being a kind of organizing statement going on above that." But, to return to Byrd's idea for a moment, has anyone really dealt with James Brown in a musicological manner? Has Chuck Berry's contribution to American music been analyzed as a *musical* phenomenon?

These are not rhetorical questions. There simply is no recognized frame of reference for evaluating the Afro-American musical continuum *in relation to* the world of "serious" music, a world whose criteria are still more or less European and more or less elitist and exclusive. Jazz may be halfway in the door, in academia and in the milieu of state-supported culture, but what about the blues or rhythm and blues? Can they be dismissed as *mere* popular music when, in the West African traditions from which they ultimately derive, *all* music is popular insofar as it is potentially communal and participative?

The European musical heritage is assumed to have . . . responded primarily to the demands of genius on the one hand and the abilities of performers on the other. In the Afro-American continuum, music responds more or less democratically to social and even political forces. The Ghanaian musicologist Nketia, in his *The Music of Africa,* describes a process in which "an approach to the practice of music as a form of social activity in community life is generally evident. . . . Moreover, because of the close integration of music and social life, it is inevitable that changes in the way of life of an African society—in its institutions, political organization, and aspects of economic life or religious practice—should lead to corresponding changes in aspects of musical practice or in the organization of performances." And since, in addition to being "popular" enough to involve and respond to entire communities, African music is "artistic" enough to have baffled European experts in transcription until the invention of phonophotography, European distinctions between art and popular music would seem to be singularly inapplicable to it. The situation is similar with respect to Afro-American music.

Before we can define American music, then, we need a set of procedures which will allow us to evaluate Charles Ives *and* James Brown. The pop/art dichotomy will not serve, but other equally European ideals may have to. For, as Dr. Byrd recently pointed out, "There are certain procedures, certain ways of studying and classifying things which are almost universally accepted. One of the stumbling blocks teachers and students of black music have faced is relating to some of these ways of studying and classifying. If your research methods are slipshod and your findings are demonstrably biased, the academic establishment can and will refuse to take you seriously. So first we need to establish our field in academic terms."

This approach will mean going against the nonproprietary American grain and attempting to materialize some kind of classifiable "order" out of the apparent chaos of American folk and popular musics. It will mean, among many other things, studying "schools" of Afro-American music. Fortunately, many of these schools have been documented, and in many cases the method and manner of documentation have been well organized and academically acceptable. Many of the researchers have not themselves been academics; many have not been Americans. But a body of knowledge does exist and, in a very real sense, a working definition of American music awaits its codification.

An example of an area of music which awaits integration into American history, an area which is of overwhelming importance if we are eventually to arrive at an estimate of how much and in what ways our music has been influenced by that of Africa, is that of black fife-and-drum music. Folklorist Alan Lomax stumbled on a living, breathing example of it in Sledge, Mississippi, in 1940, while recording for the Library of Congress. The band he recorded, which consisted of a homemade cane fife, a bass drum, and two snares, played stark, plaintive versions of turn-of-the-century popular songs and a European-sounding *Death March*, and it was generally assumed that the group represented a survival of the European fife-and-tabor tradition by way of military bands. On returning to northwestern Mississippi in 1959, Lomax heard and recorded a much more African-sounding fife-and-drum band which performed Afro-American folk and minstrel songs replete with wordless vocal moans, "hot" rhythms and cross-accents, and a degree of improvisation. Further research in the area by David Evans and George Mitchell turned up a thriving black fife-and-drum tradition, apparently of long standing, which was the "blackest" of all. Much of the material was constructed from one-measure phrases, the rhythms were even hotter, there was more improvisation, and the melodic material was blues and holler-related and primarily pentatonic. The music of the Como, Mississippi, Fife and Drum Band proved to be the most West African *sounding* folk music ever recorded in the United States.

The old arguments about African vs. European influence in Afro-American folk music need not concern us here. What is important is that an entire tradition, which can be studied as a series of regional schools with certain features in common, has yet to be placed within the context of American music as a whole. How did this tradition relate to the African heritage on the one hand and to rural brass bands and early jazz on the other? How did it relate to the blues socially, historically, rhythmically, melodically? Another line of approach would be to study the music from a performance point of view. Musicologist, saxophonist, and composer Marion Brown, who is adept at the manufacture of bamboo and cane flutes, hopes to study the construction of cane fifes in Mississippi, or Georgia, so as to preserve the physical-culture aspects of the tradition. The Center for Southern Folklore has preserved Mississippi fife making and some of the social situations in which the music is performed on film.

The rural blues is a musical genre which has been studied much more intensively than fife-and-drum music, but again a number of very basic questions about it have yet to be answered. The first dated reference to a music which is demonstrably blues is from 1903; it is W. C. Handy's frequently quoted account of hearing a guitarist playing slide guitar with a knife and singing in a metrically free manner about a railroad junction "where the Southern cross the Dog." No less an authority than Harold Courlander supposed in his *Negro Folk Music U.S.A.* that "something closely akin to blues was . . . sung in the towns and on the plantations in antebellum days," but the current consensus among blues researchers is that the blues as a distinctive genre, performed for the most part by soloists singing and playing their own accompaniment on stringed instruments, was not heard anywhere in the South much earlier than the 1890s or early 1900s. Furry Lewis and a few other "songsters" with repertoires which apparently predate the blues are still active.

Surely, one would think, it is too late to research questions like the probable date of origin of the blues, which must in any case have developed as an extension of prior forms in different areas at different times. It *is* possible, however, to find out a great deal more about the so-called "classic" period of the blues, the 1920s and early 1930s, as the case of bluesman Robert Johnson attests. Johnson's art is widely held to represent a crucial transition from rural to urban blues styles; he was the major direct influence on the postwar electric blues of Elmore James, Johnny Shines, Howlin' Wolf, Muddy Waters, and other Chicago-based performers. Until this year almost nothing was known about his life and career and there were no photographs nor even any vivid descriptions of what he looked like; he was a mystery man, known only for his gripping recordings and for his exceedingly important influence on American music and, through groups like the Rolling Stones, on the popular music of the world. But a young blues researcher named Steve LaVere, by dint of perseverance and hard work and strictly on his own recognizance, succeeded in tracking down Johnson's family, a surviving wife, and several photographs, and then proceeded to turn up a number of hitherto unknown recordings, alternate takes which offered the first real perspective on the process of Johnson's music.

We now know enough about the blues to pinpoint various critically important schools. The Bentonia, Mississippi, school produced only one "name" artist, Skip James, but was responsible for a melodically, harmonically, and rhythmically sophisticated and unique variety of country blues. Tommy Johnson and other 1920s bluesmen from the Jackson area contributed far more to the ongoing blues tradition, while Charlie Patton and Son House and Robert Johnson comprise a distinct Delta lineage which survives in the work of their pupils, including Roebuck Staples. The Texas school (metrically free, in contrast to the more rigorously structured Mississippi styles), Georgia school (extremely lyrical blues, twelve-string guitars), and many others have been preserved on 78 rpm records, most of which are now available on reissue LPs. These local cultures can be more sensibly isolated and studied as schools than can an arbitrary grouping of dissimilar New England composers centering around Ives.

Once these various blues and songster and fife-and-drum schools are duly noted and their characteristics recorded in an academically acceptable manner, American music scholars will be in a better position to understand how and to what extent white and black folk and popular music drew on one another. And the combined stream, more clearly defined, will be available for comparison with more self-consciously "artistic" American music. We will be able to say with greater authority, if not with outright certainty, how the hymns and dance tunes which figure so prominently in Ives's compositions relate to distinctly American influences. There has been a suspicion abroad for some time that only American conductors and orchestra musicians can "really" perform Ives. Certainly the magnificent Pierre Boulez, directing the New York Philharmonic's mini-festival around Ives last fall, failed to "swing" Ives's orchestral works as Michael Tilson Thomas and Leonard Bernstein did the preceding summer at the Ives Centennial concert in Danbury, Connecticut. By studying the interaction of various European- and African-derived strains in America's musical history we may someday be able to explain why this should be so.

We can gauge the impact of music emanating from America on the world at large much more accurately. In the world of art music deriving from European traditions that impact is immense, more so than at any time in American history. For one thing, the contributions of Charles Ives and of his father, George, are only now being recognized worldwide. The elder Ives, a Connecticut bandmaster, was a pragmatic experimenter whose many tests of music's resources encouraged his son in innovative pursuits. George Ives experimented with quarter-tones before Charles. In fact, he developed a veritable arsenal of tunings using violin strings and tuned glasses, and (in his best-known exploit) deployed elements of his band at opposite ends of a green or square and had them march toward him playing different tunes, the basis for Charles Ives's later use of colliding sound masses. Interestingly enough, George Ives was also a friend of Stephen Foster, the American composer who was more responsible than any other nineteenth-century figure for writing down, and therefore "legitimizing," Euro- and Afro-American folk song strains.

It was left to the younger Ives to employ these various influences he had inherited in orchestral compositions which are now recognized around the world as the first instances in modern concert music of the use of what Yates calls "the entire field of sound, bringing into relationship and contrast correct intonation, dissonance and discordance, microtonal intervals, and noise." When broken down into parts, Ives's great cataclysms of sound often consist of American barn dance fiddle tunes, patriotic anthems, ragtime, psalms and hymns of all denominations, minstrel songs, and popular piano sheet music, all in "common" or vernacular idioms but combined so as to produce clusters which still sound futuristic.

The influence of the American experimenters following Ives— Ruggles, Henry Cowell, Lou Harrison, Elliott Carter, and Harry Partch, to name a disparate few—has also been felt abroad, but the most widely discussed American composer of our own time is a maverick even by their self-sufficient standards. John Cage collaborated with Harrison and William Russell (later a dedicated New Orleans jazz archivist) in creating a new kind of percussion orchestra and a new percussion literature during the late 1930s and, in 1939, realized the first major electronic composition, his *Imaginary Landscape No. 1*. During the forties, Cage began substituting various systems of fixed pitches for the twelve-tone scale, an approach which culminated in such bewitching pieces as *Music for Marcel Duchamp*, scored for a prepared piano invented by the composer. He had established an enviable reputation as an original when, in 1952, he proposed the celebrated (or infamous) 4'33", which consists of four minutes and thirty-three seconds during which the performers sit and do nothing. Whatever occurs in the "silence" constitutes the composition. Cage's music for radios from the same period is another applica-tion of indeterminancy, or chance, an idea which Cage developed after studying Zen and which has now, largely through his example, perme-ated theater, dance, and other arts. Yates is not exaggerating when he states flatly that Cage is "the most influential composer, worldwide, of his generation."

Cage's interest in the music, philosophy, and religions of Asia is not unique; it is evidence of an enduring strain in American music. The Canadian-born composer Colin McPhee contributed to the vogue for Javanese *gamelan* music among Western composers and performers; Debussy and Ravel had been influenced by *gamelan* music during the preceding century but McPhee's exhaustive book *Music in Java* touched off a chain of events of which Cage's percussion music was only one consequence. Henry Cowell, whose early piano pieces included tone clusters to be played by fists and forearms and spawned an entirely new approach to the keyboard, used Oriental instruments and idioms in his later compositions, as did Harrison. During the sixties, a new, post-Cage school of American composers began to be heard. LaMonte Young, Terry Riley, Steve Reich, and Philip Glass have been touched deeply by non-Western music but have chosen to develop along very different paths. Young's *Dream House* presentations and *The Well-Tuned Piano* deal with the most basic and profound pitch relationships known to man, those of the harmonic series. Reich's *Drumming* constitutes a completely original approach to percussion, an approach which adapts the phasing effects common to electronic music as a means of organically shifting combination rhythms and sonorities within repeating patterns.

"Jazz," an Afro-American art music with varying stylistic boundaries in which improvisation is usually very important, has been at least as imi-tated, and certainly more widely heard abroad, than the compositions of Ives and Cage, Young and Reich. Seizing on the music's proven power to win friends and influence people where musicians working in European-derived idioms fear to tread, the U.S. State Department has been export-ing bands led by Dizzy Gillespie, Randy Weston, Louis Armstrong, and other jazzmen to the Third World for years. Film clips show that the hon-ors heaped on Armstrong in Ghana, the attention lavished on Gillespie in Pakistan, the apparently endless round of embassy parties given Weston's group in country after African country, are evidence that the combination of improvisation, kinetic rhythm, and personal, emotionally inflected instrumental sonorities communicates directly to people of many different cultures. Another variety of evidence is the internationalization of jazz. The King of Thailand is a jazz saxophonist, Manu Dibango from the Republic of Cameroon plays like a Texas tenorman, and European-born musicians like Joe Zawinul, John McLaughlin, Jean-Luc Ponty, and Jan Hammer are among the music's most popular practitioners *in America*. Serious composers have been affected by jazz, from Darius Milhaud and *La Creation du Monde*, to Milton Babbitt's *All Set*, and beyond. It's been suggested that Cage's music of indeterminancy owes a great deal to jazz as well. In both, certain elements and outlines are established beforehand but the shape and nature of the content of any given performance are determined by various temporal, physical, and psychological variables. *Who* is playing becomes as important as what is being played.

And yet the most influential of *all* American musics, and the least studied, is pop/rock, in which the identity of the player is eclipsed by his electronically projected image and the primary motive force is technology. One searches in vain through the record shops of Tangier, Morocco, for recordings of the most widespread forms of traditional Moroccan music.

Most of the sounds American composer Aaron Copland marvelled at when he visited the country with his student Paul Bowles are to be found nowhere on disc. The best that can be hoped for in most Tangier record shops is Santana; the more usual fare is second- and third-hand imitations of American rock music rendered blandly by Spanish or French or local youngsters. In Indonesia, according to an article in *The New York Times*, the village *gamelans* which once constituted a popular alternative to the rather more static traditions of the court orchestras are disappearing, to be replaced by portable sound systems broadcasting *recordings* of the music or, much more frequently, of rock.

This process is occurring worldwide and has led Alan Lomax, the late Curt Sachs, and other eminent observers to conclude that the marvelous variety of traditional musics to be found on every continent will in most cases survive another generation at best. The situation is particularly ironic in view of the fact that American composers of all stripes are drawing on the wealth of ethnic musics while this wealth is being depleted, and replaced by first- and second-hand American pop music, in the countries where it originated and grew. It is not at all difficult to envision a near future in which the only *gamelan* orchestras and African royal drum ensembles will be staffed by graduates of Wesleyan University and UCLA.

Many American musicians are turning to relatively exotic source materials because the regional cultures which once produced so much that was distinctive in American music have all but disappeared. Even in New Orleans, a regional center which has given us both original jazz and much that was original in rock & roll, musicians complain that they have to reproduce the Top 40 hits they hear on the radio, and as exactly as possible, in order to work regularly, and that younger musicians who are growing to maturity there are stylistically oriented toward the media, and not at all interested in the indigenous musical traditions around them. The complaint is an old one, of course, and there are notable exceptions to this triumph of technology almost everywhere, but they only prove the general rule that electronic media play havoc with traditional oral cultures.

Just how basic this effect is to human nature is illustrated by an incident from closer to home which Edmund Carpenter relates in his *Oh! What a Blow That Phantom Gave Me*. It seems a poet acquaintance of his had tried in vain to make his friends sit still for readings, only to be met with fidgeting, coughing fits, laughter, and outright ridicule. He then hit on the idea of putting his recitations on tape and found that people would sit quietly and listen attentively to recordings of the same poems. Similarly, a live performance by an American artist or group offers listeners in Africa or Asia the opportunity to judge the music and the musicians on their own merits. The same performance, coming to the same listener as a radio or television broadcast, seems so much more potent and *real* that familiar, traditional music will have little chance of competing with it.

Black American musicians were among the first "humanizers of technology" for musical purposes. Charlie Christian developed the capabilities of the electric guitar almost singlehanded, but a more far-reaching techno-musical revolution was effected by those originally rural bluesmen who moved to the city during the thirties and forties and used electricity to amplify their incredibly emotive expressive techniques, their sliding, whining, moaning, voicelike guitar and harmonica inflections. It was their music which was imitated by white Southern performers (Elvis Presley consciously tried to reproduce the rhythm and spirit of blues vocals by Arthur Crudup and other black recording artists) and thence by white

English performers and became the most massively popular and profitable form of music in the history of the world. Now American musicians, black and white, are humanizing the impact of electronic media in the Third World by jamming and/or studying with traditional or folk musicians on every continent, and by this example encouraging the preservation of musics which are different from their own. But the voice of the media is still a great deal stronger and more penetrating. American pop/rock, for good or ill, is effectively the paramount component in any definition of American music which seeks to account for its influence in the world.

Many other threads make up the fabric of our music. The English ballads and Morris dances and other recreational and narrative forms the early settlers brought with them got mixed up with African stringed instruments like the banjo and the resulting combination proved resilient enough to nurture the larger-than-life talents of Jimmie Rodgers and Hank Williams. Out west, the Spanish music of the conquistadors' descendants, and the English-cum-African mountain music, and the jazz, and the Rodgers and Williams songs that spoke for and to the disadvantaged white lower classes as surely as the blues spoke for the black, fused in varying combinations and resulted in Western swing, a direct ancestor of country and western music and Tex-Mex rock & roll. How about what happened to European hymns when ecstatic American revivalists got hold of them during the Great Awakening of the early nineteenth century and sang and stomped and transformed them into gospels and spirituals? How about Cole Porter and Rodgers and Hart and Hammerstein and the other tune-smiths and lyricists whose creations have introduced American music to millions of moviegoers around the world? How about the functional social music that once accompanied harvesting and sewing bees in this country and the ecstatic trance music of the Shakers of New England?

The list could go on and on. Not all the music is "good," by any definition. But all of it is American. Is it nonproprietary? Often. Is it improvisational? Sometimes. Is it individualistic? Yes, but not always. If, as the musicologist Francois-Joseph Fétis proposed, the history of music is the history of mankind, then the history of American music is the history of America, no more and no less. The only definition of American music that will stick is that it's music made by Americans.

When Is It Rock and When Rock & Roll?

A Critic Ventures an Answer

THE NEW YORK TIMES | AUGUST 6, 1978

"Baby, that is rock & roll," sang the Coasters in 1959, and nobody had to ask what they meant. Rock & roll had defined itself since it burst upon the national consciousness in the mid-1950s. According to Chuck Berry, it had a backbeat you couldn't lose. According to Jerry Leiber and Mike Stoller, who wrote the Coasters' hit, you couldn't always understand the words; if you did, "You'd really blow your lid." According to a leaflet distributed by White Citizen Councils in the South, "the screaming, idiotic words and savage music of these records are undermining the morals of our white youth in America," but on the whole this warning was not greeted with the serious consideration it merited.

Baby, what *is* rock & roll? Somehow, over the past twenty years, its meaning has become more and more elusive. Rock & roll has often been confused with rock, which is a vague enough category by itself. For some people, rock first flourished in the mid-1960s, music that was based on, but more sophisticated than, rock & roll. For others, rock continues to exist side by side with rock & roll and has to do with style rather than chronology. According to this line of reasoning, an album like *Sgt. Pepper's Lonely Hearts Club Band* is rock and an album like the Rolling Stones' *Some Girls* is basically rock & roll.

Despite the lack of a generally accepted definition for either rock or rock & roll, people use both terms as if they know exactly what they are talking about. This writer has often claimed that one performer is an authentic rocker and another one is not. He has accused some well-known rock stars of having no feeling for rock & roll and asserted that other rock stars were actually playing rock & roll and not rock. He often gets letters asking just what he is talking about, and one day recently it occurred to him that he should provide some sort of provisional answer. So here is one writer's definition of rock & roll, broken down, for the sake of convenience and clarity, into the sort of subheadings an ethnomusicologist might use in a study of the folk music of the Trobriand Islanders. Do not be misled by the scientific veneer; the opinions expressed are dangerously subjective.

I. **Historical and geographical factors.** Rock & roll was born in the South and Southwest and in some cities with high concentrations of native Southerners and Southwesterners, most notably St. Louis and Chicago. This relatively circumscribed area produced every major figure in early rock & roll: Elvis Presley, Chuck Berry, Little Richard, Fats Domino, Jerry Lee Lewis, Carl Perkins, Buddy Holly, Bo Diddley, and so on. It is true that some of the most successful early recordings in a style akin to rock & roll were made by black vocal groups in New York and Los Angeles. It is true that Bill Haley, who made some of the first rock & roll hits in 1954 and 1955, was from Pennsylvania. But the black groups were unable to score consistent successes with the white pop audience, and Mr. Haley had neither the personality nor the originality to become the first rock & roll star.

II. **Form.** Most early rock & roll songs were written in forms that had already become standard in country, blues, or gospel music. These were simple eight-, twelve-, and sixteen-bar forms. Occasionally a rock & roll songwriter might use the thirty-two-bar form of Tin Pan Alley music, and as early as Buddy Holly rock & roll songwriting began to find forms of its own. In any event, rock & roll songs never have more than one principal melodic strain, with or without a bridge, and they rarely employ more than one tempo. The suite of songs, as in concept albums and rock operas, is an idea wholly foreign to the rock & roll idiom.

III. **Instrumentation and instrumental sound.** The saxophone was the most prominent solo instrument in early rock & roll, but the electric guitar was already basic to both black blues and white country music and soon assumed a dominant role. With the possible exception of the rock & roll beat, nothing is as endemic to the idiom as certain electric guitar sounds.

These sounds are jangly, wiry, raw, and frequently distorted. In the hands of the most influential early rock & roll guitarists— Chuck Berry, Bo Diddley, Carl Perkins—the instrument stings, barks, and spits when it is not pushing insistently in tandem with the drums. The deliberate use of feedback and of malfunctioning amplifiers to achieve complex, grainy timbres was pioneered by Southern blues guitarists like Willie Johnson (of the early Howlin' Wolf Band) and perfected by Bo Diddley and his followers. The liquid, whiny, treacly toned guitar sound that is so pervasive in contemporary rock reflects a later and, to the rock & roll purist, an extremely degenerate development. Among contemporary artists, only the punk and new wave rockers and a motley handful of Southerners and Englishmen boast authentic rock & roll sounds. Amplifier and recording technologies have become too sophisticated; sound that once could be obtained simply by kicking one's battered Silvertone are now imitated with the aid of little black distortion boxes. The key word here is "imitated."

IV. **Vocal style.** As Dave Laing pointed out in his book *Buddy Holly*, the distinction between a song and a performance, a distinction fundamental to both classical and Tin Pan Alley music, breaks down when it comes to rock & roll. Songs like "Whole Lotta Shakin' Goin' On" or "Peggy Sue" have little meaning beyond the recordings of them by Jerry Lee Lewis and Buddy Holly; any attempt to record one of these songs becomes a tribute to the appropriate singer. Again, rock & roll has defined itself in the dictum "it's the singer, not the song."

Rock & roll vocal style is a maverick strain that is most original when it draws on traditional black and white mannerisms without aping either. It has been enriched by Elvis Presley's hiccup, Buddy Holly's baby talk, and other individual contributions of greater or lesser magnitude. A rock & roll singer projects a great deal of himself in something of a generalized rock & roll attitude no matter what he is singing, and what he is singing really doesn't matter the way it matters in Tin Pan Alley music or opera. As Mick Jagger once told an interviewer, "I don't think the lyrics are that important. I remember when I was very young, this is very serious, I read an article by Fats Domino which has really influenced me. He said, 'You should never sing the lyrics out very clearly.'"

V.   **Rhythm.** The roots of rock & roll rhythm are to be found in black American religion. It was in the spirituals and later in the black sanctified churches that the terms "rocking" and "to rock" first gained currency. A Library of Congress field recording from 1934 furnishes a particularly good example of a strong, heavily accented rock & roll beat in a black religious observance, a ring shout. Among the garbled lyrics, one can make out the words, "I gotta rock, you've gotta rock."

Rock & roll drumming reached its apogee in New Orleans, the only North American city where African-style drumming survived right up to the Civil War. J. M. Van Eaton, who played drums on the classic Jerry Lee Lewis records of the fifties and was himself the model for countless drummers, told this writer earlier this year that he had listened carefully to the drummer who played on Little Richard's records, which were made in New Orleans and featured the band that also backed Fats Domino.

When rock & roll is really rocking *and* rolling, it combines an irresistible forward motion, a heavy backbeat, and a certain lightness or lilt, sometimes expressed as quarter-note triplets. Charlie Watts, the Rolling Stones' exceptional drummer, is adept at giving this combination. Like Earl Palmer and the other great New Orleans drummers, he is steeped in rhythm and blues but comes from a jazz background. Compared to Mr. Watts, most rock drummers sound lead-footed. They do not rock; they thud, crunch, rumble, and flail.

VI. **Attitude.** Like the rock & roll vocal style, the rock & roll attitude says, "Look at me!" At first, in the 1950s, it was strictly an adolescent attitude, a youthful response to the public and private banalities of the Eisenhower years. It was widely perceived as a rebellion, but it was more an assertion of personality and possibility than anything else. After all, Elvis Presley always said "Yes, sir" and "No, ma'am," and Little Richard threw away his jewels and joined the ministry. A real rebel would have done neither. But then, how many rebels are genuine and how many are poseurs? Real rock & roll is always genuine.

Applying these criteria to a contemporary album like Bruce Springsteen's *Darkness on the Edge of Town*, which has been almost universally hailed as a great rock & roll album, might be illuminating. Mr. Springsteen is not rooted in or apparently even very interested in the music's Southern beginnings. He seems to have been inspired principally by the East Coast studio rock of the early 1960s, a brand of music that had one foot and sometimes both feet in Tin Pan Alley. His guitar sound will never do, and his albums are overorchestrated in a manner that has more to do with grand opera than with rock & roll. His vocal style is suitably mush-mouthed, but his self-consciously poetic lyrics, which would be enough cause for excluding him from the rock & roll pantheon by themselves, are printed on a special album insert. This is inexcusable. The rhythmic content of his music is usually one part rock and several parts bombast. His attitude, which seems to so many rock critics to be a paradigm of authenticity, strikes this listener as calculated, pretentious, only sporadically convincing. Mr. Springsteen's albums should carry a disclaimer, something like the posters advertising the musical *Beatlemania*—NOT ROCK & ROLL! AN INCREDIBLE SIMULATION!

On the other hand, the Rolling Stones' *Some Girls*, which has also been well received by rock critics, passes the rock & roll test with flying colors. The Stones know their rock & roll roots, they write in rock & roll forms using classic rock & roll chord progressions, guitar riffs, and rhythm patterns, they favor a raunchy guitar sound, Mick Jagger projects himself first and the lyrics second, and the rhythm section rocks mightily. Whether the Stones are wholly convincing is open to question, but attitude is the most subjective of all these criteria and even if they failed here, overall the Rolling Stones would still get a very high mark. Which just goes to show that even though the dictum "rock & roll will never die" is not necessarily true, rock & roll has not died yet.

THE BLUES: "A POST-HEISENBERG-UNCERTAINTY-PRINCIPLE MOJO HAND"

Why I Wear My Mojo Hand

OXFORD AMERICAN | DECEMBER 1996/JANUARY 1997

Blues and trouble, that's the cliché. The reality is: blues and chaos. Blues is supposed to be—what?—*nurtured* by trouble? So is most art that reaches deep inside and demands unflinching honesty. Is blues *about* trouble? No more than it is about good-time Saturday nights and murder most foul, sharecroppers' servitude, and sweet home Chicago. Is blues a *cause* of trouble? Not directly. But what sort of thing almost inevitably causes trouble in our oppressively regimented world? You guessed it: chaos.

The blues-and-chaos equation first presented itself to me in the mid-sixties, when a bunch of us—musicians, artists, and a smattering of smugglers and dealers—organized and presented the first Memphis Blues Festival in the Overton Park Shell. For years I believed the remarkable levels of chaos in everything remotely connected with those festivals resulted from a bunch of hippies trying to turn elderly blues singers into anarchist father figures. Now I'm not so sure. In any case, that was before I met R. L. Burnside.

R.L. was an outstanding disciple of one of the greatest of all bluesmen, Mississippi Fred McDowell, who had been a Memphis Blues Festival regular. By the early 1970s, R.L. had really come into his own. The juke joints he ran in the north Mississippi hill country were as famous for their level of violence as for R.L.'s outstanding music, which rolled out of his jacked-up guitar amp in dark, turbulent waves—sometimes punctuated by gunshots, especially on Saturday nights. In fact, R.L. has been reported waving a (presumably loaded) pistol in at least one crowded joint. If that strikes you as akin to yelling "Fire!" in a crowded theater, well, that's R.L. The man is a connoisseur of chaos; he attracts it, admires it, and then absorbs it, like a black hole sucking reality itself into the chaos of Nothing.

Back in 1993, when I found myself producing a Burnside session for the album *Too Bad Jim,* a succession of chaotic eruptions seemed to threaten the entire project. A string bass fell to pieces in the studio. Then the drum kit collapsed into kindling after being given a single light tap. A glass door fell out of its mounting and gave me a skull-rattling knock upside the head. Out of the corner of my eye I glanced over at R.L.—he was enjoying himself like a kid at a Disney movie. The performances he recorded that day were highlights of the album.

I decided, out of near desperation, to fight fire with fire. Using objects and materials you can find in any good botanica, and dedicating them with a simple, made-up ritual I thought appropriate, I made myself a chaos buster, a post-Heisenberg-Uncertainty-Principle Mojo Hand. The next time I went in the studio with R.L., the mojo was secreted on my person. The session went well. Toward the end we were taking a break when it happened again: A tall screen began to tip over, as usual for no apparent reason. It fell and hit engineer Robbie Norris on his head. This time, I was all smiles. "It works!" I crowed, giving my mojo charm a surreptitious rub. Robbie was gingerly rubbing the top of his head. "Yeah," he said, "it works *for you.*"

But of course, that's just what you expect from magic: If it affects the practitioner's reality, and in the way desired, it *works.* Chaos theory is one way of explaining the mechanics involved. Another, more poetic, and perhaps wiser way of explaining it is called "the blues." Rarely have chaos and uncertainty been so *listenable*; and I'll almost certainly be listening for the rest of my life. If I choose to pack my mojo, well, once again the blues says it best: "Ain't Nobody's Business If I Do."

Deeper into the Delta

ROLLING STONE | MARCH 5, 1992

King of the Delta Blues (Yazoo)
Charlie Patton

Founder of the Delta Blues (Yazoo)
Charley Patton

Master of the Delta Blues: The Friends of Charlie Patton (Yazoo)
Various Artists

Robert Johnson, the hellhound-haunted Mississippi Delta bluesman, didn't get his music from the devil, despite what you might have heard. He got a lot of it from Charley Patton and a lot more from Patton's playing partners Willie Brown and Son House. Someone at Columbia

Records crowned Johnson "King of the Delta Blues." Yazoo's consortium of blues scholars and record collectors think Patton deserves the honor. The Yazoo folks are probably right.

Now Patton's complete recorded works are available on two CDs, with a third disc devoted to Brown, House, Tommy Johnson, and other seminal figures from Patton's circle; maybe the "Founder of the Delta Blues" is finally going to get his due. It's about time. Patton was popping bass strings, zinging off eerie bottleneck runs, and miming obscene acts with his guitar as early as 1911, the year Robert Johnson was born. In terms of blues evolution, Johnson *simplified* the earlier music Patton created, regularizing song forms and streamlining rhythmic complexities.

After sixty-odd years, Patton's sheer focus and magnetic, almost palpable presence will still jump out of your speakers and grab you by the throat. His voice was a big, rough-edged baritone, heavy as lead when he wanted it to be but capable of blues singing's most rarefied subtleties. His lyrics chronicled the good times and the hard times of his people and his world in stark, sharp imagery. "High Water Everywhere," on *Founder of the Delta Blues*, bears witness to a disastrous flood ("The water done jumped through this town"); several of his blues celebrate the poetry of trains ("The smokestack is black and the bell it shine like gold"). He sang unrepentantly about his rowdy way of life, complaining throughout "Tom Rushen Blues" about his treatment at the hands of a local sheriff, only to admit in the song's last line, "Aw, he caught me yellin', I was drunk as I could be." And he dreamed transcendent dreams ("Safe sweet home, sweet home, baby, through that shinin' star . . . You don't need no tellin', mama, take you in my car").

Patton's guitar playing is driving, percussive, mercurial, and rhythmically complex. One of his earliest and most distinctive showpieces, "Pony Blues," also on *Founder*, alternates two-and-a-half-bar vocal lines with two-bar guitar figures; the three-line verses come out thirteen and a half bars long. As if this weren't complicated enough, the voice and guitar also weave independent, often contrasting triplet figures into the rhythm's four-beat flow. And the raps and knocks Patton bangs out with his hands and feet rarely coincide with *any* of the other accents. Yet nothing is haphazard: Each verse is exactly thirteen and a half bars long, and the play of polyrhythms remains rigorously consistent from verse to verse.

Patton's blues style may be the earliest on record, but you wouldn't want to call it primitive. He just makes it *sound* easy and elemental.

The late Nick Perls, who founded Yazoo Records in the mid-sixties in order to reissue early blues 78s on LP, compiled *Founder of the Delta Blues* as one of his first projects; it was a labor of love. His tastes ran toward hard blues and spectacular guitar playing, and on *Founder* these elements dominate; most of Patton's blues classics are included on that volume. But Patton was also an outstanding performer of country break-downs, preblues ballads, and gospel tunes, and this side of his prolix genius emerges more fully on the brand-new *King of the Delta Blues* (credited to "Charlie" Patton; the name has long been spelled both ways). The new disc may have been designed to fill in the earlier set's gaps, but a more inclusive overview of Patton's music is the happy result. *King* finds Patton playing luminous lap-steel guitar on gospel tunes, heading for the hoedown with fiddler Henry Sims on blues-a-billy stomps like "Running Wild Blues," and pushing his voice to the limit in order to match the magisterial Bertha Lee on the intense, driven-sounding gospel duets "Oh Death" and "Troubled 'Bout My Mother." There's plenty of hard blues as well, including a stunning 78 ("Jim Lee Blues Part 1"/"Some Summer Day") that was unknown and unheard when Perls was assembling the original *Founder* double album.

Perls's meticulous restoration and remastering of extremely rare 78s gave Yazoo the edge among the blues reissue labels of the sixties. But the CD version of *Founder* seems to have been transferred from Perls's sixties album master rather than from the original-source 78s. It sounds fine, but new record-restoration processes and digital remastering directly from the 78s make *King of the Delta Blues* sound considerably better. One would hope that Yazoo will get around to giving the earlier collection the same treatment.

Yazoo has cleaned up some rare and musically dazzling 1920s and '30s recordings by Patton associates, pupils, and paramours for another new disc, *Master of the Delta Blues*. The technical imperfections that remain seem minor in view of the fact that there's only one known copy of a 78 as riveting and important as Son House's two-part pow-erhouse "Preachin' the Blues," the model for Robert Johnson's later "Preachin' Blues." Tommy Johnson's spooky falsetto moans on "Canned Heat Blues," the apocalyptic imagery and otherworldly power of Willie

Brown's "Future Blues," and the barrelhouse exuberance of rough-and-ready singer-pianist Louise Johnson's "On the Wall" (the juiciest song ever written about sex standing up) are additional highlights. But *all* of the disc's twenty-three tracks are stone killers; add one or both of the Patton discs and you'll have the finest introduction to pre–Robert Johnson Delta blues imaginable.

Just as Robert Johnson borrowed from Patton and his pals, Patton, who died in 1934, must have borrowed from earlier, unrecorded musicians. But Patton's status as the primary innovator and most popular performer on the Delta's earliest known blues scene has been extensively researched and documented, most notably in the biography *King of the Delta Blues*, by Stephen Calt and Gayle Wardlow (available through Shanachie, Yazoo's distributor). And Patton has to be reckoned with in any survey of the roots of rock & roll. In fact, if you define rock & roll as a jacked-up shotgun wedding of blues and hillbilly music, Patton's music *was* rock & roll. According to eyewitness accounts, he even performed like a rocker, playing guitar between his legs and behind his back, tossing the instrument into the air and catching it without missing a beat.

Charley Patton was more than a great American musician. He was an American archetype, the first in a series of hard-living, hard-rocking ramblers that has included artists as musically diverse as Robert Johnson, Hank Williams, Jerry Lee Lewis, and Jimi Hendrix. Any of these men could have sung the final verse from Patton's "Elder Greene Blues" as his own credo: "I like to fuss and fight/Lord, and get sloppy drunk off a bottle and ball/And walk the streets all night."

King of the Delta Blues Singers

Robert Johnson: The Complete Recordings (Sony)

ROLLING STONE | OCTOBER 18, 1990

It seems odd, but probably wise, that nowhere in this definitive collection of Robert Johnson's forty-one surviving blues recordings is there a single mention of the Robert Johnson Myth. We all know it by now: the young amateur who made a deal with the devil at a dark Mississippi Delta crossroads, disappeared for a year, and then returned home to astound all the more seasoned performers who had laughed at him with music of almost supernatural power and presence and an undercurrent of impending doom.

What we have in *Robert Johnson: The Complete Recordings* are solid facts in Stephen C. LaVere's meticulously researched liner notes, brief appreciations of Johnson by Keith Richards ("He was like a comet or a meteor that came along and, BOOM, suddenly he raised the ante, suddenly you just had to aim that much higher") and Eric Clapton ("I have never found anything more deeply soulful than Robert Johnson. His music remains the most powerful cry that I think you can find in the human voice, really"), lyrics, and photos. And, of course, we have the songs—digitally clarified and, as expected, at least as powerful and affecting as ever.

Robert Johnson recorded twenty-nine songs in 1936 and 1937—alternate takes, previously bootlegged and only rarely revelatory, bring the total here to forty-one—and then vanished into the murky Mississippi Delta world of juke joints, voodoo lore, violence, grand plantation houses for whites, and perpetually indentured black sharecroppers who worked in the cotton fields all week and were serious about their Saturday nights. Johnson was fatally poisoned by a jealous husband or boyfriend shortly before fame caught up with him in the person of Columbia's John Hammond, who wanted him for the historic 1938 Spirituals to Swing concert at Carnegie Hall in New York. Fame, finding nothing left but a legend, passed him by, but only for a while. Even in these last prosaic facts, the Myth lurks. In "Sweet Home Chicago," Johnson played and sang as if anticipating the effect his music would have on the electric-blues scene in Chicago ten years later, and the last line he sang at his last session posed a question to which he would soon find the terminal answer: "Well, now, can you suck on some other man's bull cow . . . in this strange man's town?"

The Robert Johnson recordings are musical art of the highest order, as rich and transcendent as anything produced by an American musician in this century—surely only a racist or classist would argue otherwise. Was he really the greatest blues singer-guitarist-songwriter of all? Listening to Johnson in Frank Abbey's lovingly restored and remastered new versions, the question seems almost irrelevant. Johnson was a great one, all right, and a bluesman to the bottom of his soul. But at his most original, when he is also most chilling, Johnson blows genre considerations and invidious comparisons right out the window.

"Hellhound on My Trail" and "Love in Vain," both from his last session, are idiosyncratic constructions that defy time in their musical daring and emotional immediacy. "Hellhound," with its moving inner voices and dissonant, nontempered chords in the guitar accompaniment, is so vivid it's as much life as art. So are "Cross Road Blues" and "Me and the Devil Blues," but unlike the formally singular "Hellhound," these are blues to the marrow. "You want to know how good the blues can get?" asks Keith Richards. "Well, this is it."

Technically, Johnson the guitarist was an anomaly. He could sing and play cross-rhythms on the guitar, relating the parts in such complex syncopations that, as Richards notes, "You think, 'This guy must have three brains!'" Johnson also occasionally "breaks time," dropping a half beat or a half bar, apparently without realizing it ("Traveling Riverside Blues," "Honeymoon Blues"), which caused more technically conventional bluesmen to snicker. Yet could any of them have brought off the hesitations, sprung the offbeat accents and other polyrhythmic byplay—mercurial figures derived from sources as diverse as Son House, the recordings of Kokomo Arnold, and Johnson's own teeming imagination—that Johnson had mastered? More important, could any of his contemporaries have come close to equaling the sheer force and the haunted immediacy Johnson communicated? This, finally, is his bid for status as "the greatest": No other bluesman left a studio portrait that seems to come moaning and howling from the darkest recesses of his soul. The music has a power that age cannot dim. Familiarity with his work, even over many years, breeds only a finer appreciation and a more acute sense of awe.

Johnson left his mark on popular music primarily during two eras. On steady-rocking dance tunes like "Sweet Home Chicago," "I Believe I'll Dust My Broom," and "I'm a Steady Rollin' Man," he crafted complete orchestral guitar accompaniments that set a driving shuffle rhythm, accented with stinging treble-string bottleneck leads, sketched in a bass line, and even suggested figures suitable for piano chording. In Chicago in the forties and early fifties, Muddy Waters and Elmore James, among others, realized these arrangements-in-embryo as full-band numbers and made "Sweet Home Chicago" and "Dust My Broom" postwar standards. These songs had their effect on rock & roll, but they did not equal the impact of the first Johnson LP reissue, *King of the Delta Blues Singers*, on the first generation of sixties blues-based white rockers. Whether you're talking about the Stones, the Yardbirds, or Led Zeppelin, Johnson gave them all a fright, encouraged them, pushed them to play more than they knew and perhaps to find out things they did not need to know. But the last bit is part of the Myth, and every listener will finally have to come to terms with that myth in an individual, intuitively personal way.

The Myth cannot be ignored; the music can't be beat. Except for one or two questionable transcriptions that are of no great import, this singularly important reissue can't be beat, either. As Johnson sings on "Stop Breakin' Down Blues," "The stuff I got'll bust your brains out, baby, hoo hoo, it'll make you lose your mind."

Robert Pete Williams: 1914–1980

ROLLING STONE | MAY 28, 1981

"He really seemed to be almost a star-crossed or doomed person," recalled Dick Waterman, Robert Pete Williams's former manager. "He believed in every ghost, mojo, vampire—he absolutely believed in all of that. He wouldn't go near a graveyard at night. He was really a quiet, shy, gentle man, a very good husband and father. And partly because he was shy, partly because he was always very conscious of being illiterate, and partly because he was always preceded by this reputation of having done several years at Angola prison farm for murder, he tended to project a real formidable presence."

My own first memories of Robert Pete Williams are of being chilled to the bone. Waterman had booked this most improvisational and introspective of country bluesmen on a Newport–New York Jazz Festival blues show. He came walking out onto the stage of Philharmonic Hall, hit one of his rangy guitar runs, began singing in that mournful, insinuating way of his, and simply froze the place. The shiver worked its way up my spine, and I noticed other people stiffening in their seats. As Peter Guralnick wrote in *Feel Like Going Home*, it was "difficult to approve the banalities of most blues singers after listening to Robert Pete Williams. More than anyone else, he shatters the conventions of the form and refuses to rely upon any of the clichés, either of music or of lyric, which bluesman after bluesman will invoke." It's the kind of thing people say about most blues singers, but in Robert Pete Williams's case, it happened to be the truth.

Williams died at sixty-six at his home in Maringouin, Louisiana, not far from Baton Rouge, at 3:45 A.M. last December 31, after a protracted battle with cancer. News of his death took months to filter out of his tiny hometown. He'd been hospitalized, but "the disease progressed beyond medication and pain pills," according to Waterman, and Williams returned home, where he lived for several months before finally succumbing. Williams, who had often talked gloomily about having failed to heed an early call to the ministry, was buried after a traditional funeral service at Mt. Gideon Baptist Church in Maringouin. He is survived by his wife, Hattie Mae, eight sons, two daughters, twenty-nine grandchildren, and ten great-grandchildren.

Robert Pete Williams was born in 1914 to a family of sharecroppers near Zachary, Louisiana. He received virtually no education and began working in the fields when he was a child. He didn't pick up the guitar until he was twenty, and then learned only enough to re-create popular blues hits at country suppers and fish frics. But during the next two decades, while drifting from plantation to plantation in the vicinity of Baton Rouge, he developed his own blues style. It was so individual that it's never been successfully copied, not even at the height of Williams's popularity during the blues revival of the sixties. Most of the young white blues performers who readily aped Robert Johnson didn't even try to tackle Robert Pete's music. The only artist to record one of his songs was Captain Beefheart, who, accompanied by slide guitarist Ry Cooder, included a magnificent, snarling version of "Grown So Ugly" on his album *Safe as Milk*.

It was in 1955 that Williams, as he put it, "got in trouble." He had gone into a bar to drink and was accosted by a white man who apparently mistook him for someone else. As the man grew increasingly abusive, it became evident that he intended to kill Williams. He came at the singer with a knife, and Williams pulled out his gun. Williams shot him once to slow him down, but he kept coming. Williams shot again, and didn't miss. "I had to burn him," Williams told Dick Waterman. Although it seemed an obvious case of self-defense, Williams had two things going against him: He was an illiterate black, and this was southern Louisiana in the mid-fifties. He was convicted of murder and sent to Angola prison farm, where Leadbelly had served time. He languished there until 1958, when folklorists Harry Oster and Richard B. Allen visited the prison, hoping to record authentic black spirituals and work songs.

What they found in addition to these were the blues, especially the blues of Robert Pete Williams. Oster issued an album, *Angola Prisoner's Blues*, on his own Folklyric label, and it attracted worldwide interest in Williams.

Oster and Allen began petitioning the governor of Louisiana on Robert's behalf, and in December 1959 he was paroled into the custody of a local farmer. Although kept in virtual servitude, he did manage to record an album for the Prestige label, *Free Again*. Finally, in 1964, he was allowed to travel to Rhode Island to appear at the Newport Folk Festival, where he shared a program with Skip James and other recently redis-covered blues greats. After that, he toured Europe, recorded for several traditional and folk-music labels, and worked at festivals and in coffee-houses from New York to Los Angeles. But most of the time he also held down other employment (Peter Guralnick found him driving a scrap-iron truck) and spent as many weeks as he could at home with his large family. He built their home in Maringouin himself.

Onstage, Williams's blues cut like a knife, but Dick Waterman also remembers the man's more introspective side. "One morning when he was staying with me in Philadelphia," Waterman recalled, "I woke up and heard this distant music. Robert Pete was sitting at the bottom of the stairwell outside my apartment, playing very gently and melodically and singing really softly. He was startled when he realized I was standing at the top of the stairs. I told him he ought to play something like that at his concerts, and he said, 'Oh, no, I wasn't really playin' music, I was just talkin' to my wife, Hattie Mae. I take my guitar and talk to her and tell her I'll be back as soon as I play my last date, and it makes me feel not so lonesome.'"

But Robert Pete Williams's blues always sounded lonesome; they were some of the lonesomest blues around. "This is the troublest world," he told Guralnick. "There's trouble all over the world."

He had known enough of it in his lifetime, as his frightening recordings from Angola, reissued on Arhoolie Records, so vividly indicate. "Sometime I feel, feel like committin' suicide," he sang on that album. "I got the nerve, if I just had anythin' to do it with." Perhaps his bravest accomplishment was that when the choice was his again, he chose to live.

Muddy Waters: The Delta Son Never Sets

ROLLING STONE | OCTOBER 5, 1978

Muddy Waters, the master bluesman, is now sixty-three. He lives out in the suburbs, almost an hour's drive from downtown Chicago and the decaying South Side where he lived for the past three decades. His white, two-story frame house sits on a quiet corner, shaded by pine trees, with nothing to let a visitor know who owns it except the small, circumspect initials MW on the front door. Inside, it's comfortable: deep carpeting in the living room, modern furniture, a big, all-electric kitchen with grand-children and neighbors' kids constantly running through it. A few dogs, brought from the South Side where they were protectors, sleep lazily by the toolshed. It's not a pop star's house by any stretch of the imagination, but it's the kind of house very, very few of Chicago's approximately 1.5 million black people will ever own.

Muddy, who is beginning to show his age but remains a wholly commanding presence with his high cheekbones, half-lidded Oriental eyes, and undiminished aura of mannish self-confidence—"I'm a full-*growed* man," he sings, "a natural-born lover man," and you believe him—takes a visitor through the house matter-of-factly, with just a hint of pride. In the small anteroom to the den he points out framed portraits of former sidemen Little Walter and James Cotton, and in the little garden patches around the house and by the concrete driveway, he indicates his cabbage, his greens, his red and green chili peppers, and his okra. He doesn't brag about his successes, one suspects, because he knows he deserves them. But he certainly couldn't have imagined it all when he first got off the Illinois Central train in Chicago, back in May 1943. Except for a brief and not very satisfactory sortie to St. Louis and a few quick visits to Memphis, he had not traveled beyond the countryside and small towns of the Mississippi Delta, and he was twenty-eight years old.

Sunnyland Slim, the pianist and singer who got Muddy his first record date with Leonard and Phil Chess in 1947, is working in the heart of the South Side, Sixty-first and Calumet under the El stop. To find Slim, you walk into Morgen's Liquors' front door, down the bar in the middle, into the boisterous music room in the rear. Slim is sitting at a battered, red Wurlitzer electric piano, rapping out tone clusters in the treble and walking basses with all the authority of his sixty-odd years playing blues, while Louis Myers, the leader of the band and once the guitarist in Little Walter's celebrated Aces, sings blues standards.

"I don't like to play in these kind of places no more," Slim says during a break, sipping from a glass of booze and pushing his weathered face up close so he can be heard over the buzz of conversation and the B. B. King record on the jukebox. "I'll be seventy-six soon. I've just been out to California, Europe. . . . I'm just down here helping Louis out." He knows the subject of the conversation is supposed to be Muddy, and like Muddy, he is a proud man. "You want to know what made Muddy popular? Leonard Chess pushed him. At that time, see, they was still playing the blues on the radio, not like it is now. Those first records he had out, a whole bunch of us had been doin' that rockin' style for years. I brought him in to play guitar for me, on that session when I made 'Johnson Machine

Gun.' The man asked me, 'Say, what about your boy there, can he sing?' Talking about Muddy, you know. And I said, 'Like a bird.'"

Later, over on the North Side in a white singles bar with pinball machines and pizza, Jimmy Rogers, second guitarist on Muddy's classic blues records of the early fifties, is setting up for a gig with the brilliant but erratic harmonica virtuoso Walter Horton. "Muddy," says Rogers, "Muddy has a whole lot of soul. Maybe it's not the words that he says so much as the way that he says 'em. He has a voice that I haven't heard anybody could imitate. They can copy his slide style of guitar, but when the voice comes in, that's different. I know his voice anywhere I hear it."

Willie Dixon, the blues bassist, songwriter, and producer, sums up peer-group opinion in a few characteristically well-chosen words: "Everybody liked him 'cause he could really howl those blues."

What was it about Muddy that made him so widely respected and admired, that made his blues, in his own words, "deeper" than the blues of his competitors? Leonard Chess did push Muddy, but he was pushing a man with extraordinary musical gifts and an extraordinary feeling for the blues.

Conventional wisdom has it that blues melodies consist of five, six, or seven pitches or notes, with the third and the seventh and sometimes the fifth notes of the scale being treated a little funny, flattened but not quite as flat as the black keys on the piano; these are the "blue notes." But if you listen carefully to Muddy, or to any other really deep blues singer, you'll find that he systematically sings the third and, especially, the fifth notes of the scale infinitesimally flatter or sharper, depending on where in the line the pitches fall and on the feelings he's trying to convey.

Muddy is the living master of these subtleties. He gets them on guitar too—listen to his slide solo on "Honey Bee," on the Chess/All-Platinum *Muddy Waters* reissue, for example—and he's aware of getting them. "Yeah, yeah," he says when he is accused of playing microtones, or notes that would fall between the cracks on the piano. "When I plays on the stage with my band, I have to get in there with my guitar and try to bring the sound down to me. But no sooner than I quit playing, it goes back to another, different sound. My blues look so simple, so easy to do, but it's not. They say my blues is the hardest blues in the world to play."

Subtle as these inflections are, young guitarists can at least hope to learn to hear and execute them properly. But as Slim and Rogers and Dixon all noted, Muddy's great strength is his singing, something nobody has been able to duplicate. In addition to his mastery of pitch shadings, he also commands some remarkable textural effects. You can see him in Martin Scorsese's film *The Last Waltz*, screwing up the side of his face, shaking his jowls, constantly readjusting the shape of his mouth in order to get specific vocal sounds. And his timing is a kind of standing joke among musicians who have played with him. "I'm a delay singer," he says. "I don't sing on the beat, I sing behind it. And people have to delay to play with me. They got to hang around, wait, see what's going to happen next."

Muddy's sovereign control of these techniques—how many other bluesmen have had comparable mastery of them? Son House? Robert Johnson? Charley Patton?—goes a long way toward explaining the absolute, unquestioned authority he radiates. It's evident that he didn't learn them in school. They could be taught, if the teacher knew them as well as Muddy does and the student were willing to put in as much time and hard work as it takes to become, say, a first-class opera diva. But in the Delta the learning process, while no less rigorous, was more diffuse.

It's important to remember that Muddy was already an established bluesman when Robert Johnson made the first of his own keening, driven recordings in 1936. In fact, Muddy was already known in Chicago. Willie Dixon, who settled in the Windy City that same year, remembers that when talk got around to serious blues singing, people from the Delta invariably brought up Muddy. Although he heard phonograph records, the way he learned his music and the environment in which he learned it—two sides of the same coin—were almost entirely traditional.

Since Muddy was a fully formed musician by the time he arrived in Chicago, it seemed important to talk about his formative years as thoroughly as possible, and this is what we did, sitting at his kitchen table sipping Piper Heidsieck champagne and Coca-Cola. He was a little reticent at first, but soon he began recalling Mississippi scenes in more detail and really enjoying himself. We rambled through that fated countryside for hours. At times the dogs in back of the house would begin to bay like hounds; Bo, his man who grew up with him on the plantation, would say something to the children in his almost impenetrable Delta accent; a suggestion of a warm breeze would waft in the screen door, and we would *be* there.

Muddy was born McKinley Morganfield in Rolling Fork, Mississippi, April 4, 1915. He doesn't remember anything about his parents' cabin because when he was a baby his mother carried him to the country near Clarksdale, where *her* mother raised him. He got the nickname Muddy right away because he liked to crawl around in the mud and tried to eat it.

His grandmother lived three or four miles outside Clarksdale, on a huge plantation owned by the Stovall family. Not even white folks in the Delta had electricity in those days, and water came from a pump. Every day the able-bodied members of that household went out to work in the cotton fields. Nominally, they were farming the Stovalls' land and sharing in the proceeds from the crop. But since the Stovalls kept the books and charged the black families for seed and provisions from the plantation store, the sharecroppers usually ended up in debt after the year's tally. Men could also work for salaries, picking or chopping cotton or, later, driving a tractor. Families could raise their own vegetables and livestock to eat, milk, or sell. But it was still a rough, precarious existence, one that depended on the notorious vagaries of Delta weather as much as it did on any human agency.

As far as Muddy can remember, he was born musical. "When I was around three years old I was beatin' on bucket tops and tin cans. Anything with a sound I would try to play it; I'd even take my stick and beat on the ground tryin' to get a new sound. [He still likes mud and earth. Even today, nothing seems to relax Muddy as much as getting down on his hands and knees and digging in his garden.] And whatever I beat on, I'd be hummin' my little baby song along with it. My first instrument, which a lady give me and some kids soon broke for me, was an old squeeze box, an accordion. The next thing I had in my hand was a Jew's-harp. When I was about seven I started playing the harmonica, and when I got about thirteen I was playing it very good. I should never have give it up! But when I was seventeen I switched to the guitar and put the harp down. I sold our last horse for the first guitar I had. Made fifteen dollars for him, gave my grandmother $7.50, I kept $7.50, and paid about $2.50 for my guitar."

Even before he bought the guitar, Muddy was playing at country suppers and fish fries for pocket change, blowing his harp along with a guitarist friend named Scott. But once he had the guitar in his hands, Muddy learned fast. The basic Delta blues repertoire—songs like "Catfish Blues," which became the basis for Muddy's "Rollin' Stone," or "Dark Road Blues," or "Walkin' Blues"—was readily accessible, since anybody who fooled with a guitar was able more or less to get through them. For fine points, there were masters to emulate: "Charley Patton? He had so much showmanship in his thing, all this wild clownin' with the guitar, and he could *holler*! Ooh, what a voice. But Son House was the top man in my book. I always did like the bottleneck style, and he was the man doin' that then. And he had the kind of singing I liked, that preaching kind of singing."

Son House occasionally renounced the blues and preached in churches, though never for very long until he left Mississippi. I wondered if Muddy went to church. "Yes *sir*," he said, "can't you hear it in my voice? Plenty of people would stay up all night and listen to the blues and go home, get ready and go to church. Back then, there was three things I wanted to be: a heck of a preacher, a heck of a ballplayer, or a heck of a musician."

When Muddy was twelve or thirteen, a neighbor bought a record player, and he began spending hours at her house, listening to Memphis Minnie's "Bumble Bee" (the basis of his "Honey Bee"), Lonnie Johnson's "Careless Love," and Patton's "Pony Blues." When he took up the guitar, the first two songs he learned were from records: "How Long Blues" by Leroy Carr, a blues pianist who lived in Indianapolis, and "Sittin' on Top of the World" by a black string band, the Mississippi Sheiks. He played both of them with a slide, translating relatively urbane pieces into a stark, insistent Delta style.

Muddy never looked back once he established himself locally as a musician. "I didn't like farming," he said. "I always expected my guitar could beat driving tractors, plowing mules, chopping cotton, drawing water. Sometimes they'd want us to work Saturday, but—and Bo here can witness this—they'd look for me and I'd be *gone*, playing my guitar in the little town or in some juke joint. Was I a rambler? I rambled all the time. That's why I added that verse about the rollin' stone to 'Catfish Blues' and named it 'Rollin' Stone.' I was just like that, like a rollin' stone." Muddy recorded his classic rambler's boast in 1950. It furnished the name for the rock & roll band and for this magazine. "But I didn't ramble that far," Muddy added. "I was in love with my grandmother, she was getting old, and I didn't want to push out and leave her."

Muddy married when he was eighteen. His bride was around seventeen, and they both had to lie about their ages at the Clarksdale courthouse. Since Muddy now had more responsibilities and less reason to ramble, his next move was to go into the Saturday-night business for himself. "First I'd have my own Saturday-night dances. I got hip and started making and selling my own whiskey, playing for myself. I had my little crap table going in the back. I'd put coal oil in bottles, take a rope and hang 'em up there on the porch to let people know my dance was going on, and I had a lot of them lights for people to gamble by. It's pretty hard to see the dice sometimes in that lamplight. They had some fast boys with the dice down there; you had to have good eyes."

You had to have more than that. Most gamblers carried a pistol, as Muddy did off and on for years, and most had good-luck charms made by local hoodoo doctors. Sometimes a really successful gambler would disappear for a few days or weeks and reappear with a charm he claimed to have purchased in the South's most powerful hoodoo center, New Orleans. "We all believed in mojo hands, which is a luck charm. If you were gambling, the mojo would take care of that, you'd win, and the woman you want, you could work that on her and win. I won some money one night, so I went off and bought me a three-dollar mojo.

"The mojo doctor's hair was real white, he was a long, tall guy. He looked weird, and he had weird little tingalings hanging in his office. He got a little piece of paper, had writing on it, and he rolled it up tight, sealed it in an envelope, put some perfume on the envelope. And you know what? It was five years before I won another quarter." Bo, who was frying some shrimp, exploded with laughter. "Then I got mad. I got broke once in a crap game and decided I'm gonna open it and see what's in it, and it was just some little writing: 'You win, you win, you win, I win, you win, I win.' I had it read to me. It's just a con game on people's heads, you know, getting the fools. If such a thing as a mojo had've been good, you'd have had to go down to Louisiana to find one. They could have had a few things down in Louisiana doing something. But up in the Delta, nothing, I don't think."

Muddy expanded from occasional Saturday-night dances to a regular operation. By the early forties he was running his own juke house, with a policy wheel for serious gambling, one of the new jukeboxes, his moonshine whiskey, and music. Sometimes he played there alone, blowing a kazoo mounted in a neck rack and bearing down heavily on his guitar to keep people dancing. "They'd be doing the snake hips, working their butts, you know, and all those old dances, and hollering, 'Ooh shit, play it,' and I'm just blowing on my little jazz horn and hitting on my guitar. You know, the country sounds different than in the city, the sound out there be empty. You could hear that guitar before you got to the house, and you could hear the peoples hollering."

This was what was going on in the summer of 1941, when the pioneering folklorist Alan Lomax showed up at Stovall's plantation with his bulky portable recording rig. He was looking for folk music for the Library of Congress and he inquired after Robert Johnson, but Robert had been murdered a few years before and everyone recommended Muddy. "He brought his stuff down and recorded me right in my house," Muddy remembered, "and when he played back the first song I sounded just like anybody's records. Man, you don't know how I felt that Saturday afternoon when I heard that voice and it was my *own voice*. Later on he sent me two copies of the pressing and a check for twenty bucks, and I carried that record up to the corner and put it on the jukebox. Just played it and played it and said, 'I can *do* it, I can *do* it.'"

Lomax returned to Stovall in July 1942 and recorded Muddy again, as a soloist and with the blues fiddler Son Sims and his string band. These and the 1941 recordings are available on the album *Down on Stovall's Plantation*, on the Testament label, and they are phenomenal. Muddy played his steel-bodied guitar with razor-sharp accuracy, setting up hypnotic repeating patterns in the bass and filling in sharp slide figures in the treble, singing with gripping immediacy. He would rework a number of the songs he recorded for Lomax—most of which were based more or less directly on traditional pieces in the first place—into the staples of his repertoire after he got to Chicago. And once Muddy recorded for Lomax he was Chicago-bound, whether he knew it or not.

He had already been infected by a certain restlessness. "I left my first little wife, who's dead now, God bless her, for another woman," he recalled, looking a little wistful for the first and only time in the conversation. "I don't know what the hell was wrong with me; I was kind of a wild cat, man. I'd stay with her awhile and then come back and go away, and then I took this other woman from the little town next to my little town and we went and caught a train for St. Louis. But I wasn't used to the big city and I didn't like it, so we went back, and I told my wife, 'Hey, I done got married, you can move out.' What a mess will country peoples do! Later I brought this woman to Chicago with me and we couldn't get along no kind of way, I had to get rid of her. Well, I was crazy, that's all."

Muddy was bound to tangle with white authority sooner or later, and in May 1943 he had words with the overseer who ran the plantation while Mr. Stovall was away in the army. "I asked him would he raise me to twenty-five cents an hour for driving the tractor, which is what the other people were getting, and he had a fit. When he got through stomping around, my mind just said, 'Go to Chicago.' I went to my grandmother and she said, 'Well, if you think you're going to have some problem'—you know how it was down there—'you better go.' That was on Monday. I worked till that Thursday at five o'clock, and on Friday I came in sick and went on to Clarksdale to catch that four o'clock train."

What Muddy saw when he stepped off the train, still a little woozy from the all-day, all-night journey, was completely alien to the world he had known. "I wish you could've seen me. I got off the train and it looked like this was the fastest place in the world: cabs dropping fares, horns blowing, the peoples walking so fast."

Muddy slept on a couch in the living room of his sister's and her husband's apartment his first week in Chicago. But it was wartime. Industry was booming and manpower was scarce. Muddy got a draft call almost as soon as he arrived in the city—he'd been protected on the plantation because his job was considered vital to agriculture—but once the army learned he had quit school after the second or third grade and couldn't really read or write, they turned him down, to his great delight. He worked several factory and truck-driving jobs, took a four-room apartment, and eventually landed a job delivering venetian blinds. He made his run in the morning, slept in the afternoon, and played at rent parties and in small taverns at night.

His music began to change. He was concentrating more on his singing and less on his guitar, and working with some other musicians from the Delta, among them pianist Eddie Boyd and guitarists Blue Smitty and Baby Face Leroy. In 1945 his grandmother died, and it was in the spring of 1946, after he returned from burying her, that he met Jimmy Rogers, then mostly a harmonica player. They formed a little group with Rogers on harp and Muddy and Smitty on guitars, and began playing around at house parties and small taverns.

"Muddy was a little older," Jimmy says, "and he was the most like ol' Robert Johnson's style with the slide guitar. I understood the slide style quite well—I learned guitar in the Delta—so I could back him up good. Pretty soon Smitty and I just put Muddy as the leader, because he would do most of the rough blues singing."

The black neighborhoods were lawless and overcrowded. New arrivals, most of them from Mississippi and neighboring states, were pushing in every day and the whites were fighting to keep them contained on the rapidly deteriorating South and West Sides. The blues scene was transitional. Big Bill Broonzy, Tampa Red, and some other Southern bluesmen who had been popular before the war were still the kingpins, largely because of their recording connections. But Muddy and his friends were part of a new wave of musicians who played a harder, more down-home brand of blues, the kind that was being heard in Southern juke joints. In order to cut through crowd noise and compete with the volume of the jukeboxes, these younger bluesmen bought amplifiers, which became mandatory once they began to contend with the decibel level in rowdy city taverns. As the migrants continued to pour in, Muddy's electrified country blues became more and more popular.

Muddy recorded three songs for Columbia in 1946, but they were never issued. In 1947 he was in the studio again, playing guitar for Sunnyland Slim and cutting two numbers of his own for the Aristocrat label, with Slim featured on the piano—"Gypsy Woman," his first recorded blues on a hoodoo theme, and "Little Anna Mae." Leonard and Phil Chess, two Polish immigrants who had started Aristocrat that year to record music aimed at the patrons of their South Side nightclub, didn't know what to make of Muddy's raw sound and shelved the records. But early in 1948 Leonard Chess, who handled the producing end of the business, called Muddy back to cut two more sides, which turned out to be reworkings of two of the traditional blues he'd recorded for Lomax.

They were "I Can't Be Satisfied" and "I Feel Like Going Home." Singing at peak power and playing magnificent electric slide guitar, backed only by Big Crawford's string bass, Muddy was just too impressive to ignore.

Leonard Chess knew very little about down-home blues, having recorded mostly tenor-saxophone instrumentals by the jazz-oriented performers who worked at his club, but he put the record out. To his surprise, it became Aristocrat's biggest seller. From that point on the Chess brothers were sold on Muddy, and of course the record changed Muddy's life. "The little joint I was playing in doubled its business when the record came out," he recalled. "Bigger joints started looking for me. It was summer when that record came out, and I would hear it walking along the street, driving along the street. One time coming home about two or three o'clock in the morning I heard it coming from way upstairs somewhere and it scared me, I thought I had died."

At first Leonard Chess would not record Muddy's band, apparently because he thought he had found a hit-making formula in Muddy's voice and guitar and the string bass. Of course, the records weren't really hits. They sold in an area that corresponded to the spread of the Delta's black population, from Mississippi up through Memphis, St. Louis, Detroit, and Chicago, with very little action in the East or the West. But within this area, sales were strong and dependable. Soon Leonard grew confident enough of Muddy's abilities to let him bring in a few more musicians, and in 1950, the year the brothers changed the name of their label from Aristocrat to Chess, Muddy showed up for a session with a young, tough-looking harmonica player from Louisiana, Little Walter Jacobs.

Walter was the first harmonica player to use his amplifier creatively. He produced massive roars, ghostly tremolos and whoops, and punching, saxophone-like solo lines on the instrument and revolutionized the sound of Chicago blues while he was with Muddy's band.

In 1951 Jimmy Rogers joined the recording group on second guitar. With Elgin Evans on drums, this was the band that defined the sound of postwar Chicago blues and sent ripples through the world of popular music that continue to be felt. Muddy was still playing country blues, but with a beat. "My first drummer was straight down the line," he said, "boom boom boom boom. I had to get me somebody who would put a backbeat to it." Added Willie Dixon, "You know, when you go to changing beats in music, you change the entire style. Blues or rock & roll or jazz, it's the beat that actually changes it. And that's what Muddy did. He gave his blues a little more pep."

The band turned out great records in profusion: "Long Distance Call," "Honey Bee," "She Moves Me," and the searing "Still a Fool" in 1951; "Standing Around Crying" (with an initial appearance by the incomparable pianist Otis Spann) in 1952; and the seminal "Hoochie Coochie Man" in 1953. This last tune, written by Willie Dixon, is the sort of thing most people associate with Muddy—a slow, lumbering stop-time riff, lyrics that combine hoodoo imagery and machismo. It was more flamboyant than Muddy's own hoodoo blues, but it was just the kind of thing his audience wanted to hear.

"Muddy was working in this joint at Fourteenth and Ashland," Dixon remembers, "and I went over there to take him the song. We went in the washroom and sang it over and over till he got it. It didn't take very long. Then he said, 'Man, when I go out there this time, I'm gonna *sing* it.' He went out and jumped on it, and it sounded so good the people kept applauding and asking for more and he kept on singing the same thing over and over again." There was no need for further market research. The audience was right there and not at all shy about stating its preferences. Dixon wrote more hits for Muddy, most notably "I'm Ready" and "I Just Want to Make Love to You." They remain the most macho songs in his repertoire; Muddy would never have composed anything so unsubtle. But they gave him a succession of showstoppers and an image, which were important for a bluesman trying to break out of the grind of local gigs into national prominence.

Muddy's records were never huge hits, not even among the nation's blacks. "Hoochie Coochie Man" made it to number eight on the R&B charts and "Just Make Love to Me" was number four in 1954. The band would drive from gig to gig in Muddy's Cadillac, working mostly in joints on the South and West Sides of Chicago and in the South, with occasional forays to the East. Even though he had fewer hits once rock & roll came along, Muddy was in the game for keeps. "Rock & roll," he said, "it hurt the blues pretty bad. People wanted to 'bug all the time and we couldn't play slow blues anymore. But we still hustled around and kept going. We survived, and then I went to Newport in 1960 and it started opening the door for me."

His first crack at a white audience came in 1958, when the English

promoter Chris Barber brought Waters's band to England on Big Bill
Broonzy's recommendation. At first the tour seemed to be a disaster.
"Oh man," said Muddy, "the headlines in all the papers was SCREAMING
GUITAR AND HOWLING PIANO. Chris Barber said, 'You sound good, but
don't play your amplifier so loud.' Then I came back to England in the
early sixties and everybody want to know why I didn't bring my amplifier.
Those boys were playing louder than we ever played."

"Those boys" were the Rolling Stones, the Yardbirds with young
Eric Clapton, and other white blues groups that had sprung up in England, following the lead of older performers like Alexis Korner and Cyril
Davies, and been among the few enthralled by Muddy's volume and raw
power in 1958. The Stones and their contemporaries were still kids in
1960 when Muddy scored a direct hit with the folk audience at Newport,
but they eagerly bought his Newport album, which included the classic
extended version of "Got My Mojo Working." In fact, those blue-and-
white Chess records from America were as important to them as eating
and sleeping. They listened hard to Chuck Berry, whose first recording
date was set up by Muddy, and to Bo Diddley, who also came out of the
South Side. But Muddy's records had a special, mysterious luminosity.
They were so distinctive, so "deep," that they couldn't really be copied,
not like Chuck and Bo, though the Stones tried with a brooding rendition of "Can't Be Satisfied" that Muddy terms "a very good job." (In mid-
July 1978, Mick Jagger, Keith Richards, Ron Wood, and Charlie Watts
surprised Muddy by showing up to jam with him at Chicago's the Quiet
Knight. Mick and Muddy had a high time trading vocal licks on "Mannish Boy," and Keith played some stinging slide guitar.)

In the States too the music was reaching young whites, who were
coming in, literally in many cases, through the back door. Johnny Winter, who grew up in Beaumont, Texas, remembers that "Muddy was one
of the first people I fell in love with. I guess I was about eleven. My
grandparents were fairly well off and they had a maid and a guy that'd
been working for them for years, and they'd have the black radio station
on. I just couldn't believe that music; as soon as I heard it I was obsessed
with finding out what it was and hearing more of it. Pretty soon all the
record shops in town were saving me a copy of every blues record that
came in." The process had been going on since the early fifties, when
record-store proprietors began to notice whites showing up and buying

race records "for my maid" or "for my yardman"—records they'd heard their maids and yardmen bopping to and wanted to bop to themselves. By the early sixties young white musicians were emulating the music on those backdoor records, Johnny Winter among them.

For Muddy, though, the sixties were an unsettled and unsettling period. It was true that young whites were beginning to appreciate his blues—outside Chicago, they made up the major part of his audience. But he was much more concerned with the blacks who were turning their backs on the blues. "When the Rollin' Stones came through the States," he said, "they came to record at the Chess studios. When that happened, I thinks to myself how these white kids was sitting down and thinking and playing the blues that my black kids was bypassing. That was a hell of a thing, man, to think about. I still think about it today. Some of these white kids are playing *good* blues, but my people, they want something they can bump off of. I play places now don't have no black faces in there but *our* black faces."

Muddy's recording scene was unsettled, too. His brand of blues was no longer selling, and although he continued to put together strong bands with the help of Otis Spann, his pianist, bandleader, and right-hand man from the mid-fifties until his death in the late sixties, Muddy never again found sidemen as creative, sympathetic, and cohesive as Little Walter and Jimmy Rogers. (Walter left him in 1952 when "Juke" became a hit, and Rogers split in 1955 to put together his own band.) Leonard Chess's son Marshall and other young executives at Chess began trying to package Muddy, starting with albums like *Muddy Waters, Folk Singer*, which was a reasonable acoustic album, and *Brass and the Blues*, culminating in the dreadful *Electric Mud* and *After the Rain*, which pleased nobody. Then Chess was sold and resold. For two decades Muddy had enjoyed a family-style relationship with the Chess company. Now he belonged to a succession of faceless conglomerates.

The picture began to brighten during the early seventies. He took on Scott Cameron, a shrewd, hardheaded manager who helped him in a number of ways. They sued Arc Music, the Chess publishing company, for back royalties on scores of his compositions, and although nobody will discuss the terms of the eventual out-of-court settlement, apparently Muddy was at least partially satisfied. And finally he pulled free of his Chess entanglements altogether and signed in 1976 with Blue

Sky Records, the Columbia-affiliated label managed by Steve Paul. With Johnny Winter as producer he made two splendid albums, *Hard Again* and *I'm Ready*. Winter wisely avoided trying to duplicate the Chess sound, but he did put Muddy back in a raw-edged, pure blues context, with sympathetic backing from former sidemen like Jimmy Rogers, Big Walter Horton, and James Cotton. Winter mimicked Muddy's guitar style so accurately, especially on *Hard Again*, that it was virtually impossible to tell which one was playing.

The records sold fifty to sixty thousand copies each and are still moving briskly, making them the best sellers of Muddy's career. He began getting better jobs for better money, especially after an all-star tour with Cotton and Winter that furnished material for a third, soon-to-be-released Blue Sky album. And he was as impressive as ever on that tour. He would start each performance sitting on his stool, letting his voice carry the music, but then he would pick up his guitar and play a wrenching slide solo, the band would begin to fly, and soon he would be up working the lip of the stage, weaving and bobbing to the music and roaring out his lyrics as if they mattered more than anything else in the world.

"This is the best point of my life I'm living right now," Muddy said with great finality near the end of our last conversation. I wondered how he felt about having taken so long to get to this point and he looked at me like I was a plain fool, his eyes shining with the irony that informs some of his greatest records. "Feels good," he said, "are you kidding? I'm glad it came before I died, I can tell you. Feels great."

Lightnin' Hopkins at 68:
Still Singing Those Blues

THE NEW YORK TIMES | OCTOBER 31, 1980

"I want my money," said Lightnin' Hopkins. He was flashing a gleaming, gold-toothed smile, and his powder-blue suit was the brightest thing in the dingy nightclub basement, but his eyes were hidden behind dark sunglasses and it was impossible to read what was in them. He took a swallow of whiskey, shook his head slowly from side to side, and looked up at the club owner, who was standing in the doorway of the dressing room. "You've got one more show to do, Lightnin'," he said. Mr. Hopkins tapped a bulge in his hip pocket significantly; it could have been a wallet or a flask, but on the other hand. . . . "If you want it now, Lightnin', that's no problem," said the club owner. Mr. Hopkins smiled even more broadly. "Yes," he said, "I want it now." The club owner disappeared and Mr. Hopkins leaned back in his chair, emitting a short, dry laugh.

An aura of vaguely defined but palpable menace hovers around Lightnin' Hopkins, the sixty-eight-year-old singer and guitarist from Houston, whose vivid, often bitter lyrics are among the more striking verbal inventions in the blues tradition. The menace is part of his survival equipment; after growing up on a Texas farm, hoboing around the state as a teenager, and serving time on the Houston County Prison Farm in the late 1930s, Mr. Hopkins settled in Houston for good in the mid-forties, and he's lived there ever since, frequently working in bars and juke joints where at least the veneer of toughness is a necessity.

In truth, there's no evidence that Mr. Hopkins is a violent man, and in fact people who know him well describe him as a generous friend. But he tends to keep his own counsel, and while he's capable of building up a steamroller momentum with just his guitar and voice, his blues are often so personal and introspective he could almost be ruminating to himself. . . .

Sam Hopkins was born in Centerville, Texas, in the middle of the Cotton Belt and about halfway between Dallas and Houston, on March 15, 1912, and when he was eight years old he made his first guitar out of the archetypal cigar box.

Joel Hopkins, his older half brother, taught him some basic guitar blues, enough to get him started as a musician. When he was young, possibly as young as eight or ten, Sam Hopkins left school and began traveling around Texas as a hobo, occasionally stopping to work as a farmhand and at other jobs and sometimes playing the guitar and singing at country picnics and parties. During the course of his ramblings he encountered Blind Lemon Jefferson, the most popular Texas blues singer of his day and an artist who recorded prolifically, beginning in 1926. Mr. Hopkins also met his cousin Texas Alexander, a tough man with a voice like barbed wire who sang but didn't play an instrument and took the young guitarist on as his accompanist.

Texas Alexander recorded some of the most powerful blues of the 1930s, and although Sam Hopkins never backed him on records, their partnership was long lasting. They were working together at Houston's Rainbow Theater as early as 1927 and they were still working together on Houston street corners and city buses in the early 1950s. . . .

Because Mr. Alexander was used to singing by himself, he tended not to follow a set metric scheme, and he always sang personally; even when he was using a traditional blues text he would alter it in some way so that it fitted his own situation more closely. Sam Hopkins also expresses his thoughts in music without recourse to a regular metric pattern, and he personalizes everything he sings.

But his voice isn't as heavy and gruff as Mr. Alexander's was; he tends to sound more like Blind Lemon Jefferson when he sings, and Mr. Jefferson's unpredictable guitar accompaniments, with their sudden bursts of speed and equally sudden silences, their flurries of notes and sharp, hammered punctuations, became the basis of Mr. Hopkins's style.

During the thirties Mr. Hopkins wandered around the South, working as far afield as Yazoo City in the Mississippi Delta. But by 1945 he was back in Houston, where he became well-known around Dowling Street, the main thoroughfare of the city's mostly black Third Ward. It was there that he was found by Lola Anne Cullum, a blues enthusiast and budding businesswoman who managed a local pianist and future rhythm and blues star, Amos Milburn.

Mrs. Cullum had already arranged for Mr. Milburn to record in Los Angeles, where a number of small labels were making money with disks aimed at black record buyers. When she took Mr. Milburn to Los Angeles for his second recording session, she also took Sam Hopkins and a pianist he sometimes played with, Wilson Smith. It was at this initial 1946 session that a record-company employee nicknamed Sam Hopkins Lightnin'; Wilson Smith, who soon dropped from sight, became Thunder.

Mr. Hopkins wasn't interested in traveling to promote his early recordings; they made him a star in Houston, and that was enough. His song "Katy Mae" became a local hit, and soon he was recording in his own town, for Houston's Gold Star label. Gold Star's Bill Quinn would pay him one hundred dollars in cash when he came up with a few new numbers, and Mr. Hopkins, who'd been making songs out of things he saw and things that happened to him for years, found that coming up with new numbers was easy.

He recorded perhaps more prolifically than any other postwar blues artist. There wasn't much musical variety to his recordings, just that parched, knowing voice and sparse, dramatic electric guitar for the most part. But the lyrics were another matter. Though blues musicians are often called "folk poets," most of them are heavily dependent on traditional lines and stanzas. Mr. Hopkins is a real folk poet, a chronicler of his life and his community who's the closest thing to the tradition-bearing "griots" of West Africa and Alex Haley's *Roots* that one can find in the United States.

Mr. Hopkins was still selling records to black blues fans in the late fifties, when he became one of the early heroes of the blues revival. By the end of 1960 he had recorded for Folkways, Tradition, and World Pacific, three labels catering to college students and other white folk-music aficionados, and he performed at the University of California Folk Festival in Berkeley, where he began a long association with Arhoolie Records.

Some of his best albums are still available in the voluminous Arhoolie catalog—*Early Recordings*, volumes one and two, for example, and *The Texas Bluesman*, which includes several gripping narrative songs and the stark "Slavery." These days, Mr. Hopkins travels when he wants to but still spends a great deal of time in his customary Houston haunts.

On past New York visits, Mr. Hopkins has performed at Carnegie Hall and opened for rock groups at the Palladium, but he's usually at his best in a small club, especially when the audience is willing to interact with him.

His visit to Tramps this weekend provides a welcome opportunity to watch a master at work in a setting that's often been particularly convivial for blues.

Black Snake Moan: The History of Texas Blues

GUITAR WORLD | SEPTEMBER 1996

No matter what you may have heard or read, nobody knows where the blues began—or even if it *did* begin in a particular place, as opposed to springing up in several places more or less simultaneously. The Mississippi Delta is often credited with being the "cradle of the blues," but there is evidence that the music was flourishing in Texas at least as early as it was in Mississippi. When asked for his opinion, pioneering blues and folk scholar Alan Lomax used to quote a traditional, anonymous lyric he had encountered early in his travels: "The blues came from Texas, loping like a mule."

Blues is by nature something of a gumbo—part field holler, part guitar ragtime and songster balladry, part barrelhouse boogie, with a seasoning of gospel, jazz, and even hillbilly music. In Texas, a big, big state with a number of immigrant communities and small farmers in addition to its large cotton plantations, early blues musicians were exposed to an unusually broad range of influences: mariachi bands and flamenco-inspired guitarists from Mexico; French-speaking Cajun and zydeco bands; the polkas and other accordion-driven dance music of German and Eastern European settlers; a widespread jazz scene, with sophisticated music heard not only in the cities but out in the rural "territories" as well; old-time hoedown music. To some degree, Texas blues absorbed all these influences. And the blues was a prime ingredient in later Texas styles such as Western swing, honky-tonk, and rockabilly.

Texas's blues pedigree is unsurpassed and the Lone Star state, along with its bordering territories (parts of Louisiana, Arkansas, and Oklahoma), also played a formative role in the development of boogie-woogie, the pounding, rocking eight-to-the-bar rhythmic foundation for all subsequent developments in rock & roll. The origins of boogie are generally attributed to anonymous black pianists who entertained workers in the isolated, backwoods lumber and turpentine camps of eastern Texas and western Louisiana, probably around the turn of the century.

A traveling pianist and songwriter from New Orleans, Clarence Williams, reported hearing a Texas pianist playing boogie-woogie bass figures in Houston in 1911, more than fifteen years before the first boogie-woogie recordings. (The Texas pianist George Thomas was the patriarch of a piano-playing family that included early recording artists Hociel and Hersal Thomas and their sister, better known as the classic blues singer—and Bonnie Raitt idol—Sippie Wallace.) In 1917 or 1918 another pianist, Sammy Price, heard blues guitarist Blind Lemon Jefferson playing bass-string boogie riffs. The term Jefferson knew, however, was "booger rooger," which was something like an all-weekend house party, what East Texas Cajuns called a "La La." You can hear Jefferson's jamming, loose-limbed approach to the "booger rooger" rhythm in the final choruses of "Easy Rider Blues," his version of the Texas standard of pre–World War I vintage. As with so much of the history of American music, nobody knows for sure whether boogie-woogie was invented by pianists and later adapted to the guitar, or the other way around. However it went down, it probably went down in Texas.

The First Guitarists

Guitars seem to have found their way into the hands of black musicians in Texas earlier than in other parts of the South. The long border the state shares with Mexico meant there was widespread contact with Spanish-speaking immigrants, whose culture has cherished the guitar since the Moors brought prototypes to Spain in the Middle Ages. Centuries later, back in Texas, the first wave of black guitarists we know about had already developed their own style and repertoire well before the initial wave of popularity for the blues. Huddie Ledbetter, better known as Leadbelly, roamed the countryside, playing a rolling, bass-heavy style of twelve-string guitar (then a novel Mexican import) and singing narrative ballads, hoedown tunes, and other dance music that predated the blues. "Texas" Henry Thomas was a hobo who ferociously strummed his guitar while blowing on a set of cane panpipes that was rack-mounted around his neck like a harmonica.

Thomas left an impressive body of recordings, including "Going Up the Country," made famous by Canned Heat. Of all the Texas songsters (archetypal wandering bluesmen, except that they performed more ballads, breakdowns, and ragtime than blues), Mance Lipscomb was one of the longest-lived and best-loved. Unlike Leadbelly and Thomas, he generally stayed in one spot and farmed, rather than brave the juke joints and barrelhouses, where murder and mayhem could be counted on to spice up most any Saturday night.

During the first few decades of this century, blues slowly eclipsed the old songster ballads and hoedown tunes as the rural dance and entertainment music of choice. In most of the South, there were considerable social as well as musical barriers separating blues musicians from those who played jazz or sang gospel. Blues was "country," associated with the "down and out," and considered musically moronic to many jazz musicians, the devil's music to pious churchgoers. Texas, once again, did things differently. From the beginning, Texas blues and jazz enjoyed a fruitful relationship, one that worked to the advantage of both. Even the most unreconstructed, musically primitive bluesmen, such as the influential singer Texas Alexander, often recorded with a sympathetic jazz player or two as featured soloists. The jazz musicians, for their part, didn't share the disdain for the blues that many of their peers expressed.

In fact, jazz bands from Texas and Oklahoma largely built their reputations playing loosely arranged, rhythmically compelling jump blues. This was as true of the Blue Devils, twenties precursors of the original Count Basie Band, as it was twenty years later, when Houston's Milt Larkin Orchestra introduced a whole new generation of honking, big-toned Texas saxophonists—bluesmen all.

Blind Lemon Jefferson

But when it comes to blues, Blind Lemon Jefferson was the most influential artist Texas produced until the post–World War II arrival of seminal electric guitarist T-Bone Walker. As early as 1915, Jefferson was known around Dallas and in the surrounding countryside as an itinerant street singer. Beginning in 1926, he enjoyed a string of hit records that continued, off and on, until his death in 1929. Nowadays, Charley Patton, Robert Johnson and other Mississippi Delta bluesmen are best remembered among Lemon's near-contemporaries. But he was arguably a more significant blues artist than any of them. According to blues historian Steve Calt, a Patton champion and biographer, Blind Lemon Jefferson was "as important within the scheme of blues as Elvis Presley is to rock" and "the most famous male blues singer who ever lived, rivaling Bessie Smith for popularity among record buyers of his time."

Many rural bluesmen habitually drop a beat or a bar or add a half-bar or more to the standard twelve-bar verse, resulting in actual verse lengths of twelve and a half, thirteen, or thirteen and a half bars—often in the same tune. On first impression, Jefferson's playing was even more anarchic than that. While singing, he would strum quiet chords or softly mark the beat, but his guitar fills, generally tumbling, single-note lines inserted between vocal verses, were liable to meander almost anywhere. Calt describes these fills as "impromptu-sounding riffs of no fixed order or duration." This edge-of-your-seat approach to improvisation is what makes Jefferson classics like "Match Box Blues," "See That My Grave Is Kept Clean," and "That Black Snake Moan" perennially rewarding and surprising.

In effect, Jefferson developed and popularized "lead guitar" as a style of blues accompaniment. T-Bone Walker, who listened to Jefferson and followed him around Dallas as a youth, later amplified the single-note lead lines he'd inherited. Walker's combination of melodic invention, bluesy string-bending, and jazz-flavored chord voicings inspired virtually every blues-based guitarist who's come along since—including Delta-bred stylists as influential in their own right as B. B. King and Robert Jr. Lockwood.

Electric Texas

Texas musicians took to the electric guitar as rapidly and enthusiastically as they had taken up the guitar itself at the beginning of the century. Eddie Durham, a guitarist from San Marcos, Texas, made his first "amplified" guitar in the early thirties, using a tin pan as a resonator. Soon he had graduated to homemade pickups, playing through radios and phonographs, and leaving a trail of burned-out appliances behind him. When DeArmond came out with its pioneering pickup in the thirties, Durham was among the first to use it. In 1937, he met another young local guitarist, Charlie Christian, and they traded amplification arcana.

Paralleling these developments, amplified guitar and lap-steel guitar made quick inroads into the Western swing music scene. The most startling of the early electric steel players was Bob Dunn, a featured soloist with Milton Brown and his Brownies. Dunn played pedal steel like a modernist-leaning trumpeter: isolated bursts of notes, daring harmonic choices, unpredictable phrasing that could be jagged one minute and flow like honey the next. By the end of the thirties, Milton Brown's band had broken up (following the leader's death on the highway) and the best-known, most influential Western swing pickers were guitarist Eldon Shamblin and steel guitarist Leon ("Take it away, Leon!") McAuliffe, both featured with Bob Wills. Nobody who's heard Bob Dunn's twisted steel lines come cascading out of a charming piece of Milton Brown square-dance hokum can forget the experience. The guy was one of a kind, and his few recordings must only hint at his weird genius.

After World War II, electric guitars and guitarists continued to proliferate, challenging and eventually supplanting the saxophonists as vernacular music's principal solo voice. Iconoclastic, quasi-free-form blues guitarists in the Blind Lemon tradition—Lightnin' Hopkins, Frankie Lee Sims, the Black Ace, and others—plugged in and rocked the juke joints and taverns. But the T-Bone Walker mode was dominant, and in the forties and fifties Texas produced an astonishing number of influential, wildly kinetic, and competitive lead guitarist/blues singers. Even a limited list would have to include iconic figures such as Clarence "Gatemouth" Brown, Pee Wee Crayton, Freddie King, Albert Collins, Johnny Copeland, Lowell Fulson, Cal Green (Hank Ballard and the Midnighters' axman), Clarence Garlow, Roy Gaines, Goree Carter (whose 1949 "Rock Awhile" is a worthy candidate for "first-ever rock & roll record"), not to mention legendary session guitarists such as Wayne Bennett and Clarence Holloman and lap-steel-playing bluesmen Sonny Rhodes and Hop Wilson. Most of these guitarists fronted bands with a small horn section of saxes and brass as well as the standard piano, bass, and drums; the close connection between blues and jazz in Texas was still very much in evidence.

Artists such as these often performed locally, bringing their shows not just to cities and towns but to rough, rural dance halls. This rich musical environment had everything to do with the growth and development of younger musicians coming of age in the sixties. For electric guitarists Johnny Winter, Jimmie and Stevie Ray Vaughan, and Doug Sahm, as well as for acoustically minded pickers like Willie Nelson and Townes Van Zandt, blues was much more than a musical language acquired from obscure phonograph records. Blues was a language they shared with the form's mostly black creators, often from early childhood. As a result, Texas guitarists seem to have a genuine, deeply rooted feel for the blues, whatever their color. When Stevie Ray soared on minor-key blues changes, or when Van Zandt picks and sings one of his ten- and eleven-bar originals, there can be no doubt: This is the blues. We shouldn't be surprised; from Bob Dunn to honky-tonk's Lefty Frizzell to rockabilly's Sleepy LaBeef, Texas guitarists have been playing and singing idiomatic, natural blues for generations.

Big State, Bigger Questions

Why is this significant and substantial musical culture still relatively little known and underappreciated? Texas was *a*, perhaps *the*, incubator for blues and boogie-woogie at the beginning of this century, and later for electric blues, honky-tonk, and important developments in country-swing and rock. Yet we hear and read much more about the Delta, Robert Johnson, and Muddy Waters. In part, Delta blues has attracted fans and boosters with its rawer, more in-your-face approach featuring aggressively driving, syncopated cross-rhythms. And Delta music has a potent mystique—hellhounds on your trail, blues and the devil walking side by side, selling your soul to the dark man at the crossroads. To some degree, this mystique was calculated from the very beginning; early bluesmen such as Tommy Johnson, Son House, and Muddy Waters knew that invoking hoodoo not only played to the beliefs and fears of their audience in the joints, it was image-making that sold records. Texas has its own brand of hoodoo, and it has seeped into tunes like Hop Wilson's odes to his baby's black-cat bone. But the deep, heavy, serious metaphysical baggage that comes with so much Delta blues is rare in Texas, where blues is, above all, music for entertainment and dancing or for chronicling the ups and downs of day-to-day experience, as in the autobiographical blues of Lightnin' Hopkins.

Delta blues is a kind of sacred music, opposed to the church but espousing its own African-rooted spiritual values. In Texas, on the other hand, blues tends to be resolutely, unapologetically secular, sensuous, even carnal—like rock & roll. The blues scholars may not all get it, but musicians do; there isn't a blues guitarist alive who hasn't picked up something from T-Bone Walker or one of his disciples, just as no jazz guitarist for decades has remained untouched by the innovations of Charlie Christian. Among Texas guitarists, musical standards are particularly high, which is why you'll find even B. B. King worshipping at T-Bone's feet. That Texas blues just keeps loping along, but these days it's more like an express train than a mule.

Out There in the Dirt

Liner notes for *All Night Long* by Junior Kimbrough & the Soul Blues Boys (Fat Possum, 1993, produced by Robert Palmer)

Crawling around in the dirt. Crawling around in the dirt between the rows of blooming, blinding white cotton in the field to the side of Junior's old country juke, and this woman, Lord she must have been sixty, she was out there crawling around in the dirt *with* me, I'm not lyin'! Both of us out there in the sun, drunk on white lightnin' in the middle of the day! And it was *Sunday*! Amps turned up all the way inside the shack, drums making the floorboards boom, you could hear it fine. Yeah out there in the dirt.

Sometimes the music inside would be so *intense*, you'd think twice about going in. People would be clustered on the front porch, perched on the front railing like birds, drinkin' out of mason jars. And that one big room was most of the house, that would be just *throbbing* with Junior's beat, Junior's rhythm. . . . You went in that room, got in there between the band and the people dancing off it, you'd be dancing too, before you'd know it was happening. Like trance dancing, everybody breaking a sweat and the song would go on until their eyes were rolled back in their heads. You'd be dancing and then somebody would be dancing with you, and pretty soon the two of you would be out there crawlin' around in the dirt again. Now how about that!

David "Junior" Kimbrough is the *man*, all through there in that north Mississippi hill country. Junior has been throwing weekly house parties or running his own juke joint for more than thirty years. And even before that he was playing in those places. He grew up there, in the north part of Marshall County, near the Tennessee line, outside a town called Hudsonville. His brothers and sisters all sang and played, and they'd hear neighbors like Fred McDowell and Eli Green play too, and pretty soon people were asking Junior's father to bring *him* around to the party to play. He's been doing it ever since.

Charlie Feathers, the rockabilly innovator, and Stan Kesler, the Sun Records session musician, both remember listening to Junior and learning from him when they were growing up. Feathers and Kesler wrote songs together in the fifties; Elvis recorded several of their tunes. Later on Kesler produced some of the all-time killer rock & roll singles, such as Sam the Sham's "Wooly Bully." In whatever form, the Junior influence is there. It was Feathers who said Junior was "the beginning and the end of music." As a description of his music it isn't all that far-fetched. You'll hear him sing something that sounds like a preblues field holler while he's playing a guitar rhythm like Memphis soul music, and when the bass and drums come in on one of Junior's riffs, the music might sound like some kind of hillbilly-metal-funk that hasn't been heard yet— except around Junior's place. David Nelson described it in an article about Junior that appeared in *Living Blues*: "Kimbrough's music carries the emotion and soul of the deepest blues, yet his music can also match reggae in its hypnotic qualities, as well as stand up to any rock 'n' roll for sheer intensity. . . . Bass, drums and guitar . . . anticipate and feed off each other and know where the songs are going, becoming one big churning *force*."

Until now Junior's music has been heard of more than heard. Two 45 singles (on Philwood and High Water) and a couple of cuts on anthologies (*National Downhome Blues Festival Volume Two*, on Southland, and *Deep Blues*, on Atlantic) were his only recordings. His music was never designed for the recording studio; the crowd at Junior's cues the music's tempo and pacing and the beginning and ending of songs with their shouts of encouragement and their dancing. Even the Soul Blues Boys' overall sound is enveloped and shaped by the acoustical resonance of the room they're playing in.

The wooden shack that inspired crawling around in the dirt outside gave the music a fat, booming bottom. Junior played there each week for sixteen years. His newest joint is a former sanctified church, about ten miles west of Holly Springs, Mississippi, on Highway 4, and there the same music sounds different. It's more hard-edged, with sharper definition and a welter of high harmonics that ring and ricochet up in the vaulted ceiling above the band. We recorded Junior and the Soul Blues Boys in this comfortable environment, the music filling the room with a pervasive sonic drone.

Bluesman R. L. Burnside and his family live close by, and between the Burnsides and Junior there's always music to be heard. The music on this disk, like the scene at Junior's, is very much a family affair. R.L.'s son Gary Burnside plays bass and Kenny Malone, Junior's son, is on drums. They negotiate the often idiosyncratic structures and grooves of Junior's tunes with deceptively casual skill.

As we set up one afternoon to record at Junior's the sky began to darken. The cotton rows and the empty stretch of two-lane blacktop made for a uniform landscape devoid of life, except for our steepled juke. The clouds rolled in suddenly, and as Junior was singing a slow blues, lightning struck the juke joint itself, causing him to trail off at the end. "Slow Lightning" was the result. The rest of the songs are Junior's choices for this, his first album. The performances are as they happened: no editing, no overdubs. You don't need that kind of stuff when lightning strikes. That keeps you rockin' *all* night long.

JAZZ: "A KINETIC KALEIDOSCOPE"

The Dominion of the Black Musician

ROLLING STONE | JULY 26, 1979

It's worth remembering that in the forties, many bebop fans damned Charlie Parker with faint praise while they worshipped Charlie Ventura; that during the fifties, the West Coast jazz of Shorty Rogers and Stan Kenton was touted as the most significant music of its time, while Sonny Rollins and Thelonious Monk were making some of their most enduring recordings; that a prominent jazz critic of the sixties refused to acknowledge the breakthroughs of Ornette Coleman and John Coltrane, preferring to proclaim vibraphonist Gary Burton, a fine but hardly revolutionary musician, the wave of the future.

These items are particularly worth noting if you read Mikal Gilmore's essay on the state of jazz in *Rolling Stone*'s recent jazz supplement (RS 295). Among other things, Gilmore wrote the following: "It may well be that the music is becoming less a chronicle of the black American experience than the meeting place of schooled musical sensibilities, both black and white." That would have been easy to believe in the forties, fifties, or sixties — if Ventura, Shorty, or Burton were your idea of the last word in jazz innovation.

The above statement can be read as a prevalent misunderstanding of jazz's history. But it's perfectly logical if one accepts the perspective that jazz-rock (or fusion music) and the sort of Euro-American jazz classicism purveyed by ECM Records are "two of the main movements in contemporary jazz," with Weather Report and Keith Jarrett as their most talented representatives. Noting the failure of Weather Report and Jarrett to set the entire jazz world aflame, he concludes that "no younger artist (or movement) in the seventies has yet been able to catalyze jazz the way Parker, Coltrane, or Davis did. . . . Now that jazz has become more popular, it seems unable to replenish its diminished supply of leaders."

This is a widely accepted overview; among people who follow jazz casually, it probably represents a consensus. My own view of the contemporary jazz scene is very different. It's shaped by my residence in New York, which allows me to follow the latest developments without having to depend on records, but more than that, it's shaped by the study of jazz history. That history tells us that jazz has always been an experimental music; the most important players have been those who moved the music forward. They have also been black. We've had great white jazzmen, from Bix Beiderbecke in the twenties to Charlie Haden today, but no white player or composer has moved the music forward as radically or as effectively as Louis Armstrong, Duke Ellington, Lester Young, Charlie Parker, Miles Davis, John Coltrane, or Ornette Coleman.

Weather Report and Keith Jarrett — and the fusion and neoclassicism they represent — are marginal if not wholly irrelevant to the evolution of jazz. During the sixties, Weather Report's Joe Zawinul was writing catchy, commercial jazz-funk tunes for Cannonball Adderley. Today he is writing catchy, commercial funk-jazz tunes for Weather Report. His tunes and orchestrations are ingenious, and there can be no doubt that Weather Report stands head and shoulders above the fusion pack. But fusion is not an essentially experimental music. It's a musicianly, semi-improvisational, but essentially popular music; the popular bias is most clearly evident in its consistent use of dance rhythms. Significantly,

Weather Report's considerable impact has been almost entirely within the sphere of fusion and related popular forms.

Keith Jarrett is a brilliant pianist, but his music is just as irrelevant to the ongoing evolution of jazz, and so is the studied classicism of many of his ECM labelmates. In fact, all the contemporary musicians we've been discussing are more retrogressive than progressive. Their harmonic and melodic vocabularies have been shaped primarily by the jazz of the late fifties and early sixties, in the case of Weather Report and many of ECM's European artists; by late-nineteenth- and early-twentieth-century European romanticism, in Jarrett's case; or by blues, soul, and gospel music, in the case of most conventional fusion music. Rhythmically, they either swing as jazz groups did in the fifties, use ostinato bass patterns like the John Coltrane of the early and middle sixties, or investigate their own variants of rhythms from contemporary popular music—rock or funk.

Armstrong, Ellington, Young, Parker, and the rest of the authentic black innovators forged ahead into unexplored territory harmonically, melodically, and especially rhythmically. And, to return to our original premise, their innovations got the necessary approval from younger black musicians, who built on what they had created in order to effect innovations of their own. There is no evidence that many serious young black jazz musicians are listening to Weather Report or Keith Jarrett.

Jazz musicians were playing in racially mixed groups at least as early as the twenties, yet after all these years of musical integration and cooperation, the significant breakthroughs in jazz have continued to come from the black musicians. Why? The answer would require a book, but it seems evident that rhythmic innovation and virtuosity have been vital components of every advance in jazz, and rhythmic sophistication is an integral part of black culture. This isn't necessarily innate, but it is learned by black children at such an early age—through the movements of their parents, the rhythms of black life and black music, children's games, and so on—that it might as well be. Black musicians speak the language of jazz—and that includes the subtle inflections of the blues, which are related to black speech, as well as the rhythms—more naturally and more fluently than their white counterparts because they have a head start in mastering both the music's basics and its fine points.

So if we're looking for the really significant musicians in contemporary jazz, we'll have to find musicians who understand the resources of the jazz tradition, have brought something original to that tradition, and have created new extensions of the tradition that are being accepted and emulated by numbers of younger black players. Who are these musicians? First we should take note of the continuing relevance of Ornette Coleman. His innovations in the sixties probably altered the shape of jazz more tellingly than the work of any musician since the early Louis Armstrong, and he has influenced the seventies by befriending some of the key innovators, teaching his advanced theories of improvisational interaction and, with his group Prime Time, opening up electric music to the same freedoms his acoustic bands announced two decades ago. We should also mention Cecil Taylor, whose insistence that even musical freedom requires careful structural thinking has become a touchstone of this decade's new jazz.

Moving into the seventies, we come to the Art Ensemble of Chicago. Along with Anthony Braxton, Muhal Richard Abrams, and some of the other members of Chicago's pioneering black musicians' cooperative, the Association for the Advancement of Creative Musicians (AACM), the Art Ensemble has altered both musical and business aspects of jazz. These players have made significant rhythmic breakthroughs. Braxton and the Art Ensemble's Roscoe Mitchell don't swing like any musicians who came before them, but in their oblique way they *do* swing. The Chicago movement has also contributed an increased awareness of the composer's importance in organizing improvisational music making. Because of the AACM, avant-garde jazz is no longer "free" jazz. It is every bit as structured as the jazz of the fifties, but the structures are more varied.

Some other jazzmen—the remarkable young tenor saxophonist David Murray and his companions in the World Saxophone Quartet; pianist Anthony Davis; and alto saxophonist Arthur Blythe—are more interested in redefining traditional approaches to swing and in reaffirming the continuing relevance of the music's blues roots than in the structuralism of a Braxton or a Roscoe Mitchell. They are an important counterbalance to the cooler, more abstract tendencies of some of the Chicagoans.

But all these musicians, formalists and firebrands alike, are advancing the music while preserving its roots and respecting its integrity. They have catalyzed seventies jazz as surely as Miles Davis and John Coltrane catalyzed the jazz of the late fifties, a comparable period of consolidation and significant but cautious innovation. And they are inspiring legions of younger musicians who seem primed to carry the music into the eighties. As long as this effective system continues to operate, jazz is in no danger of becoming "less a chronicle of the black American experience." Nor will it become anything less than what is has always been—a medium for self-expression in which any musician can realize his or her potential as an artist.

Musicians in Quest of Language

THE NEW YORK TIMES | OCTOBER 4, 1987

Lionel Hampton, who has been a jazzman for some sixty years, made a relevant point in the course of a recent conversation. The subject was college courses in jazz musicianship, which Mr. Hampton supports. The question was whether students who learn to play in classrooms will make the same kind of jazz musicians as students who learned the way Mr. Hampton did.

"Well, I learned to play by playing, mostly in bars and dives," Mr. Hampton recalled. "We had to learn all the tunes people wanted to hear, and we learned to edit ourselves. Now I hear a lot of younger musicians who have learned the tunes, but when they start to improvise, it sounds like they're playing right out of their exercise books. What they're playing doesn't relate to the tune at all. And that isn't jazz."

In jazz, an improvisation doesn't have to consist of variations on the theme at hand. A few jazz musicians, ranging from Louis Armstrong to Stan Getz, have excelled at subtly altering the melody and chords of standard tunes. Others, Dizzy Gillespie for example, are at their best developing ingenious new melodies on familiar chord structures. Ornette Coleman showed musicians how to improvise on the sound, the mood, the feeling of a tune, and many followed his example.

But all these improvisers are fundamentally alike and each one has developed a distinctive musical syntax, a personal dialect of the language we call jazz. And they speak the language in their own way whether they are playing a theme they have written, paraphrasing someone else's theme, or purely improvising. There is an understanding that the "deep structures" of a distinct, self-consistent, cross-cultural musical language will unify the composed and improvised portions of any given performance.

Indian classical music, which, like jazz, emphasizes improvisation but grows out of completely different musical assumptions, has its own inherent structural imperatives. There are fundamental melodic patterns, or ragas, on which melodic material in every performance is based; often a celebrated musician's elaboration of the raga, preserved by oral tradition, provides further material for development and elaboration. There are also talas, or cycles of rhythms to adhere to, and an overall form that requires the player to begin with a reflective melodic exposition and then move, as in a classical suite, through variously structured sections.

Jazz is not unique because it emphasizes improvisation, nor because theme and variation are unified by a common musical syntax. The heart of jazz is the source of its language, and the heart of the language is the blues.

From the standpoint of European musicology, blues can be defined by a three-line verse form, often twelve bars in length, and a particular melodic flavor, distinguished by its "blue notes," the flat third and seventh. But despite this taxonomy, not all three-line stanzas are blues, nor does every melody with a flat third and seventh sound bluesy. If blues is essential to the deep structure of jazz, then it must function in a more complex manner than these definitions provide for, analogous to the way the patterns and praxis of raga and tala function in Indian music. And in fact, one can show that it does.

Musicians who are close to the blues talk about a recognizable "blues sound." Everything the superlative alto saxophonist Charlie Parker played had this blues sound, whether he was tracing the theme of a popular standard, jamming with a Latin band, or spontaneously inventing twelve-bar blues choruses. The blues sound is a way of conceptualizing pitch—as a player or a listener—and organizing melody, rooted in black vocal music and in centuries of African tradition. It's also a certain subtlety of inflection, related to the localized stresses and rhythms of vernacular speech. The inflection is more important than where the note falls in the European scale.

The blues has another major structural imperative, that most basic form of communication, the dialogue, often expressed musically as call and response. As Ornette Coleman once noted, "If you play a phrase that asks a question or makes a statement, and then in your next phrase you answer that first phrase, then that's a form of blues." And in blues-based music, the voices and instruments debate with each other.

Last week at the Kitchen, several Japanese musicians who had been featured in a weeklong festival of new music from that country took part in unstructured improvisations with various American collaborators. Sato Michihiro, who plays a three-stringed lute called the samisen, comes from a tradition that has developed a rich improvisational language over a long period of time. His playing was assured and coherent, even in a free-form context; he understood how to combine elements of musical syntax to structure and improvise performance.

Japanese and American musicians who were grounded in jazz were able to play together naturally, developing group improvisations that had both variety and direction. But the musicians oriented toward rock, a musical form that has not yet developed an improvising tradition of real depth, tended to settle into rambling jam sessions, parading licks and effects and fragments of diverse subgenres without ever quite arriving at a common focus. In this context, the players' country of origin wasn't as important as their grasp of an improvisational language, or lack of it.

This listener has been encountering the sort of musicians Lionel Hampton was worried about in settings ranging from a recent improvisation festival at a downtown jazz club to new music venues to an all-star rock concert for Chuck Berry. The musicians have formidable technical skills and are adept at stringing ideas together, but they have trouble forging written and improvised materials into a satisfying, consistent whole.

They haven't learned to analyze the underlying structures and active processes of jazz and Indian music and other major improvisational traditions. And they haven't transcended their sources to forge a musical language of their own.

As more and more improvising musicians look beyond their own tradition for inspiration, drawing on the world of music that electronic media have made available, the problem of developing a voice and language becomes a crucial one. The musicians who are able to solve that problem for themselves, in a way that makes sense in a global culture and an age of almost instantaneous communications, are going to shape the improvisational, multicultural music of the coming century.

Count Basie: The Explosive Catalyst

THE NEW YORK TIMES | AUGUST 15, 1982

William (Count) Basie, the septuagenarian bandleader and pianist, has been getting some long-overdue recognition recently. A few months ago, the Black Music Association presented a tribute to Mr. Basie at Radio City Music Hall, with performances by Lena Horne, Stevie Wonder, Quincy Jones, and other black superstars. The new CBS cable television network devoted the first of what it promises will be a series of hour-long specials on jazz to another Basie tribute that featured Tony Bennett and Sarah Vaughan, among others. The Book-of-the-Month Club has released a three-record boxed set, *Count Basie: The Early Years*, that traces his career from the mid-1930s through the early 1950s, and other reissue albums are on the way.

Several of the participants in the recent Basie tributes, including Mr. Basie himself, have noted that artists can only appreciate such recognition while they are still alive. Duke Ellington did not die unappreciated, but there were no elaborate celebrations like the Basie gala at Radio City Music Hall. More disturbingly, Mr. Ellington was nominated for a Pulitzer prize in composition, only to suffer the humiliation of being passed over in favor of a more ordinary white composer working in a European-derived contemporary classical idiom.

America's cultural custodians and tastemakers (the committee members who award Pulitzers, for example) have been slow to acknowledge the artistic validity and worldwide impact of the black American art music called jazz. Duke Ellington wrote symphonic music, extended suites for his jazz orchestra, sacred music, and an enduring body of popular songs in addition to numerous jazz classics. His rejection by the Pulitzer committee was a shameful farce. Now, almost a decade after his death, he is widely recognized as one of the outstanding American composers of this century.

But Count Basie is not likely to receive this sort of recognition in the foreseeable future. Although he wrote or cowrote "One O'Clock Jump" and a few other swing-era gems, his contribution to American music cannot be accurately measured by his composer credits. The composer, all-important in the European classical tradition, is rarely as significant in jazz as the catalyst who can refine and blend traditional elements from black vernacular music into fresh new styles, or the bandleader who can fuse a disparate bunch of gifted musicians into a performing unit greater than the sum of its parts, or the inspired instrumentalist who in turn inspires his fellow musicians.

Count Basie has certainly been a great instrumentalist and a great bandleader. But above all, he has been the great catalyst who combined the latest Southwestern jazz innovations and the old, irreducible essence of the blues into an explosive new mixture—the first authentically modern jazz.

It is true that some of Louis Armstrong's early recordings still sound modern, with their hints of bitonality, their freedom from the European conventions of "proper" tone production, and their radical expansion of the range and the expressive capabilities of the trumpet. But Mr. Armstrong was also a blues player, firmly rooted in New Orleans traditions and suspicious of new musical developments like the bebop of the 1940s. Count Basie's original big band, the band that set the jazz world on fire when he brought it to New York from Kansas City in 1936, was imbued with what can be seen in retrospect as a thoroughly modern sensibility, and so were the bands he led during the next two decades.

At first, this modern sensibility was most evident when Mr. Basie was prodding and provoking his brilliant and unorthodox tenor saxophonist, Lester Young, with offbeat dissonances, percussive thumping, and daring, extended silences. But it was also evident in the way the band used blues riffs, which became both the basic building blocks of "head" or extemporaneous brass and reed section arrangements, as well as thematic material to be developed or retooled by individual soloists.

After the Second World War broke up the original Basie band, and especially during the early 1950s, when Mr. Basie started over with an eight-piece band and then built it into an orchestra, repeating his transition from small band to big band in the mid-1930s, his modernism shone with added luster. Modernism in jazz may have meant bebop in the 1940s, but today's modernism is more a spirit or an attitude than a style. It involves a thorough knowledge of the history of jazz, including the principal styles of each jazz era; the willingness to use elements drawn from any or all of these eras, as needed; and the caliber of musicianship and insight that enables a player or bandleader to transform traditional materials into new music that is fresh and personal. This is exactly what Mr. Basie was up to in the 1940s and 1950s, as one can hear on several recent record releases, most notably Book-of-the-Month Records' *Count Basie: The Early Years*.

Like the extensive series of jazz reissues produced by Time-Life Records (who have not released a Count Basie set yet, though one is planned), *Count Basie: The Early Years* attempts to strike a balance between comprehensiveness (to appeal to novice listeners who are just beginning to build jazz collections) and rarity (a few unreleased or long-unavailable selections to appeal to more serious collectors). The set begins with Basie the sideman, working in the Bennie Moten band of the early 1930s. The Basie–Lester Young partnership is represented by the superb (but frequently anthologized) small-group performance "Shoe Shine Swing" and by a few familiar big-band numbers like "Roseland Shuffle" and "I Left My Baby" (a Jimmy Rushing blues feature). These are among the masterpieces of recorded jazz, but they are also readily available on Columbia's compendious *The Lester Young Story* (five two-record sets) and on several MCA/Decca reissues. The (uncredited) compilers of the album have also included an entire side of 1939 quartet numbers featuring Mr. Basie and his definitive rhythm section, numbers that were recorded for Decca but have not been widely available on American reissue albums.

Surprisingly (since compilations of this sort frequently have a traditionalist bias), *Count Basie: The Early Years* gives equal time to the less frequently reissued Basie recordings of the 1940s and 1950s. Don Byas, Buddy Tate, and Illinois Jacquet are among the soloists who make the 1940s recordings so memorable. But Basie the modernist really shines on the six selections from 1950–51 that comprise the collection's final side. Three are by an octet that was surely, man for man, the finest band Mr. Basie ever led, with the possible exception of his original 1936 big band.

The saxophonists Wardell Gray and Serge Chaloff (two gifted improvisers who recorded much too little and died much too young), the young clarinetist Buddy DeFranco, and the slyly inventive trumpeter Clark Terry are all at the height of their powers on the Basie octet's "Song of the Islands" and "I'll Remember April," and these performances are also remarkably successful fusions of bebop, Kansas City–style swing, blues riffing, and the older East Coast stride and ragtime piano styles that were the New Jersey–born Mr. Basie's original specialty. Anyone who listens with open ears to the way Wardell Gray's tenor saxophone lines sail effortlessly over Mr. Basie's oompah stride playing on "Song of the Islands," or to the heady mixture of swing tempo and bebop lyricism on "I'll Remember April," can only conclude that these performances are modern, in the best, most all-embracing sense of the word, and also timeless. And so are "Nails," "Little Pony," and "Beaver Junction," big-band selections from 1951 that offer equally sublime Clark Terry and Wardell Gray as well as the more muscular tenor of Lucky Thompson.

Two albums that were originally issued by Verve in the 1950s and have recently been reissued in high-quality Japanese pressings by Polygram shed additional light on Count Basie's modernism, and particularly on his unique reconciliation of swing, bop, and the blues. "Jam Session 4," an early jam-session album supervised by Norman Granz, finds Mr. Basie and a compatibly swinging rhythm section (Buddy Rich is superb on drums) backing solos by several alumni of the early-1950s Basie octet and big band—Wardell Gray, Buddy DeFranco, and the trumpeter

Harry Edison—as well as Stan Getz, Benny Carter, and Willie Smith. Mr. Gray's relaxed but ravishing lyricism lights up a charging "Oh, Lady Be Good," and Mr. DeFranco proves once again that he was the greatest modern clarinetist.

On Verve/Polygram's *Count Basie at Newport*, the 1957 Basie band encounters charter Basie band members Lester Young, Jo Jones, and Jimmy Rushing, as well as Illinois Jacquet and Roy Eldridge, for an unforgettable, supercharged concert performance that renders even the announcer, John Hammond, practically speechless. On some of the Basie-Young recordings from the late 1930s, "Roseland Shuffle" for example, one can hear Mr. Young deliberately using "false" or unorthodox fingerings to draw bluesy moans, slurs, and quarter-tone effects from his saxophone. His use of these devices was certainly avant-garde in 1936, but Mr. Young and Mr. Basie sound equally avant-garde on their 1957 Newport recording. One of their choruses on a wildly exciting "Lester Leaps In" finds them using so many offbeat accents and jarring dissonances that they sound, fleetingly but unmistakably, like Charlie Rouse jousting with Thelonious Monk. Performances like this one suggest that the swing vs. bop controversies of the 1940s were more personality clashes than cases of musical incompatibility. The music on *At Newport* and *The Early Years* subsumes swing and bop into something grander and more lasting than any particular style. It subsumes everything from the simplest blues motifs to the most angular, skewed rhythmic displacements into a brilliant personal synthesis. Call it jazz, call it great black music (as some younger musicians do), call it what you will; this music is as worthy of a Pulitzer prize, and of any other honors a grateful America might bestow upon it, as any sounds this country has produced.

C. Mingus Ain't No Jive Bassist

ROLLING STONE | JANUARY 20, 1972

New York—Composer, autobiographer, and master bassist Charles Mingus, his magisterial presence spread over a chair in the Columbia editing room, sang along with a recorded section of one of his new compositions, correcting the lead player's phrasing from time to time. Rusty, the soft-spoken, red-haired engineer from Alabama, was busy with a pair of scissors, trying to follow Mingus's directions.

"This is too long," Mingus said. "See, this phrase"—he sang the brief, ascending motive—"should go right into the next one . . . there!" He gestured abruptly, and waited while Rusty spliced. "Now the next one should follow just like this"—he sang the next two phrases as one continuous phrase. Rusty asked if cutting there might not interfere with the drum-roll backdrop. "Naw, it's just a press roll," Mingus said. "You won't be able to tell the difference."

Soon the introduction was trimmed to half its original length. It had the flow of an off-the-cuff remark, and the drum part sounded absolutely intact. Lengths of wide sixteen-track tape were draped over the table, and Mingus picked up a segment of press roll and tried it on. "Might make a good tie but it's too short," he said, discarding it.

"They're good for hula skirts," Rusty said.

Teo Macero, the Columbia producer who works with artists like Miles Davis and Bill Evans, bounced in to hear the shortened introduction joined to the rest of the piece. Elated with the results, he sang back answering parts when Mingus sang the melody lines. The roar of the twenty-eight-man band filled the tiny editing room—snarling saxes and trumpets tumbling crisscross lines over one another, then quieting down to a waltz-time interlude for bowed bass and piano. It was real Mingus, the kind of emotional yet formally perfect music that has graced albums for Savoy, Bethlehem, Candid, Fantasy, RCA, Columbia, and Impulse over the past fifteen years.

"What are you calling that?" Teo asked as the last note faded. "'The Shoes of the Fisherman's Wife Ain't No Jive-Ass Sandals,'" Mingus said with a grin. "Or 'They Are Some Jive Sandals.' Or . . . you can say 'ass' these days, right?" Teo cracked up. His friendly, collaborative relationship with Mingus is hassle-free for good reason—Teo was the tenor saxophonist in one of the earliest and most demanding editions of Mingus's Jazz Workshops. The group cut half an album for Savoy around 1955, and the music—not so different from "Fishwife's New Shoes"—represented the earliest successful incorporation of twelve-tone writing and other advanced compositional techniques into the improvisatory music called jazz. For the first time a bowed bass stepped out front for an eerie lead that could have been written (but probably not played) by Darius Milhaud. And it was the first attempt at a "free" counterpoint of the kind perfected much later by a younger generation of players: Ornette Coleman, Cecil Taylor, Archie Shepp.

In 1955, Mingus put it this way: "Since I don't believe that such music can be classified as 'atonal' or 'weird music' . . . I would identify it as 'a little beyond the elementary.' If and when these present constructions are accepted, I will venture to delve a little more into the so-called dissonance of free-form improvisation." Today, Teo says, "I wonder how many of these horn players now could've cut those parts."

It may be that Mingus thinks and moves in broad, epochal circles.

That same night, at the Village Vanguard, his quintet launched into an extended essay on the Duke Ellington–Billy Strayhorn evergreen "Take the 'A' Train." The tune has long been a Mingus favorite, since Ellington is up there with Charlie Parker and Art Tatum in Mingus's panoply of demigods, but this time he took the music way back to traditional roots. Al Dailey, the pianist, was striding like Tatum, throwing in dissonant punctuations like Ellington, and laughing almost maniacally while trumpeter Lonnie Hillyer growled and roared through his horn, drifted into and out of "Muskrat Ramble," and then warned an alto player sitting in, "No bebop, now." Mingus was so happy he was twirling his bass around and around like some character in a forties film clip, and the musicians were laying the free expression of the sixties and seventies into the two-beat rhythm slyly and seamlessly. Suddenly Mingus yelled, "Break!" and the swirl subsided for a succinct bass solo. "Head!" he shouted, and they took the tune out.

The blend of spontaneity and control that characterizes Mingus's music is rooted in his vocal approach. Whether he is directing his small group with one-word exclamations or singing individual parts to musicians in a large orchestra, the connection with songs that can be sung—and with the blues and black church music, both essentially vocal idioms—is always in evidence. Even Mingus's classical music, such as "Adagio Ma Non Troppo," from his upcoming Columbia album, scored for six basses, two pianos, English horn, and orchestra, breaks down into parts that can be sung. In fact, it's a transcription of one of Mingus's ad-lib piano solos. The music's overall complexity and depth rests on this bedrock of strong individual lines. Classical? "Black faces aren't expected to play classical," Mingus once said. "But they do. We, too, went to school. We, too, studied music."

Mingus continues to confound people who want to put music into bags. His physical and mental agility, which [match] his girth and the size of his accomplishments, has led certain writers to refer to "many Minguses." For instance, there was the Mingus who brought a new intensity to jazz with searing albums like *Pithecanthropus Erectus* and *Tijuana Moods*; there was Mingus at the Monterey Jazz Festival in 1964, who won a standing ovation for his "Meditations" and gave each of his eleven musicians an affectionate bear hug; there was proud, angry Mingus, defending his music and his blunt honesty against philistine critics and businessmen; Mingus the prose writer, whose *Beneath the Underdog* is as scorching and exhilarating as his music.

Mingus is a man of his word. He fulfilled his 1955 promise to get into free-form improvisation with his incomparable 1960 quartet that featured Eric Dolphy, and with his later interactive masterpiece, *The Black Saint and the Sinner Lady*. Then, when it seemed he was about to write the definitive aural textbook for the New Music, he returned to an older format that reflected his continuing affection for the music of his departed friends and collaborators, Charlie Parker, Fats Navarro, and Tadd Dameron. He hit a slump in the mid-sixties, a period that came to a head when New York City evicted him from his loft. That event was chronicled in a documentary film, *Mingus*, which included footage of Charlie blasting away at the walls of his former home with a rifle. He kept a "low profile" for several years after that, issuing an occasional recording on his own label, curtailing all public appearances.

Mingus's comeback was slow and determined. He was out of practice at first, and his group played standards and some of the older, simpler originals. Gradually he built up momentum, and now he is looming. His quintet, which most recently featured veteran Lee Konitz playing crystalline, pure alto sax, still gets by with a minimum of compositional structure, but the new album is full of overwhelmingly powerful music, with plenty of talented players to fill out and interpret the scores and Mingus's sung instructions. The new music bridges the "classical" and "jazz" idioms effortlessly, and Mingus will present it, along with the looser music of the quintet and some even newer music, written after the album's completion, at a February 4 concert in New York's Philharmonic Hall. The plan calls for Bill Cosby to MC, and for Teo Macero to conduct the large orchestra that is being assembled. The concert will showcase Mingus's earliest and very latest works, and for once all the "many Minguses" will be occupying the same space/time coordinates.

Well, almost all the Minguses. There's more to the man than he could possibly give at any place and time, even if he wanted to. He was sitting at a table at the Vanguard the other night, playing with a mean-looking Luger pistol that was really a cigarette lighter, adjusting the length of the flame and lighting people's smokes from a foot away. "They tell me you can click the chamber this way," he said, "and shoot all that fire out at once, like blam! But if you do that, it's all gone, and the damn thing doesn't work anymore."

Liner Notes for *Kind of Blue* by Miles Davis

(Columbia/Legacy re-release, 1997)

Playing gigs at the Fillmore East during the sixties made it easier for you to get in and catch other bands, even if tickets were sold out. As a young saxophonist in a rock band, I played there several times and attended numerous concerts; the one group I never missed (unless I had to be on the road) was the Allman Brothers Band. More specifically, I went to see their guitarist, Duane Allman, the only "rock" guitarist I had heard up to that point who could solo on a one-chord vamp for as long as half an hour or more, and not only avoid boring you but keep you absolutely *riveted*. Duane was a rare melodist and a dedicated student of music who was never evasive about the sources of his inspiration. "You know," he told me one night after soaring for hours on wings of lyrical song, "that kind of playing comes from Miles and Coltrane, and particularly *Kind of Blue*. I've listened to that album so many times that for the past couple of years, I haven't hardly listened to anything *else*."

Earlier, I'd met Duane and his brother Gregg when they had a teenage band called the Hourglass. One day I'd played Duane a copy of Coltrane's *Olé*, an album recorded a little more than a year after *Kind of Blue* but still heavily indebted to it. He was evidently fascinated. It's rare to see a musician grow that spectacularly, that fast; I'm not sure there's any guitarist who's come along since Duane's early death on the highway who has been able to sustain improvisation of such lyric beauty and epic expanse. But the influence of *Kind of Blue*, even to the point of becoming a kind of obsession, wasn't unusual at all; it was highly characteristic of musicians of our generation, mine and Duane's. Of course, listening to an album isn't going to turn anyone into a genius; you can't get more out of the experience than you're capable of bringing to it. Duane brought something special, even unique to the table, but it seemed that everyone was sharing the meal. This was true among musicians categorized as "rock" or "pop" as well as among those labeled "jazz." In fact, the influence of *Kind of Blue* has been so widely spread and long lasting, it's doubtful that anyone has yet grasped its ultimate dimensions. We know *Kind of Blue* is a great and eminently listenable jazz album, "one of the most important, as well as sublimely beautiful albums in the history of jazz," in the words of Miles biographer Eric Nisenson. But there is more to it than that.

Music fans, not to mention critics and even more musicians, can be an opinionated and contentious bunch, even when it comes to works and artists almost universally admired as classics. It often seems no "great work" is sacrosanct. Not all rock aficionados share a high opinion of the Beatles' opus *Sgt. Pepper*, for example; to some, it's uneven, self-indulgent, overproduced, underwritten—and dated, a flower-power curio. The recent elevation of the late Robert Johnson to "King of the Delta Blues" has provoked grumbling from some scholars, who point out that Johnson sold few records in his lifetime and was never as influential among other musicians as Charley Patton, Son House, or even Muddy Waters. Or consider the case of John Coltrane, whose breathtaking solos on *Kind of Blue* would seem to be an integral aspect of its charms. One influential critic, Martin Williams, gives Ornette Coleman his due but includes only one brief and somewhat atypical performance by any of

Coltrane's bands on *The Smithsonian Collection of Jazz Music*. There's no "Giant Steps," no "Chasin' the Trane," no "A Love Supreme"—all, presumably, "classic" jazz.

Kind of Blue distances itself from even this exclusive company by having few, if any, notable detractors. Of course, we can always depend on at least *some* critics to miss the boat on its maiden voyage, and in fact, some early reviews of the album described Miles's playing as "morose," "maudlin," even "sluggish [!] and low in energy output." But a number of critics immediately recognized *Kind of Blue* as a modern masterpiece, and in recent years little has been heard to the contrary. Not even the sort of after-the-fact analysis that has managed to make certain other recorded masterworks all too familiar, draining them of a great deal of their "magic" or "charge," has dimmed the luster of *Kind of Blue*. Miles Davis never liked "explaining" his music, and when it comes to *Kind of Blue*, the other musicians he chose as participants have managed to avoid analyzing the proceedings to death. Somehow, the experience of *Kind of Blue* insists on retaining at least a touch of the ineffable.

Consider the circumstances. Miles took his musicians into the studio for the first of two sessions for *Kind of Blue* in March 1959. At the time, "modal" jazz—in which the improviser was given a scale or series of scales (or "modes") as material to improvise from, rather than a sequence of chords or harmonies—was not an *entirely* new idea. Miles himself had tried something similar in 1958 with his tune "Milestones" (also known as "Miles"), and when he and Gil Evans were recasting the songs from Gershwin's *Porgy and Bess* around that time, they rewrote "Summertime" to include a long modal vamp with no chord changes. Originally, the idea for this kind of playing was the concept of composer George Russell, but his program for "modal jazz" came imbedded in an elaborate, all-embracing musical/philosophical theory, the "Lydian Chromatic Concept of Tonal Organization." Miles saw the approach, at least in part, as a way of drastically *simplifying* modern jazz, which was then pushing against the outer limits of chordal complexity. "The music had gotten thick," Davis complained in a 1958 interview for *The Jazz Review*. "Guys give me tunes and they're full of chords. I can't play them . . . I think a movement in jazz is beginning away from the conventional string of chords, and a return to emphasis on melodic rather than harmonic variation. There will be fewer chords but infinite possibilities as to what to do with them." Technical though it may seem to non-musicians, Davis's statement can be reduced to a single, simple proposition: *a return to melody*. *Kind of Blue* is, in a sense, all melody—and atmosphere. In essence, Miles Davis was looking for new forms that would encourage his musicians to improvise in streams of pure melody, which is an aspect of music as easily appreciated by the layman as those who speak modal.

It's worth noting that Miles didn't just write out some simple, almost skeletal compositions, pass them around the band, and hope for the best. He chose his players carefully, bringing back the already-departed pianist in his sextet, Bill Evans, for three sessions only. His group's new pianist, Wynton Kelly, was something of a blues specialist, and he was asked to play on one tune only, the blues "Freddie Freeloader." Some of the musicians credit Miles with "psyching" Kelly into playing that would fit seamlessly alongside Evans's work on the rest of the album. Perhaps. As Nisenson points out in his *'Round About Midnight*, "The recording in and of itself was an experiment. None of the musicians had played any of the tunes before; in fact Miles had written out the settings for most of them only a few hours before the session. . . . In addition, Miles stuck to his old recording procedure of having virtually no rehearsal and only one take for each tune." Nisenson quotes drummer Jimmy Cobb as saying of *Kind of Blue*, "It must have been made in heaven," which may be as revealing an explanation as we're ever going to get. Because there *is* something transcendent, poetic, perhaps even heavenly about the music on *Kind of Blue*. To check it out, go right to the only unused first take of the sessions, the alternative version of "Flamenco Sketches."

On any other Miles Davis album, the first, previously unheard take of "Flamenco Sketches" (the last selection on this disc) would have been a highlight. Listened to on its own, it is a group performance of the highest quality. The supple strength and firmly centered tone of Paul Chambers's bass (heard here with a clarity unmatched by earlier reissues) is much the same on both performances. So is the precise clarity and unquench-able swing of Cobb's drumming. The solos by Miles, pianist Bill Evans, and saxophonists John Coltrane and Cannonball Adderley are different from the solos on the familiar, issued version of "Flamenco Sketches," as one would expect from improvisers of this caliber. Adderley, however, can be heard formulating and organizing melodic materials that coalesce into an altogether different sort of melodic statement on his second try, the issued take. And this, it seems to me, is precisely where *Kind of Blue* comes into its own as a monument to sheer inspiration and creativity. Every solo seems to belong just as it is; it isn't so much theme and variations or a display of virtuosity as it is a kind of *singing*.

Kind of Blue flows with all the melodic warmth and sense of welcoming, wide-open vistas one hears in the most universal sort of song, all supported by a rigorous musical logic. For musicians, it has always been more than some beautiful music to listen to, although it is certainly that. It's also a how-to, a method for improvisers that shows them how to get at the pure melody all too frequently obscured by "hip" chord changes or flashy fingerwork. But no matter how much a musician or a listener brings to it (for this is one of those incredibly rare works equally popular among professionals and the public at large), *Kind of Blue* always seems to have more to give. If we keep listening to it, again and again, throughout a lifetime—well, maybe that's because we sense that there's still something *more*, something not yet heard.

Or maybe we just like paying periodic visits to heaven.

Liner Notes for *Homecoming: Live at the Village Vanguard* by Dexter Gordon

(Columbia, 1976)

The excitement Dexter Gordon created in New York in 1976 surprised almost everyone who was a part of it. The hard-core jazz fans were startled when overflow crowds showed up for his engagements and cheered and pounded tables, serving notice that the saxophonist's greatness would never again be the secret of a handful of connoisseurs. The new fans, who had read that Gordon was John Coltrane's initial inspiration or simply heard that he was worth hearing, discovered a master musician at the very pinnacle of his art. And Gordon himself discovered a new, young public ready to embrace his music and revere its creator, a public schooled in the intricacies of modern jazz and positively clamoring to hear it played by one of the greats. He had created a pleasant life for himself in Copenhagen, far from the clamorous, competitive antagonisms of the American jazz world as he left it in 1962, but this was something else!

After his first triumphant evening at the Storyville club, where he had to plead exhaustion at 3 A.M. to avoid demands for an encore, and a second night playing for an audience which was even larger and more vociferous, Gordon began rehearsing for a week-long engagement at the Village Vanguard, a basement club where some of the greatest moments in modern jazz have occurred. Charles Mingus, the bassist and composer, who had first played with Dexter in a high school jazz band, spent the afternoon at the Vanguard, looming over a table close to the bandstand and urging the saxophonist on with shouts and laughter. "Yeah, yeah," he would exclaim whenever Gordon played a particularly felicitous phrase, "you're gonna be teaching New York some *stuff*, man. Some *lessons*."

After the rehearsal, Dexter sat down to talk in the Vanguard's dark, crowded little kitchen. He was still elated by the ovations he had received at Storyville. "That was just overwhelming," he said. "I've noticed that in Europe, where I live and work, there are a lot of new young fans, but I wasn't prepared for this reception. What can I say? It made the heart glad."

Listening to Gordon talk was not unlike hearing him play. His voice, like his sound on the saxophone, was warm, self-assured, deep, and resonant. He also had a way about him, a certain magnetism. One might call it charisma, although these days charisma is often manufactured, and Dexter's brand was natural and genuine. Perhaps one should simply say that he was a charmer. In any event, as he was talking the Vanguard's telephone rang, and since nobody on the club's staff was about, he answered it. "Village Vanguard. No, it's the Thad Jones–Mel Lewis band tonight. On Tuesday, Dexter Gordon. Who's this? This is Dexter." There was a long stretch during which the party on the other end talked and Dexter listened, his grin growing wider and sunnier by the second. "Why, thank you, sweetheart," he finally said, as suavely as a king acknowledging the adoration of his minions. "Yes, we'll be here through Sunday."

On the bandstand, Gordon's royal *savoir faire* was even more evident. He was a striking-looking man, tall and handsome with a smile bright enough to light a room. He announced tunes in a mellow, liquid baritone, often quoting at length from the lyrics to a standard he was about to play. When he finished a solo, he acknowledged applause by holding his tenor saxophone out in front of his abdomen, parallel to the floor, as if he was sharing the adulation with it. But of course Gordon's playing was the most aristocratic thing about him. His sound was huge and encompassing, from his booming lower register all the way up to a rich falsetto range. He was a master of harmonic subtleties and a master of timing. He was a prankster who enjoyed inserting little musical jokes—quotes from "Santa Claus Is Coming to Town" or "Here Comes the Bride"—into the most passionate improvisations. Above all, he was an architect of sound. His choruses have an ineluctable solidity to them. They are balanced and logical, classical, really, in the best sense of the word. The individual phrases are handsomely blocked out and warmly inflected, but ultimately the stories told by choruses and entire solos are even more impressive.

Gordon's music is rooted in the creative ferment of the mid-1940s, when modern jazz erupted onto the scene and brought the swing era to an end. He was born Dexter Keith Gordon in Los Angeles on February 27, 1923, and his father, a doctor who treated Duke Ellington and Lionel Hampton, made sure he heard plenty of jazz. He was impressed by Lester Young, the most progressive tenor saxophonist of the late swing era, and then by Charlie Parker, the fountainhead of the emerging modern jazz movement. As early as 1945, when he began making records under his own name, he had his own style together. It was really the first saxophone style to synthesize the towering influences of Young and Parker, and as a style in its own right it influenced just about every musician who subsequently took up the tenor saxophone, not to mention players on other instruments. Among the saxophonists most heavily indebted to Gordon's breakthroughs were Sonny Rollins and, especially, John Coltrane.

Unlike many of the musicians of his era, Gordon did not stop developing. The records he made in the 1960s for Blue Note are an advance on his original Savoy sides from the 1940s, and after he moved to Europe, he developed even more. "Of all the people of his generation," said the producer of this recording, Michael Cuscuna, at the time, "Dexter has stayed youngest. He is the most modern player to have come out of that period. He influenced Rollins and Coltrane and then, when they became more advanced, he learned from them. He's still learning and still growing." This recording is a testament to the veracity of that statement.

After his initial week at the Village Vanguard, Dexter went out on the road, with the Woody Shaw–Louis Hayes group backing him. By the time he returned to the Vanguard to fulfill demands for another week—the club had been packed the first week, with lines of people snaking up the stairs and into the street—more people had heard about him and the lines were even longer. Fans would wait for hours, until other listeners dragged themselves home and there was room for them to hear the last set of the night. They rubbed shoulders with a remarkable collection of musicians, who between them made up a very discriminating audience. Squeezing into the club on various nights of Gordon's second week, the week when these recordings were made, were Charles Mingus, Cecil Taylor, John McLaughlin, Art Blakey, Jimmy and Percy Heath, Yusef Lateef, Jimmy Owens, Horace Silver, Cedar Walton, Stanley Turrentine, Barry Altschul, Julius Hemphill, Billy Higgins, and Dave Liebman, among many others. Phoebe Snow came, heard a single Gordon ballad solo, and was moved to tears.

With the roadwork behind them, the quintet you hear here was able to present a varied program. Shaw, who made his professional debut with the late Eric Dolphy and has always shown a penchant for the jazz style associated with John Coltrane, contributed two tunes, "Little Red's Fantasy" and "In Case You Haven't Heard," which brought out the very modern side of Dexter Gordon. The wonderfully bright "It's You or No One" and the Thelonious Monk gem "'Round Midnight" are distillations of Gordon's classicism, while the opener, "Gingerbread Boy," and closer, "Backstairs," portray the saxophonist's prowess in the twelve-bar blues form. "Fenja," which Dexter wrote for his wife, has chorus after chorus of warm, lyrical invention by the saxophonist, and then Shaw scoots in with a skittering ascending phrase that seems to be saying, "Don't forget, I'm here too." Ronnie Mathews, whose sturdy chording and fleet solos are highlights of the set, contributed the medium-uptempo burner "Let's Get Down." Throughout the proceedings, bassist Stafford James and Louis Hayes, Woody's co-leader, provided a wonderfully fluid drive.

We are fortunate that before he left us, Dexter committed his masterful portrayal of an expatriate musician not unlike himself (with traces of Lester Young and Bud Powell) to Bertrand Tavernier's film *Round Midnight*. Many felt he deserved an Oscar for that performance, but while the acting was transcendent (when all is said and done he was playing a character, not himself), Dexter communicated best on the bandstand, with his tenor, that cavernous, lived-in voice, and his special, magnetic presence. This recording captures a particularly vivid high point in his career, his triumphant return to New York City as a jazz star after years of living abroad. Listen. The triumph is in every note.

Sun Ra Casts Special Light on Jazz

THE NEW YORK TIMES | DECEMBER 29, 1978

Sun Ra, the jazz bandleader and visionary, took his Arkestra, as he calls it, to Egypt a few years ago. "I went to the Great Pyramid," he said, not long after their return, "and that pyramid is the pyramid of Ra. The number of Ra is nine. So when I got to the King's Chamber, I stopped and said the name Ra nine times. And when I finished, all the lights in the pyramid went out."

The conversation was taking place backstage in a Manhattan theater, where Sun Ra and his troupe of between twenty and thirty musicians and dancers had performed one of their astonishing programs of traditional and avant-garde jazz, electronics, African drumming, theater, and poetry. Just as Sun Ra finished his story, just as he said, "went out," all the lights in the theater went out. Sun Ra, his musicians, and the interviewer were plunged into total darkness. After a few seconds the lights came back up, and Sun Ra continued as if nothing had happened.

Things like this don't happen very often in the real world, but they seem to happen with some regularity around Sun Ra, who says his music speaks of "unknown things, uncharted paths for people. . . ."

Sun Ra has been expanding the range of his music lately by turning his Arkestra into a kind of repertory company, playing great jazz from the past as well as his own "music of the future." In addition to free-form dialogues and exotic percussion pieces, one is likely to hear Duke Ellington's "Lightnin'" or Fletcher Henderson's "King Porter Stomp." Or Tadd Dameron's "Lady Bird." Sun Ra is especially close to the music of Fletcher Henderson, in whose band he says he worked briefly during the late 1940s.

"As a so-called child," Sun Ra once told the writer, "I was always playing Fletcher Henderson records, even before I could read."

Although Sun Ra is not very forthcoming about his childhood, it is generally believed by jazz researchers that he was born in Birmingham, Alabama, around 1915. He apparently toured with territory bands during the 1930s and '40s, eventually settling in Chicago, where he played the piano behind visiting jazz stars such as Coleman Hawkins and Stuff Smith. He took the name Sun Ra and put his first Arkestra together during the mid-fifties.

The first Sun Ra Arkestra played hard bop, the reigning black jazz style of the period. But it was hard bop with extensions. The band included the tenor saxophonist John Gilmore, who is still a member and featured soloist, and two percussionists, one of whom was a symphonic tympanist. Sun Ra played an electronic keyboard instrument of his own invention in addition to the piano. There were tunes with tempos that went up and down deliberately and tunes that employed African polyrhythms. The music was a fascinating mixture of discipline and freedom. "In rehearsal," Sun Ra has said, "we do just like a football team. I give them their little exercises, but when you get on the field you don't do exercises. Then it's part of the game, and you just do what you have to do."

During the sixties Sun Ra made the first important use of the Moog synthesizer in improvisational music, innovated in the use of slides and light shows to accompany his music, and reintroduced traditional elements such as dance and vocals into avant-garde jazz. He hired some talented musicians, some of whom—Pharoah Sanders, Rashied Ali—went on to individual careers while others, such as the saxophonist Marshall Allen, became permanent members of the Arkestra. And Sun Ra has kept moving into the seventies.

"People have tried to build a better world," Sun Ra says, "but they've failed because they don't have a blueprint. You can't tear something down, you know, unless you've got something better. I've got my equations, and *these* equations are *valid*. I'm not doing any of this on faith or on what I think. I'm not even dealing with intellect. You have to have this intuitive plan. The whole thing is a wilderness and you've got to have some pioneers to go out there and discover and achieve."

Ornette Coleman and the Circle with a Hole in the Middle

ATLANTIC MONTHLY | DECEMBER 1972

The image on the screen is a village street in Nigeria. Brightly dressed people are clustered in a circle playing drums, giant calabashes, double-reed horns, and a sort of violin with horsehair strings. Ornette Coleman is standing in the middle of the circle, switching from alto saxophone to trumpet and back, laying alternations of skittery runs and long, expressive blue notes into the simmering stew of cross-rhythms and gutty, jagged melodies. The picture focuses and refocuses cyclically on the face of a woman, sad or blank or unknowable like the whitewashed walls of the village. Her ululating rises sharply above the music like the barking of dogs.

Behind the television set a collage covers a brick wall. There is an empty space helmet, a tube oozing green paste, the convolutions of a naked brain, an ARVN officer with a pistol shooting a suspected terrorist through the head. The victim is falling in multiple exposure, changing color from flesh tones to a washed-out gray. A corner is hung with the spirit images of Z. K. Oloruntoba, a Nigerian who paints ghosts and gods into rich, stylized color canvases full of disembodied eyes and mysterious protoplasmic movement. Z.K. is hanging his first New York show downstairs, in the storefront where Ornette often rehearses. Ornette is in another corner, sighting down a pool cue. "Take aim, then hit it," he says, dropping one of his stripes into a side pocket. "If you wait, you lose your aim." The cries of children in the SoHo street float in through the open third-floor window.

Ornette's sparkling green tunic creases and his brow knits as he arches over the pool table. He lives in a world of clear, endlessly permutating images of global musics, folk and classical and jazz, that interpenetrate. Not so long ago he was dissuaded from putting out an early mix of his Columbia album *Science Fiction* that had on it an inordinate amount of echo in the horns. He liked it, he explained, because the echo "made the sound visual, like a mirror." He calls his orchestral piece *Skies of America* "a kinetic kaleidoscope composition." On the television, the Nigerian videotape has been replaced by the Ornette Coleman quartet performing in Milan. Ornette's trumpet and Dewey Redman's musette are playing a loose unison, both their voices distinct, like the unisons in the Nigerian music. On a table in the center of the large loft are a score for ninety-piece orchestra, notes for Coleman's as yet unpublished book on his Harmolodic Theory, and a box of specially painted postcards announcing the opening of Z.K.'s show. "Aren't his things beautiful?" Ornette asks as he makes another cushion shot. "I met him when I was in Nigeria, bought his work. And just having it in my possession I learned that, you know . . . it's harmless and it's there. Eight ball in the corner pocket."

Whack! "You know, most artists think they're above show business, but an artist is not a different person; he just has a different title. The fact that you're an artist doesn't mean that you're not supposed to learn to read and write and count. It just happens that if you're an artist, you haven't had any time to be doing lots of other things. I know that when I was going to school I was learning geometry, history, and science, and also I had an art class. So education must include all those things as having something to do with the concept of value in relation to intelligence. I never thought of myself as being a person that just dealt with music and everything else was irrelevant. I like the involvement of bringing things into existence that better the life of people. I love that concept. And whatever it's called, to me that's art. Do you want to rack up the balls for another game?"

Ornette's conversation is often like his painting *The Circle with a Hole in the Middle*, which graces the cover of his Atlantic album *The Art of the Improvisers*. His music manifests the same thought pattern, circling around the theme, moving far afield, returning to the starting point when you least expect it, and moving away again, progressing by variations of feelings and ideas, balanced like Humpty Dumpty on the edge of the void, the hole in the middle of space and time.

The Ornette Coleman quartet that debuted in New York at the old Five Spot, in the fall of 1959, approached the void and, at times, tumbled into it. The listeners that first night included Leonard Bernstein, Gunther Schuller, Nesuhi and Ahmet Ertegun, John Hammond, and almost every musician in town. Some heard formlessness and chaos, others a sound that would radically alter the course of jazz and inform the work of a generation of musicians to come. "In the music we play," Ornette said, "no one player has the lead. Anyone can come out with it at any time." This new approach to group playing looked ahead with its polyrhythms, geared to exploration rather than to predetermined patterns, and its melodies that proceeded through a complex of unstated modulations rather than riding on a cushion of traditional chord progressions. But the music looked back through the jazz tradition with its collective improvisations and its personal, speechlike approach to intonation and phrasing, so much like the ensemble and solo styles of the early Southern and Southwestern blues and jazz musicians. In the fall of 1971, Ornette reassembled his original quartet to record *Science Fiction*. In twelve years the style had become classic, distilled into the kind of unique, breathtaking perfection that characterized the work of Lester Young, Charlie Parker, John Coltrane, and a handful of other black innovators.

By the beginning of 1972 twenty-one Ornette Coleman albums were listed in the Schwann catalog. All but one were small group recordings, and all but two or three of the compositions were Coleman originals.

"I started writing before I started playing," he explains. "I didn't start playing until later, because nobody would hire me. But when I went to audition my tunes for Les Koenig [of Contemporary Records, Los Angeles], he liked me playing my own music, so I got the date. And yet it's been twelve years and they're still saying I haven't paid off the cost of the record." For a decade Ornette channeled his compositional ideas into providing frameworks for his combo to improvise on. Somehow he found time to write a string quartet and a piece for strings and woodwinds. Then he was awarded a Guggenheim, which allowed him to devote more time to writing, and last summer *Skies of America*, a full-length work for soloist and symphony orchestra, was given its premiere at the Newport-in–New York jazz festival.

In a sense, the composition is "about" the many things that have happened to Ornette Coleman since March 19, 1930, when he was born in Fort Worth, Texas, "under America's skies." More specifically, it is about being black, feeling exploited, working for recognition as an artist and a man in a society that has often been aloof, condescending, or hostile. He started on the alto saxophone at the age of fourteen, switched to tenor two years later, and played in numerous Texas rhythm and blues groups. He first left Fort Worth as a teenager, with a carnival band. He was dismissed from the tent show for playing bebop, stranded in New Orleans, threatened by racist sheriffs in Mississippi. In Baton Rouge a gang of roughnecks beat him up and threw his tenor off a hill, so he went back to the alto, which is still his principal horn.

He went to Los Angeles with Pee Wee Crayton's blues band and spent the better part of the fifties there, working at various odd jobs, studying music theory, practicing and composing whenever he could. He continued to develop his own expression, and gradually a few musicians began to understand, especially the trumpeter Don Cherry, bassist Charlie Haden, and drummers Ed Blackwell and Billy Higgins. Ornette, Cherry, Haden, and Higgins worked with pianist Paul Bley at Los Angeles's Hillcrest club in 1958, and struck out on their own later that year.

During the sixties he was the subject of numerous articles, which either idealized or vilified him, and a series of "misunderstandings" with record executives and club owners made him more and more distrustful of the white middlemen who still control the presentation and dissemination of jazz and popular music in America.

"America is a very good country for a Caucasian human being," he says, "because regardless of what his native tongue is, if he changes his name and speaks English he could be of any Caucasian descent. And believe me, that is a very successful form of freedom. If you're black you can change your name, you can do anything you want to, but the color of your skin defeats you from having the same privileges as what I just spoke about. This is the tragedy of America.

"John Lennon says women are the niggers of the world. Well, I guess the Jewish, the Italian, and the Irish people were the niggers of the white world. But you can take any Irish or Jewish or Italian person, and when they return from their job and go home they are returning to an original concept of who they are as a person. When they're on the street, selling their merchandise or doing anything to relate to the country in a land-of-the-free, home-of-the-brave situation, they speak English, take an English name, and that's it. When they get home, whatever their name is or whatever they are knowing in their ancestral background, they can live that. And I think that is very beautiful for a human being to have, where he can go out in the world and make a living for himself and then come home and have his ancestral roots still intact. That is one thing that black people here have never yet had. I'll tell you, man, I'm so tired of feeling that being black in America has something to do with not being white in America that I find I can no longer be involved in social functions that have to do with intellectualism or art or racial questions. Knowing the things I've just said to you, I find myself being totally . . . paranoid about some person trying to get ahead in life when I'm one of the many persons he can use to get ahead without feeling that he's doing anything wrong.

"I would like to have the same support for *Skies of America* as any artist that the public has heard and enjoyed. And everybody in their heritage and natural state of being wants success; no one is basing their involvement in anything on a negative attitude. I'm speaking about success humanly, intellectually, racially, financially, and religiously. I mean success in those senses of knowing that they have something to do with having less enemies and more friends, or less debts and more objects, less evil and more love, or less hatred and more happiness. And I don't want someone to pat me on the back and not truly listen or try to understand the piece of music. I get lots of lip service that has to do with the value of my work having to always be dictated to me by people who have no interest in my welfare at all. I've written lots of music, but not because I wanted to have someone say, Oh, isn't he a wonderful writer. I wrote the music because I *could* write the music, and then secondly I wrote it because if I hadn't written it down I wouldn't have had any way of keeping it and explaining it to others.

"One day I finally realized that all the music I had heard, someone had made it possible for me to learn or hear it by simply writing it down or repeating it. So since I became aware that it had something to do with writing, I decided that was what I wanted to be. That's the concept of *Skies of America*: to give people an insight into things that I've done and to show them that they could also participate with me in doing it.

"Anywhere you go," he says, "you're going to have some problems with people not getting into your music. And you're going to get lip service."

The modern black American composer-improviser is particularly subject to this lip-service syndrome, and to what Ornette calls "a very New York cliché thing: people satisfying you mentally but never giving you anything that you want." One reason is that the music of an Ornette Coleman, a Cecil Taylor, an Anthony Braxton, or a Sun Ra draws on a much wider spectrum of influences than many listeners have been exposed to. In addition to past and present jazz, there is the repertoire of modern concert music, the amplification and pulselike beat of rhythm and blues and rock, and the infinitely diverse musical traditions of the emerging nonwhite nations. The black composer may use in a single piece elements from any number of these primary sources. Living as he does in Western urban centers, wired into the output of cultures he would never have come into contact with a few decades ago, he hears, and uses, any music that comes naturally to his particular sensibility.

The more he hears, the more connections he makes. The vocalized scream in Ornette's sound, for example, is a tone split into its harmonics or overtones. This practice was characteristic of blues musicians and singers as far back as the beginnings of "race recordings," and it can be heard in pure African music. Ngbaka (central African) soloists on the musical bow are able to draw a multitude of harmonics from the single "ground" tone of the bow's string, just as a saxophone virtuoso like Ornette runs harmonics over a root that is sounded simultaneously. But modern European and American "classical" composers are also interested in harmonics. Iannis Xenakis, for instance, often indicates in his scores which particular partials of a given tone are to be sounded. The complex African polyrhythms currently in favor with many jazz groups were finding their way into modern concert music as early as Varese's 1931 *Ionization*. And many of today's major jazzmen were playing "jazz/ rock" long before its current vogue, often because the only jobs they could get were with rhythm and blues bands.

This unusual number of reference points has left much of the new black music in a commercial vacuum. The music is often too intricate and demanding for the traditional smoke-filled nightclub, but it has yet to attract the widespread private and foundation support that would make regular concert hall performances possible. While some of Coleman's contemporaries, such as Cecil Taylor and Ken MacIntyre, have accepted positions in the black-studies programs of Eastern universities, others—Pharoah Sanders, Sun Ra—continue to function in the nightclub milieu. Ornette, who continues to write for his quartet as well as for orchestra, and whose recently completed theory book is potentially a major shaping influence on the younger generation of black composer-instrumentalists, hopes to utilize all these outlets, provided, of course, that they become available to him. Since *Skies of America*'s premiere he is beginning to feel that maybe he's on an upswing.

Downstairs, Z.K.'s show is opening. Champagne is being served to a mixed crowd of musicians and artists. The Nigerian videotape is playing and Ornette Coleman, dressed in a neat, conservative suit, walks from circle to circle, greeting friends and making conversation. The scene in the gallery and the image on the screen merge into a continuum of circles, with Ornette in the middle of each one.

THE ORIGINATORS: "WHERE THE *HELL* DID THIS MAN COME FROM?"

The Fifties

ROLLING STONE | APRIL 19, 1990

For some of us, it began late at night: huddled under bedroom covers with our ears glued to a radio pulling in black voices charged with intense emotion and propelled by a wildly kinetic rhythm through the after-midnight static. Growing up in the white-bread America of the fifties, we had never heard anything like it, but we reacted, or remember reacting, instantaneously and were converted. We were believers before we knew what it was that had so spectacularly ripped the dull, familiar fabric of our lives. We asked our friends, maybe an older brother or sister. We found out that they called it rock & roll. It was so much more vital and alive than any music we had ever heard before that it needed a new category: Rock & roll was much more than new music for us. It was an obsession, and a way of life.

For some of us, it began a little later, with our first glimpse of Elvis on the family television set. But for those of us growing up in the fifties, it didn't seem to matter how or where we first heard the music. Our reactions were remarkably uniform. Here, we knew, was a sonic cataclysm come bursting (apparently) out of nowhere, with the power to change our lives forever. Because it was obviously, inarguably *our* music. If we had any initial doubt about that, our parents' horrified—or at best dismissive— reactions banished those doubts. Growing up in a world we were only beginning to understand, we had finally found something for us: for us together, for us alone.

But where did it come from? How did it get started? Thirty-five-odd years after rock & roll first burst upon us in all its glory, we still don't have a simple, definitive answer to these questions. Of course, they are trick questions. Where you think rock & roll came from and how you think it grew depends on how you define rock & roll.

Fats Domino, the most amiable and pragmatic of the first-generation rock & roll stars, was asked about the music's origins in a fifties television interview. "Rock & roll is nothing but rhythm and blues," he responded with characteristic candor, "and we've been playing it for years down in New Orleans." This is a valid statement: All fifties rockers, black and white, country-born and city-bred, were fundamentally influenced by R&B, the black popular music of the late forties and early fifties. R&B was a catchall rubric for the sound of everything from stomping Kansas City swing bands to New York street-corner vocal groups to scrappy Delta and Chicago blues bands. As far as Fats Domino was concerned, rock & roll was simply a new marketing strategy for the style of music he had been recording since 1949. But what about the rest of the fifties rock front-runners?

When we get down to cases, we find that several of the most distinctive and influential rock & roll performers of the mid-fifties were making music that could not, by any stretch of the imagination, be defined as a continuation of pre-1955 R&B. There was no clear precedent in R&B for an artist like Chuck Berry, who combined hillbilly, blues, and swing-jazz influences in more or less equal measure and wrote songs about teenage life and culture that black and white teens found equally appealing. (Louis Jordan, the early idol of both Berry and Bill Haley, came closest, but his jump 'n' jive story songs were aimed as much at adults as teens, and any hillbilly flavor in his records was strictly a comedic device.) Certainly, mainstream popular music had never seen a performer whose vocal delivery, stage moves, and seamless integration of influences as diverse as down-home blues, white Pentecostalism, and hit-parade crooning remotely resembled Elvis Presley's. And where, outside the wildest, most Dionysian black storefront churches, had anyone heard or seen *anything* like Little Richard?

Sam Phillips, the rock & roll patriarch whose Sun label first recorded Elvis, Jerry Lee Lewis, Carl Perkins, Johnny Cash, and other first-rate talents, has suggested that the true import of fifties rock & roll had very little to do with musical content, let alone musical innovation. And it's perfectly true that once you strip the music down and analyze it, riff by riff, lick by lick, you find a mélange of blues conceits, prewar big band and Western swing, gospel, and other existing vocabularies. For Phillips, rock & roll's real significance was twofold.

First, it was the only form of popular music that specifically addressed and was tailored to teenagers—there had been adult records and kiddie records, but nothing for that burgeoning bulge of the baby-boom population caught between childhood and adulthood. Second, rock & roll enabled "marginal" Americans—poor white sharecroppers, black ghetto youths, and, not coincidentally, storefront record-label operators in out-of-the-way places like Memphis—the opportunity to express themselves freely, not as purveyors of R&B and C&W, whose audiences were limited, but as a dominant force in the popular marketplace. Elvis was transformed from hick truck driver to idol of millions in less than a year. Suddenly, it seemed, the sky was the limit, if there was a limit at all.

The coming of rock & roll in the mid-fifties was not merely a musical revolution but a social and generational upheaval of vast and unpredictable scope. It also represented a major reversal in the *business* of popular music. There were no pre–rock & roll counterparts to Sam Phillips, who parlayed a tiny Memphis label with a staff of one into a company whose artists sold millions of records throughout the world. In record-business terms, rock & roll meant that small, formerly specialized labels like Sun, Chess, and Specialty were invading the upper reaches of the pop charts, long the exclusive domain of the major corporate record labels and old-line Tin Pan Alley music-publishing interests.

Concentrating on high-volume sales and bland, lowest-common-denominator pop disposables, the majors were caught napping by an unholy coalition of Southern renegade radio engineers (Phillips), Jewish immigrant merchants (the Chess brothers), black ex-swing-band musicians, and raving hillbilly wild men. These were the "marginal" Americans who had been recording for specialized audiences since the majors had virtually ceded them that territory at the end of World War II. The ghetto-storefront, nickel-and-dime record operation of 1949–53 suddenly emerged an industry giant in 1955–56, accounting for many and often most of the records at the top of the pop charts.

Because many of the same small labels that had taken over the R&B market were also dabbling in country and western music, and vice versa, these musics had been drawing closer together. The younger generation of C&W fans were also listening and dancing to black music, and as a result white country musicians were encouraged to record R&B songs and play with a heavier, emphatically rocking beat.

Meanwhile, many blacks growing up in isolated pockets of the rural South listened to and were influenced by the country music on radio programs like the *Grand Ole Opry*, from Nashville. Black performers like Chuck Berry and Bo Diddley found that when they performed a song that was vaguely hillbilly in style or derivation, black audiences went for it. Despite the still-rigid racial segregation of the fifties, the white and black underclass of music fans and performers was finding more and more common ground.

With the flowering of the postwar baby boom, teenagers, especially white teenagers with money in their pockets, represented a potentially enormous and largely untapped consumer group. It didn't take a genius to realize, as Sam Phillips and other early-fifties indie-label owners did, that more and more of these free-spending kids were listening to black records, spun on local radio stations by a new generation of black-talking but mostly white-skinned disc jockeys. If a white performer with an R&B style and teen appeal could be found . . .

The runaway success of Bill Haley and the Comets following the use of their "Rock Around the Clock" in a key sequence of the 1955 juvenile-delinquent movie *The Blackboard Jungle* was a clear signal that R&B and C&W (Haley's Comets were a former C&W band recording R&B tunes in a style resembling Louis Jordan's) weren't going to remain ghettoized from the pop-music mainstream much longer. But Haley wasn't exactly teen-idol material. It took an assiduously groomed and promoted Elvis Presley—who, legend has it, walked into Sam Phillips's tiny office to make a record for his mother's birthday—to assure the triumph of rock & roll.

To succeed in the teen marketplace, the new music—new, at least, to the teenagers who embraced it—needed a name. Rhythm and blues was a dated term with exclusively black connotations. Alan Freed, the white R&B disc jockey whose move from Cleveland to a top-rated New York station in 1954 was as crucial to the emergence of rock & roll as the timely appearance of the Pelvis, came up with the name. It must have amused Freed and other insiders a great deal that the term *rock & roll* was black slang for sex—and had been as early as 1922, when blues singer Trixie Smith recorded "My Man Rocks Me (with One Steady Roll)." It was a secret shared by the disc jockeys, the performers, and the kids: Astonishingly, "responsible adults" didn't seem to "get it." Certainly, nobody who was in on the joke was going to spell it out for them. Teenagers were developing their own codes of in-group complicity, expressed in clothes, in accoutrements (from girls' earrings and pins to greasers' switchblades), and increasingly in their own slanguage. The medium that spread this underground teen culture was rock & roll.

From its earliest days the rock & roll label covered a broad musical terrain. The cliché is that rock & roll was a melding of country music and blues, and if you are talking about, say, Chuck Berry or Elvis Presley, the description, though simplistic, does fit. But the black inner-city vocal-group sound, which itself was diverse enough to accommodate the tough, soulful Midnighters and 5 Royales, the neo-barbershop harmonies of "bird groups" like the Orioles and the Crows, and the kid sound of Frankie Lymon and the Teenagers or Shirley and Lee, had little to do with either blues or country music in their purer forms.

The Bo Diddley beat—which, once Bo popularized it, began showing up on records by everybody from the former jazz bandleader Johnny Otis ("Willie and the Hand Jive") to the Texas rockabilly Buddy Holly ("Not Fade Away")—was Afro-Caribbean in derivation. The most durable (read "overused") bass riff in fifties rock & roll, as exemplified by Fats Domino's "Blue Monday" or Lloyd Price's and Elvis Presley's "Lawdy Miss Clawdy," had been pinched by Dave Bartholomew, Domino's canny producer and bandleader, from a Cuban *son* record. The screaming, athletic saxophone playing that was fifties rock's dominant instrumental voice before the electric guitar moved front and center was straight out of forties big-band swing, as were typical rock & roll arrangers' devices such as riffing sax sections and stop-time breaks. Traditional Mexican rhythms entered the rock & roll arena through Chicano artists, most prominently Ritchie Valens. Rock & roll proved an all-American, multiethnic hybrid, its sources and developing substyles too various to be explained away by "blues plus country" or any other reductionist formula.

At the height of the initial pandemonium, in 1955–56, a select number of front-runners emerged, stars whose personalities and performing antics set the stage for all that was to follow: Elvis, of course; Chuck Berry, whose definitive guitar style (rooted in swing jazz and the uptown-band blues of T-Bone Walker) was as widely emulated as his brilliant, vividly economical lyrics of teenage tribulations and triumphs; Little Richard, the archetypal rock & roll screamer and ambisexual striptease artist, with the toughest, most influential road band of the period, the mighty Upsetters; friendly, reliable Fats Domino, who mixed New Orleans blues and jazz with Tin Pan Alley pop and quietly racked up more hit records than anyone but Elvis; Jerry Lee Lewis, the prototype of the rock & roll wild man, his stage persona and lifestyle perfectly matched; Buddy Holly and the Crickets, the paradigm of the singer-songwriter-fronted guitar band; Sam Cooke, Ray Charles, the 5 Royales, and a young James Brown, all of whom enacted Pentecostal religious ecstasies on the rock & roll stage and spawned the sixties soul men in the process; and Eddie Cochran, who combined teen-idol looks with a probing musical intelligence and who understood early on that the recording studio was a musical instrument.

Certain behind-the-scenes figures were arguably as important as even the brightest singing stars in building and shaping rock & roll as a viable musical idiom, with a future as well as a spectacular, slam-bang present. The producer Milt Gabler, who applied what he learned producing Louis Jordan's forties jump-blues novelties to Bill Haley's breakthrough hits. Dave Bartholomew, the New Orleans trumpeter, bandleader, songwriter, and record producer, whose musicians powered most of the hits by Fats Domino and Little Richard. Bartholomew's drummer, Earl Palmer, who defined rock & roll rhythm in New Orleans and moved on to first-call status among the Los Angeles studio elite, playing uncredited on a staggering number of the era's most influential records, from Richard's "Tutti Frutti" to Cochran's "Summertime Blues." If any single musician can be credited with defining rock & roll as a rhythmic idiom distinct from jump, R&B, and all else that preceded it, that musician is surely Earl Palmer. But it was another drummer and Little Richard associate, the Upsetters' Charles Connor, who first put the funk in the rhythm, as even James Brown admitted.

Atlantic Records' Tom Dowd introduced true stereo and gave Atlantic singles by the Coasters, the Drifters, and many others a unique clarity and presence. Sam Phillips was as significant for his ingenious engineering, his feel for echo and ambience, as for his talent spotting and genre mixing. And Phillips's multiracial populism, an unpopular stance for a white Southerner in the fifties, to say the least, had a lot to do with defining what we might choose to call either the spirit of rock & roll or its politics. It was Phillips who expressed most clearly, through his recording policies and his public utterances, the vision of rock & roll as a dream of equality and freedom.

Much has been made of sixties rock as a vehicle for revolutionary social and cultural change, but it was mid-fifties rock & roll that blew away, in one mighty, concentrated blast, the accumulated racial and social proprieties of centuries. What could be more outrageous, more threatening to the social and sexual order subsumed by the ingenuous phrase *traditional American values*, than a full-tilt Little Richard show? There he was, camping it up androgynously one minute, then ripping off his clothes to display for a packed house of screaming teenage white girls his finely muscled black body.

It is a measure of fifties rock's genuine revolutionary potential (as opposed to the revolution-as-corporate-marketing-ploy so characteristic of the sixties) that while sixties rock eventually calmed down, was co-opted, or snuffed itself out in heedless excess, fifties rock & roll was *stopped*. Cold.

Rock & roll's takeover of the pop-music marketplace in the mid-fifties was as threatening to the entrenched old-line music and entertainment business as it was to professional authority figures everywhere. RCA had Elvis, but most of the early rock & roll hits were on regionally rooted indie operations. Most of the major labels, as well as the established music publishers that had been the industry's backbone for more than a century, reacted slowly to the rock & roll onslaught, and most were definitely not amused by it.

It took a coalition of these Tin Pan Alley interests and publicity-hungry congressmen to bring rock & roll to its knees with the payola hearings that so ingloriously capped a truly tumultuous decade. The payola hearings managed to pillory Alan Freed, who had always played original black recordings rather than the bland white "cover" versions being offered by squeaky-clean opportunists like Pat Boone.

At the same time a combination of economic forces and the gradual takeover of record-distribution networks by major labels made running a small label more and more difficult. The indie labels that had launched the music and sustained it during the two or three years when it ravaged the land either caved in to the pressure and quietly wound down their operations, like Sun and Specialty, or diversified and became corporate giants themselves, like Atlantic.

On top of all this came a series of mishaps in the careers of some of rock's leading lights. The army and Colonel Parker conspired to make Elvis safe. Chuck Berry was busted and spent time in jail. Little Richard quit at the peak of his powers to preach the gospel. Jerry Lee Lewis married his barely pubescent cousin and was blackballed. Holly, Valens, and the Big Bopper went down in an Iowa field. Alan Freed's fall from grace ended at the bottom, with his death as an alcoholic recluse.

During the few brief years when high-octane rock & roll ruled unchecked, the possibilities seemed mind-boggling, even limitless. Viewed with hindsight, the whole affair turns out to have been the cultural vanguard of a movement toward racial, social, and sexual equality that was then only beginning to assume an explicitly political form. It's no mere accident of history that Rosa Parks's refusal to move to the back of a segregated Alabama bus, the germinal act of what became the civil-rights movement, occurred during the brief pop-music ascendancy of performers like Chuck Berry and Little Richard, black men whose every sound and sign communicated their refusal to respond to the racist's traditional "C'mere, boy!"

If fifties rock & roll failed to realize the creative and social aspirations it so eloquently expressed, on a purely cultural level it succeeded beyond the wildest dreams *anyone* could have entertained at the time. Not only has it proved more than a passing fad or an episode of youthful folly, it has provided the model, the template, the jumping-off point for virtually every subsequent wave of pop-music innovation. The best of fifties rock & roll may have promised a utopia that was not to be, but as long as the music survives, the dream will live on.

Liner Notes for *Bo Diddley: The Chess Box*

(Chess, 1990)

Guys kind of piss me off trying to name what I'm doing, and a lot of times I tell people I don't know what it is, I just play it. It's mixed up with spiritual, sanctified rhythms and the feeling . . . I have a feeling of making people Shout. I put it in the Shout mode, and I got it locked right in there. And that's what you got to do. If you can't lock them into that mode, they don't move.

BO DIDDLEY, 1990

If the musical copyright laws of the United States more accurately reflected the way American vernacular music is created and disseminated, Bo Diddley would be a wealthy man today. Over the years, a who's who of rock & roll royalty has recorded Diddley's *songs*, from Buddy Holly's fifties cover of "Bo Diddley" to the multitudinous sixties covers of Diddley staples like "Mona," "Road Runner," "I'm a Man," and "Who Do You Love" by the Stones, the Yardbirds, the Who, the Pretty Things (who named their band after a Diddley song), Ronnie Hawkins, the Doors, Quicksilver Messenger Service, and Bob Seger, among many others. You *can* copyright a song, and some royalties came Bo Diddley's way, although his record company, Chess, usually claimed half his song-writing royalties, like virtually every other rhythm and blues and rock & roll label of its time. But you can't copyright a rhythm, a beat, a guitar sound, or a riff pattern. American copyright law follows the European tradition that a song is words, melody, and chords, and "The Song," defined in this narrow sense, is the thing; everything else is secondary.

But it just so happens that this "everything else" is the area in which Bo Diddley made many of his contributions to American popular music. The Bo Diddley sound and the so-called Bo Diddley beat—actually more a rhythmic complex, and a philosophy of rhythmic orchestration, than simply a "beat"—have been the resilient framework on which numerous artists have built their hit records, and on which some lesser artists created entire careers. In the fifties, hits like Buddy Holly's "Not Fade Away" and Johnny Otis's "Willie and the Hand Jive" and "Crazy Country Hop" were pure Bo Diddley in sound and feel. In later years, performers such as the Rolling Stones and Eric Clapton have rerecorded these Diddley-inspired songs and made them hits all over again. The Bo Diddley rhythmic vocabulary had so thoroughly seeped into the bedrock of pop and rock music by the 1980s that when the British postpunk group the Smiths used a Bo Diddley rhythm to underpin one of their most memorable British hit singles, "How Soon Is Now," that country's music press hardly seemed to notice how much the song's beat, tremolo guitar sound, and atmosphere owed to Papa Bo. In none of these cases did Bo Diddley write the lyrics or melodies of the songs; when other artists turned his ideas into hits, he received no remuneration and precious little recognition.

All of this is common knowledge in rock & roll circles. It is, sadly, all too typical in the annals of American popular music, especially where black originators and white imitators are concerned. In Bo's case it has become almost a cliché—"The Story of Bo Diddley" for real. But it is not the whole story, and its repetition over the years may well have played a part in limiting our understanding of the true scope of Bo Diddley's art and innovation. All too often, it has encouraged rock & roll historians to depict Bo as a limited, single-minded performer whose essential contribution to the music was one great idea—a sound, a beat. One listen to *Bo Diddley: The Chess Box* should go a long way toward dispelling this misconception.

The selections in this set make it clear, for example, that Bo was a singularly important catalyst in one of the most far-reaching transformations of post–World War II American music: the absorption of black gospel music, especially in its more deeply rooted, down-home, "sanctified" manifestations, into the pop mainstream. As Bo himself testified, he considers the Shout—the oldest and most fundamental known form of black American religious rhythm music—the essential source of his own music's characteristic feeling and momentum. When we think of performers who led the way in "sanctifying" popular music, we think first of men like Ray Charles and Sam Cooke. But Charles's first success with a gospel tune turned into a dance number, "I've Got a Woman," appeared in 1955, the same year Diddley records like "Diddley Daddy" and "Bring It to Jerome" introduced jubilee-style vocal group harmonizing (on the former) and an all-out, testifying Shout call-and-response format (on the latter) onto the pop charts. Sam Cooke's first significant efforts in these directions, and milestones such as Charles's "What'd I Say" and the Isley Brothers' "Shout," were still several years down the pike.

Similarly, Bo Diddley and his right-hand man, maracas player Jerome Green, were the first popular artists to seize on black street-corner culture—children's games and game songs, the ritualized rounds of bragging and insults known as "the dozens," the mode of tall-tale-telling called "toasting"—as the stuff of pop hits—hits that crossed racial and social boundaries, appealing to teenagers black and white, rural and urban, middle-class and poor. "Say Man" and "Who Do You Love" are the classic early examples. Records like the former, which Bo describes as "signifying," make a strong case for Bo Diddley as one of the Godfathers of Rap, and some of his fifties chop-rhythm guitar patterns make him an early avatar of funk.

Bo was also a tireless sonic experimenter, and seems to have been one of the few fifties rockers to effectively, if not officially, produce many of his own sessions. He was also one of the very first to take the next step in control of his own recording, the building of a home studio in his late fifties Washington, D.C., home. He even recorded in stereo, having wired together a two-track Scully and a three-track Presto. One example of Bo's home recordings in this collection is "Spend My Life with You."

Add to these achievements Bo's remarkable flexibility and power as a lead vocalist; his ability to work tightly with established vocal groups in a gospelish doo-wop style (the previously unreleased "You Know I Love You," with the Flamingos, is a glorious find); his singular abilities as a bandleader-arranger; his prescient anticipation of some of the sixties guitar sounds achieved with overdriven amps, sustain, and feedback; the variety and resourcefulness of his songwriting; and his early understanding of the importance of establishing a performing alter-ego, with his self-reflexive lyrics, influential stage moves, the square-bodied and flying-vee guitars he introduced, and his celebrated "Bo Diddley Is a Gunslinger" outfits and original record cover designs. A view of the man begins to emerge that far transcends the cliché of the clever rhythmatist with one great idea. Nor has the nature and scope of Bo Diddley's rhythmic concepts been adequately examined. What we have here, emerging clearly, perhaps for the first time, from the careful, balanced programming of *The Chess Box*, is a portrait of one of the most versatile, innovative, and *complete* musical talents of our time.

One of the apparent paradoxes of the Bo Diddley story is how the fifties rocker with perhaps the most "down-home" style and persona of them all developed it in an urban environment. After the age of eight or nine, Ellas McDaniel was a city kid who rarely returned to Mississippi. He arrived in Chicago between the two great waves of black immigration from Mississippi and neighboring states triggered by the two world wars and the opening up of jobs in war-related industries. Most of his fellow Chess artists made the move north some years later—Muddy Waters in the early forties, Howlin' Wolf at the beginning of the fifties. One has to remember the ethnic and geographical makeup of Chicago in the thirties and forties, when McDaniel was growing up there. The city was known as "Little Mississippi," and for good reason. Its black population had been increasing exponentially since the first world war, and the new arrivals were crammed into two long, narrow, densely populated, sharply defined tenement strips—one on the South Side, where the McDaniel family lived, the other, developing somewhat later, on the West Side.

Within the teeming South Side strip, an overwhelming majority of the residents were either born in Mississippi and its vicinity or were the young children of former Mississippi agricultural laborers. An enterprising family member would make the move north, find a residence, and write to relatives, who often as not ended up settling in the particular neighborhood where their relatives and former friends were already established. Entire blocks of tenements were dominated by Mississippians from a single rural county, or from the vicinity of a major delta town like Clarksdale. In effect, an entire culture was being transplanted, and the change from country to city living did not disrupt the old ways to nearly the degree one might imagine, precisely because the new arrivals stayed as close as possible to their own "kind."

The attitudes with which the more established met the newer arrivals were neither simple nor cut-and-dried. On the one hand, new arrivals were often disparaged for acting "country," and Bo remembers "a big change, because I ended up being taunted by other children for being 'country.' " But the same children who taunted young Ellas were also preserving down-home ways, in the form of sayings, slang, games and game songs, and other forms of cultural expression their parents and older siblings seemed all too eager to forget. This is evidently the source of much of the down-home folklore Bo later worked into songs like "Bo Diddley," "Diddley Wah Diddy," "Who Do You Love," and the Southern-style train song "Down Home Special." "Signifying," or "the dozens," the basis of "Say Man" and Bo's other call-and-response insult-games with Jerome Green, was a Southern children's tradition that flourished, becoming more verbally inventive, aggressive, and scatological in the tougher Chicago environment. As Bo recalls, this children's lore also seems to have been the source of Ellas's nickname, Bo Diddley.

It also happens that in certain backwoods areas of Mississippi, including the southern Mississippi area where Ellas spent his earliest years, a children's game that was popular for generations involved making a toy instrument, a kind of one-string guitar or musical bow, often simply by nailing a length of broom wire to the side of a cabin. A rock is inserted under the string as a movable bridge and the wire is played, bottleneck guitar–style, with some sort of slider. The instrument is called a diddley bow. Furthermore, as folklorist David Evans pointed out when he first raised this issue in the groundbreaking article "Afro-American One-Stringed Instruments" (*Western Folklore* 23, 1970), the rhythm most typically played on the diddley bow is a kind of "hambone" or "shave-and-a-haircut-six-bits" rhythm—virtually the "Bo Diddley beat." When the young diddley-bow players grow up, they apply the techniques they've learned to the guitar and begin playing "blues," the area's "adult" music.

Bo Diddley's first single, Evans continued, perfectly illustrates this process. The top side, "Bo Diddley," is a song in the style of a children's game, played with the "diddley bow" rhythm associated with children's music-making in Mississippi. In many ways, it is a song *about* childhood. The record's flip side, "I'm a Man," is just as emphatically a song about adulthood, performed in the adult musical idiom, the blues. How are we to square Bo's own account, which he has stuck with all his life, and the evidence of his first record? Surely all this adds up to more than mere "coincidence."

Coincidence is, of course, a loaded word. It simply means that, while we notice an *apparent* connection between *apparently* disparate or unrelated facts or events, we are unable to *pinpoint* a connection that makes sense in cause-and-effect terms. Rather than admit that our events or facts may indeed have a significant relationship that *cannot* be explained by a simple, rational, linear process of cause and effect—the kind of relationship characterized by psychologist C. G. Jung as "synchronicity"—we simply dismiss the whole thing as "coincidence." What we are in fact saying is that because we sense a meaningful relationship but can't explain or understand it, it isn't really meaningful, and therefore isn't a "real" relationship.

The key to *this* particular mystery, I think, is the material on the Shout quoted at the beginning of these notes. Bo describes his distinctive sound, which others have seen simply as a rhythm pattern, as something "spiritual," and specifically "the feeling of making people Shout." Few recordings of authentic old-style Shouts are in existence, but these recordings (mostly on the Library of Congress and Folkways labels) document an overall rhythmic feeling with the same sort of accent patterns heard in Bo Diddley's music. The most characteristic Shout rhythm of the Georgia Sea Islands, for example, has been identified with the "Habañera," an African rhythm that became a popular Cuban dance-hall rhythm into the first half of the nineteenth century and left an imprint on certain American popular music at that time. The Bo Diddley-ish 3/2 accent pattern (three strokes, a rest, and two more strokes spread over a four-beat measure) is in fact the rhythmic foundation of Afro-Cuban music, the clave pattern, named for the wooden sticks that are struck sharply together to delineate the pattern while other percussion instruments weave polyrhythms around it.

So the Cubans call it clave; black shoeshine boys of the nineteenth century called it hambone; Southern blacks in nineteenth-century rural churches used it as the basis for a shuffling, counterclockwise religious dance called the Shout or ring shout; ragtime composers of the late nine-tenth century used the pattern in the bass for many piano rags, often identifying it as Habañera; in New Orleans, pioneering jazz composer-pianist Jelly Roll Morton used it in tunes like his "Black Bottom Stomp"; in the first decades of the century variants of the pattern were associated with both the black bottom and the Charleston dances, which astute observers even then traced back to the Shouts of isolated Southern plantations and country churches. No wonder such a rhythm turned up in the music made by young Mississippi blacks on their diddley bows; it's practically ubiquitous in African and African-American music where the dominant African cultural influences have been (Nigerian) Yoruba and Kongo—particularly in Cuba, Haiti, Louisiana, and Mississippi.

To young Ellas McDaniel, growing up in the "little Mississippi" that was South Side Chicago in the thirties and forties, that basic polyrhyth-mic kernel, implying in its concise construction both the principles three-against-two and five-against-four, would have been something in the air, something in people's walk, in the way they talked, something almost as natural as breathing. And Bo himself knew very well that in *his* frame of reference, its source was the sanctified holy dance of the more ecstatic black Christians—the Shout. As for the Bo Diddley–diddley bow connection, black vernacular is known for its rapid changes in emphasis and meaning, for using the same words or variants to mean different things in different contexts. In Mississippi, a diddley bow was a children's one-stringed instrument, but Bo never messed with one, or with a guitar, until he had lived in Chicago for some five years. Among black school-children in Chicago, a "Bo Diddley" was probably a big, black bully, or something of the sort. And how did Bo's first (and fantastically success-ful) single come to represent, musically, rhythmically, lyrically, and with a folklorist's verisimilitude, the transition from childhood to adulthood? You could call it genius, or art, or synchronicity. You could attribute it to the tremendously strong and resilient basic cultural patterns passed on from generation to generation as part of the African heritage slave owners worked so hard to suppress, patterns that have surfaced and resurfaced in our popular culture without their popularizers always being fully cognizant of their origins. You could think of it as hoodoo, as plain, simple down-home magic; wasn't Bo always portraying himself on records as a kind of super hoodoo-man, a larger-than-life, almost mythic figure with a supernatural whammy? Or maybe you prefer coincidence. It's up to you.

In any case, things are often not as simple as they seem, and Bo Diddley's music is certainly a case in point. It also happens to be a particularly vital example of how the most deeply rooted oral folk traditions and the latest "uptown" musical fads and developments interacted, in the midst of a period of rapid social change and turmoil, to produce the explosive hybrid we call rock & roll.

Some of the sources of Bo's music are indeed surprising, and have little or nothing to do with down-home roots. His first musical experience was as a violin student, playing in an orchestra organized by Professor O. W. Frederick that rehearsed at Chicago's Ebenezer Baptist Church. The orchestra played European classical music, and Bo was going at it for several years before hearing John Lee Hooker's rocking electric-guitar hit "Boogie Chillen." Years later, Bo would occasionally use the violin on Chess records like the atmospheric after-hours blues instrumental "The Clock Strikes Twelve." But his violin studies also influenced his guitar playing in an unexpected manner—he applied his violin technique to the choppy, choke-rhythm guitar playing later associated with mid-sixties funk.

The first black pop performers who inspired Bo to take up music were urbane swing-era figures like jive-man supreme Cab Calloway and balladeer Billy Eckstine. His first band, the Hipsters, included Samuel Daniel, who handled Billy Eckstine–style vocals and also danced as a "sandman"—a staple of the period's black show business in which certain dancers would specialize in dancing on a tray of sand, using their feet to make a swishing sort of rhythm of the sort Bo later featured on his records in the form of Jerome Green's maracas.

During the forties and early fifties, the Hipsters, being too young for regular work, mostly played on the streets. Sometimes they plugged into a store's electrical outlet in the bustling Maxwell Street Market, where their competition was mostly hard delta blues played by the likes of Robert Nighthawk or Little Walter. Here Bo absorbed a deeply personal feel for the blues to add to his eclectic influences from sanctified church music, street rhythms, vocal-group harmonizing, and big-band swing. With the addition of ace harmonica player Billy Boy Arnold, the Hipsters changed their name to the Langley Avenue Jive Cats, their sound becoming harder, bluesier, in keeping with the resurgence in popularity of down-home blues that was sweeping Chicago with the rise of more recent Mississippi émigrés such as Muddy Waters.

During the late forties or early fifties, Bo met Jerome Green, whom he taught to play the maracas and whose comic timing and lusty, unrestrained singing made him the perfect foil for Bo's equally intense but more personably modulated approach. With the musicians getting older, the group began getting more and more club gigs. During the early fifties, Bo, Jerome, and bassist Roosevelt Jackson (later joined by drummer Clifton James) began working at a popular blues tavern, the 708 Club.

Bo and his gang had been scrappy street-corner entertainers, ready to play anything from a Cab Calloway tune to something in a country and western vein, which Bo had long had a fondness for. (Hear "Cadillac" in this box.) Gigging regularly at the 708 gave the musicians a chance to shape their influences into a sound all their own. And they certainly had that sound when they walked into Chess Records in March 1955. From that point on, the sound is documented, and can be heard at satisfying length and in illuminating depth in this collection.

Even in 1955, when new artists such as Chuck Berry and Little Richard were turning American popular music upside down, everything about Bo Diddley's records sounded different. There were the game songs, the boasts, the high-spirited verbal exchanges, the shimmering, fluid tremolo guitar. But from today's perspective, for a listener who has seen black music develop from soul into the more skeletal song forms and harder rhythmic edge of funk to the current emphasis on rhythm and verbal inventiveness in rap, the most strikingly original quality of these recordings is Bo's utterly unique reorganization, or reimagining, of the rhythm section.

If we forget for the moment the blues, gospel, doo-wop, and country-flavored material that makes this such a varied set and concentrate on the material generally thought of as more "typically" Bo Diddley, we find a radical approach to rhythmic organization that can only be compared to the effective re-Africanization of the music consolidated by the James Brown bands of the mid-sixties. As with James Brown, it isn't necessary to posit a familiarity with African cultural sensibility lending form and substance to individual creativity. The rhythmic emphasis in traditional African music is comparable to European music's concentration on harmony and Indian music's on melody. And the principles used to organize cross-rhythms in African percussion music are a fundamental part of overall cultural patterning (see Yale professor Robert Farris Thompson's *African Art in Motion* for essays linking the music to patterning in sculpture, weaving, and other arts). Time and again these patterns seem to have submerged in our pluralistic American culture, only to reemerge through a visionary artist like James Brown or Bo Diddley.

In African percussion orchestras, each distinct rhythm line is carried by an instrument or combination of instruments with a clearly defined timbre. In the African-American ring shout, this principle was simplified but still employed. Feet rhythmically slapping the wooden floors of churches provided the deep, bass rhythms and the music's fundamental time line. Handclapping patterns, high-pitched and sharply accented as opposed to the more booming drumming of the dancers' feet, carried counter-rhythms, often at double the tempo of the dancing. In parts of the Americas where drumming was not as widely banned as in what is now the U.S.—Haiti or Cuba, for example—additional rhythm patterns, often overlapping each other in complex cycles, are also carried by instruments or groups of instruments with distinctive timbres of their own—an iron double-bell and a pair of shakers or maracas, for example, have such different sounds that when different rhythms are played on them, both are clearly audible.

This is what we hear on Bo Diddley records such as "Bo Diddley," "Pretty Thing," "Say Man," "Hush Your Mouth," "You Can't Judge a Book by Its Cover," and many others. Generally, the drummer concentrates almost entirely on his various tom-toms, the bass drum, sometimes the snare. One rarely hears a cymbal pattern. Instead, the handclapping-speed cross-rhythm assigned to the ride and sock cymbals (when the principles of African drumming were applied to a kit played by a single musician) are handled here by Jerome Green's maracas. The maracas are heavily favored in the recording balance, given just as much presence as the tom-tom and bass drum. Bo's electric guitar, sometimes played through a tremolo device or other rhythmic/vibrato modifier, often handles two different rhythms simultaneously, on two distinct levels of pitch and timbre. His treble-string picking and high harmonics ride above the rich, fat swish of the maracas, weaving in and out of their double-time patterning, while the middle and bass registers of the guitar lay down a proto-heavy-metal riff structure that locks in with the deeper drum patterns into what Bo calls "the Shout mode."

Add occasional claves and other percussion instruments, occasional minimal bass lines, judicious seasoning from piano and/or harmonica and/or second guitar, and Bo's own wizardry in the use of deliberate distortion and feedback, delicately plucked bell-tone harmonics, and fluid, watery textures, and you have a concept or philosophy of rhythmic orchestration that is much more varied and mutable than it initially seems. A careful listen to the tracks included in this collection reveals that no two tunes use the same "beat," the same combination of rhythms orchestrated in the same way. The rhythmic emphasis ranges from a heavy backbeat (heard in the African-derived music of Cuba and the Southern U.S. but not in most other African-American cultures) to an equally insistent emphasis on the first and third beat of every measure, as in "Crackin' Up," which is "on the one" in the manner of calypso, reggae, or modern funk. Different layers of rhythm are given to different instruments on different records, and the patterns vary. Far from being an artist with one great idea, Bo Diddley has created a whole musical, rhythmical world.

And there is so much more here than one of the most original and fertile rhythmic intelligences of our time. There is the work of a singer with steely chops who can shout with the best of them, cut off his phrases as percussively as he chokes his guitar, handle blues shadings and more complex gospel colorations with equal aplomb, project an instantly identifiable personality and sense of humor, and still hit every note with a full-bodied sound and squarely on the head. There's a songwriter who has rarely been spoken of in the same breath as Chuck Berry or Leiber and Stoller or Buddy Holly, but should be. And presiding over this feast is the hoochie-coochie dude his bad self, in his cobra-snake necktie and Western boots and ten-gallon hat, cracking that grin, and enduring.

Sam Phillips: The Sun King

MEMPHIS MAGAZINE | DECEMBER 1978

Back in the mid-fifties, the Sun Records studio at 706 Union Avenue was the epicenter of a sudden, wrenching shift in world consciousness. Tremors had been felt for several years, and then, one afternoon in early 1954, Sam Phillips was busy with routine work in the tiny studio when Destiny walked in.

Actually, Destiny, in the person of a handsome, painfully shy but flashily dressed young man with longish hair and greasy sideburns, paced up and down the sidewalk outside for some time before summoning the courage to actually walk in the door. Phillips, a thirty-one-year-old radio engineer from Florence, Alabama, who'd opened his studio in 1950 and begun making distinctive yellow-label Sun records of local blues talent in 1952, watched the boy idly through the storefront building's window.

The kid said his name was Elvis. He was there to make a record for his mother, and Sam turned on the machine that pressed private messages—songs, greetings, remote recordings of wedding or funeral services—onto acetate discs. Elvis ran through his song, the Ink Spots ballad "My Happiness," a couple of times and Sam, who'd already proved he had a sharp ear for talent by making some of the first recordings of Howlin' Wolf, B. B. King, and other seminal black artists, cocked an ear. The kid had something.

Within two years that something was going to shake RCA, CBS, and the nation's other giant record companies to their foundations, inspire paroxysms of angry rhetoric and record-burning by clergymen and politicians and disc jockeys, dig a crevasse between young people and many of their elders, and bring millions of black and white Americans together socially for the first time in the country's history. That something that Sam Phillips heard in the voice of Destiny would be banned in Boston and in Red China, accused of inciting rioting and juvenile delinquency, attacked in the U.S. Senate, savaged and defended in public debate. It was the sound of a white man with a look, a style, and a genuine feeling for the vitality that America's minority musics—white country, black rhythm and blues—had in common. It was rock & roll.

When Elvis Presley walked into Sun Records that first time he was painfully timid. "He tried not to show it," Sam Phillips says today, "but he felt so *inferior*. He reminded me of a black man in a way; his insecurity was so *markedly* like that of a black person." But less than two years later, the shy kid was a national phenomenon. Sam had found Elvis a band, worked with him in the little studio on Union, and made five single records, each of which featured Elvis singing a blues song on one side and a country song on the other. The records were so successful that RCA bought Elvis's contract out. For that, Sam got $35,000, a fee that seems pitiful today but was unheard-of at the time. And he turned right around and recorded Carl Perkins's "Blue Suede Shoes," the first record to become a top ten hit in every major market—country, popular, and rhythm and blues. Another Sun discovery, Johnny Cash, was selling steadily to the nation's fans. And in the next few years Phillips recorded Jerry Lee Lewis, Roy Orbison, Charlie Rich, Carl Mann—the list goes on and on and on. "This man had a knack," says Carl Perkins. "He had the capability of spotting raw talent. Because look at the guys he spotted, check 'em out—they're damn near all still around."

A spotter of raw talent with a record that no other figure in the history of American popular music has matched, Sam Phillips was much more as well. He did not just find talents that were waiting to be polished, packaged, and promoted: he *perceived* talent in individuals who might otherwise have kept it locked up within themselves. Elvis Presley hid an overwhelming drive to success beneath his timidity, but how long would it have taken him to break into the music business through conventional channels, and what other producer would have taken weeks and months to work with him, patiently searching for something he couldn't even name or define?

Jerry Lee Lewis and Carl Perkins both tried their luck with Sun. Perkins's family had been the only white sharecroppers on a huge Tennessee plantation, and Lewis had been banging out the blues and boogie numbers since he was twelve or thirteen. Phillips wasn't worried that they were too country and too black for conventional country music tastes. In fact, he was intrigued, just as he'd been intrigued by something he heard in Elvis. As a longtime booster of black music, Sam was very aware that young whites, especially in the South, were listening to it. "When I first formed my label," he says, "the input I got from the distributors, jukebox operators, and retailers was that white teenagers were picking up on the *feel* of the black music. These people liked the plays and the sales they were getting, but they were concerned, saying, 'We're afraid our children might fall in love with black people.' At that time, you know, three categories of music—pop, country music, rhythm and blues—were just miles apart, and yet, if you took a Southern country person and a Southern black, they were so damn close together. Still, that line came right down. So, in no way to undermine the black people that gave me my start in this industry, I felt that if we could get plays on radio stations and generally better acceptance for this music because white people were doing it, it would help. It couldn't *hurt* the black man, because he can hold his own in music with anybody in the world."

But Phillips wasn't looking for white singers who would simply copy black records or the mannerisms of black singers, as white pop and country and jazz vocalists had been doing for years. He was looking for a singer who could approach black idioms as naturally as he approached country music, and in Presley, Perkins, Lewis, and most of his other white rock & roll artists he found just that. It was a matter of trial and error. "If it took a week or a month to get in or out of a person what they really, truly had to say," Sam continues, "this is what we did. A lot of times you've just got to *unlock* that person."

Right now, interest in what Sam Phillips and his Sun artists accomplished is more intense than at any time since the fifties. Rockabilly, a term Phillips hates but a generally accepted description of a kind of music he made, is the rage of England and the continent. There, every record company with the rights to a major American catalog has released a rockabilly compilation. *CBS Rockabillies, Mercury Rockabillies, Capitol Rockabilly Originals, The M.G.M. Rockabilly Collection,* and the rest are really tributes to Sun. For the most part they chronicle the mid-fifties reactions of established country stars, up-and-coming hopefuls, and panicky record executives to the Memphis juggernaut.

That interest isn't limited to people who purchase fifties rock & roll collections. A strong rockabilly flavor runs through contemporary pop, from superstars like Linda Ronstadt, who included a few rockabilly numbers on each of her multimillion-selling albums, to English cult figures like Dave Edmunds and Nick Lowe. Punk rockers—New York's Robert Gordon, Memphis's own Alex Chilton, a whole phalanx of English groups—flatter Sun rock & roll by attempting to copy it. Carl Perkins, Ol' Blue Suede himself, is making a spectacular comeback on the CBS-distributed Jet label. After a decade making albums that were mostly barstool country, Jerry Lee Lewis is rocking again. And, of course, Elvis is an even bigger star in death than he was in life.

Historians are beginning to chronicle the Sun years, or trying to. The problem is that Sam Phillips, the man who started it all, hasn't talked to any of them. Without his input, books like *Catalyst: The Sun Records Story,* which was published in England in 1975, and Jerry Hopkins's *Elvis: A Biography* are less than definitive. In fact, Phillips quarrels with Hopkins's account of Elvis's days at Sun, an account pieced together with the help of Sam's former secretary Marion Keisker, on several significant points. As interest in the Sun story continues to grow—and it is an essential story for anyone who wants to understand American popular culture in this latter half of the twentieth century—that story becomes increasingly obscured by half-truths and outright fantasies.

But recently Sam Phillips pried himself loose from his radio station and his other business interests long enough to come again into the public eye, especially to supervise the restoration of the original studio at 706 Union. A few weeks ago he agreed to talk to this writer. The interview he gave was his first major interview, and it lasted a good six hours.

Phillips lives on a quiet suburban street in east Memphis, in the same house he owned when Sun was at its zenith. He doesn't look his fifty-five years. In fact, he doesn't look much like the grinning, crew-cut young man with the somehow pixieish nose whose picture is in so many histories of rock & roll. He has a lot of hair and a full, red beard, and you have to look at him hard to discern those same distinctive features. But the spirit is there, and so is the headstrong individualism that led him to leave a secure job with WREC in the early fifties to plunge into the extremely risky business of recording black blues musicians. "I thought it was vital music," he said as soon as he had settled himself on the couch in his wood-paneled den. "I don't know whether I had too many people agree with me immediately on that, but I thought it was vital and I tried my best to let people be individuals. I think that if I contributed anything, it was the ability to discern in people a natural talent, be it unpolished or semi-polished or almost crude—I feel prouder of myself for that ability than for any other achievement."

Eventually the conversation got around to establishing some facts. Sam Phillips was born January 5, 1923, on a small farm near Florence, Alabama, at a bend of the Tennessee River. As a child he worked in the cotton fields, like so many of the artists he recorded for Sun, black and white alike. "And I never did see white people singing a lot when they were chopping cotton," he says, "but the odd part about it is, I never heard a black man that couldn't sing *good*. Even off-key, it had a spontaneity about it that would grab my ear."

Sam played drums and sousaphone in the high school band, took the lead in organizing a school dance band, and even convinced his band director to let him organize a benefit concert so the budding musicians could buy capes and some decent instruments. "I think some leadership quality came out," he says, thinking back, "the ability to possibly convince somebody that change is not always bad. It might be fun, and it might even be good." As a teenager, his burning ambition was to become a criminal defense lawyer, but his father died, the family had a deaf-mute aunt to look after, and his older brother, one of eight Phillips children, went into the Marines. Sam had little choice but to quit school and begin working for a living. Luckily—although it may be stretching the point to call anything that happened to such a self-willed individual "luck"— Sam had impressed the manager of a Muscle Shoals radio station, WLAY, when he announced numbers for his high school band, and he went to work spinning white gospel and hillbilly records. He moved on to stations in Decatur and Nashville, and in 1945 he arrived in Memphis.

"The first thing to remember about Sam," says Stan Kesler, who played steel guitar and bass at Sun and wrote songs for Elvis Presley and other Sun artists, "is that he was a great audio man, a radio engineer. And what made Sam great, Sam was not afraid to experiment." Already, the young man had a reputation for audio excellence. He began engineering live broadcasts by big-name bands from the Peabody Skyway, and starting in 1946 his broadcasts fed directly into the CBS radio network every night. It was customary for stations to record these remote broadcasts; the next day the bandleaders would drop by to see how they had sounded. They began to encourage Sam Phillips. Then one day the bandleader Art Mooney needed to make a record in a hurry in order to cover a fast-breaking hit by Pee Wee Hunt, "Oh!" Sam arranged to record the Mooney band at the studios of WMC, in the old Goodwyn Institute Building, and ran wires from the studio all the way to a long, straight stairwell in the back of the building. That stairwell was his first echo chamber, and Mooney's "Oh!" was a smash.

One would think this kind of success might have emboldened Sam Phillips to go into business for himself, but he denies that it did, and it isn't difficult to believe him. Unlike most young people who came from rural poverty to the relative sophistication of a career in the city, Sam was still concerned with, maybe even obsessed by, his roots. He remembered Silas Paine, a blind black man who had lived on his family's farm when he was very young and who sang him perhaps fifty or a hundred blues and folk songs. He remembered passing a black church there in Alabama, on the way home from the Baptist church he joined when he was sixteen because he found his family's Methodism insufficiently emotional and too formal. "I would tell people, 'Why doesn't *our* music sound that good in *our* church?' I mean, hearing them was *inspiring*, you'd get *happy*, and although back then you were taught to look upon it as, well, you know,

'Those niggers are really getting with it,' I felt that they *were* getting with it, in the *right way*. They were letting it all hang *out*. Wish I'd known that expression then, but you couldn't have used it, could you?"

These were the experiences that fired Phillips with the desire to open his own studio, a move he made with the express purpose of recording black talent. There was plenty of it around Memphis. Beale Street had been a black Main Street for the entire Mid-South since the early years of the century, and it was still going strong. Sam went to a few shows there—occasionally there would be a roped-off section for whites, or a balcony, or a whole show—and heard a young Mississippian with a big, booming, gospel singer's voice and a fleet, polished guitar style—Riley "Blues Boy" King. But for the first time in Memphis's history, whites didn't have to go to Beale Street to hear black music, they could simply turn on their radios. WDIA had switched to a black format, against considerable community opposition, and was enjoying success with performing disc jockeys like King, Rufus Thomas, and the one-man band Joe Hill Louis. Some of these artists played Mississippi Delta blues and appealed to blacks with strong country roots, while Thomas, King, and others were more urban. All of them were good enough to get it on records, but Memphis didn't have a record company, or even a commercial recording studio.

All this time, the major record companies were largely ignorant of the shifting tastes of black record buyers. The war years had seen an epic black migration from the rural South to the nation's cities, and these newly urbanized country people wanted music that combined deep roots with a metropolitan veneer. The companies that were providing this music were small, one-man or family operations—Specialty, Imperial, and Modern in Los Angeles, Chess in Chicago, Atlantic in New York. Often the men who ran these companies would load records into the trunks of their cars and make whirlwind tours of the South, where much of their audience still lived, visiting radio stations, bribing disc jockeys, hawking records, and looking for talent. Several of them had already visited Memphis when Sam Phillips opened his Memphis Recording Service at the beginning of 1950.

"I knew that it wouldn't be easy," says Sam. "My boys Knox and Jerry were born in '45 and '48, and I couldn't save too much on fifty, fifty-five dollars a week and raise a family, even then. But I managed to save and with my own hands built a little studio and wired it. I was also working for WREC as an engineer—I finally quit in June of '51—and taking care of the convention PA system for the entire Peabody. So I was a pretty busy cat. Recording black musicians was what I wanted to do, but in the meantime I recorded conventions, funerals, weddings, anything I could to keep the doors open while I was trying to do some of the things I personally wanted to do."

Even if Sam Phillips had never started the Sun label and never recorded Elvis Presley or any of his other white artists, his place in the history of American popular music would be assured. Through his studio passed the cream of the Mid-South's black musicians, men who would go on to leave an indelible imprint on the whole world's popular music—B. B. King, Bobby "Blue" Bland, Howlin' Wolf, Junior Parker, Rufus Thomas, James Cotton, and more.

In March 1951, Sam Phillips recorded his first big hit. Ike Turner, later half of the very successful Ike and Tina Turner team but then a young bandleader and disc jockey from Clarksdale, Mississippi, showed up at the Memphis Recording Service with his band, the Kings of Rhythm. Unlike older Delta bands, which still played the down-home blues, the Kings of Rhythm looked to the urban jump blues that was then emanating from Texas and the West Coast for their inspiration. Their lineup boasted Ike's piano, electric guitar, bass, drums, and a section of saxophones. Unfortunately, the group's equipment was not on a par with its aspirations. They had all packed into one car to make the drive up to Memphis, and on the way guitarist Willie Kizart's amplifier had fallen off the top and onto the highway, bursting its speaker cone. Sam's knowledge of audio and willingness to experiment saved the day. "We had no way of getting it fixed," he recalls, "so we started playing around with the damn thing, stuffed a little paper in there and it sounded good. It sounded like a saxophone."

The distorted, fuzzy-sounding guitar played a rocking boogie figure all the way through "Rocket 88," a song about cruising around in a fancy automobile that boasted a convincing vocal by saxophonist Jackie Brenston and a searing, all-out saxophone solo from Raymond Hill. "Rocket 88" was snapped up by Chess Records and became one of the best-selling black discs of 1951. It has often been hailed as the first real rock & roll record because of its loud guitar sound, rocking beat, raunchy saxophone, and teenage-automotive lyrics. Later that year, a young white country musician named Bill Haley made his own recording of "Rocket 88." It was his first venture outside the strictures of conventional country and western music.

Soon Sam produced another hit for Chess, Rosco Gordon's "Booted." But encouraging as these experiences must have been, the first few years of the Memphis Recording Service left him deeply frustrated. Legal wrangling, and some questionable business tactics on the part of some of the record companies he dealt with, deprived him of the services of some of his most talented black artists. He especially regretted the loss of Howlin' Wolf, who agreed to record with him for a year but was lured away to Chicago by Leonard Chess after the first sides he recorded with Phillips stirred up interest there.

It was frustrating, too, to have no control over the commercial fortunes of artists he really believed in. Dr. Isaiah Ross, a harmonica- and guitar-playing bluesman from Tunica, whose recordings combined fire-breathing intensity with novelty lyrics, catchy melodies, and a chugging beat reminiscent of the rockabilly to come, never really got off the ground, and neither did Jimmy DeBerry, a Delta bluesman in the old style whom Phillips greatly admired. Neither did Harmonica Frank Floyd, a white hobo who fascinated Sam because he had an innate feeling for black music, even if it was the black music of the 1920s and 1930s.

"I thought about it long and hard," Sam says. "My devotion was in creating, or attempting to. I kind of have an evangelistic way about me. I don't go for all this religion as it's structured today; my evangelism is, in my own peculiar way, letting people out of themselves. I got pure gratification, far more than what recompense I got monetarily, in unlocking or helping these people unlock their lives. So with the help of my old friend Jim Bullet, who had the Bullet label out of Nashville years ago, we started Sun." The yellow label, with its sunburst, crowing rooster, and musical staff line, was designed by a man named Parker who played with Sam in the high school band in Florence.

The first fifteen Sun releases were by black musicians. There were deep blues by the likes of Joe Hill Louis and Walter Horton, jazzy jump music by some artists who have since faded into obscurity, and three hits. The first, "Bear Cat" by WDIA disc jockey Rufus Thomas, was evidence of far-reaching changes in American popular music. Early in 1953, a Texas blues shouter named Willie Mae Thornton had had a hit with a song called "Hound Dog." It had been written for a black singer and aimed at a black audience but the authors were two young whites, Jerry Leiber and Mike Stoller. Within a few years they would be writing rock & roll hits for black groups like the Coasters and for Elvis Presley. But Sam Phillips had no way of knowing that when he concocted "Bear Cat" as an answer record to "Hound Dog." "I should have known better, though," Sam says ruefully. "The melody was exactly the same as theirs, and we claimed credit for writing the damn thing." The result was a lawsuit. It was settled out of court and the record sold much more than any of Sun's previous efforts, but the whole incident left a bad taste in everyone's mouth. Rufus Thomas was dissatisfied with the record because his roots were in jazz and the slick novelty music of Louis Jordan, and Sam had put him together with a studio band that featured the country-style blues guitar of Joe Hill Louis. Even today, Rufus takes perverse delight in pointing out the wrong notes in Louis's solo.

The second Sun hit was the Prisonaires' "Just Walkin' in the Rain," and the third was a bristling boogie record, "Feelin' Good," by Little Junior's Blues Flames, led by bluesman Junior Parker. Gradually some white country artists appeared along with the blacks, beginning with an unaccompanied vocal group, the Ripley Cotton Choppers, followed by Earl Peterson ("Michigan's Singing Cowboy") and the haunting, unforgettable "Troublesome Waters" by a blind guitar evangelist, Howard Seratt. It was inevitable that Phillips would record more and more white musicians, because more and more blacks from rural Mississippi, Arkansas, and Tennessee were leaving the area altogether for better salaries in Detroit and Chicago. Almost all the black musicians who recorded at the Memphis Recording Service and during the early days at Sun followed the migration northward. Only the most stubbornly countrified bluesmen remained, along with a handful who had good, steady jobs, like Rufus Thomas.

And then in walked Elvis. There has been considerable confusion about what happened during the first few months he was working at Sun, and

Sam's story differs from the most widely accepted account, as told by Marion Keisker to Jerry Hopkins in *Elvis: A Biography*. According to the Hopkins account, Sam was out, and Marion, who worked part-time as his secretary while still holding down a position at WREC, was in on the day Elvis first came to the studio. According to Hopkins, Marion turned on the big, bulky machine that made custom acetates, but when she heard Elvis's voice she also turned on the tape machine so that she could save a copy for her boss. "The reason I taped Elvis," she is quoted as saying, "was this: Over and over I remember Sam saying, 'If I could find a white man who had the Negro sound and the Negro feel, I could make a billion dollars.' This is what I heard in Elvis. . . ."

"I hate like the Devil taking anything away from Marion," says Sam, "but the *record* has to be set straight. And the record *is* that, number one, I was there busy in the little control room and I saw Elvis through the windows, trying to get up the courage to come in. Number two, I recorded him. Marion didn't even know how to record an acetate record, and it was put on acetate directly. There wasn't a copy put on tape, period. This was a record that he bought and paid for, and if you want to know the truth I wasn't going to use any tape for it. Tape was *expensive*. But his voice really interested me, even singing the Ink Spots song. It was *there*, no question about it. I mean I saw it by the *yard*. I wrote down and hung on the spindle 'Good voice. See if I can find a song. . . .' Something like that.

"So I talked to Elvis and asked him had he been playing with any musicians. Usually if you were that interested in music you would, but Elvis was a total loner, based on the fact that he was extremely timid. So I told him, 'Look, I'll get on the phone and call some musicians. I'm going to call Scotty Moore, who's very interested in working with us over here, and possibly Bill Black, and y'all can do a little woodshedding.' And that's how it happened. I called Scotty and he was tickled to death to do it. I explained to Scotty and Bill that Elvis *was* an extremely shy person and just to really make him feel at home, no matter if they did it at his house—Elvis's bedroom where he played so much—or at Scotty's, or if they came over to the studio when it wasn't busy. Bill reported back that he didn't see much in Elvis."

Sam laughs. "I was real busy trying to keep my label going, so my time frame is not too secure, but Scotty and Bill fooled around with

Elvis and they were in four or five different times. I'd listen to what they were doing, and they'd go back and work some more. It was treated as an informal thing with no promises to anybody, because I felt this was his one chance. From the first time he heard 'Without Love' until I actually got them to recording, it was somewhere between three and six months.

"We cut some good stuff, and of course you didn't save much then because you had to save tape. Aww, God, the stuff I recorded over! We worked on I don't know how many songs. I knew he had it, and I liked the simplicity of Scotty's guitar and the slap of Bill's bass; nothing was encumbering anything there. There was no question in my mind that this kid had it in him. It was a challenge for me to see if it was possible for us to get it out of him somehow. Then one night"—records show that it was July 6, 1954—"we were just about ready to give up for that session, and I walked out and I said, in jest or tongue-in-cheek a little bit, 'Elvis, ain't there something you know that you can sing?' And when he cut down on 'That's All Right, Mama'. . . Of course, I *love* Big Boy Crudup, and it was amazing to me they even knew a Big Boy Crudup song. That just knocked me *out*."

Sam ran back in the control room, and after he offered some advice on the song's tempo, Elvis, Scotty, and Bill recorded "That's All Right" (as the label read) in a burst of energy. The flip side of what was to be Elvis's first record took a little more time; "Blue Moon of Kentucky," a well-known country song by Bill Monroe, went through several changes. By this time Phillips must have known he had something, for several early takes of the song were saved. On a Dutch bootleg album called *Good Rockin Tonight* you can hear its step-by-step transformation from a straight country song with an unconventional instrumentation—no fiddle, no steel guitar—into a jumping jukebox number, hillbilly with a beat.

The story of how Dewey Phillips introduced the record on his *Red Hot and Blue* show, received so many calls he had to play it over and over, and eventually fetched Elvis out of a movie theater to come and be interviewed, has been told and retold. What one hears less often is that Sam Phillips's efforts to break the record outside Memphis were some of the hardest and most dispiriting of his career. He would leave Memphis driving his black '51 Cadillac on a Sunday afternoon and crisscross the heart of the country, Oklahoma City to Dallas and Houston, down to

Shreveport, into Mississippi, stopping at every little radio station along the way, checking with his distributors, pushing new releases, getting reactions. Nobody would play Elvis's record. One disc jockey, a longtime friend, told Sam, "You know, Mr. Phillips, this man is so country, he got no business at all singing after the sun comes up." Finally, a distributor in Dallas began moving on the record. It went on to sell around 300,000 copies in the South, more than enough to encourage Sam to persevere.

The most encouraging signs, though, were Elvis's personal appearances around Memphis. "His first show," Sam remembers, "we played him at a little club up here at Summer and Mendenhall, I went out there that night and introduced Elvis. Now this was kind of out in the country then, out on the highway, as they say. It was just a joint. Here is a bunch of hard-drinking people, and here is a kid up there onstage, and he ain't playing country, and he ain't necessarily playing rhythm and blues, and he didn't look conventional like they did. He looked a little greasy, as they called it then. And the reaction was just *incredible*. Then there was a show at Overton Park Shell with Slim Whitman, who was hot with 'Indian Love Call.' Slim was supposed to wrap up the show, and I felt sorry for him, because when he came out those people just wanted more Elvis. Those people came to see Slim and wound up with Elvis, that's a fact."

Sam has often been criticized for selling Elvis's contract to RCA when he could have held on to it for another eighteen months. "I just needed the money," he says. "I had struggled so long, and I made a damn proposition that I didn't think they would take. I didn't think they'd be *fool* enough to take it. And it was the eleventh hour before they *did* actually take it. The price doesn't sound like anything today, but damn! Columbia paid twenty-five thousand dollars for Frankie Laine's contract from Mercury, and they had less time to go on his contract than I had on Elvis's. What I needed was money to just get out of the bullpen so I could *maybe* get on the mound and throw to a batter. If I've been asked once I must have been asked a thousand times, did I ever regret it? No, I did not, I do not, and I never will."

Sam Phillips did get on the mound with the $35,000 from RCA—it was closer to $40,000 because RCA also paid Elvis around $5,000 that Sun owed him in royalties—and his aim was true. Johnny Cash was already a country star—he had been selling household appliances door-to-door when he came to Sun—and by the end of 1955, before RCA was able to make a new record with Elvis, Carl Perkins had a nationwide smash with "Blue Suede Shoes."

Carl Perkins has always maintained that he was playing rockabilly before he heard Elvis, or at least country music with a beat. Sam Phillips maintains that Carl was more or less a straight country artist and that making him a rocker took him somewhat out of his element. Both men are probably telling the truth. Carl's music probably did have a jumping boogie beat, but it must have been closer to the hillbilly boogie of black-influenced country groups like the Delmore Brothers than it was to Presley's rawer, sparer, bluesier sound. In any event, Carl's Sun recordings—"Blue Suede Shoes," "Glad All Over," "Honey Don't," and "Matchbox" are some of the best—were, like Cash's, a self-contained body of work, not country, not blues, not rock & roll, just pure Perkins.

The third member of Sun's post-Presley triumvirate arrived at 706 Union not long after Sam had hired Jack Clement as producer. "I had a little station over in Marked Tree, Arkansas," Sam says, "and we went over there for a little open house. When I got back to Memphis, Jack Clement had recorded Jerry Lee and everybody was just ecstatic. Well, I don't know if I told Jack this, but I had been saying I wanted to get off this guitar scene and show that it could be done with other instruments. And they put that tape on, 'Crazy Arms,' and I said, 'Where in the *hell* did this man come from?' He played that piano with abandon. A lot of people do that, but I could hear, between the stuff he played and didn't play, that spiritual thing. And I told Jack, 'Just get him in here as fast as you can.' Now you talk about *talent*."

With the help of his brother Judd, an experienced country music promoter, Sam made Jerry Lee Lewis into an international phenomenon. His singles sold in the millions, and after shooting a movie with Mamie Van Doren, *High School Confidential*, he left for a tour of England. Unfortunately, the English press found out that he was married to his teenage cousin and he was hounded out of the country. That was the end of his career, for all practical purposes, until he came back as a country singer in the sixties. Sam lost him to Mercury and he lost Johnny Cash and Carl Perkins to Columbia. But there were other Sun hits, ranging from Roy Orbison's regional successes to smashes on the new Phillips International label by Charlie Rich and Carl Mann. There were plenty of great records that never quite made it, by rockers like Billy Lee Riley, Warren Smith, and Sonny Burgess.

Riley says flatly of his Sun almost-hit "Red Hot" that "Sam Phillips let that record die. He canceled orders on it so that he could fill orders for Lewis's records; I stood right there in the office and heard him do it. I guess he could handle just so many artists at once, and he had a big record with Jerry Lee, 'Whole Lotta Shakin' Goin' On.' Well, I got mad and drunk and came in the studio one night and kicked a hole in the bass fiddle."

Riley is not the only star to have expressed dissatisfaction with Sun. Jimmy Van Eaton, the brilliant session drummer who powered Jerry Lee Lewis's most incendiary recordings and those of many other Sun rockers, told an English interviewer a few years back that "things really started falling apart at Sun after Jack Clement and [arranger] Bill Justis got fired. We were in a groove and it just disappeared. After the hits stopped coming, they started screwing the musicians. I was pretty dissatisfied with Sun by the time I left."

You'd think Riley and Van Eaton would bristle at the very mention of Sam Phillips's name, yet they speak of him warmly, and still with a trace of awe, and both of them have been working in the Phillips studio on Madison these past few months, along with Knox and Jerry Phillips, cutting hard, raw rock & roll just like the old days. An initial single, Riley's moving ode to the Sun sound "That Good Old Rock and Roll" with a churning "Blue Monday" on the flip side, has been released on the Southern Rooster label. "I tell you," says Riley, "back then we had *fun*, and that's what's happening here."

Time ran out for Sam Phillips and Sun not because he lost the feel — his astonishing gift for getting the very most out of an artist and reacting spontaneously in the right way at the right time, as he did when Ike Turner showed up with a broken guitar amplifier and when Elvis half-jokingly began singing "That's All Right." Time ran out because of the very thing he had been working for, because of success. Jack Clement and Bill Justis made some excellent records for Sun, using saxophones, vocal choruses, and the other sweetenings that other record companies were using. But one suspects that once Sam Phillips had to devote more of his time to running his hit-making company, once he could no longer spend as many hours as he wanted roaring around his little studio and working with his artists until they yielded up their treasures, he began to lose interest. After the early sixties, Sun returned to being basically a local label. It was inactive for a year before Sam sold a controlling interest to Shelby Singleton in 1969.

· By that time, Credence Clearwater Revival was at the top of the nation's record charts with a sound that was as close to the Sun sound as they could get, and a new generation of American and English rockers was coming along that would pay homage to Elvis, Carl Perkins, Jerry Lee Lewis, and the rest, as the Beatles, the Rolling Stones, and so many others had done. But try though they did, none of them quite managed to duplicate the essentials of the Sun sound — its simplicity and its feel. "Everything's too complicated anyway," said Sam Phillips late in the interview. "Why make music complicated? You'll notice my records never did have too much in the way of instrumental cushion. I knew in my mind's eye what I was looking for when I would go into these sessions. Maybe not the lyric, maybe not the melody pattern, but the *feel*. And with this approach and with an awful lot of patience, I think that each person developed that feel in working with me. It was a mutual type of thing."

Pop records aren't made that way anymore. They're made a step at a time, starting with the drums and bass and adding instruments one or two at a time and the vocals last, sometimes weeks later. The ingredients aren't mixed together right there on the spot, when the juices are flowing and everyone is concentrating on the task at hand. Nowadays records are mixed by highly paid technicians with the help of elaborate computerized consoles. Record companies don't decide who they're going to record the way Sam Phillips did, by instinct. They decide in board meetings, after studying whether the artist can be promoted as this or that and plotting his demographics. And records don't *sound* like Sam Phillips's records anymore. A good 99 percent of today's popular music sounds dull and lifeless by comparison. It doesn't have that spark, that feeling of going for the big one as if nothing else mattered. It doesn't have the soul. But more and more people are finding Sam Phillips's recordings to their liking, and who knows? Maybe someday records will begin to sound like Sun records again.

Rock at the Wop-Boppa-Lu-Bop Crossroads

THE NEW YORK TIMES | APRIL 1, 1990

"Keep the spirit, but don't go to such extremes," Little Richard was told by his producers during a mid-fifties recording session. That advice had the effect of goading the singer into the frenzied performance of "Good Golly Miss Molly" that was released as a single and became one of his biggest hits.

Extremes were what Little Richard was all about. Elvis Presley popularized rock & roll, but Little Richard provided the big bang, that first explosion that made all that followed possible. He was the most influential vocalist and band leader of fifties rock, and unlike most of his contemporaries his influence extended through the sixties, when former Little Richard imitators like James Brown and Otis Redding developed his original style into modern funk and soul.

Born Richard Penniman in Macon, Georgia, Little Richard burst onto the pop music scene late in 1955 with his first hit, "Tutti Frutti," an all-out blast that made everything else on the radio sound tame. Pat Boone recorded a white-bread version of the song, and Elvis Presley performed it on several of his earliest television appearances. But nothing could match the incendiary fervor of Little Richard and the New Orleans studio band that backed him on "Tutti Frutti," and for the next two years the singer enjoyed hit after hit.

When he decided to leave rock & roll for born-again Christianity, he didn't just quit. He tore off his gold jewelry and diamond rings and threw them in the Pacific Ocean. In religion, as in just about every other aspect of his life, Little Richard seemed positively to revel in going to extremes.

But if the energy and flash of Little Richard's fifties recordings tended to dazzle, the musicianship and artistry involved were often obscured in the process. *Little Richard: The Specialty Sessions* finally gives Little Richard's music the attention this definitive fifties rocker has long deserved.

The set has been released in two versions. The British Ace box, available here as an import, includes up to five different takes of every song Little Richard recorded for Specialty, plus demo tapes, studio chatter, even a commercial for Royal Crown hairdressing. The box issued by Specialty in the United States dispenses with many of the alternate takes, while still offering at least one version of every tune from every session. Both sets have been digitally remastered from the original master tapes and include a compendious thirty-two-page booklet with photographs, essays, and a discography.

Add to either box the German single-CD reissue *Little Richard: The Formative Years 1951–53* (Bear Family BCD 15448) and you have ample material for an in-depth study of Little Richard's music from the fifties. The Little Richard of the 1951–53 recordings and the first Specialty session from 1955 was a gospel-rooted blues shouter in the vein of Roy Brown and Clyde McPhatter, both early influences. "Tutti Frutti," recorded at the end of Little Richard's second Specialty session on September 14, 1955, marked an abrupt departure from the journeyman rhythm and blues of the earlier recordings, an eruption of gleeful, manic intensity that can be seen in retrospect as pure rock & roll.

Originally, "Tutti Frutti" had been a risqué tune performed by Little Richard in some of the South's wilder whites-only clubs; he found that it provoked delirious reactions from whites, and little or no reaction in his more customary all-black performing venues. The Specialty version gave the original lyric a thorough whitewash but preserved the song's flavor of sensual dementia.

"Tutti Frutti" was also the first successful result of a musical alchemy involving Little Richard and the New Orleans studio band that had been playing on rhythm and blues sessions since the early fifties. The band, drawn from a group led by Dave Bartholomew, had mastered the art of capturing musical excitement on tape while backing Fats Domino and other New Orleans recording artists. But the intensity, power, and drive of Little Richard's singing and piano playing presented them with a fresh challenge, and their response defined the musical parameters of first-generation rock & roll. Describing these sessions, Specialty's owner, Art Rupe, noted that "everything was planned, very organized, very disciplined so that it would come out sounding undisciplined."

Mr. Rupe and Little Richard had an ongoing disagreement about the merits of the New Orleans studio band as opposed to Little Richard's touring band, the Upsetters. The Little Richard boxes, especially the more complete Ace set, shed some light on the two bands' similarities and differences. The earliest Upsetters session, a two-song demo that Little Richard recorded in a Macon radio station in February 1955, displays a band that was already consolidating regional variations in rhythm and blues stylings into a fresh approach—a rock & roll approach.

In Charles White's 1984 biography, *The Life and Times of Little Richard: The Quasar of Rock,* Mr. Penniman recalls trying to convince Mr. Rupe to record him with the Upsetters, a group the singer considered superior to the New Orleans recording band. The British Ace box provides enough versions of the same songs by both groups to suggest that both sides of the argument had their merits.

The New Orleans band's long studio apprenticeship gave their playing a disciplined fullness that was ideal for recording purposes. The early Upsetters sessions present a band that lacked studio polish, but made up for it with a remarkable ensemble cohesion and rhythmic creativity. The Upsetters' drummer, Charles Connor, has been credited by no less an authority than James Brown with sparking the rhythmic transition from fifties rock & roll to sixties funk. On the evidence of these records, the Upsetters matured into a unit that collectively anticipated funk by playing as if every instrument, from drums to saxophones, guitar, and piano, was a rhythm instrument.

Interesting as these contrasts are for students and historians, it is Little Richard's astonishing energy and vocal prowess that lift these recordings above the crowd of fifties rock & roll hopefuls. His pioneer years encompassing the full range of gospel-derived vocals in a dance-music context pointed the way to sixties soul music, and the multiple versions included in the Ace box prove that his vocal musicianship was astonishingly consistent.

Even Little Richard's most elaborate melismas find him hitting each note squarely on the head, and his innovative use of percussive vocal phrasing displayed an extraordinary affinity for drum patterns. If modern jazz, or bebop, began with rhythmic onomatopoeia such as "oop-bop-she-bam," rock & roll can be said to have begun with the urgent "wop-boppa-lu-bop" that introduces Little Richard's "Tutti Frutti." Popular music hasn't been the same since.

Big Boss Man: Working with the King

ROLLING STONE | SEPTEMBER 22, 1977

One night in 1955, a ten-year-old named Knox Phillips was hanging out at Sun Records, a small, narrow building next to a parking lot at 706 Union Avenue in downtown Memphis. He hadn't come to audition for Sam Phillips, Sun's proprietor, as hundreds of young hopefuls from all over the South had. Sam Phillips was his father and he had come to see four of his discoveries—Elvis Presley, Jerry Lee Lewis, Carl Perkins, and Johnny Cash—make a recording together. The four men had longish, greased-back hair and were wearing loud clothes, but they were singing white country spirituals, looking reverently up in the direction of heaven while Lewis pounded out a sanctified accompaniment on the Sun studio's piano.

Knox had his ducktail Brylcreemed and was dressed to the nines in his cat clothes in emulation of Elvis, his idol. During a break between takes, Presley spotted him, broke into a broad grin, walked over, and hugged him. "Stay with me, son, stay with me," the singer said, clasping young Knox close. "And," Phillips added twenty-two years later, the day after Presley's death, "he meant it. I think he saw me coming up as an embodiment of the Southern rebel thing and the other things he represented."

Presley was largely a Southern phenomenon that night in 1955, but already he was shaping the style and attitude of a younger generation, the first rock & roll generation. He would move on to the movies, to Las Vegas, to an increasingly elaborate musical presentation, but he always came back to Memphis, and onstage he always came back to gospel music and rock & roll. This rooted, self-consciously Southern Elvis Presley was the Elvis many of the music people who worked with him—instrumentalists, singers, producers—remembered in the days following the announcement of his passing. He came, as Knox Phillips said, "from poor, deprived people who were also fundamentally religious people," from a part of the country where poor whites knew intimately and to a great extent shared the lives of poor blacks. Like these people, he was impulsive and shy, self-willed and humble, wild and spiritual, courtly and crude. He was a Southern man.

He was also a Southern musician, not the first and not the last, but surely the most important. He learned to sing in the fundamentalist First Assembly of God Church in Tupelo, Mississippi. In Memphis, with the help and encouragement of Sam Phillips, guitarist Scotty Moore, and bassist Bill Black, he spent hours, days, weeks, and months transforming the white and black gospel, blues, folk, and country music of his childhood into something people would call rockabilly, which we recognize today as archetypal rock & roll. And it was largely in Nashville that the raw sound of rockabilly was refined—or emasculated, depending on one's point of view—into songs the whole world could sing.

There can be little doubt that Sam Phillips played the crucial role of midwife in the birth of the new music, that without him there might never have been an Elvis Presley. White boys who sang black were nothing new in the South. Carl Perkins, playing with his brothers in Jackson, Tennessee, and Jerry Lee Lewis down in Ferriday, Louisiana, were making music much like Presley's when Elvis was screwing up his courage to go in and make that first record for his mother. Country boogie groups had been covering black hits in a more or less black style for years; that went back to prewar recordings of people like Jimmie Rodgers and Bob Wills. But white singers who sang *very* black and also jumped and boogied to the beat were considered low class and disreputable even by hillbilly musicians.

Presley came to Sun with all his musical influences digested, but he was starstruck and tried at first to imitate the popular crooners of the day. Sam Phillips, who is fond of saying, "If you aren't doing something different, you aren't doing anything," tried cutting the country ballad "I Love You Because" with him, then, during a break, Elvis grabbed his guitar and launched into "That's All Right, Mama," a blues by Arthur Crudup. Scotty Moore and Bill Black fell in behind him and Phillips knew immediately that what another producer might have taken for a bit of lighthearted country clowning, a break from the serious work, was in fact one of the most serious cultural events of the twentieth century. Presley never forgot this moment. He had tried, and failed, to make the kind of music mainstream Americans accepted. From now on he would make music that came, naturally and instinctively, from his roots.

When RCA's Steve Sholes bought Presley's contract from Sam Phillips, his young assistant, guitarist Chet Atkins, was given the responsibility of helping to arrange the singer's first Nashville sessions. "I thought he was a black guy when I heard his Sun records," Atkins recalls. "When I found out he was coming I hired the Jordanaires, Floyd Cramer, and some of the other musicians to work with his group. Everybody knew he was going to be the hottest thing in show business, he was already so hot in Arkansas, Texas, Louisiana."

Elvis came to Nashville with Moore, Black, and D. J. Fontana, who'd been staff drummer for the *Louisiana Hayride*. Fontana was used to playing conventional country music, and he freely admits that "I didn't understand what they were doing. I had listened to a lot of music but I wasn't that familiar with what was happening in rhythm and blues. When they first played on the *Louisiana Hayride*—this was when he was on Sun—Elvis was playing rhythm and Bill Black played a drum kind of thing, slapping that bass. Scotty had his thing. They had a feel and a sound all their own and didn't really need me. But somehow it all fell into place."

It didn't always fall into place when Presley recorded with Nashville musicians. Many of the early RCA tracks sound chaotic and clattering compared to the sleek, spare sound of the Sun recordings.

The RCA sessions took place in New York and Los Angeles as well as in Nashville, but always with the touring band as their core. Often they went on all night. Chet Atkins, a family man, stopped playing on them when they no longer took place in the daytime, but as a Nashville RCA executive, he kept track of how they went. "They would begin setting up around eight P.M. and Elvis would come in after nine. He would do karate, swap stories. I remember at the early sessions he would come in with pockets full of press clippings and show them to his friends and laugh. Anyway, they would start cutting around eleven or twelve and then they'd send out for a hundred Krystal burgers or some other kind of fast food. They'd eat, and around two or three A.M. they'd take a little siesta. Then it would be back to work."

The night hours were necessary because of Presley's notoriety; he simply could not go out during the daytime. He kept the same hours when he returned to Memphis, but he always managed to see Sam Phillips nevertheless. "Elvis would call at three in the morning," Knox remembers, "and my mother would get up and cook eggs for him and the twenty or so people he brought with him. It would always be Memphis people with maybe a Hollywood starlet. They would stay up all night shooting pool and listening to records."

Presley toured a great deal during the late fifties before he was inducted into the army, and it was hard work. The group, which had fleshed out its spare sound with the vocal harmonies of the Jordanaires, depended on house public-address systems, except for Scotty Moore, who had a custom-built amplifier. "We had to do the best with what we had," says D. J. Fontana, "and play hard." Presley was still very much a country musician. Several of his early Sun records—"Milkcow Blues Boogie" in particular—were virtually country blues, with the singer dropping beats and whole bars of music and the band following him like a hound on a possum. These rough edges were smoothed out on the RCA recordings, but not on the road. "As far as dropping beats and things," Fontana recalls, "he would do that all the time. We'd know to change chords by his hand movements."

If Elvis was a natural, instinctive musician, he was also a thorough professional. Jerry Leiber and Mike Stoller wrote for him frequently after he had a hit with their "Hound Dog," and they had a number of chances to watch him work in the studio. "He was one of the most phenomenally consistent performers," Leiber says. "Rarely did a take flag down or drop in energy. He'd prefer one take because of a certain note he hit or a turn of phrase, but they were all good. He was very fast and seldom made more than four or five takes of any number. And he was very high-strung. He would crack jokes with the boys from Memphis, jump to the piano and play a few bars, pick up a guitar, slap somebody on the back, hit three notes on the bass. But then he'd say, 'Okay, let's make it,' and get in front of that mike and get it in a few takes."

Leiber and Stoller had been writing for and working with black artists almost exclusively since the early fifties, and they shared with Presley a fascination for and intimate knowledge of black culture. But otherwise they were poles apart. Leiber and Stoller's music was shaped by city blues, and Elvis was brought up on country blues and gospel. They wrote sensitively for him, including some of the music from *Jailhouse Rock* and *King Creole* and the delightful "(You're So Square) Baby I Don't Care," but perhaps their most successful song for him, "Love Me," was originally recorded by a black gospel duo they'd persuaded to do secular material.

Colonel Tom Parker had seen to it that Presley was kept away from the public and even insulated from most of the people he worked with, but Elvis seems to have been content, at this point at least, to carry his culture around with him in the person of his Memphis cronies. Leiber and Stoller remember him being polite but standoffish. The Colonel was not as polite. Once, when Stoller went to visit Elvis in a Los Angeles hotel suite, the singer nervously and with some embarrassment told him that the Colonel said he had to leave.

"After Elvis got out of the army," says D.J. Fontana, "his music changed. He wanted a bigger sound and hired more musicians." This was the period when Presley began to sing the most banal and inappropriate sort of material. It was what the Hollywood studios wanted, it seemed to be what the fans wanted, and it was what the Colonel wanted. But Elvis's musical orientation remained the same.

"Elvis always loved gospel music," says J. D. Sumner, the bass singer who hits the double-low C on the current Presley single, "Way Down," and a friend since Elvis was fourteen. "He would go to the National

Quartet Convention almost every year, and he was always showing up at performances in out-of-the-way places. I first met him when I was singing with the Blackwood Brothers quartet and we had to let him come in the back of the auditorium because he couldn't afford to pay to get in. He'd show up after that. We'd sing in Long Beach or Nashville and there he'd be.

"We spent many hours together singing gospel. You know, he wanted to sing with a quartet before he started recording for Sun. He came from a strictly evangelistic bringing-up. I remember he used to like to sing spirituals, and of course those came from the blacks. He would sit there and teach the feeling to me, and it would take me two or three hours to get it. A black singer will jump the beat, get behind the beat, and Elvis would do all that naturally. You know, with black gospel singers it's like wringing a dishrag, getting all the water out of it. They take a word and do the same thing. Elvis could do more with one word than any other man I ever heard sing. He could squeeze the world out of a word."

Presley hired Sumner and the Stamps quartet to sing with him in 1972, and the bass singer found that Elvis still recorded in the old way. "He wouldn't overdub. They tried to get him to do that, or to sing in one section of the studio with us in another one. 'It'll bleed onto the other tracks if you have everything here in the room,' they'd tell him. He didn't care. He had to have his people around him so he could get the feel of it. He needed the assurance of his family being together. He said, 'Let it bleed.'"

Larrie Londin, who filled in for regular Presley drummer Ronnie Tutt on Elvis's final concert tour, had to throw his normal working methods out the window. "His people sent me tapes two weeks in advance of everything he might do," the drummer remembers. "It was like four hundred songs! So I sat down at the house and listened to them and wrote out charts for all the ones they said he was most likely to do. Then they flew me to his mansion in Memphis to rehearse. He came down and sang a few bars of this song, a few bars of that song, and had me play along. Then he said, 'Great, it's gonna be all right,' and went back upstairs to bed.

"We went out onstage cold, and I was worried. He started the first number and it didn't go like the tape. He stopped the band and said, 'Larrie, watch me.' Well, it turned out I couldn't read the charts. I just had to watch him. He was liable to stop one song in the middle and start another one. I must have sweated off twenty pounds the first two weeks of that tour, but he sweated as hard as I did. He really worked, and he expected his people to work too. And for what he was paying us, he was right to expect that."

By 1977, Presley's music-by-feel—a feel he kept alive by surrounding himself with Southerners, keeping himself steeped in his Southern roots—was almost an anachronism. But the musicians, songwriters, and producers who worked with Elvis nevertheless stand in awe of his contribution to their art. For some, it had its negative side. "Ever since he came along, we've been losing our musical identities," says Chet Atkins. "There used to be pop *and* gospel *and* country and so on. Now they're all fusing together. You can hardly tell the difference between a James Taylor record and a Waylon Jennings record." J. D. Sumner sees this process differently: "One day there won't be any more pop or country or rhythm and blues. It'll just be named American music, and Elvis Presley did as much to make it that as anyone who ever lived."

The Devil and Jerry Lee Lewis

ROLLING STONE | DECEMBER 13, 1979

"I'm the toughest son of a bitch that ever shat out of a meat ass," Jerry Lee Lewis said, deliberately. Having just done a show, he was sweating, stripped to the waist, and balancing precariously on a rickety wooden chair in the wine cellar of a would-be honky-tonk on New York's Upper East Side. Some well-meaning but inexperienced promoters had commandeered the place, a former German restaurant, and paid Lewis a considerable sum to open it. Unfortunately, the lights didn't work, the sound was tinny, the piano was atrocious, and the surly mob that had descended on the place from heaven knows where to hear the Killer pound the eighty-eights was packed in so tightly he had to wade through it to get on and off the stage. The wine cellar, the best the club could do for a dressing room, adjoined the urinal; any fans, male or female, waiting for an audience with Lewis had to watch hapless customers pissing their beer away.

Despite the primitive working conditions and Lewis's consumption of what was reported by the club's staff to be an unbelievable amount of whiskey ("It wasn't *nothin'*," he later countered. "I used to have to drink a fifth of tequila to sober up and do my shows"), the first set was spectacular. The Killer (nickname since high school) roared through "Whole Lotta Shakin' Goin' On" and his other rock & roll hits, sang a "Big Legged Woman" that was slow, throbbing, and utterly lascivious, and mixed country ballads and pop tunes with rhythm and blues and spirituals, giving all of them everything he had. He interrupted the show only twice, once to tell the audience, "This piano ain't worth shit," and again to muse that "I've seen so many friends and loved ones die away, I just thank God I'm still here." His father, Elmo Lewis, a champion drinker and hell-raiser who'd always given Jerry Lee's musical career his unstinting support, had died three weeks earlier.

Once the show was over and Lewis was back downstairs, it was evident that the sleazy club and, especially, his father's death were weighing heavily. He glared moodily at no one in particular, swigged from a bottle of Scotch, and tossed an empty glass higher and higher in the air, catching it and muttering to himself, "I'm the *meat* man," a litany that seemed to take on metaphysical implications. At one point the glass he was tossing ricocheted off his palm and sailed across the room, missing J. W. Whitten, his wiry, capable road manager, by inches. Whitten, who's used to far worse, didn't even blink. Then the Killer began to amuse himself by throwing punches at various friends and well-wishers, stopping his fist about a millimeter from their faces. "Did you ever hit anybody doing that?" I asked him when he tried it on me and my wife. "I *never* hit anybody," Lewis said. He smiled wickedly and added, "unless I want to."

Lewis's teenage daughter Phoebe appeared and blessed him with a wet kiss on the cheek, and his mood began to lighten. He stopped muttering and started singing snatches of songs—"Ramblin' Rose," one went, "ramblin' Rose/Where she rambles, Jerry Lee goes"—and talking about his music. "I had to leave Mercury," he said, referring to the company he recorded for from the mid-sixties until 1978, when he signed with Elektra. "They were tryin' to put me in a bag, strings and all that shit. I play rock & *roll*! Don't ever call me a hillbilly. I'm a *rocker*." When Whitten told him it was time for the second show, he bounded up and into a clean shirt and went out the door singing "Give my regards to Bro-o-oadway/And tell 'em they can kiss my ass. . . ."

A few months earlier, I had checked into a North Hollywood motel where the Killer, his manager, Bob Porter, and Whitten were staying while they prepared for the Los Angeles Country Music Awards show. First Porter, a young, Alabama business-school graduate, checked me out. Then I sat down in the motel coffee shop with Whitten, and we discovered we were both from around Memphis, both the same age, and both Jerry Lee Lewis fans from the first. "Jerry has a heart as big as this building," Whitten said. "He's not the mean rounder people think. We played a benefit for the St. Jude Children's Hospital in Memphis last month, canceled thirty thousand dollars' worth of shows to do it for nothing. Now, he is a hell-raiser, that's a fact. But man, that's rock & roll."

That afternoon a limo pulled up to take Lewis, Whitten, and Porter to a CMA rehearsal. "I've told Jerry you're all right," Whitten advised me. "You just come in the car with us." I got in and there was the Killer, steel-blue eyes flashing behind a grin that looked a little silly and more than a little shy. "How're you?" I asked. I couldn't understand a single word he said in response. I'm *Southern*, but his accent was impenetrable. Before long I grew more accustomed to it, but I found that the only way to really track it was to down a few drinks. "Well, uh, how are things in Mississippi now, got a big spread, a lake. Memphis is a ridiculous place. They have lost their *minds*. Naked women dancin' on every corner." He chuckled softly to himself. "Really?" I said. "You sure? Which corners?" This time Lewis laughed out loud. "This is gonna be all right. Let's stop and get us a fifth. Naw, better make that two fifths."

We pulled up to the parking lot behind the theater around two P.M. and found our way to the Killer's dressing room, which was in a trailer like everybody else's. The first bottle of Scotch was already open and Lewis was feeling expansive. "Who's next door?" he asked as we all crowded into the tiny room. "*Priscilla Presley?*" He leaned over in the direction of the ventilator and began crooning the Conway Twitty hit "Hello Darlin'." "Uh, Jerry," said Porter, "she can hear everything you say if you talk into that, man. It's just like an intercom." Lewis cackled. "Inter*come*," he said. He eyed my tape recorder and added, "She's a really wonderful person, really. A *lady*." That's Lewis's highest accolade for members of the opposite sex.

"Go on," said Whitten, "ask him some questions. This is as close as you're gonna get." I had a notebook of carefully considered lines of inquiry, but suddenly it didn't seem very relevant. "Is it true about you setting that piano on fire?" I asked. The story goes that during the fifties, the Killer, who never opens for anybody, was somehow made to go on before Chuck Berry. So he climaxed a scorching performance by setting the piano ablaze in the middle of "Great Balls of Fire" and pounding the keys while it flamed.

"Burned it to the ground," Lewis said. "They forced me to do it, tellin' me I had to go on before Chuck. I was supposed to be the star of the show." "How did you do it?" I wondered. "Lighter fluid and a lighter?" "Naw, gasoline. Took a Coke bottle full of it onstage with me. I once pushed another piano in the ocean. They tried to give me a busted piano that wouldn't play. I pushed it off the stage, across the dance floor, out the door, and then I played it on the sidewalk and pushed it into the ocean."

There was a knock at the door. It was Mickey Gilley, a cousin of Lewis's who grew up with him in Ferriday, Louisiana, and began making records in the late fifties that sounded exactly like him. He had blossomed in recent years into a major country star, with a string of hits and his own celebrated Houston honky-tonk, Gilley's, where John Travolta and company had been filming *Urban Cowboy*. "Mickey and me used to go around together in Ferriday," Lewis said by way of introducing us. "Used to go down and hear the music at Haney's Big House, a colored place. They were *rockin'*." He pronounced the word with spirit and reverence, the way some people say "heaven" or "Jesus." "Best music in the world," he added. "Wilder than my music."

Gilley looked slick and well-fed in his tailored Western attire, especially next to Lewis, who is still lean and was wearing slacks and a knit T-shirt. "Siddown, boy," the Killer commanded. Gilley eyed the rapidly disappearing Scotch. "Have a *drink*." Lewis personally mixed a stiff one with Coca-Cola and passed it over. "Well now," said Gilley after he'd had a taste, "don't you agree with me that if God made anything better than a woman, he'd have kept it for himself?" It was a decent enough opener, but Lewis wasn't buying it. "You got that from me," he said, "just like you got your music." "You agree with it, don't you?" asked Gilley, holding his ground. Lewis just smiled. "I *know* it. But I keep tryin' to get *away* from these women. They just won't let you."

Gilley chuckled. "The reason these women won't let you alone," he asserted, "is that they're sinful."

Lewis set down his paper cup. He suddenly looked very serious. "It's the man's fault," he said, "not the woman's."

"You don't really believe that, do you?" asked Gilley.

"Why, naturally. The man is stronger."

"Well, yeah, but . . ." Gilley was momentarily at a loss for words. "But who enticed him with the apple?"

"The demons," Lewis said, his eyes clouding. "The Devil did."

"Now wait a minute. In the Garden of Eden, Eve's the one that got . . ."

Lewis snapped forward in his seat. "The *snake* done it," he said decisively.

"We*lll*," said Gilley, pondering the idea. "I ain't gonna fuck with no *snake*." The dressing room exploded with laughter; Lewis was chortling so hard he was crying. Then, abruptly, he was serious again. "Now I'm gonna tell you something," he said, addressing us all with the declamatory emphasis of a country preacher. "The snake was the most beautiful creature. He walked and talked and was just like a man. He got Eve and she was weak. Enticed her into eating this apple." He whirled in his seat, turning toward his cousin. "Can you tell me what the last scripture of Revelation says?" Gilley was caught off guard. "I . . . I don't read the Bible much," he muttered glumly, like a kid caught playing hooky from Sunday school. "Used to . . ."

"We both *used* to," Lewis trumpeted scornfully. "I'll tell you what it says: 'Do not add or take away from these words, for if you do, you're taking away your part out of the book of *life*.' "

"I never read that," said Gilley, now genuinely defensive. "I'll take your word for it."

"Well *study* it," Lewis thundered. He looked his cousin up and down, brow furrowed, eyes flaring. "Boy, you're *weak*. That's where it's at. Got that damn club down there in Texas . . ."

"I get letters from churches," Gilley said. "They say they heard Jimmy Swaggart talk about me on television, about how I used to go to the Assembly of God church in Louisiana and now I've got this club." His voice rose to a ministerial stridency in imitation of their cousin, the Reverend Jimmy Swaggart, who along with Lewis and Gilley used to get shooed away from the back door of Haney's Big House when they were all children and who is now a phenomenally successful television and radio evangelist. "And these letters say, 'My . . . daughter, she went out and got a divorce, and now she's goin' to *Gilley's*!"

Lewis took a swig of Scotch. "What the hell are you takin'?" he asked. Again, the room was convulsed with laughter. "But it's the truth," he added. "That's what makes us so bad: Jimmy's fans." He grinned wickedly.

"That's *right*," Gilley said. "They hear him preachin' about how sinful we are and then they come to us wantin' to get screwed."

"That's the *truth*," Lewis bellowed, kicking at the door with his boot heel, "the damn truth."

Eventually the hilarity wound down. It occurred to Gilley that he was going to have to make some announcements and open some envelopes a little later on, so he left after a cordial parting exchange. "I didn't know Swaggart was your cousin," I said. "He came down and pulled me off the fuckin' stage," said Lewis. "I had five thousand people at my show. This was in Baton Rouge, must've been three or four months ago. I was strung out on pills, and I don't know how, but he knows everything I do. I was singin' 'I'm the meat man, ya oughta see me eat, man,' gettin' to where I was really *rockin'*, the place *packed*, and all of a sudden there stands Jimmy Lee, right on the stage. I said, "H*eeey*, Jimmy, how you doin'? Nice-lookin' shirt you got on.' It looked like a damn pajama top. He said, 'Boy, you're comin' with me.' I said, 'Well, let's go.' I was feelin' *good*, I didn't care."

Lewis poured himself another drink. "The promoter came runnin' up and Jimmy said, 'Just talk to my lawyers.' He took me home, poured all my whiskey down the sink and all my pills down the commode. I sat in my chair and we talked for a while. About four o'clock in the mornin' I was ready to *fight*. No good, though, Jimmy just come and put his arm around me and said, 'You'll be all right, pal. Have some more malted milk and shrimp.' That's all I got for a week! I guess it saved my life. Nobody else had sense enough to say anything to me about it. They'd say, 'Boy, you're doin' great.' And I was strung out like a wild Comanche."

"I read a while back that you believe you're a sinner and going to hell for playing rock & roll," I said. "Is that true?" Lewis looked me right in the eye. "Yep," he said. "I *know* the right way. I was raised a good Christian. But I couldn't make it. . . . Too weak, I guess." But, I argued, why would playing rock & roll damn you to hell? Lewis looked at me as if I'd just asked an impossibly stupid question. "I can't picture Jesus Christ," he said evenly, "doin' a whole lotta shakin'."

When you get down to it, that's the source of Jerry Lee Lewis's formidable authority, the tension that powers his transformation of *rockin'* from a black euphemism for sex into a numinous, supercharged mojo word that defines not just his music but his entire life. Jerry Lee Lewis knew from the very first that he was going to hell for playing rock & roll, and he went ahead and rocked anyway.

Lewis was born September 29, 1935, on a farm outside Ferriday, Louisiana, a little town a few miles from Natchez, Mississippi. When he was three a truck hit his brother, Elmo Lewis Jr., in front of the house, killing the child instantly. Until the arrival of the first of his youngest sisters several years later, Jerry Lee was raised as an only child, and his mother and father doted on him. Except for the fact that his ears stuck out, he was a strikingly handsome boy, a real charmer who usually got his way.

His mother, whose death in the early seventies sent Lewis into a tailspin of depression, practically worshipped the early country star Jimmie Rodgers, but there were all kinds of popular music in the house, including swing and Bing Crosby. When Jerry Lee was in his early teens he would spend Saturday afternoons sitting transfixed in the alley behind the Ferriday movie house. "I would listen to Gene Autry sing," he told me one night. "It only cost a dime to get in, but you could hear the sound back there. Gene Autry was my idol." But Lewis also heard music more powerful than Autry's: rocking music, both in local black joints like Haney's and in the Assembly of God church, where rhythmic hymns were sung and people getting the spirit and speaking in tongues weren't uncommon occurrences.

When he was eight years old or thereabouts, Lewis spotted a piano in the home of an aunt. He'd never played one before, but he sat down and knocked off a recognizable version of "Silent Night." "All black keys," he remembered with a grin, "but my mother said, 'He's a natural-born piano player.' They mortgaged the house to buy me my first piano, and I've still got it. There's no more ivory on the keys; I wore 'em down to the wood." In 1949, around the time of his fourteenth birthday, Lewis made an initial public appearance in the parking lot of the Ferriday Ford dealership to celebrate a new line of cars. He sat in with a local country and western band, but the showstopper of his set was "Drinkin' Wine, Spo-Dee-O-Dee," a black rhythm and blues hit of that year. He must have rocked the place, because the crowd came up with thirteen dollars for him. Elmo Lewis, who barely supported his family with carpentry work and produce from the farm, began driving his son and the piano around in the back of a truck; they'd stop, play, take up a collection, and move on.

Soon, Jerry Lee Lewis started working in a Natchez nightclub, playing drums and occasionally piano. He landed his own twenty-minute radio show on WANT, which often featured his cousins Mickey and Jimmy Lee. When he was fifteen he married seventeen-year-old Dorothy Barton; before long the marriage fell apart and he was running around with Jane Mitcham. Jane got pregnant, her brothers came after Lewis, and soon he was married again. He named their son Jerry Lee Lewis Jr.

After he graduated from high school, Lewis was sent to a fundamentalist Bible college in Waxahachie, Texas. "At night," he recalled, "I'd tie sheets together, slip out of the window, head for Dallas, and *rock*—go to the picture show, ride the rides at the carnival, get the guy that ran the Tilt-a-Whirl to just turn the thing wide open. Then one night I was playin' 'My God Is Real' for a school assembly in the chapel, and I played it boogie-woogie style. I had 'em *rockin'*. I mean, I thought that was the way you should do it. First tune I learned to play, 'Silent Night,' I played it rock & roll style. Me and Jimmy Lee Swaggart learned to play on the same piano, and we just *always* liked to rock it. But in Waxahachie, they said, 'We can't have this around here. You don't boogie-woogie when you say your prayers at night. You're expelled for two weeks.' I said, 'I'll take the whole year.'"

Lewis has often insisted that he always played rock & roll, and since his style springs from no single apparent source and has changed very little if at all since he made his earliest recordings, there are no serious grounds for doubting him. You can hear intimations of the Lewis piano style in the forties recordings of such black jump-blues pianists as Amos Milburn and Cecil Gant, who were in turn influenced by a history of black piano boogie that began long before Lewis was born. By the time the Killer was rocking in public, several popular white pianists were singing in a quasi-hillbilly style while playing with a driving boogie beat, among them Merrill Moore and Moon Mullican. Lewis never passes up an opportunity to talk about his favorite singers, among whom are Autry, Rodgers, Hank Williams, and Al Jolson, but he stonewalls questions about piano influences. He told me he'd never heard of Cecil Gant, and he once silenced another interviewer who was persistent about Mullican by asserting that "*he* couldn't influence a *toilet* bowl."

My guess is that the Lewis Boogie, as he called it on an early Sun single, was a mixture of local black influences, the hillbilly boogie and rhythm and blues that were popular on Southern jukeboxes when he was growing up, and—the most crucial ingredient—the Killer's staunchly individual musical genius. There has never been another American pop musician with Lewis's particular mixture of egotistical self-confidence, innate taste and sensitivity, eclecticism (he will play Chuck Berry, Hoagy Carmichael, Jim Reeves, Artie Shaw, spirituals, blues, low-down honky-tonk, or all-out rock & roll, as the mood strikes him), formidable and entirely idiosyncratic technique (both instrumental and vocal), and sheer bravura.

"Listen to the amazing piano solo he did on 'Number One Lovin' Man,'" says Bones Howe, who produced Lewis's first and soon-to-be-released second Elektra albums. "He did that in one take. When we finished we played it back, and one of the backup singers said, 'That oughta be a union test for a rock & roll piano player. Okay, you think you're hot? Play *this*.' 'Cause there's *nobody* that plays like that." Sam Phillips, who supervised the recording of Lewis's early classics for Sun, is still just as enthusiastic. "You talk about a *talent*," he says. "Good God almighty! I'm not talking about voice, piano, any *one* thing. He is one of the great talents of all *time*, in *any* category."

Phillips is the man who brought that talent to the public. When he began recording whites who sang in a heavily black-influenced idiom, beginning with Elvis Presley in 1954 and continuing with Carl Perkins, Roy Orbison, and others in 1955 and 1956, country boys who'd grown up on black music and were rocking everything they played came flocking out of the backwoods to the Sun studio in Memphis. One of them was Jerry Lee Lewis, whose father sold thirty-three dozen eggs to finance the trip and drove up with him.

"Where the *hell* did this man come from?" Phillips remembers asking when he returned from a short vacation and heard the tape his assistant,

Jack Clement, had made—Lewis's loping, utterly original version of the country weeper "Crazy Arms." "He played that piano with abandon. A lot of people do that, but I could hear, between the stuff that he played and didn't play, that spiritual thing. Jerry is *very* spiritual, very close to God, and yet he's very vain. He is trying his best, and has all along, to get into trouble."

Fame and trouble came together, and quickly. Lewis moved to Memphis, staying at the home of his second cousin, J. W. Brown, while he worked at coming up with a hit for Sun. "J. W. Brown was an electrician," explains Kay Martin, an early president of the Jerry Lee Lewis fan club and a longtime fan of his. "He was one of the first people to play an electric bass. J.W. and his wife, Lois, made a home for Jerry, Jane, and Jerry Lee Jr. there in Memphis. A little later on, when Jerry started going out on the road, the Browns' daughter, Myra, Jerry's third cousin, would babysit for Junior."

In early 1957, Lewis and two musicians from Billy Lee Riley's band, the Little Green Men—guitarist Roland Jones and drummer Jimmy Van Eaton—recorded "Whole Lotta Shakin' Goin' On." Judd Phillips, Sam's brother and Sun's promotion man, gambled the company's future on the record. After it had sold around sixty thousand copies in the South, Judd Phillips took Lewis to New York, successfully auditioned him for *The Steve Allen Show*, and sank most of Sun's capital into pressing enough copies to supply stores all over the country. The Steve Allen appearance did for Lewis what Ed Sullivan had done for Presley, and for a while the two were running neck and neck in terms of popularity; Lewis and Sun records enjoyed a series of million sellers virtually unprecedented for such a small label: "Whole Lotta Shakin'," "Great Balls of Fire," "Breathless," and "High School Confidential." Lewis's live shows more than lived up to the fire in the grooves. Meanwhile, in December 1957, having left Jane, he married thirteen-year-old Myra Brown. "They kept it a secret," says Kay Martin, "mostly because everybody told them to. She was with him quite a bit on the road, but by that time J.W. was playing electric bass with him, so whenever anyone said, 'Who's that?' somebody would say, 'That's J.W.'s daughter.'"

Lewis arrived in England for his first overseas tour in May 1958, but the tour was cut short when the English press discovered Lewis and Myra were married. To this day, Lewis blames Sun Records for panicking at the adverse publicity and issuing "The Return of Jerry Lee," a comedy single that made light of the scandal and is hilarious today but wasn't so funny then. According to Kay Martin, "Jerry was being managed by Oscar Davis, and when he came back from England, Davis booked him into a New York nightclub, some place on Broadway. Jerry's fans weren't old enough to get in, and he was totally out of his element with all these girls, like Las Vegas, and the bubbles. . . . It was a pure disaster. That and general mismanagement had a lot to do with the fact that it was hard for him to recoup after England." Whatever his reasons, there's no denying that Lewis played an important part in his own downfall. When he found out what the English press was doing to him he was cocksure and defiant to the point of parading Myra onstage. But then what would you expect from a country boy who sincerely believed he was playing the Devil's music?

Paradoxically, it was during the next nine years that the Jerry Lee Lewis legend really took hold. Crisscrossing the country, playing in gymnasiums, nightclubs, and roadhouses, at county fairs and on grueling package shows, Lewis got serious about his drinking and his pills. "I'd be out on the road with the band," he remembered one night in Los Angeles, "and we'd take Biphetamine and be wa-a-ay *up*. Then we'd decide we'd try Placidyls and go wa-a-ay *down*." Whitten laughed. "First time they got busted," he said, "it was in some motel in Texas. The cops claimed they found seven hundred pills. Two hundred of 'em were for the boys, the rest were Jerry's." At the same time, Lewis worked harder than he'd ever worked. He still wouldn't allow anyone to follow him onstage, still insisted on rocking out at peak intensity in every joint and whistle stop, still bragged that he put on "the greatest live show on earth." And in 1968 he confounded everyone who'd written him off by scoring the first of a string of top-ten country hits, "Another Place, Another Time." He prospered as a top country star, making records that ranged from elemental honky-tonk to tepid country pop, though none lacked the stamp of his personality.

On the surface, then, Lewis is an American success story. But just under the surface, demons lurked. In 1962, Steve Allen Lewis, his son by Myra, drowned in the family pool. In 1970, Myra left him. "It was my fault," he says. "She caught me cheating."

In 1973, Jerry Lee Lewis Jr., who had reportedly been involved with drugs before finding salvation at a tent revival in Mississippi, died in an automobile accident. In September 1976, Lewis shot bassist Butch Owens in the chest with a .357 Magnum. "Is it true that you shot your bass player?" I asked him late one night, when liquor had boosted my courage. "I shot him," Lewis said flatly. "Was it an accident?" "Of *course* it was an accident." Later in '76, Lewis overturned his Rolls-Royce near Collierville, Tennessee, where he was living with his fourth wife, Jaren (they've since been divorced). In May 1977 he checked into a Memphis hospital, where his gallbladder was removed and he was treated for a collapsed right lung, pleurisy, and a back injury from the accident in the Rolls.

There was also the celebrated incident in November 1976 at Graceland, Elvis's Memphis mansion. Lewis showed up at the front gate in the middle of the night, and when the guard wouldn't let him drive in, he reportedly began waving a pistol. "Elvis had called and asked me to come over," he insists. "Of course I was drunk as a skunk. I was so loaded that when I tried to roll the window down in that Lincoln I rolled the seat all the way back. So I threw a champagne bottle out the window, and boy, there were six squad cars, surroundin' me. The next day Elvis drove out to my house and waited around for me for three hours. I was off somewhere, still drunk." Lewis's intense feeling of rivalry with Presley is no secret, but when he talks about that night, the missed meeting the next day, and the calls he swears he continued to receive from Elvis, he seems genuinely pained. They never saw each other again.

Many people believe that of the two, Lewis is the greater talent. Lewis, for one, is firmly convinced that if it hadn't been for the scandal involving Myra, he would have become "the biggest thing going." But there's more to it than that. "Jerry's appeal was never as broad as Elvis's," says Kay Martin, "because he really only appealed to men. I ran his fan club for eight years, and if I had twenty girls in it at one time, that was a lot. He turned them off; I think he frightened them. Because if you were gonna go with Jerry Lee Lewis, he didn't want to cuddle you like a teddy bear, he wanted to show you his great balls of fire. Plus, he chained himself to the piano with his style. It was very difficult to separate him from that and put him in another context, whereas Elvis, you could put *him* in those movies."

At the Los Angeles Country Music Awards broadcast, Lewis offered a short speech. Before he started his number, "Rockin' My Life Away," from the first Elcktra album, he looked squarely into the camera and said, "I'd like to say that me and Elvis Presley never won an award, but we know who the Kings of rock & roll are." After the show, as we poured ourselves into the limo and took off for a Hollywood party, he was unusually quiet.

"I get crazy sometimes," he said, "upside-down. But I've been accused of more things. If everything they say I've done is true, I'd have been put in the penitentiary long ago." He turned to me. "Did you believe I was telling the truth when I said I pushed that piano in the ocean?" I nodded. "If I did, I swear I don't remember it. A lot of times people make up things, and I just go along with 'em." For the next ten minutes he talked about how much he loves pianos, how careful he is not to hurt them when he's playing with the heel of his foot or clambering inside one.

The party was a whirl of country stars, movie stars, and unidentifiable slicks. Lewis made a grand entrance and was soon the center of an admiring knot of people. The execs from MCA Records, who were throwing the party, looked a little nonplussed. Conway Twitty, one of the label's brightest country stars and an ex-rockabilly singer, came over to pay his respects. "Say," he asked Jerry, "you remember the Peppermint Lounge in Miami?" Twitty turned to me. "I'd been playin' there two weeks—this was back in the rock & roll days—and I'd told this club owner some stuff about what Jerry had done to pianos. The guy went out and got an old beat-up piano with boards across it. Jerry showed up at the club the afternoon before he was gonna open, took one look at the piano, and kicked it all the way out of the building, across the parking lot, and into the water. Then he came back in, blew cigar smoke in the club owner's face, and said, 'Now get me a goddamn piano.'"

Later, in the limo, Lewis puffed coolly on a cigar. "The next motherfucker that gives me a bad write-up," he mused, taking the cigar out of his mouth and looking it over with a Jack Palance sort of glaze over his eyes, "I'm gonna hunt him down and blow his fuckin' head off." He slowly shifted his gaze in my direction, and then he cracked up. "Nawww, I ain't gonna do that. Just tell 'em I'm a drunken oaf. They ain't heard too much about Jerry Lee Lewis except that he's always sayin' he's the greatest." "Well," I said, "aren't you?" "I never considered myself the greatest," he replied. "But I'm the best."

The past few months have been difficult for Jerry Lee Lewis. An Australian tour had to be cut short when a fan picked a fight with him onstage and the two of them, scuffling, fell against a monitor speaker. Lewis emerged from the fracas with several fractured ribs. He returned home to find the Internal Revenue Service, which had confiscated all his vehicles once before for alleged nonpayment of taxes, had paid another visit and confiscated them again. To add insult to injury, they had him busted for marijuana and cocaine they said they found on the premises. The last time I saw him, he was looking puffy and out of it. Several people told me they were afraid he was drinking himself to death. But just before this article went to press I called up a friend in Memphis who had done some recording with Lewis. "I just saw Jerry," he said, "and he's been in the hospital, getting straight. He looks *great*. I don't understand how a man can do what he does to himself and bounce back like that." I could almost hear J. W. Whitten saying, "But man, that's rock & roll."

SOUL AND R&B: "IT HAD TO COME FROM SOMEWHERE, AND THE CHURCH IS WHERE IT ALL CAME FROM."

Liner Notes for *Ray Charles: The Birth of Soul*

(Atlantic, 1991)

They called him "The Genius" at Atlantic Records. "We started calling him that simply because we genuinely thought of him as a genius," Atlantic co-founder and chairman Ahmet Ertegun explained. "His whole approach to music has elements of genius in it, his concept of music is very, very different from anybody else's. His equipment is different, his style of piano playing and his style of singing are very personal to him. He has many imitators, a lot of them are great, but it's not the same thing, they're not Ray Charles." Charles himself has maintained and succinctly expressed a divergent and characteristically iconoclastic point of view.

"I got a lot of criticism," Charles recalled when interviewed in the early 1980s about his "classic period," the Atlantic rhythm and blues years. "There was a crossover between gospel music and the rhythm patterns of the blues, which I think came down through the years from slavery times, you know, because this was a way of communicating. But when I started doing things that would be based on an old gospel tune, I got criticism from the churches, and from musicians too. They thought it was sacrilegious or something, and what was I doing, I must be crazy. But I kept doing it, and eventually, instead of criticizing me for it, the people started saying I was an innovator." Charles vented a sharp, ironic chuckle. "It's like a manager who makes a decision. If it works, he's a genius, and if it doesn't, he's an ass. What we did worked. So I became a genius for it."

A decade has elapsed since Ray Charles spoke those words into my tape recorder, but my mental picture of the day and the man retains its clarity, long after most of the events of that time have been shunted off into the musty back-files of long-term-memory storage. We were facing each other across a folding card table in a comfortable but anonymous hotel room in Cleveland, where Charles and his orchestra—the ace road warriors of American music—were beginning an extended engagement. Charles was chain-smoking, a small tin ashtray close at hand. We talked for three hours, intensely at times, and Charles never dropped so much as a flake of ash anywhere but into the ashtray. At one point he got up, walked unerringly across the room to a window, opened it, and walked just as unerringly back to the table, gracefully skirting all the furniture and with no tentative or wasted motion. He was more assured than I would have been in a strange hotel room, and I can see.

Charles navigated, as he has navigated the course of his life and music, straightforwardly, with a firm, squarely centered sense of personal direction and a highly evolved and sensitive sonar. Talking music, down to the strengths and idiosyncrasies of past band members and the drum and cymbal patterns on twenty-five-year-old records, the man seemed more a force than a presence.

Singers can get overconfident if enough people praise their "genius" often enough. But Ray Charles still practices: He sings in the shower. "I think that the voice is really the instrument," he said. "You always need to know what you can get your voice to do, under the worst conditions. Not the best. Because there will be nights when you may be hoarse, you got a cold or whatever, and you need to know what you can make your voice do. I'm always singing something, trying to discover little things, and, although people make a lot of jokes about it, one of the best places to actually practice is in the shower. If the shower's an average-size shower where the sound can wallow around in those tile walls, you can really hear yourself. If you should get out of tune, you hear it right away, immediately. I practice constantly like that, just to find out how my voice is doing. You've got to constantly keep fooling with it, just like you do a horn. You've got to keep it up the way you'd keep your house up or your property up, because anything that you don't use, you lose."

Imagining this Promethean musical polymath, blender and creator of idioms, setter of styles and trends, methodically bouncing sonic resonances off shower tiles . . . well, it was a heady proposition. I thought of him homing in on the exact balance of timbre, tonal weight, and intonation that would precisely fill, but never overload, such an acoustically "live" space. And I kept asking him to retrace his steps musically, but the question I really wanted to ask had already been posed, by Raelett Mary Ann Fisher, on one of Charles's most incandescent, unforgettable Atlantic singles: Ray Charles, "What Kind of Man Are You?"

To understand the great and particular significance of Ray Charles's fifties R&B recordings for Atlantic — covering a period in which he grew from being an especially versatile and clever musical chameleon into the indelibly original master we revere today — one has to look into where, and what, he was coming from. He is perhaps the ultimate musical exemplar of that old Firesign Theater maxim: "You've gotta start young if you're gonna stick it out." Charles was born September 23, 1930, in Albany, Georgia, a contemporary of Sonny Rollins and Ornette Coleman; it was a good year for future musicians who would excel at obliterating boundaries of style and turf, or as we now say, "pushing the envelope." His family moved from Albany to Greenville, Florida, "more of a village than a town" according to Charles, when he was about six months old. "So all I really know is Florida," he said in our interview. "I was raised in Greenville and I went to school in St. Augustine, to a state school for the deaf and blind." His father was a no-show early on and he was raised by his mother. "Even compared to the other blacks in Greenville, we were at the bottom of the ladder," he wrote in his characteristically head-on autobiography *Brother Ray.* "Nothing below us, 'cept the ground."

"Back in there in the thirties and forties, the people in the South were very religious minded," he recalled. "Most of the black people in Greenville were Baptist, and there was no such thing as not going to church every Sunday. And whenever there was a revival meeting, which could be during the week, you went to that." A neighbor, Wylie Pittman, owner of a little store and a sometime juke joint, initiated him into the church of blues and boogie-woogie. "He didn't consider himself to be a professional piano player, but I thought he was damned good," Charles remembered. "The kids would flock to his little store after school, to play the jukebox and stuff like that. But whenever he sat down at that old upright and started to play, if I was in the yard, having fun with the other kids, I'd always go over there, and he'd let me sit on the piano stool or in the chair next to him and bang on the piano with him. I know I wasn't playing anything. How could I? He could have easily made me stop and run me away. But he must have had some kind of foresight: I guess he thought any kid that was willing to give up his playtime to come in and listen to music, why then, maybe it was music in his blood."

As a child, Charles heard a wider range of blues on Pittman's jukebox. "But on the other hand," he emphasized, "I also heard some swing things—Count Basie, Jimmy Lunceford, Lucky Millinder, Erskine Hawkins. Then there was Artie Shaw and Benny Goodman—in other words, we heard just about all the popular music, the white music along with the black. I also listened to the Grand Ole Opry every Saturday night. I would never miss that for nothing. Once I started going to school, then I got exposed also to classical music. And naturally I was always around church music."

When Charles talks about the world of sounds he lived in as a child, he makes those days sound idyllic. They were not. Before he gradually lost his sight, between the ages of five and seven, he saw his younger brother George drown in a washtub. He was only fifteen, still attending the state school in St. Augustine, when he got the news that his mother had died. There were no sisters or brothers, and his seldom-seen father died the following year. Charles was well and truly orphaned, his family and one of his most crucial senses torn away from him by forces he could neither fight nor fathom, before he was sixteen. He had to virtually create a new world to inhabit, a sonic world, and his restless intelligence drove him to furnish that world with as many views and vistas as he could access. He was reportedly able to arrange and score every part for big band or orchestral music by the age of twelve.

In May 1945, still only fifteen, he left home for Jacksonville, Florida. "My mother had instilled in me that you don't beg," he said, "and I thought that because Jacksonville was a city, maybe I could find some work. It was rough, you know, it was very rough. But one thing about being young, you can take an awful lot, if you're really trying to get someplace." Charles was definitely going places, running, as he put it, on "sheer determination."

The genius had hit the road.

When Charles calls making it in the city on his own "rough," he must be drastically understating the case. But if his heritage was small town/rural, his musical scope was already broadly urbane. "I've never been any certain kind of piano player," he said when discussing his music during these scuffling years. "I've always been one of those kind of people to tackle anything that I like. If it was just plain boogie-woogie, I would play that. But I would also play 'String of Pearls,' 'Jersey Bounce,' 'After Hours'—these were some of the songs I was playing back in those days. I tried to play whatever was popular at the time, whatever was called for." Whatever his initial discouragements, Charles was soon playing in a small band, then another, and another, barnstorming around Florida.

From a little combo of Louis Jordan copycats he jumped to a white hillbilly band, the Florida Playboys. At times he was able to front his own trio, working in a terrain mapped by his main man at the time, Nat "King" Cole. Cole was a fine jazz pianist who was also able to parlay his smooth singing and some catchy "pop" material—"Straighten Up and Fly Right," "Route 66"—into hit records that appealed to both black and white audiences. At the time, the mid-forties, Cole and another Charles favorite, Louis Jordan, were the leading wedge of black musicians' first significant inroads into the white pop market. They were the exceptions. The rule, Charles explained, was that "what was a hit in the black community did not cross over to the white community, but a big hit in the white community often became very popular in the black community.

It was kind of a one-way street." Charles was destined to take the lead in the transformation of that one-way street into a two-way thoroughfare.

By 1948, the eighteen-year-old Charles was a road-seasoned musician. He even bought an early wire recorder and recorded some home demos in Tampa, including "St. Pete Florida Blues" (a.k.a. "I Found My Baby There") and "Baby Let Me Hear You Call My Name." These first recordings dispel any notion that the early Ray Charles was entirely a "cover" or bar-band musician, regurgitating the songs and styles then popular. The church intensity and rawness is as evident in his singing as the swing and bebop influences in his jabbing piano fills. But Charles decided he was getting nowhere in Florida, and after hoarding some gig money he left for the West Coast, winding up in Seattle. There he met future movers and shakers such as Bumps Blackwell, later producer of the original Little Richard hits, and Quincy Jones. He also assembled a new, improved trio, the McSon Trio. The "Mc" part denoted a Tampa associate who'd followed Charles west, Gosady McGee. The Son was Charles himself. He had been born Ray Charles Robinson but soon dropped the last name to avoid confusion with boxing hero "Sugar" Ray Robinson.

Before long, the trio attracted the attention of Jack Lauderdale, whose Downbeat (later Swingtime) Records was one of the first post–World War II black-owned indie labels. Lauderdale was enjoying some success on the black sales charts with Lowell Fulson and Lloyd Glenn, the latter a pianist whose feel for Afro-Cuban rhythms may have influenced the Latin flavorings that emerged on several key singles during Charles's Atlantic tenure. In 1950, at Lauderdale's urging, Charles left the trio and moved to Los Angeles, where he shared a house with Lauderdale's secretary. His first Downbeat single, "Confession Blues," had been a solid seller in 1949. Soon Charles was on the road again, playing in guitar bluesman Lowell Fulson's band. When Fulson met up with fellow Swingtime artist Lloyd Glenn in Texas, Charles met Glenn's saxophonist, David "Fathead" Newman, later the star soloist of Charles's Atlantic-period band. In 1951, Charles recorded another substantial hit in the black community, "Baby Let Me Hold Your Hand."

On these and many of his other Swingtime singles, Charles worked in a Nat Cole/Charles Brown vein. Brown was then an extremely popular R&B singer-pianist who was bluesier than Cole but every bit as polished. "I tried very hard to sound like Nat Cole, 'cause I loved him so much, and like Charles Brown," Charles admitted. "But the reason I tried to sound so much like them was, I could get work, especially club work. And I did that on my first hits. But some of my other records from that same time—'Snow Is Falling,' 'Kiss Me Baby'—are all me. On those I didn't sound like or imitate anybody." The records bear out Charles's point of view. "But I didn't have anybody I could talk to who would advise me," Charles added, "and I had mixed emotions. I was getting over with imitations, but I didn't know if people would accept me as I am. It took me a while to get the nerve to really go whole hog and just do only Ray Charles. Even when I went to Atlantic, I was still afraid to really turn it loose."

By 1951, label owner Jack Lauderdale had racked up enough major R&B hits to overextend his resources. He had to trim his artist roster, and since Charles's hits had been Cole- and Charles Brown–oriented, failing to establish a strong, individual identity, the singer-pianist fell prey to Lauderdale's cost-cutting. The Swingtime boss put out the word that Charles's contract was for sale.

Herb Abramson, one of Ahmet Ertegun's original partners in Atlantic, explained to author and researcher Colin Escott how Charles came to Atlantic: "One of the good connections we had was the booking agent Billy Shaw. After we signed Joe Morris and Ruth Brown, we brought them to Billy Shaw for bookings. We had already heard Ray Charles doing 'Baby Let Me Hold Your Hand.' It sounded like Charles Brown, but it was good, very good—very soulful. Billy Shaw told us . . . that Ray Charles had left Lowell Fulson and that he [Shaw] was thinking about placing Ray with Joe Morris when they came east." Morris was the leader of an R&B combo whose musical standards were exceptionally high: on his early recordings; band members included some of the major players in the emerging modern jazz movement—pianist Elmo Hope, bassist Percy Heath, drummer Philly Joe Jones.

Shaw also told Abramson he thought he could buy Charles's contract from Swingtime. "Ahmet and I agreed to pick up his contract," Abramson recalled. "Ray flew into New York and we booked him into the Braddock hotel for his first session."

Ertegun reminisced: "At the time, we were struggling to get the company going and I thought Ray Charles was just about the best artist I'd ever heard that we had a chance to sign. When we found out from Billy

Shaw that Ray's contract might be available, we contacted Jack Lauderdale, and signed up Ray Charles without ever seeing him. I believe at the
time we paid $2,500 for his contract."

For Charles's first Atlantic sessions, the company put him together with
a group of New York studio players under the direction of Jesse Stone.
These musicians' resumés were at least as varied and eclectic as Charles's
musical personality; few out-and-out honkers and screamers would have
been quick or flexible enough to work efficiently against the studio clock.
The nucleus of the group was present on the first ten selections in this
anthology, and their backgrounds may seem surprising to younger listeners used to more rigid musical categorizations. Stone himself offers an
excellent example of the continuity that runs in an unbroken line from
some of the earliest recorded jazz into the rock & roll years. He was
leading a jazz band popular in the Southwest, and making records,
before the end of the 1920s, a first-generation Kansas-city-style jazzman
who went on to write "Shake, Rattle and Roll," "Money Honey,"
and other early rock & roll standards under the pseudonym Charles
Calhoun.

The guitarist—the only guitarist prominently featured on any of
Charles's Atlantic recordings—was Mickey Baker. Best known as the
Mickey of Mickey and Sylvia, who teamed up for the rock & roll hit
"Love Is Strange," Baker is one of a select handful of black electric guitarists who were exploring high-volume effects, deliberate tonal distortion, and a screaming, in-your-face solo style, a good fifteen years before
groups like the Yardbirds made such "innovations" a permanent part of
the rock guitar lexicon. The drummer was Connie Ray, best known for
his work with the Modern Jazz Quartet. Lloyd Trotman was a rock-solid,
big-sound, nail-down-the-tempo bassist, perfect for studio work.

According to researcher Colin Escott, Stone complained about
"Charles's unwillingness to take direction." Later, when Charles was
able to form his own band, it became apparent that he was much better
at giving directions than taking them. If there was a tug-of-war between
Stone and Charles at that first session (September 11, 1952) then the
artist scored at least a partial victory. "The Sun's Gonna Shine Again"
is pure R.C., a crying, sandpaper-throated gospel-blues, and a Charles

composition. If Stone hoped the formulaic novelty tune "Roll with My Baby" would be more commercial, Charles must have dashed those hopes with his spiky tone-cluster piano fills, which effortlessly conflate gospel piano and bebop à la Monk. The third Charles tune of the date, "Jumpin' in the Morning," is notable mainly for its proto-ska groove, a harbinger of the rhythmic explorations that would be such an important part of Charles's achievements on Atlantic.

Charles was still unsure of himself and admits he "still did a little bit of Nat Cole" on his first Atlantic dates. His second, last, and longest date with the New York session aces (tracks 5–10, volume 1, recorded May 17, 1953) nevertheless produced some exquisite music. "Losing Hand," a "Charles Calhoun" blues, features a deft, deeply felt blues conversation between Charles's piano and Baker's guitar and is perhaps the first of the Atlantic tunes to create its own palpable mood. "Mess Around," a contribution from the pen of Atlantic's Ahmet Ertegun ("A. Nugetre"), borrowed liberally from boogie-woogie master Cow Cow Davenport's "Cow Cow Blues." It inspired Charles to turn in the session's most burning vocal performance, and it rocked liked crazy.

"You see, when I was writing rhythm and blues songs," Ertegun explained, "I was going back to a lot of the blues records I bought as a very young kid, records by Cow Cow Davenport and by others, like Cripple Clarence Lofton or Pinetop Smith. These records were big hits among Southern blacks and the music was played all over. I thought 'Mess Around' would strike a chord in Ray Charles and in the Southern audience. I wrote it for him because no New York players could play the blues or that kind of jump-boogie blues like Ray Charles. It was a Southern tradition and part of a kind of subconscious memory. So I sat with him and showed him the song and somehow he immediately remembered 'Cow Cow Blues' and 'Pinetop's Boogie.' It came naturally to him and he performed it very well. It wasn't a huge hit, but it was a hit. It was a precursor of 'What'd I Say,' because that had a lot of the same elements, except that 'What'd I Say' was very up-to-date."

The Memphis Curtis talking blues "It Should Have Been Me," which struck a fine compromise between Charles's headstrong individualism and the commercial realities of the R&B marketplace, gave our genius his first Atlantic hit—a year and a half after signing with the label. It combined the sort of wryly humorous cross-talk that would become a hallmark of the Coasters' Atco sides with a stop-time riff of the kind then associated with the Muddy Waters/Willie Dixon school of Chicago blues.

Looking back on that second session, Ertegun explained: "What we did was try to really go for hits. Jesse Stone wrote one song, I wrote two. Memphis Curtis wrote 'It Should Have Been Me,' a novelty-type song which Ray liked very much. He told me at the time that he had stopped at a gas station, and the attendant had a very strange drawl. On that record, he was imitating the station attendant's voice as he remembered it, singing in a different accent than his own. I think we sang harmonies, Jesse and I and whoever else was at the session.

"Ray was never just another artist to us, he was always somebody very important. At first, we didn't know how to bring out of him what we knew was there and we really didn't hit our stride until we let him do what he wanted to do. In the first two sessions, we were trying to guide him into what was our formula, the Atlantic formula for making R&B hits. It took us a little bit of time to understand that he had something else all of his own. When we heard him on the road, we realized we had a genius of sorts, an artist who had a lot more to offer than just writing a song and singing it. He had a whole conception of what his band should sound like, of what the track should sound like, and of what he should sound like."

During much of 1953, Charles worked out of New Orleans, where producer-arranger Dave Bartholomew and his hand-picked session band were well on their way to developing the ensemble style and rhythmic grooves that they deployed with such devastating effect on early rock & roll hits by Fats Domino and Little Richard. In New Orleans, Charles arranged and played piano on a Specialty Records session for bluesman Guitar Slim. Out of that session came the biggest R&B hit of 1954, Slim's "The Things I Used to Do." Charles had not written any of the arrangements for his earlier Atlantic sessions; "The Things" proved that his comprehensive musical vision could also be highly commercial, if we take that word to mean "selling lots of records."

Since Charles was in the middle of extended stays at New Orleans's Pelican Club and Dew Drop Inn, Atlantic's Ahmet Ertegun and Jerry Wexler recorded him in New Orleans, using reliable New Orleans musicians, on August 18 and December 4, 1953. The August session, apparently intended to capitalize on Ray's role in the making of Guitar Slim's hit, found him covering an earlier Slim single, "Feelin' Sad." But this was clearly not the way to go. Slim's own version may have featured horns and piano that were woefully out of tune, but it fused feeling and atmosphere into perhaps the most powerful slow gospel-blues recorded up to that time. Charles's cover has higher musical standards and is much more professionally recorded, but if an exceptional atmosphere was generated at the session, it doesn't come across on the record. In itself, Charles's version is a solid, even moving performance, but Slim's rendition is sheer magic, out-of-tune instruments and all.

This stay in New Orleans represents both the last and the most controversial period of what might be called R.C.'s formative years. In his autobiography, Charles wrote, "There were good musical sounds in New Orleans then—and I sat in with as many of the cats as I could. The blues were brewing down there and the stew was plenty nasty. I was experimenting with my own voice and doing fewer and fewer imitations." This somewhat neutral statement is hardly an admission of heavy New Orleans influences in Charles's music. How much the city's trailblazing R&B bands did influence him has become something of a bone of contention among historians of American music. Some writers have heard a considerable New Orleans influence in the arrangements Charles began writing when he formed his first band. Yet in my interview with him, he stated unequivocally that "when I went to New Orleans, I was already pretty much into what I was doing. New Orleans had very little influence on me, if any."

My own ears place me somewhere in the middle of these polarized opinions, but closer to Charles's point of view. Guitar Slim's impassioned, churchy singing style may have encouraged Ray to cut loose a little more, but on no recording could one man's singing be mistaken for that of the other. New Orleans, already moving into the swamp-funk feel that surfaced more definitively in the early sixties, influenced all the fifties R&B that wasn't strictly swing or boogie based, including, no doubt, Ray Charles's R&B. "I Got a Woman" is more Texas lope and Kansas City swing than it is New Orleans oriented, rhythmically. And while most New Orleans R&B arrangements, especially for horns, were firmly rooted in the big band era, Charles used his small, tight horn section like a percussion instrument, chopping away at riffs that were often radically syncopated in relation to the drum accents. Charles's mid-fifties band arrangements seem much closer in concept to the sixties idiom developed by James Brown's bands than they do to the New Orleans R&B of the fifties. For some musicians, including Brown, New Orleans exerted an undeniable influence. For a musician like Ray Charles, it would be safer to say that New Orleans is a good place to discover one's personal identity.

Ertegun's perspective on the issue goes as follows: "There is no doubt that living down there for several months and hanging out, you certainly couldn't help but feel the excitement of New Orleans music. However, I think Ray Charles must have influenced some of the people down there more than he was influenced by them. He really had found himself by then, and that first [New Orleans] session was the beginning of his playing with musicians he liked and getting into his groove."

From New Orleans, Charles went to Dallas, where he finally was able to put together his own band. Escott's interview with trumpeter Renald Richard, Charles's first bandleader, fills in much valuable detail on this crucial period. "I was in Houston and had just finished a gig with Ivory Joe Hunter," Richard remembered. "Someone mentioned to Ray I was available and I went to see him. Right away we went out on the road with Ruth Brown, starting in El Paso, playing dance halls with her all the way to Florida." Shortly after saxophonist David "Fathead" Newman joined the three-reeds-two-trumpets-three-rhythm lineup (September 1954), another road trip provided Richard and Charles with the opportunity to get to know each other better, jive around a bit, and come up with the seminal "I Got a Woman."

"We had just played South Bend, Indiana, and we were on our way to Nashville," Richard related to Escott. "We were listening to gospel on the radio like we often did, and there was some spiritual that had a good groove to it." Escott reports that this was probably an Alex Bradford hymn. "We used to clown a lot when we were traveling," Richard continued, "and we started singing 'I Got a Woman' to the tune on the radio. Ray said, 'Can you do something with that?' I said, 'Sure!' And the next morning I had the lyrics written. In fact, I had already written most of them for a song that was never published." Out of this casual exchange came a sound that would ring out the R&B era and ring in the years of soul.

In November 1954, Charles asked Atlantic executives Ahmet Ertegun and Jerry Wexler to meet him on the road in order to hear his new band and new material. They met at the Peacock Club in Atlanta. Ertegun remembers that "by that time, he had his own orchestra, and we were amazed to find he had everything prepared for the session. The band had been rehearsed, they were totally familiar with what he wanted them to play. He had every note that was to be played by every musician in his mind, he had the whole thing down and knew exactly what he wanted to hear and say. It was a real lesson for me to see an artist of his stature at work. You could lead him a little bit, but you really had to let him take over. For the first time, we heard something that didn't have to be messed around with, it was all there. And he only got better, he got more commercial without trying to make hits. He was doing what he wanted to do naturally, but the music and the songs became better and stronger."

Wexler recalls that Charles "counted off and led into an amazing succession of songs. I was stunned. I knew that he had hatched. I knew something fantastic had happened. Zenas Sears [Atlanta's number one R&B disc jockey] got us studio time at the Georgia Tech station WGST. They had this old engineer and we'd say, 'Bring up this pot, there's a sax solo coming in about four bars,' and about twelve bars later he'd say, 'What did you say?' We had to break every hour during the session so that they could read the news."

The relatively primitive recording conditions may actually have been more a help than a hindrance. The founders of Atlantic had consciously set out to make R&B records that had higher musical values, a cleaner, sharper sound, and more polish than the competition. If any general criticism can be levelled against the label's early-fifties productions, it's the arguable proposition that high standards sometimes subordinated feel and mood to a certain tidy clarity and definition. In Atlanta, under difficult conditions, Ertegun and Wexler got a record out of Charles that had the best of both worlds—feel and production values—and gave R.C. his first number one R&B hit. "I Got a Woman," released in January 1955, pressed the ecstasies of black church music into the service of a Dionysian sensuality. The record's rhythmic tension, with the sharply percussive horn and piano parts actually jerking away from the New Orleans–tinged skip-rope shuffle laid down by drummer William Peeples, perfectly complements the striking contrast between church-hymn musical cues and overtly sexual intent. Wexler may have understated his case when he called "I Got a Woman" "the first intimation of greatness from Ray Charles." Actually the record doesn't intimate, it confirms. The genius had arrived.

Further confirmation of Charles's arrival as a mature musical force came with the follow-up release to "I Got a Woman." RC's next single, "A Fool for You," also went to number one on the R&B charts. By this time it was 1955, and within the music business, change was in the air. Songs recorded by black artists, which had previously reached white listeners through more or less insipid copies or "cover versions" by white singers, were beginning, in a few cases, to outsell the whitebread competition. Smooth black vocal groups had "crossed over" to pop-chart success, followed by the black country-rockabilly of Chuck Berry's "Maybellene," Fats Domino's smooch/slow-dance favorite "Ain't That a Shame," and finally by the unbridled passion and rampant omni-sexuality of Little Richard. White artists, label owners and employees, managers and bookers still controlled the industry, but the big corporate record labels were being bested in the marketplace by small indie companies, operating with one- and two-man staffs and low overheads. Rhythm and blues, or at least some of its leading performers, was becoming rock & roll— mainstream popular music, at least potentially.

Prescient label owners had seen it coming. White teenagers were searching out and buying more and more indie records by black artists, and the music that failed to cross over from rhythm and blues to rock & roll seemed to be getting rawer, more rootsy. Memphis's Sam Phillips, of Sun Records and early Elvis fame, was among the first to capitalize on the apparent erosion of racial barriers in popular music. Presley himself was something of a Ray Charles fanatic—he covered "I Got a Woman" on his first album and in live performance on several national TV shows, including the top-rated Ed Sullivan circus. Charles received his first substantial composer royalties for the song, and it must have been tempting bait. Atlantic's founders had spotted the new trend as early as Phillips; they suggested changing the term rhythm and blues to "cat music" before Alan Freed made "rock & roll" the official byword.

They were naturally interested in the vastly increased sales possibilities of the white pop marketplace, and were having some success in that direction with La Vern Baker, Big Joe Turner, and others.

At this crucial juncture in Ray Charles's career, a very surprising thing happened. Charles refused to compromise his music with the simpler beat, more adolescent lyrics, and smoother singing that white rock & roll fans seemed to favor. He continued to write, arrange, play, and sing from his soul, and his records continued to sell almost exclusively within the black community. Even more remarkably, Atlantic, an enlightened company but one that needed to sell records as much as any other label, backed Charles all the way. His music suffered no dilution. In fact, mid-fifties Charles landmarks such as "Come Back Baby," "Drown in My Own Tears," and "Hallelujah I Love Her So," all recorded during rock & roll's breakthrough period from late 1954 to late 1955, were more soulfully incendiary, churchy, and rootsy—more "black," if you will—than many of his earlier discs.

"Atlantic, yeah, I give them some skin," Charles said later, "compared to other labels. And one of the things that Jerry Wexler did with me when I was over there was that he never ever told me what to do. They would send me material, but if I didn't like it, I'd sit down and write whatever I wanted to write. This is how I wrote so many songs in that period: They'd send me material I didn't like, I'd have to record, so I'd go in the studio and show them what I had written. And they'd say fine, go ahead and record it, and that was that. After all, by producing myself, doing my own songs and arrangements, I was saving the company money. They didn't have to go out and get Jesse Stone or somebody to supervise the sessions. And Atlantic has always done an excellent job with promotion. Even back in 1954, when they had a studio about the size of this hotel room or smaller, they already had a great rapport with the media people, radio station disc jockeys, and so on. Like I say, I have to give them some skin."

Along with that "skin" came plenty of great music. With more than thirty-five years' hindsight, we can appreciate that music on its own terms; it isn't necessary to categorize it as "R&B," "rock & roll," or "soul" in order to enjoy and be moved by it. Charles would certainly prefer that we listen in that spirit; he has never been fond of imposed boundaries within the broader arena of American vernacular music.

Charles has been credited as both a rock & roll innovator and as the artist who led the way from black rock & roll into the overtly gospel-based soul music of the sixties. But Charles refuses to take responsibility for any of this. "When people ask me what I think about soul music," he admitted, "I don't know what the hell to say. I think all these terms are names that the media give the music in order to try to describe what they mean. I don't know the difference between rhythm and blues, soul music, and the black version of disco; the rhythm patterns are the same. As far as putting more church into the music, I don't think I created anything there, really. You *can't* get away from your roots, and since I was reared in the church, a lot of church was within me. Naturally a lot of that had to come out in my music; I just didn't try to hide it."

Similarly, writing in *Brother Ray*, Charles insisted that "I never considered myself part of rock & roll. I've never given myself a lick of credit for either inventing it or having anything to do with its birth. My stuff was more adult. It was more difficult for teenagers to relate to; my stuff was filled with more despair than anything you'd associate with rock & roll. Since I couldn't see people dancing, I didn't write jitterbugs or twists. I wrote rhythms that moved me. . . . [My] style requires pure heart singing."

In order to catch Charles even paying lip service to categories, you have to dig back into a 1959 issue of *Billboard* in which, astonishingly, he defined the still-emerging rock & roll phenomenon as primarily a guitar-band idiom, much the way it's generally thought of today. "When they get a couple of guitars together with a backbeat, that's rock & roll," he said then. "Rhythm and blues is genuine down-to-earth Negro music."

I've often thought that the determinedly original and protean musical innovators credited with creating new musical idioms singlehandedly were in fact playing in no idiom but their own. The "great man" theory of history, in which a few larger-than-life individuals lead the way and the masses follow, sheeplike, in their wake, doesn't necessarily apply to American vernacular music. Recordings, live radio, stage shows, and encounters with a variety of other musicians, combined with roots and natural inclinations, are more likely to produce what we call a "style" through a complex synthesis or synergy.

Elvis Presley's Sun recordings, for example, may have inspired rockabilly, but they are not rockabilly, or rock & roll, themselves. There are no saxes, no drums, one country-simple electric guitar, and a voice that seems to draw equally from R&B, black and white gospel singing, country music, and mainstream pop. The Presley Sun sides are strong enough to stand out on their own: They need no claims of musical primogeniture to validate their singular excellence. I like to think of Ray Charles's music in the same way, even if we limit our discussion to the fifties Atlantic sides in this set. Call the Charles Atlantics whatever you wish: List all the categories, from gutbucket blues to uptown jazz, hillbilly ballads to Tin Pan Alley, church cadences to swing-band horn voicings to Latin rhythms. All of them figure in the mix; none of them individually offers more than a hint of the essential musical personality, let alone the scope, of Ray Charles.

Take a record like "Greenbacks," for example. An inner-city storefront church service provides the façade for a tighter-than-tight horn arrangement Jimmy Lunceford would have appreciated; the seasonings include passing chords derived from bebop and a snapping, percussive bite in the playing of Charles's exceptional band. The even more churchy "Drown in My Own Tears" bends gospel cadences in a blues-and-jazz direction. "Rockhouse" is down-and-dirty backroom piano combined with an acuity of tonal weight and sonic texture worthy of a more down-home Gil Evans.

As for commercial performance, "Hallelujah I Love Her So," basically a revamping of Dorothy Love Coates's "Hallelujah! I Love Him So," got some airplay on white pop radio in 1956. Perhaps that had to do with its unusually light-hearted feel, reminiscent of the sort of catchy gospel-based novelties recorded by Sister Rosetta Tharpe and the Lucky Millinder band in the early forties. "Drown in My Own Tears," not a Charles original, took a blues recorded by Lula Reed with Sonny Thompson deep into transcendental territory, and continued Charles's R&B winning streak while proving "too black" for pop radio. "Lonely Avenue," whose gospel inspiration seems to have been the Pilgrim Travelers' "How Jesus Died," and "Leave My Woman Alone," a tune known to churchgoers as "You Better Leave That Liar Alone," followed the commercial pattern set by "Drown in My Own Tears" and most of R.C.'s other mid-fifties Atlantic singles.

The path connecting white and black popular music was still running mostly one way. Of all Charles's tunes from the mid-fifties, only "Swanee River Rock" sounds like a possible concession to the rock &

roll market. It was Charles's first really significant pop hit, reaching number thirty-four on the *Billboard* chart. But if the song itself belongs to the world of nineteenth-century Americana, the rhythmic treatment Charles gave it was, typically, distinctive. R.C. requested a conga player for the session, and Jerry Wexler brought in Afro-Cuban heavyweight Mongo Santamaria. "Mongo was playing all these complicated Cuban fills, and Ray didn't want that," Wexler has recalled. "He'd say, 'Man, cut it back.' Mongo couldn't really understand too much English, but he simplified it to the point where he was playing a pattern, which Ray then wanted reversed. Ray went to Mongo and said, 'No play tick-a-tock, play tock-a-tick.' "

Charles employed every instrument and section in his band percussively when arranging a song, making sure each part was simple enough rhythmically, and syncopated properly to mesh with the other parts. The resulting polyrhythmic brew was then honed to an even sharper edge, for maximum impact.

It helped enormously that every man in Charles's touring band was a formidable player, equally adept at extemporization and part-reading, and that Charles was able to practice songs at his shows before taking the band in to record them. This was unusual in the fifties, when most artists were under the absolute dominion of their producers or record label owners. Little Richard, whose record sales far exceeded Charles's in the mid-fifties, waged a long and frustrating battle with the Specialty label's Art Rupe, who insisted on recording Richard with handpicked studio musicians despite Richard's insistence that he should go into the studio with his smoking stage band, the Upsetters. Serving as songwriter, arranger, song-selecter, and de-facto producer or co-producer of his own records, Charles enjoyed the kind of artistic freedom groups like the Beatles and the Yardbirds were still having to fight for in the mid-sixties.

Perhaps Charles could have accomplished as much with a substantially different band. And perhaps not. Originally assembled in Dallas, the group fully justified Charles's proud assertion, years later, that his fifties crew comprised "one of the best little bands in the country. You know, in those days, a lot of the guys didn't read [music]. Fortunately for me, the guys in my band could read, but they could also go the other way. I could say, 'Hey, man, set a riff behind me,' and hum some common riff. And each horn would find a harmony part to that riff and follow it. It was different from many musicians today; you try to set a riff and they don't know how to follow you. I was lucky to have cats in my small band who were able to play any kind of way you wanted them to play. Nowadays musicians are specialists; you might find a really good rock drummer, but when you want to play some jazz, they're lost. Lost! In the forties and fifties, there were so many musicians coming up, and coming out of the army and so on, that leaders could pick the cream of the crop, the musicians who could really play. There was a lot of competition; you had to be a good musician just to survive.

"We played dances in those days, and my band could carry a dance. Basically you're talking about three and a half hours of music, and the band would play instrumentals, good dance music, to get the people to come alive, and bring them in. Get them in, get them socializing, get them happy, and then stir them up! You really had to get a groove going, and keep it going. And I didn't wait to come out onstage. Up until around 1959, I had just two saxophonists and I was the third, playing alto sax. During that first hour of the show, which was instrumental, I stood up and played alto with the band for that hour. And I kept playing alto except when I was singing; then I'd sit at the piano."

At first, Amos Milburn alumnus Don Wilkerson was the band's tenor saxophonist and star soloist. He was a stomping, hard-driving player with that big Texas tenor sound, as he proved in the early sixties when he recorded with the superb bebop pianist Sonny Clark for Blue Note. It's Wilkerson playing those tough tenor solos on "I Got a Woman," "This Little Girl of Mine," and "Hallelujah I Love Her So," to name three of his more enduring efforts. David "Fathead" Newman was another Texan from the state that seemed peculiarly suited to nurturing saxmen with big, swaggering sounds and a booting way with rhythmic momentum. At first, Newman doubled on alto and baritone saxes. With Wilkerson's departure in 1956, Newman moved over to tenor and rapidly earned the reputation for excellence and fire he still enjoys. In 1957, when Memphis saxophonist Hank Crawford joined up, first on baritone, then as Charles's replacement on alto—the genius decided to concentrate on his singing and piano, once he could afford an extra man.

Finally, as the fifties were drawing to a close, Charles found Leroy "Hog" Cooper, the baddest, biggest-sounding baritone saxophonist who ever kicked an entire band along singlehandedly. With Crawford on alto (and copying and scoring much of the music), Newman smoldering on tenor, and Cooper anchoring it all with that foghorn baritone, Charles had found his definitive sax section. The two-man trumpet section included, at one time or another, the rock-solid lead man Joe Bridgewater and an astonishing technician and jazz improviser, Marcus Belgrave. William Peeples was the band's primary drummer until the late fifties, and Roosevelt Sheffield the most frequently employed bassist. I was fortunate enough to hear this band play dances around 1959–60, and they more than justified Charles's hard-won praise; their exhilarating tightness was matched only by the key players' magnificent solo turns.

But by 1957, this band was being called upon to play much more than the punchy R&B that had made their reputation. Between 1957 and 1959, Charles expanded his recorded repertory with big band standards, timely revivals of 1940s Louis Jordan jump 'n' jive, Latin proto-funk, and the first of what would be many forays into country and western music. Like Hank Snow, "The Singing Ranger" whose song he covered, the Ray Charles of the late fifties was "Movin' On."

When Ray Charles envisioned additional voices to cushion and contrast with his own, he heard women's voices. His first recruit was the gospel-trained Mary Ann Fisher, whose lovely, expressive voice seemed to have an inner core of spun steel—her strength was a tensile strength, springy, flexible; it would twist and bend, but it would never break. Fisher sang torch songs and some duets with Charles at live shows, and he celebrated her arrival with "Mary Ann," heard on volume 2. Around the same time, Jesse Stone, the Atlantic session leader, composer, and songwriter who had supervised Charles's early recordings for the label, came to his aid one more time. Stone had trained and developed a "girl group" originally known as the Cookies. Charles hired them, added Mary Ann Fisher, and presto!—the Raeletts. This group of backup singers played an increasingly important role in the maestro's music from 1956 through the end of Charles's original tenure with Atlantic. In addition to Fisher, the Raeletts included Darlene McRae and the especially incandescent Margie Hendrix.

"I'd always liked the sound of girls' gospel groups," Charles wrote in *Brother Ray*. "I could have had four men and formed a regular all male gospel quartet . . . but instead I wanted the flavor of a man's voice— my voice—set against women. I hadn't heard anyone do that in popular music before." But, Charles added, with the determined individualism typical of him, "I didn't really care whether it was an old idea or a new one. I just knew that was what I was searching for."

"What Kind of Man Are You" deftly balanced the elemental Raeletts vocal blend, an intense lead vocal by Charles, and a featured spot for Mary Ann Fisher, whose performance generates enough electricity to light up a switchboard. This single achieved a level of intensity and spiritual fervor that made listening, or more precisely feeling the music, one of those ineffable adventures of the soul some psychologists refer to as a "peak experience." As always, Charles refused to let an artistic breakthrough degenerate through repetition into a formula. He seemed particularly restless from 1957 through '59, and his recordings chart his mercurial experiments.

His musical sources continued to broaden. He dipped into the late-swing-era Kansas City canon for "I Want a Little Girl," which he made his own with some especially imaginative phrasing—listen to the way he embroiders the melody when he comes to the words "nylon hose." "Yes Indeed" was drawn from the more polished, uptown side of swing-era jazz, as represented by the song's composer, the arranger-bandleader Sy Oliver. Rhythmically, though, Charles's "Yes Indeed" is light-years beyond the swing era. There's a hint of New Orleans–style "slow drag" pulling against the steamroller swing of the rhythm section, another of Charles's anticipations of the rhythmic devices later codified as "funk." "I Had a Dream" returns us to deep gospel—so deep the record sounds capable of raising spirits, or at least goose bumps, until Charles subtly lightens up, defusing the spooky intensity—the performance has built up just as it begins to wind down of its own accord.

"Tell All the World About You" is another significant milestone, a further development of Charles's ongoing rhythmic workshop. Mongo Santamaria is back on congas, playing a clear, specific counter-syncopation that builds tension by pulling at the momentum with an opposing tilt, but periodically releases that tension by snapping back squarely into the pocket. On this level the record is a meticulously orchestrated rhythmic counterpoint with hair-trigger balance and a kind of controlled plasticity. Somehow the push-pull of staggered accents and tension/release cycles lock into one monolithic groove that's almost heavy metal.

The folk-pop evergreen "My Bonnie" sounds like it should have been Charles's next big hit. Instead, Charles scored with an atypical "cover" of a record by another gospel-blues pioneer, Nappy Brown. "The Right Time" (which Brown himself had borrowed from a 1937 piano blues record by Roosevelt Sykes, "Night Time Is the Right Time") featured a lead vocal that followed Brown's performance to a degree unusual for Charles. But the Raeletts brought a richer texture to Charles's version, and instead of emulating Brown's screaming emotional peak, the genius gave Margie Hendrix room to raise the rafters on her own terms. Add "Fathead" Newman's preaching alto saxophone solo and the resulting mixture sounds hot enough to scorch your eardrums. But despite a four-month stay on the R&B charts, "The Right Time" saw little pop-chart success. Much pop music, after all, deals in fantasy, and Charles's records like "The Right Time" are nothing if not the Real Thing.

"What'd I Say," Charles's first million-seller, was another of his original compositions, but he didn't come up with it entirely on his own. The central importance of call-and-response in "What'd I Say"—Charles sings or moans, the Raeletts repeat his phrase, and the voices keep up a running dialogue with horns and rhythm—was no fluke. Like the early spirituals, and before them West African tribal music, "What'd I Say" began as an improvised interchange between lead singer, band, and audience, or, in gospel terms, between the preacher and his congregation. The difference was that in "What'd I Say" Charles was preaching what he described in his autobiography as "the sweet sounds of love."

I asked Charles for a full account of the song's genesis when I interviewed him, and he went into more detail than he allowed "What'd I Say" in his autobiography. So this telling should be compared to the one in Brother Ray, though the two differ only in detail. During late 1958 and early 1959, Charles was playing a series of dances in the Midwest. At one of these dances—"I believe it was in some little place right outside of Pittsburgh, called Brownsville, Pennsylvania," he said—a combination of fast-tempo performances and long working hours left the evening's final fifteen minutes open. "I had sung everything I could think of," Charles recalled. "I really had. So I said to the guys, 'Look, I'm gonna start this thing off. I don't know where I'm going, so y'all just follow me.' And I said to the girls, 'Whatever I say, just repeat after me.' I started with that bass line, the one you hear on the record, and we got to the part where the girls and me were going 'unnh' back and forth at each other, and it went on. To make a long story short, the people were dancing like hell off this thing. When the dance was over, a lot of them came up to me and asked, 'Where can I buy that record?' I didn't know what they were talking about.

"And they said, 'You know, that last thing you played, that was wild, we loved it.' I said there wasn't any record of that, and they all said, 'What??!' So the next night I thought, well, I'm going to try this thing again. So we kept trying it, going from town to town, and we got the same kind of reaction: People just went crazy. And they loved that little 'unnh,' 'unnh,' especially when the girls started doing it. The people would start to answer, too. Finally I decided that if that many people seemed to like this thing, I'm going to go into New York and record it. So it was a made-up song, made up on the spot, and you can tell if you listen, because the verses don't really have anything to do with each other. They're just made-up verses, but that isn't what the people cared about. I think what they liked was that rhythm, and of course the 'unnh—unnh.' Everybody knew what that meant."

In a nutshell, the record's initial appeal was that it was sexy, a fact Charles freely admits and has never apologized for. "Isn't it funny," he mused years later, "how that was considered vulgar in those days, and now people sing and do almost anything on radio and TV. When we did it, it was forbidden territory, but *that was what the people loved*, that little sexy sound in it. Because it did suggest something, there's no doubt about that. But hell, let's face it, everybody knows about that. It's how all of us got here. So I don't know what the world wants to hide from it for. But even when it started selling in the black community, the white radio stations wouldn't play it. It was too suggestive for them until Elvis did it, and then, of course, it was all right."

"What'd I Say" was truly a record beyond category. On the surface it was pure gospel call-and-response, but there was also a distinct Latin influence—listen to the syncopations drummer Milt Turner plays on his cymbals against the left-hand Latin boogie of Charles's electric piano. The new keyboard, a Wurlitzer Charles had bought for road work after one too many bouts with out-of-tune house pianos, was a fresh sound in 1959, and that helped make the record distinctive as well. It was Charles who decided to bring the Wurlitzer to his recording session on February 18, 1959.

Even after Charles, his band, and the Raeletts recorded "What'd I Say," there was more work to be done in the studio. "I mixed 'What'd I Say' three times," recording engineer Tom Dowd recalls. "I edited out a lot. They [Atlantic] wanted some of the more suggestive parts out, so I scissored it and resequenced the recording. We also needed to make it shorter, because the record could have gone on for ten minutes." As it was, there was enough of "What'd I Say" for a double-sided single, labelled Part One and Part Two. And the "sweet sounds of love" still came through loud and clear. The single peaked at number six on the pop charts and, of course, number one on the R&B charts.

During the brief time remaining under his Atlantic contract, Charles continued to experiment widely, almost feverishly, as if he was in a hurry to show the world, or another record company with more money, just how much he was capable of. While still at Atlantic he recorded with strings, with an all-star big band, and with hand-picked jazz combos, while continuing to make the R&B singles collected in this box. Even on the R&B front, he ranged restlessly from idiom to idiom. "I'm Movin' On" and "I Believe to My Soul," recorded back to back, could hardly have been more disparate. The former tune had been a country and western hit for Hank Snow, "The Singing Ranger," in 1950. Charles again used a flavoring of Latin rhythm and the well-developed call-and-response between his own voice and those of the Raeletts. A steel guitar was even added, possibly to make the song's provenance more immediately evident. Otherwise, it sounded like pure Ray Charles. And so did "I Believe to My Soul," which anticipates mid-sixties soul music as surely as "I'm Movin' On" presaged Charles's later successes with country songs. "I Believe to My Soul" burned from beginning to end, and serves as an appropriately incendiary climax to the singer's Atlantic R&B years. It also includes another kind of first. If you listen closely, you may be able to tell that the Raeletts who answer Charles's lead vocal throughout the song are not the Raeletts at all. They are Charles himself, multitracked. Tom Dowd remembers that "the girls couldn't get it right, and Ray said to me, 'Hey, pardner, you got enough tracks?' I said 'Yeah' and he did all four female parts on the remaining tracks. One take on each part." No wonder the folks around Atlantic called him a genius.

When Charles's Atlantic contract expired late in 1959, ABC made the singer an incredibly lucrative offer for the time, one he could hardly afford to turn down. He was guaranteed at least $50,000 a year in advances, a 5 percent royalty, and another percentage for his services as producer of his own material. He also was guaranteed eventual ownership of all his ABC master tapes. This was an unusual deal for any artist. For one who had proved his worth almost entirely in the R&B marketplace, it was unprecedented. Atlantic simply couldn't match it at the time, but if ABC was gambling, their gamble paid off handsomely. Charles hit for them with "Sticks and Stones," "Georgia on My Mind," the *Modern Sounds in Country and Western Music* albums, and the other breakthroughs that have made his name a household word in white and black households around the world.

The folks at Atlantic heard about Ray's imminent departure through the grapevine, as Ertegun recently explained to Yves Beauvais, one of this set's producers: "He didn't know he was leaving. He called up from New Orleans, I remember very well, to tell us he was coming to New York to record. I'd heard two days before that a contract had been filed with the musicians' union from ABC-Paramount for a Ray Charles session. I told him I'd heard that rumor and he said: 'Well, I don't know about that, I'm coming to record for you, I think.' I replied, 'That would be great, but you know, we have to clear up what this is,' and eventually we found out that whoever at the time was advising him had made a deal elsewhere. To this day, I really believe it was not his own intention to leave Atlantic.

"It was a terrible loss for us, because we had just expanded into different types of music with him with the *Genius of Ray Charles* album, which Nesuhi [Ertegun] produced. It was an album of standards with a big band and strings, and that's the direction he wanted to go into. This was his first real departure into a big band phase which is still with him now. His leaving the label was certainly a great disappointment for us; we would have done anything to keep him."

If Charles's later years were a gratifying commercial success, artistically the Atlantic sides captured him at his zenith. During these years he grew from imitation into true originality. He fused heretofore disparate musical idioms. He wrote his own tunes (something he rarely did after leaving Atlantic) and arranged and recorded them with his own crack touring band.

Although a certain amount of pride can be discerned, Jerry Wexler of Atlantic was entirely justified in stating that, "In terms of purity and musical value, he cut his best sides for us. It was righteous roots music. It was intrinsically great music." And, Wexler might have added, this was music that would always sound fresh. Searching for hits while refusing to compromise his personal vision, Ray Charles created a body of work for Atlantic that still stands tall—work as enduring as anything in the history of American vernacular music.

Liner Notes for Sam Cooke's *Night Beat*

(RCA, 1995 reissue)

I could tell from all the way across the local newspaper's marbled lobby that something was wrong with my friend who worked in the coffee shop. She was going about her usual business, wearing the uniform dress and disposable apron our Little Rock newspaper deemed appropriate for "kitchen help," but there was a look of profound sadness on her face instead of her usual radiant smile, and her eyes were brimming with tears. And there was something else about her, something she'd never let me see before: maximum anger, held in check under maximum pressure. I thought of a song, Sam Cooke's "Laughin' and Cryin'." "I keep on trying to hide my feelings," he sang, "trying to hide my soul." My friend was trying hard.

It was the winter of 1964, my friend and I were both in our teens, but in certain ways we were strangers. She was, as far as I knew, the newspaper's only black employee; I worked part-time after school, moving immense rolls of newsprint around the basement. What we had in common, the whole basis of our friendship, really, was music. It was all we talked about when we got together on coffee breaks or after work. We each had our individual heroes and solid senders, our "wait-till-you-hear-this" discoveries, but when it came to naming the greatest of them all, we were in complete agreement: Sam Cooke ruled.

And now my friend was telling me, "They shot Sam." Who shot him, I asked, knowing there was only one Sam that meant that much to her, or to me. "I don't know," she said, no longer able to hold back her tears. "They said—who cares what they said. SAM COOKE IS DEAD." And with that she straightened her dress, wiped away the tears, and went back to work, serving hamburgers and Cokes to people who were utterly unaware that anyone of importance had passed. Most people who grew up in the 1960s remember exactly where they were and what they were doing when they heard of the Kennedy assassination; the day I recall with preternatural clarity is the day we lost Sam Cooke.

Cooke meant many things to many people. To some, he was the most gifted pop vocalist of his time; no more, no less. He was a spellbinding performer; my friend and I had seen him play in Little Rock a few short months before his death, and we weren't just captivated, we were utterly entranced and illuminated, along with everyone else. It was the gritty, soulful sort of show captured on *Live at the Harlem Square Club*, chock full of hits, most of which Cooke himself had written, arranged, and in effect produced. But seeing him that night was more like going to church than going to an R&B show.

I didn't realize at the time that from 1950 to 1957, before he'd ever made a pop or R&B record, Sam Cooke was already a star in the world of black gospel music as lead singer with the Soul Stirrers, one of the most popular and respected groups of its time. Many of his earlier pop fans, after he made the switch to secular music with his spectacular first hit, "You Send Me," had seen him sing in their own church or town hall; some resented his abandoning gospel for the more lucrative world of pop, but many more cheered him on. Whether the text was addressed to "my Lord" or "my baby," people continued to attend Sam Cooke shows expecting to "have church," and church, at its most inspirational and transcendent, is what he gave them.

His music was so spiritually resonant and nurturing, it preached so eloquently and prayed for a better day with such contagious fervor, that it could penetrate the deepest despair, find a glimmer of hope even in the heart of darkness. After far too many disappointments and casual indignities had bruised the spirit and sapped the will, Sam Cooke's music could actually make life seem worth living again.

And he was inspirational in other ways. While paying his bills playing R&B shows on the "chitlin circuit," he was slowly and methodically working up a more "uptown" presentation he could take into a Las Vegas hotel or a major club like New York's Copacabana. His first attempt at playing the Copa was a disaster. Cooke learned from the experience and returned to the Copa in triumph. Similarly, he started his own record label, SAR, as another step in the crossover of pop and gospel music—a crossover Cooke first conceptualized, then worked to make a reality. He was one of the first popular artists to take a firm stand against the segregation of concert audiences by race—and the first with enough earning power, determination, and sheer charisma to have his way and make it stick.

White record buyers were largely unaware of this side of Sam Cooke, but to many black musicians and would-be record-business tycoons, Cooke was a hero and a role model. The battles he fought were their battles as well, and he opened doors many more black Americans would walk through in the coming years.

Much of what Sam Cooke meant during his tragically foreshortened career is history now. Thankfully, the music remains. The best of his singles, collected on *The Man and His Music,* are as original and virtuosic as one could wish. He wrote most of them, gave his arranger Rene Hall specific rhythm section, horn, and string parts to orchestrate, and served as de facto producer at all his sessions, whether for his own records or for releases by other artists on his SAR roster. The problem with the best of Cooke's own recordings is simply that there aren't enough of them. There are the singles; his earlier gospel recordings with the Soul Stirrers (Cooke at his very best, according to many aficionados); and two splendid live albums, one from the Copa and one, considerably more muscular, from a black dance hall in Miami, the Harlem Square Club.

But when Cooke was making records, singles were the name of the game. Even the Harlem Square album went unreleased until more than twenty years after Cooke's death. In those days, an "album" was usually one of several hit singles and a lot of "filler." In Cooke's case, the "filler" was often Broadway-style tunes and standards for which he seemed to have little natural affinity. He could certainly hit the note, as the more carefully chosen and sympathetically arranged standards on the albums handily demonstrate. What is lacking in the less successful album tracks is some evident emotional connection between the singer and his material. What isn't lacking—but should be—is overdone orchestrations and chirpy "pop" vocal choruses, which only made matters worse.

This brings us to *Night Beat*, an anomaly in the Cooke discography. Backed by a superbly supple and attentive soul combo, Cooke sang his heart out on these informal, late-night recording sessions from winter 1963. There isn't even a hint of filler. The result is a vocal tour de force, and just under the music's gracefully melodious surface, the emotional waters run deep.

The remarkably consistent mood of the album is a 2 A.M., last-call sort of feeling. It's a blues mood, but the diversity of the songs—from spirituals to bluesy ballads to Cooke's sophisticated gospel-rooted originals—and the singer's ability to make every song his own, regardless of genre, keep it from becoming a "blues album."

Above all, this is a *Sam Cooke* album—his greatest, according to many. Of all his records, it's the one you'd put on to show the uninitiated what an extraordinary vocal musician and communicator the man was. It's also by far Cooke's most intimate album, sounding for all the world like you're sitting in a dark, late-night bar listening to a man pour his heart out. Even as he worries and embellishes the lines about "trying to hide my feelings, trying to hide my soul," he's revealing, not hiding. We can only speculate as to what masterworks Cooke might have given us if he'd had the time and the opportunity to make more of his own albums in his own way, with only himself to satisfy. Thankfully, we do have one such album, this one, and a glorious album it is.

Even Rene Hall, the bandleader, arranger, and session musician from New Orleans who worked with Cooke throughout the singer's career, speaks for his former associate in tones bordering on awe. "I rate him as being a genius," says Hall, "as a person who was able to create as he did with no formal musical training whatsoever. He could hum a part to you, and what he would hum would be in perfect sequence with the orchestrational concept. Or Sam would tell me, 'I want the bass to play this,' and hum the part, and he was never musically incorrect. I never had to say, 'Sam, this isn't the right note for the bass'; it just never happened. He could hear the entire orchestra, the string lines, the bass lines, the horn lines, the backing singers' lines. And as a spiritual singer, he had never dealt with these things before. Cliff White [Cooke's longtime guitarist] would hear Sam do things and think they'd never work, like the way he went from major to minor chords in his version of 'Summertime.' Things like that, Cliff was going, 'Jesus Christ!' and then he'd do what Sam asked for, not believing that it would work, and when he tried it, it did. Even at the beginning of his career, just before he left the Soul Stirrers, he was trying to cut his first pop session, but he said he didn't get the feel of the songs. Then he told me that if I showed him a few chords on the guitar, he said, 'Maybe I can come up with a tune.' So I showed him three chords, and on the three chords he learned, he composed 'You Send Me.' He said, 'Man, this is gold; I can write a lot of these things.' I consider something like that a gift, a special talent."

Cooke was such a protean musical figure that even though he can legitimately be considered the original soul singer, the first successful gospel artist to understand and effectively utilize hard gospel elements in a deliberately "pop" context, this reputation rests on a relatively small part of his recorded output. Certainly his training and his most enduring stylistic orientation were in gospel, and Cooke-penned singles like "Shake," "Another Saturday Night," "Soothe Me," and "Bring It on Home to Me" were among the first and deepest soul hits.

But as Rene Hall observes, "Sam had a very strange ear, different from even gospel singers. Because most gospel singers deal in sevenths—like blues-type changes—and Sam dealt in sixths. Like you hear him do his yoo-hoo-hoo, that's sixths. I had played jazz, and we did a lot of sixths and ninths and so on, but it was strange for me to hear that from a gospel singer . . . because Sam wasn't actually singing proper gospel, he was singing a pop concept of his own. The entire concept or approach to melody that Sam used was completely original. Even when he did a standard tune, and he did quite a few standards in his day, he would approach them with his original version of the melody."

Cooke altered melodies the way a jazz musician will, as a way of personalizing a tune. He drew on gospel, blues, and related idioms for his basic stylistic orientation, but while his melodic embellishments had a gospelish fluidity and timing, the intervals he sang were more common in jazz than in gospel or blues—more sixths than sevenths, as Rene Hall put it.

What does it all add up to? None of our tired old genre clichés is inclusive enough to describe, let alone contain, the artistry of Sam Cooke. It's great American music—Sam Cooke music, a genre in itself. It may not have the special emotional relevance for you that it has for me, but I'm sure it will get to you, too, in its own way. Because as soon as you put on *Night Beat* and hear Cooke's first mellifluous tones, riding nothing but a light bass, an occasional tap on the snare drum, and his own sovereign command of rhythm and inflection, something magical begins to happen. Cooke and his musicians—who include pianist Ray Johnson, organist Billy Preston, lead guitarist Barney Kessell, alternating drummers Hal Blaine and Ed Hall, bassist Cliff Hils, and Cliff White and probably Rene Hall on rhythm guitar—are going to take you to church.

Just stand back and let the man sing.

Ernie Isley: The Family Way

PENTHOUSE | APRIL 1977

"Some of this disco music is the pits," said a sweat-drenched Ernie Isley as he draped himself over a folding chair backstage at Madison Square Garden. He was wearing an unlikely looking combination of leather, furs, and something that appeared to be vinyl, and he had been playing so hard that the furs were wringing wet, the leather soggy, the vinyl streaked.

"On the other hand," he continued, "some disco music is actual dynamite. The thing is, the public wants dance music, something with at least the insinuation of a backbeat. Rock & roll is going back to where it was at the beginning; you could always dance to Chuck Berry or Elvis or the early Beatles. Another thing you have to remember about discos is that people are exposed to a lot of new, progressive music there. Around 1967–68, you could go to the Cheetah in New York and they'd be playing records like Jimi Hendrix's 'Purple Haze.' It may be that whatever the people arc dancing to is what's actually happening."

Ernie had just finished stirring up a near-capacity Garden crowd with one last screaming, super-amplified guitar solo while his three older brothers, Ronald, Rudolph, and Kelly, chanted and grunted and shouted and shrieked. Although he is only twenty-four, he has been a member of the family band since 1969. The original Isley Brothers began as a vocal trio back in 1957. No other rock group can match this longevity record. What's more, the Isleys are maintaining their present level of popularity without trafficking in nostalgia. Even Elvis Presley still performs his early hits. Yet the Isley Brothers never do "Shout," their 1959 million-seller, or "Twist and Shout," its equally successful 1962 sequel, or their influential 1969 single, "It's Your Thing." Nor do they directly invoke the specter of Jimi Hendrix, their former lead guitarist. The Isleys may be veterans, but they remain determinedly fresh and contemporary.

In fact, the disco-conscious 1970s have been their most consistently productive period. Every album they have released since mid-1973, when they began recording for Columbia, has sold well over one million copies, and "That Lady," "Live It Up," and "Fight the Power" were all gold singles. Although a change-of-pace album, *Harvest for the World*, contained mostly ballads and didn't yield a single hit, it went gold anyway, within weeks of its release. Yet the Isleys are rarely written about in the rock press, and many pop radio stations ignore their records entirely.

The Isley Brothers' music is and always has been very, very black, not too black for the many white fans who buy their records, but too black for many white rock writers and disc jockeys.

"Black music has always been kept in some sort of corner," complained Ronald Isley, the group's chunkily handsome lead singer, when he was asked about publicity and air play. "White friends of ours from out of town will say, 'I didn't hear your record,' when I happen to know that it sold, say, eight hundred fifty thousand copies. Certain stations just didn't want to play it. Right now the one big outlet for black music is the discos."

Ronald gave Ernie a fatherly hug, as all the older brothers do when he has played particularly well, and left to change his clothes. Kelly, whose heavy frame filled a bright yellow jumpsuit, added, "We never tried to follow any other act, never tried to cut a 'disco' single. Remember, 'Shout' was a six-minute-and-something record with two different tempos in it. People said it would never get played. The fact of the matter is that we move people, and we enjoy doing that. It's really a carry-over from gospel music, which moves people automatically."

Most contemporary black vocalists were gospel singers first, but the Isleys never really abandoned the gospel sound. Ronald, Rudolph, Kelly, and their brother, Vernon, sang with their mother before they entered grade school. Vernon was killed by a truck while he was riding his bicycle, but the other three carried on. In 1957, when Ronald turned sixteen, the Isleys decided to seek fame and fortune in New York City. A chance meeting on the Greyhound bus they caught led immediately to auditions with various record companies and to a management agreement. Soon they were performing at black theaters like the Howard and the Apollo, and although they were still imitating hit groups, notably Frankie Lymon and the Teenagers, they made good money.

After several unsuccessful records, the brothers made "Shout" for RCA. It was a thinly secularized slice of gospel hysteria, the sort of music one might hear in a storefront church in any American ghetto. But such music had never been heard on pop radio. When "Shout" was released, in 1959, *American Bandstand* banality was gaining the upper hand in pop. The record seized the imaginations of rock-starved whites as well as the affections of blacks, who knew that "shouting" was something people did in church when the spirit moved them. After several years more of stabs at the Top Ten, the brothers recorded "Twist and Shout." A year after its release, it was revived by the Beatles on their first album. The three Isleys toured England, where they hung out with up-and-coming rockers like the Rolling Stones.

After an on-again-off-again relationship with Motown, the Isleys added the young Jimi Hendrix and began to revamp their style in the direction of progressive rock. Then younger brother Ernie came in to fill Hendrix's shoes; Marvin, another younger brother, was added on bass; and Isley brother-in-law Chris Jasper joined as keyboard player. By 1969 they were a self-contained family unit except for their drummer, and on records Ernie began to play the drum parts as well as guitar.

The new sound was a kind of black rock: still gospel shouting on top, but now supported by a lean, loud, aggressive instrumental quartet. Songs stretched longer as Ernie began matching his older brother's churchy vocal improvisations with long, searing guitar solos.

Of all the brothers, he is the most openly enthusiastic, and more and more his extraordinary musicianship dominates the group's performances. His recorded guitar solos—the best is the full-throttle improvisation on "Hope You Feel Better," from the album *The Heat Is On*—are the most bracing examples of the art since Hendrix. But they are personal extensions, not out-and-out copies, like the work of so many white Hendrix imitators.

"I just love the guitar," he said. "The sound of it, the feel of it, the way it looks. I never know what I'm going to do when I play a solo, and, really, that's why I love rock & roll. It's free—that's what makes it. You can't take one song or one form and define the style."

The lights in the dressing room flickered on and off. It was time to be going back to Teaneck, New Jersey, where the Isleys live separately but practically within shouting distance of each other (the younger, unmarried members still in the same house with their mother). "I think the reason the group survived so long is that our roots are the church," Ernie said as he got up to leave. "We stuck together and believed in 'Honor Thy Father and Thy Mother' and in God." To which Ronald Isley, passing by on his way out, could only add: "That's the foundation of this whole business, the foundation of rock & roll music. It had to come from somewhere, and the church is where it all came from."

Monkey Hips and Rice: The "5" Royales Anthology (Rhino)

ROLLING STONE | AUGUST 11, 1994

"Don't try to figure out where I come from," "5" Royales guitarist and songwriter Lowman Pauling warns at the beginning of "The Slummer the Slum," the group's 1958 social-protest-as-dance-craze single: "I could be a smart guy from Wall Street, or I could be the Purple People Eater's son."

And it's true that Pauling, whose compositions for the Royales included "Dedicated to the One I Love," "Think" (covered by James Brown), and "Tell the Truth" (covered by Ray Charles), was a hard one to figure. He penned soul-deep ballads and rockers that chronicled depression and discrimination, advised listeners to "get something out of it, take what's yours," and indulged in a mature, explicit sexuality far beyond the bounds of the period's teen-slanted double-entendres.

But perhaps the biggest mystery is why the Royales still aren't recognized as the definitive late-fifties rock & roll vocal group and the leading-edge innovators of the coming soul era—and why Pauling's name doesn't automatically come up whenever the music's greatest songwriters and most influential electric guitarists are enumerated.

Rhino had the right idea. In putting together their latest batch of classic R&B reissues from the King label's rich catalog, Rhino limited the likes of Little Willie John and Hank Ballard's Midnighters to a single CD each while lovingly assembling a two-disc set, *Monkey Hips and Rice: The "5" Royales Anthology*, from the best of the "5" Royales' King and earlier Apollo label material. For the first time, one can go to a single source to sample the Royales' brilliant body of work—not just the pre-Shirelles "Dedicated" and the other hits but riveting obscurities like "Say It," with its unexpected snarls of overdriven electric guitar, and a great 1957 proto-soul outing in which Pauling notes almost matter-of-factly that being broke and lonely "makes me feel like *messin' up*." Memphis soul supremo Steve Cropper has named Pauling as his major guitar influence, and veteran musicians like Dr. John have praised the gospel-rooted "5" Royales as the most creative and musicianly of all the vocal groups making the late-fifies rock & roll circuit.

But the Royales' reign as R&B hit makers didn't last much past the fifties, and since then musicians (and a handful of writers such as this set's compiler, Ed Ward) have been the group's only advocates. *Monkey Hips and Rice* may or may not help remedy this neglect, but it does provide the best opportunity yet for contemporary listeners to connect with one of rock's richest hidden treasures.

Savor it; Lowman Pauling himself advises, in one of his uniquely philosophical lyrics: "Don't go too fast/The faster you go, the quicker you will get to the end."

Danger: High Voltage from Stax

ROLLING STONE | MAY 16, 1991

The Complete Stax/Volt Singles: 1959–1968 (Atlantic)
Various Artists

The soul music recorded at the Stax/Volt company's Memphis studio during the sixties is a deep well that just won't run dry. It has been a primary influence in rock from early Creedence, Eric Clapton, and Bonnie Raitt, right up through Peter Gabriel's electro-Stax "Sledgehammer" and on to the latest album by Robert Cray. But the records made at Stax in its sixties heyday—from the collected works of Otis Redding to seminal dance disks like Rufus Thomas's "Walking the Dog," Eddie Floyd's "Knock on Wood," and Sam and Dave's "Soul Man," as well as seldom-heard masterpieces like Mabel John's "Your Good Thing (Is About to End)" or Barbara and the Browns' "In My Heart"—remain unsurpassed.

What made those records great has been the subject of much debate. Credit the musicians who played on almost every Stax/Volt release while making their own classic records as Booker T. and the MG's and the Mar-Keys. Credit a stable of exceptional vocal talents. Credit the in-house songwriting and producing and the deliberately dry, acoustically "flat" engineering, studiously imitated by the Band on that group's two first and best albums.

Insiders talk about the funnel-shaped studio, a converted movie theater, where the sound of musicians at the narrow end seemed to grow bigger, fuller, more resonant as the room widened. And there is Stax's close relationship with the surrounding community. The movie theater's former candy stand was converted into a record store where newly recorded songs were tried out on customers from the black inner-city neighborhood surrounding the building; singles were sometimes released or canned depending on those man-in-the-street reactions.

Atlantic Records distributed Stax/Volt singles and albums until 1968, when, with flagship artist Redding gone, the company's delicate record-making chemistry began to deteriorate. During this period, Stax/Volt made enduring albums that ranged from Otis Redding's *Dictionary of Soul* to bluesman Albert King's *Born Under a Bad Sign*, which signaled a challenge—and in many ways a change in style—for every blues-based guitarist in rock. But singles were the name of the game in those days, for soul-dance labels at any rate. And in that game Stax's track record was one of almost astonishingly consistent quality, as this nine-CD box set handily demonstrates.

The Complete Stax/Volt Singles: 1959–1968 includes every A-side and many outstanding B-sides released under the Stax and Volt imprints in the singles format during the company's glory years. The set is definitive; for once, everything has been done right. Stax's stereo mixes for albums never compared to the label's superb monaural pressings, so the music in this set has been remastered in mono, using a "specially modified and restored Ampex 350 full-track mono machine with original tube electronics." Bill Inglot, best known for his award-winning work at Rhino, was in charge of the remastering process.

Inglot's stated intention—"to re-create the Stax sound on today's stereo systems without compromise"—has been fully realized. There is a sharp increase in definition and clarity, dramatic enough to bring out nuances in even the most familiar material, but the characteristic, never-duplicated Stax sound remains, its integrity intact. The meticulous work by reissue producer Steve Greenberg and booklet author Rob Bowman are equally praiseworthy.

And American music doesn't get any better than this. The set begins with Chips Moman's 1959–1962 productions, an intriguing key to the early development of the Southern soul sound. Traces of influences are still apparent—a bit of Allen Toussaint's early Minit-label productions here, a touch of the Curtis Mayfield–produced Chicago sound there. A surprising undercurrent of Latin rhythms runs though these sides as well.

The spontaneous combustion that resulted when the racially inte-grated Stax studio band honed its chops to a razor's edge can be followed single by single, from the days of Moman's departure to start his own stu-dio, American, through early hits like the Mar-Keys' "Last Night" and on into the full flowering that came with the arrival of Otis Redding, Eddie Floyd, and Sam and Dave. Once the rhythm section solidified into the core quartet of guitarist/producer/songwriter Steve Cropper, organist Booker T. Jones, bassist Duck Dunn, and drummer Al Jackson Jr.—ably supported by Wayne Jackson, Andrew Love, and the other Memphis Horns—all the right elements were in place.

As one moves progressively through the box—warning: It can be highly addictive—surprises abound. Relative unknowns, especially over-looked Stax soul women such as Barbara Stephens, Wendy Rose, and the mighty Mabel John, turn in scorching vocal performances that at least approach the heights scaled by Otis Redding and Sam and Dave. Art-ists often considered second-stringers—William Bell, Carla Thomas—emerge as versatile, resourceful stylists, real musical heavyweights. Bell in particular ties the entire Stax legacy together, with records ranging from the deepest gospel-blues ballads to jazz-flavored material to catchy, original pop tunes. Bell was to Stax what Marvin Gaye was to Motown.

But the real surprise is how stirring and special *all* this music is. Out of 244 songs, there are no more than a dozen out-and-out bombs, and several of these were vanity records featuring talentless but influential disc jockeys. The rest—and that's a lot of music—ranges from the merely fine to the utterly transcendent. What other American label can equal this track record? Not even the Chess and Sun catalogs are as potent, song after song after song.

Willie Mitchell, the Memphis producer of hits by Al Green and other artists, has spoken of Memphis music's unique rhythmic peculiarities, which are fully displayed in this collection. There's a lazy, behind-the-beat *feel*, set by Al Jackson's outstandingly creative drumming and the supple, loping Duck Dunn bass lines. But, as Mitchell noted, just when you think the tempo is almost dragging, there's a kind of "sway," and suddenly the whole band is right on top of the beat.

This rhythmic legerdemain is first evident in the almost infinitesimal delays that follow the stop-time breaks in the Mar-Keys' seminal instrumental hit "Last Night." The late Al Jackson Jr. admitted, when interviewed during the late sixties, to taking regular vacations in Jamaica, and one does hear grooves that hybridize Southern fatback with rock steady and reggae. A certain fondness for rumba blues on some of the earlier Stax releases also figures into this equation.

But in the end the timing that's so important in this music eludes precise analysis. It's a kind of aural sleight of hand. At least one thing is certain: Hearing Stax music clearly and at length, in all its rhythmic permutations, leads to the conclusion that the staff musicians should be credited as pioneers of funk on a par with the great New Orleans studio players and the mid-sixties James Brown Band.

Obscure but startling nuggets abound, and the clarity of the remastering reveals new detail even in the classic vocals of Otis Redding. But ultimately, the whole is greater than the sum of the parts, and the parts, especially in these original mono mixes, mesh too finely to be exhaustively isolated and catalogued. Still, trying can be fun; this outstanding set will give analytical listeners as much pleasure as those more taken with the music's energy, purity of conception, and heavy emotional payload. Finally, after years of apparent indifference, Atlantic has given its Stax masters the memorial they have long deserved. The result is one of few boxes amid the current glut that fully justifies the adjective *monumental*.

CLASSIC ROCK: "MUSICALLY, WE WEREN'T AFRAID TO GO IN ANY DIRECTION WHATSOEVER."

Portrait of the Band as Young Hawks

ROLLING STONE | JUNE 1, 1978

The Last Waltz blends concert and sound-stage footage with director Martin Scorsese's interviews with members of the Band. They discuss the group's history, including its early-sixties beginnings as the Hawks, backup band for rockabilly trouper Ronnie Hawkins. Robert Palmer played saxophone in many of the same Southern clubs as the Hawks and relived that era with Robbie Robertson as work on The Last Waltz was being completed.

The long black Cadillac ground to a stop in the Delta Supper Club's dusty parking lot and gave a shudder, as if it were glad to be rid of the weight of the trailer it was pulling. The six young men who got out, squinting in the bright Arkansas sun, were dressed for the road, in blue jeans and plaid or cowboy shirts. The older one, Ronnie Hawkins, was in his late twenties, beefy, filling his tight clothes, his hair teased and greased with a spit curl hanging down over his forehead. The others were kids in their late teens, gangly, miming the by-now-ritualized attitudes of rock & roll cool. They looked around at the West Helena afternoon for a minute, sizing up two locals who were giving them the eye from a weather-beaten Chevy pickup truck, and then Hawkins led them into the club and over to the bar, not to drink, though they could hold their own at that, but to look.

Ronnie felt along the wooden bar until he found a jagged seam. "Well boys," he said in his rangy Ozark drawl, "here it is." The seam ran all the way down the bar and all the way through the thick wood. It seems that one night a Billy Bob or Jimmy Lee from the country around Helena had gotten into a fight and been evicted from the establishment. Being smashed on rotgut whiskey and not about to take that kind of treatment, he stumbled to the back of his pickup, pulled out his chain saw, burst through the front door of the club, and let the thing rip. All the good old boys went scrambling out the windows and the door, but Billy Bob didn't even see them. He just went straight for the bar, lowered that whirring blade, and sawed the bar in two. That was the genesis of the famous chain-saw story, which musicians all over the South heard and told, even if they didn't believe it. "Yep," said Hawkins, almost reverently, "this is where it happened. See, here's where they glued it back together."

It was 1961, and Robbie Robertson, who'd replaced Fred Carter Jr. as lead guitarist in Hawkins's backup band, the Hawks, just a few months earlier, was still walking around this fabled country in a daze. He was seventeen, but he'd been around, playing rock & roll in his native Toronto since he was thirteen, writing a couple of hot tunes and going to New York when he was fifteen to watch Hawkins record them, getting that call when he was sixteen—"We need us a guitar player, come on down"— and riding a Greyhound from Toronto all the way down to Fayetteville and then to West Helena, on the Mississippi River, smack in the middle of the Delta. It was blues country. Those gravelly voiced singers and storming black metal guitarists Robbie had been hearing on the radio, on clear Toronto nights when he could pull in John R.'s show on WLAC from Nashville, actually stalked these dark bottomlands, cypress swamps, clusters of board-and-tar-paper croppers' shacks, and cotton fields baking in the sun.

Robbie knew the music; along with James Burton, Dale Hawkins,

Roy Buchanan, and a few other punks, he was one of a handful of white guitarists who were playing it. But the music was one thing; the place was something else. Levon Helm, the intense, wiry drummer who was to initiate him into its mysteries, met him at the Helena bus station and took him out to the Helm farmhouse, which was built on stilts to keep it dry during spring floods when the Big Muddy overran its banks. Levon's dad, a cotton farmer, told tales that made them split their sides laughing, and his mother cooked food that made them split their sides eating. Later, with Levon at the wheel, Robbie had a look at the town. There were black folks everywhere—he could remember seeing only a few in his entire life—and even the white folks talked like them, in a thick, rolling Afro-English that came out as heavy and sweet as molasses but could turn as acrid as turpentine if your accent or behavior were strange.

By the time Robbie had been with the Hawks a few months, the original Arkansans, except for Levon, had been replaced by Canadians. Earnest young Rick Danko, who knew some country fiddle and mandolin but had been smitten by rock & roll fever when he was in his early teens in the Canadian tobacco belt, was first. Then came Richard Manuel, a smoky-voiced screamer and master of the art of rhythm piano. "The piano was used as a rhythm instrument, with solos on organ or guitar or sax," Robbie explains. "So when you stopped playing rhythm to play a solo, the rhythm wouldn't drop out—the piano was still holding it." The last to join was Garth Hudson, who'd been classically trained and agreed to come only after the others promised him a token fee in exchange for regular lessons in music theory and harmony. It seemed to satisfy his parents, who imagined a different kind of musical career for their son.

The musical director was Levon, who'd come to the Hawks from a Helena group called the Jungle Bush Beaters and liked his rock & roll hard and raw. Hawkins had had some hits in the brash rockabilly vein of the late fifties and early sixties—"Odessa," "Mary Lou"—and liked Levon's style, but by 1961 or '62 there were changes in the air. The band added saxophonist Jerry Penfound so it could play soul tunes like Bobby Blue Bland's "Turn on Your Lovelight." With Garth on organ they sported two keyboards and a sax; with Garth on sax they had a soul band's horn section. And despite his classical training, Garth developed a saxophone style in the classic mold. Even today, he will tell you that the art of rock & roll saxophone playing was all but lost in the late fifties and the early sixties with the introduction of the Otto Link metal mouthpiece and the arrival of King Curtis and Boots Randolph and their strangled, chicken-clucking sound.

"When the music got a little too far out for Ronnie's ear," Robbie remembers, "or he couldn't tell when to come in singing, he would tell us that nobody but Thelonious Monk could understand what we were playing. But the big thing with him was that he made us rehearse and practice a lot. Often we would go and play until one A.M. and then rehearse until four. And I practiced incessantly; I could go for it until my fingers were just raw. I was interested in doing what those other people couldn't do; I really wanted to be good."

They all drove from gig to gig in the Cadillac, with their equipment in the trailer. The circuit extended from Arkansas, Mississippi, and Tennessee up through Missouri. Then there was the Canadian part: Toronto and out into Ontario. Sometimes they would drive hundreds of miles, from warm, almost tropical weather into sheets of freezing rain or snow. Levon remembers Hawkins looking out at an icy Canadian landscape from the speeding Caddy, turning to him gravely, and saying, "Son, it's as cold out there as an accountant's heart."

But Arkansas, Ronnie's and Levon's home state, was their headquarters and prime stomping ground. Across its length and breadth they were legends, and not just for their music. Local bands did copy their arrangements note for note, and budding guitarists got both their kicks and their licks from catching Robbie at national guard armory dances or country roadhouses. "But the Hawks could eat and pop pills and fuck with the best of 'em," remembers a veteran Arkansas rocker. "Ronnie knew every whore between Helena and Toronto."

The lifestyle was decidedly fast. In central Arkansas, for example, they often played the Club 70, a big barn of a place just off the two-lane blacktop of Highway 70 between the Little Rock city limits and the Jacksonville air force base. There was a brisk business in amphetamines in the parking lot. To get into the club you had to get past a bouncer who sat in a little glassed-in booth under a blue light, checking IDs. Sometimes a local with his T-shirt sleeves rolled up to his shoulders would sit down in front of the bandstand, chug-a-lug a quart of vodka, chug down a quart of beer for a chaser, and dare anybody to start a fight. Sometimes a gang of tough Yankee slum kids from the air base would mock the

Arkansas Razorback cheer, "Sooiee Pigs," by yelling "Soooieee, Pigshit," and then there would be real trouble: chairs and tables flying, bottles breaking, black eyes, and more money out of the till to pay off the cops. After a night of that, the Hawks would pack, get in their Caddy, and drive up into the Ozarks to Fayetteville, Razorback Valhalla, where they sometimes had to wade across a floor that was literally knee-deep in beer cans in order to get to the stage. Mostly, though, they played roadhouses. "You'd just be driving along," says Robbie, "and there'd be this place, out on the road somewhere. At night people would come from all around, it would be packed. You could tell by looking at it that it was only gonna be there for a short while, that somebody was gonna torch it at any given moment. It happened a lot. We'd play in a club and go back a year later and they'd have burnt it down and built a new one."

The Hawks split from Ronnie Hawkins in 1963 and worked for a time under Levon's feisty, determined leadership. And they almost became Sonny Boy Williamson's backup band instead of Bob Dylan's in the mid-sixties.

"We were in West Helena, just hanging out and talking about the music," says Robbie. "Levon had grown up listening to Sonny Boy on King Biscuit Time [broadcast over KFFA radio in Helena] and we thought about him and said, maybe he's here. So we went down to the holler—Levon knew where everything was—and we asked some people if Sonny Boy was around. They said, 'Yeah, he's playing down at the café.' We went down and there he was, a big tall man in a bowler hat, white hair and a white goatee, wearing a suit he'd had made in England that was gray on one side and black on the other, and the reverse on the back. He looked kind of . . . fine.

"Levon introduced himself and said, 'Can we go somewhere to play some music?' Sonny Boy took us to these friends of his, this woman had a place where she sold bootleg corn liquor. Well, that stuff is outrageous. We got drunk, *drunk*, and we all played. Man, he played the harmonica inside out. He'd put the whole thing inside his mouth and play it. I kept noticing him spitting in this can. I thought maybe he was chewing tobacco. I was wandering around at one point and I looked in the can and it was blood, he was spitting blood. It was a gruesome sight, and I was *so drunk*. . . .

"Things got a little weird there. There were all these young guys around trying to hustle us, and they were afraid of Sonny Boy—he was the only legend around the neighborhood, and it was also a known fact that if you fucked with him he would cut you. But eventually there were just too many people. So we all left and smuggled him into our motel— they didn't allow black people in there, you understand—and we just played and played, and he couldn't believe it. He'd been to England and played with the Yardbirds and some other groups, and he told us, 'They're awful. They want to play the blues so bad and they play it *so* bad. . . .' Anyway, we really got on, and we made all these plans, things we were gonna do together. Then we went to play in New Jersey and we got this letter from Sonny Boy's manager or whoever he was, saying that he had passed. Tuberculosis."

Levon and the Hawks didn't spend all their time in the South, not by a long shot. They would play in New Jersey and Pennsylvania and pop into New York to see some of the Brill Building songwriter types they'd met when they recorded there with Hawkins: Neil Diamond, Doc Pomus, Leiber and Stoller. They spent some time in Chicago, where they got to know Paul Butterfield and Mike Bloomfield and went with them to blues clubs on the South Side. They gigged regularly in Canada. It was on one of their northern swings that they met John Hammond Jr. Hammond and Mary Martin, who worked in Albert Grossman's office and knew a lot of Canadian musicians, both told Bob Dylan about them.

"Dylan called when they were working in New Jersey," says Jonathan Taplin, who was the Band's company manager from 1968 to 1971 but knew their music much earlier. "Evidently, he went down to listen to them, returned to New York, and called up Levon. He asked if they'd like to play with him at the Hollywood Bowl and at Forest Hills Stadium. And Levon's reply was, 'Who else is on the bill?' Because they were just beginning to hear 'Like a Rolling Stone' on the radio. They never bought albums, they just listened to the radio, so they had no idea how big Bob was. The way it ended up, just Levon and Robbie went to the Forest Hills gig, and Dylan got Harvey Brooks and Al Kooper to play bass and organ. See, Levon and Robbie wanted to be sure that he'd really sold out these big places. . . . Then they got the other three guys to come on up."

"We'd heard a couple of his records and we knew he was really good," Robbie says of Dylan, "but we were a rock & roll band. We didn't play his kind of music, we just appreciated it in the same way you would listen to Big Bill Broonzy and appreciate it. But once he started wanting to change his music, it was an interesting challenge. It was easy to play with him, but it was hard getting everybody to play with him at the same time because he would break meter, and all of a sudden you wouldn't know where you were, you'd get mixed up. Sometimes we didn't know if we were playing great music or nonsense. A lot of it had to do with . . . Well, it was a strange experience, going around the world in a private plane and getting booed. An interesting way to make a living, but definitely strange. Everybody was telling Bob to get rid of us, that we were sent from the devil and putting this dirty, vulgar music on a pure folkloric tradition. That's what the attitude was. And *then* everybody just forgot about that and accepted the whole thing as if it had always been accepted."

When Dylan's first electric tour hit Memphis—*Highway 61* was on everyone's turntable; *Blonde on Blonde* was still several months in the future—some of the Arkansas rockers, hearing that this new kid Dylan was playing with the Hawks, drove up along the twisting Delta highway to see them. It was an unforgettable show. Dylan did the first part unaccompanied, introducing "Visions of Johanna" and driving everybody half crazy with lines like "the ghost of electricity howled in the bones of her face." Then he brought out the Hawks, who looked pretty much like they'd always looked, street casual, not too much hair, jeans, old sports jackets. The music was loud, intense, possessed. Robbie played wrenching solos from back near Levon's drums, hardly moving a muscle. Dylan, playing rhythm, mimed the throes of a convulsion whenever Robbie tore into a break, and everybody but the Arkies thought *he* was soloing.

Jonathan Taplin caught the group later in that same 1965 tour. "It was astonishing," he remembers. "They were louder than any band I'd ever heard. At that time, there was nothing like it. As it went on, into 1966, they got even more daring. I have live tapes from England with Robbie playing outrageous high-note blues guitar. Nobody was playing like that. Then, when everybody else got into that kind of style, he began to look for a new sound, a more delicate, less bluesy kind of thing. He's just a killer musician. On that record he made with John Hammond in 1964, they had Robbie playing the guitar and Mike Bloomfield on piano. I mean, it was obvious who was the better player then. But you know, they're all killer players. The funny thing is, when they became the Band, they constantly tried to play down solos, musicianship, that kind of thing, in order to be an ensemble, when in fact they were the best solo players in the music at that time. Whenever there would be a jam session, Garth was a far better organ player than anybody, and Robbie, when he'd get together with other guitar players, would amaze everybody with his rides."

Taplin was going to Princeton and acting as road manager for the Jim Kweskin Jug Band, another Albert Grossman act, when he met the Band. Dylan was in seclusion following his motorcycle accident, but they all were seeing a lot of each other in Woodstock, getting together, trading songs, making the recordings that later surfaced as *The Basement Tapes*. "By then," says Robbie, "the give-and-take was an everyday procedure, whether we were traveling around the world or hanging out in somebody's kitchen. It was an education for all of us, and it was fun." You can hear a strong mutual fascination on *The Basement Tapes*. Dylan, the urban-folkie-turned-rocker, found in the Hawks a direct connection with the roots of rock—blues, country, rockabilly—and the Band found in Dylan a new understanding of what rock could become. Robbie was writing songs again. "Bob taught me a certain liberty," he says. "How to tell a story in a short form without necessarily having to go from point A to point B. I mean, he broke down a whole lot of the tradition of songwriting right before my very eyes. With all the rules broken, you could go ahead and tell the truth without having to do some kind of fancy dance. But I was never too hot for the messages and the poetry, that side of it, because I just didn't come out of that school. I never thought I was writing poetry; they were songs."

The songs Robbie ended up writing came out steeped in the South's bottomlands and shacks and cotton fields, steeped in the Baptist and Holy Roller churches where folks in the throes of religious hysteria invented the duck walk and all the other classic rock & roll moves. During the first months in Woodstock the songs had come slowly, and maybe that was because Levon, who'd tired of the road shortly before Dylan's European tour and gone back to the South, wasn't with them. They recorded a lot of the music on *The Basement Tapes* without him, but they found that they needed that razorback spirit and never-say-die Confederate orneriness to be a real band. When Levon rejoined them and sunk roots in Woodstock—today he is the only member who still lives there—the transformation was complete. They were no longer the Hawks, a band; they were the Band.

Taplin helped the Band move into Sammy Davis Jr.'s old house in Hollywood to record their second album in the winter of 1968. They built a makeshift recording studio in the pool house, where Levon lived for the duration of the sessions. Once the place was set up, Jonathan went back to finish at Princeton. When he returned, the Band sat him down and played him "The Night They Drove Old Dixie Down."

"It was May," he says, "and they'd just finished it the night before. They said it'd come out fast and hard and clean. It was just the most moving experience I'd had for, God, I don't know how long. Because for me, being a Northern liberal kid who'd been involved in the civil-rights movement and had a whole attitude toward the South, well, I loved the music but I didn't understand where white Southerners were coming from. And to have it all in just three and a half minutes, the sense of dignity and place and tradition, all those things . . . Well, the next day, after I'd recovered, I went to Robbie and asked him. 'How did that come out of you?' And he just said that from being with Levon so long in his life and being in that place at that time . . . It was so inside him that he wanted to write that song right *at* Levon, to let him know how much those things meant to him."

To the world at large, *Music from Big Pink* and *The Band* were the remarkable beginnings of a remarkable new group. In reality, they were the crowning fruition of a career that had spanned almost a decade. Of all the rock groups making music during those heady years, the Band was the one that was most in touch with the music's history and its heartland, the one that realized most clearly how inseparably music, past, and place were linked. After they completed the second album, they went out on their first tour as the Band, a tour that has been chronicled elsewhere, most notably in Greil Marcus's book *Mystery Train*, and, perhaps, in some of the lyrics on the Band's third album, the aptly titled *Stage Fright*. When one suggests to Robbie Robertson that the tour really was the beginning of a new ball game, he nods his head. "You're right. For us it was, anyway. The first two albums were really like the fulfillment of something."

Cut to Los Angeles, early 1978. Robbie is in his small office on the MGM movie lot, taking care of detail work, fulfilling his responsibilities as producer of Martin Scorsese's *The Last Waltz.* In the office next door, Jonathan Taplin, who went on from his work with the Band to produce Scorsese's *Mean Streets,* is serving as the new film's executive producer. "The road didn't really change that much," Robbie says over a Styrofoam cup of coffee and a chain of cigarettes, "just different-class hotels, different-class transportation. I guess the first stage could have been more deadly just in terms of how physically dangerous it was. The second stage was dangerous too, but more on a head level. It really was kind of a mindfuck." And so is the movie. All those faces from the early days, the period with Dylan, the second stage. The energy in the music and its weathered, lived-in quality—every phrase, every note sighs from sixteen years on the road—are almost too intense. "We would watch the footage and not be able to watch it again for a day and a half," Scorsese said the night before. "We would come home drained."

The important thing is that the Band didn't go down in a plane crash or on the highway, or down in spirits and chemicals like so many of their contemporaries. They flirted with the edge, some members more hungrily than others, but in the end they set a date for their demise as a touring unit, arranged for it to take place where they played their first engagement as the Band, threw a party instead of a wake, got to do some of their favorite songs one last time with their favorite artists and friends, and captured the whole thing for their grandchildren. How many other rock & roll bands have been able to say as much?

Excerpt from *The Rolling Stones* (1983)

The Stones' tax exile was the first in a series of moves intended to give the band the complete control and financial mobility of the Swiss-bank upper crust. The next step came in April with the creation of their own label, Rolling Stones Records. The Stones chose Atlantic Records to distribute their releases and hired Marshall Chess, the son of Chess Records founder Leonard Chess and a hipster roughly their own age, to serve as the company's president. Before the month was out, Rolling Stones had issued its first single, "Brown Sugar."

Listeners had to work to make out the words to "Brown Sugar," which had been mixed down into the instrumental track and partly obscured, in typical Stones fashion. Mick has recalled being profoundly influenced by an interview with Fats Domino in which the rotund hitmaker advised, "You should never sing the words out very clearly." Some of the lyrics on "Satisfaction" and other Stones singles were deliberately obscured, partly to make the records more mysterious and intriguing and partly to hide drug and sex references from the censors. This was the origin of the so-called Stones mix—a vocalist fighting to be heard over a wall of careening guitars and a big bass and drum sound.

The first phrases most listeners pulled out of the din of "Brown Sugar" seemed like a welter of antifemale gibes and dubious racial slurs. The song set a pattern for controversy, the kind of public do-they-or-don't-they that the Stones loved to provoke—leading up to the feminist controversy over the advertising campaign for *Black and Blue* in 1976 and the Reverend Jesse Jackson's criticism of "Some Girls" in 1978. As usual, though, the taunts in "Brown Sugar" were a red herring. The full lyric, three compact verses, follows a slave ship's cargo from the Gold Coast to a plantation in the English colonies. Mick notes with a certain ironic relish that sexy black slave girls always made "cold English blood" run hot, and finally relates his own conquests of black women to the tradition of slave mistresses and the exploitation of blacks by his slave-trading ancestors.

The song also has a subtext—the fascination with black culture and black expression that brought the Stones together in the first place. In those early days, black blues was almost a religion to them, and they proselytized for their religion everywhere they went—even in America, where they insisted on sharing their first guest spot on the network television show "Shindig" with bluesman Howlin' Wolf. Such cheek was unheard of, but the incident wasn't isolated. The Stones hired black performers to open most of their subsequent tours—B.B. King, Ike and Tina Turner, Stevie Wonder. They had taken a great deal from black music and thought it was only fair to give something back. But by the early seventies, the Stones' borrowings were being called rip-offs by critics and politicos. "Brown Sugar" answered the charge with tongue in cheek, pleading guilty to the exploitation of blacks with disarming candor and catching the band's most humorless detractors off guard.

"Brown Sugar" was the first single with the lapping tongue logo of Rolling Stones Records on the label; *Sticky Fingers* followed a week later. The bulging male crotch on the Andy Warhol cover and the lubricity of the title suggested that the accent would be on sex, and there is some supremely sexy rock & roll on *Sticky Fingers*—the seductive insistence of "Can't You Hear Me Knocking," the yearning intimacy of "Wild Horses," the juice and heat and drive of "Bitch" and "Brown Sugar." But the album is at least as concerned with drugs as it is with sex; Stones fans who habitually combed the band's LPs for drug references had a field day with it. "Brown Sugar" was a slang term for brown heroin, they noted, and the album ended with the hard-drug trilogy of "Sister Morphine," "Dead Flowers" (heroin again, as in crushed poppies), and "Moonlight Mile" ("with a head full of snow," cocaine). On *Sticky Fingers*, Mick and Keith seemed to be making a serious attempt to get something out of their drug experiences besides a rush.

But *Sticky Fingers* wasn't the triumph it might have been. Some of the arrangements lacked focus—there were too many guitars chugging away in the introduction to "Bitch," and the Santana-like instrumental tag to "Can't You Hear Me Knocking" seemed gratuitous, tacked on. And too many of the songs attempted to provide hard-boiled accounts of lives lived on the edge but ended up sounding like druggy soap operas. ("Sister Morphine" was the worst offender, with its lurid Hollywood treatment of drug withdrawal.) All these defects were symptomatic of a more serious problem: a potentially debilitating self-consciousness was creeping into the Stones' music, and with it came a certain amount of overacting and cheap melodrama.

The Stones returned to Nellcote from July to November 1971 to record *Exile on Main Street*. It was more convenient for the band to come to Keith than for Keith to come to the band, for by this time the guitarist's drug addiction was the most pressing problem confronting the Rolling Stones. At least at Nellcote, privacy and the Stones security team made a bust less likely. And the band could work at its own pace, unhampered by studio schedules. The result was a double album that captured a confident rock & roll band at the height of its musical prowess. The rough, defiantly muddy sound emphasized the ensemble's guts and drive, burying Mick's vocals in the densest of all Stones mixes but capturing the Richards-Taylor twin-guitar assault at its most slashing and spirited, and the great Stones rhythm section sounding fiercely, urgently kinetic.

Some of the lyrics were disguised very efficiently indeed, perhaps because they were among the most personal the band had ever committed to vinyl. The Gram Parsons–influenced "Torn and Frayed," for example, commented on Keith's hard-drug problem with unsentimental clarity, successfully avoiding melodrama. In the "ballrooms and smelly bordellos/ And dressing rooms filled with parasites," Joe the guitar player

(Keith transparently disguised) found himself getting more and more restless, and no wonder: "Joe's got a cough/Sounds kinda rough/Yeah, and the codeine to fix it/Doctor prescribes/Drugstore supplies/Who's gonna help him to kick it?" The band was learning to live with Keith's problem, out of loyalty and because the music was still transcendent: "Just as long as the guitar plays/Let it steal your heart away." Perhaps some of the other songs were addressed to the prodigal son as well. Hey you, soul survivor? You, turd on the run? C'mon, stop breaking down!

Exile on Main Street was released less than a month before the Stones kicked off their 1972 tour. Compared to *Let It Bleed* or *Beggar's Banquet*, or even *Sticky Fingers*, it sounded at first like a chaotic, sprawling mess. Stones albums often sounded impenetrable at first but always kicked in sooner or later. But critics, forced by newspaper and magazine deadlines to listen fast and take sides, registered disappointment and frustration at the music's blurred edges, the indecipherable lyrics, the apparent lack of contrast. Why was there filler like "Turd on the Run" and "Ventilator Blues" scattered among new classics like "Tumbling Dice," "Torn and Frayed," and "Happy"? *Exile's* reputation soared only after the Stones followed it with the most abysmal records of their career. When it was new, one could compare it only to the uneven but frequently captivating *Sticky Fingers* or to the near perfection of *Let It Bleed* and *Beggar's Banquet*. In this company, *Exile* comes up wanting.

Beggar's Banquet and *Let It Bleed* are classics of another sort; they are collections of superb rock & roll *songs*, and fine as the individual performances and the ensemble playing are, it's the songs and what they are saying that matter most in the end. *Exile,* on the other hand, is a great, defiant chunk of rock & roll *noise*. It defies the listener to delve into its murky depths, and it defies the seventies' notion that rock & roll is above all an entertainment.

It's true that songs like "Tumbling Dice" and "Rip This Joint" are supremely entertaining, but even these songs have a careening momentum that sounds dangerous, a momentum that threatens to spin giddily out of control. And songs like "Shine a Light," "Torn and Frayed," the Robert Johnson blues "Stop Breaking Down," and "Soul Survivor" are entertaining only if you ignore their momentum and their message. Listen carefully, and they are intensely disturbing vignettes, warnings that decay and death are waiting in the wings and may even be calling the tune. Several lyric excerpts are reprinted amid Robert Frank's photo images of a Main Street America that died more than a decade ago. "I don't want to talk about Jesus," says one, "I just wanna see his face." The other: "I gave you the diamonds, you give me disease." Barbed, deadly lines like these poke out of the thick, swirling sound mix at every turn, and the music just roars along toward some unimaginable apocalypse — until the final track, "Soul Survivor," which announces that *this* rock & roll band is determined to survive, whatever the cost.

Eric Clapton: The *Rolling Stone* Interview (excerpt)

ROLLING STONE | JUNE 20, 1985

Eric Clapton joined the Yardbirds in 1963 and was recognized almost immediately as one of the most dazzling guitarists in popular music. Like jazzman Charlie Parker and a few other virtuoso improvisers before him, he was deified by his most devoted followers, who scrawled CLAPTON IS GOD around London. Also like Parker, he attempted to deal with the adulation, and with the pitiless creative urges that drove him, by deadening his nerve endings with drugs and drink. But unlike many who go down that road, he lived to tell about it.

From John Mayall's Bluesbreakers to Cream, from Blind Faith to Derek and the Dominos, from his first solo album to the new *Behind the*

Sun, Clapton has consistently maintained exacting musical standards. His audience, expecting superhuman playing from him no matter what the context, has sometimes been disappointed by his records and, to a lesser extent, by his shows. But if his music has sometimes lacked fire, it has never lacked consummate craftsmanship. . . .

Clapton is an intensely private man who was never a talkative interview subject. He hadn't been interviewed in depth in some seven years when we first talked, by telephone, during his 1983 tour. I figured that it might pleasantly surprise him to talk to a journalist interested in music rather than in scandal, and sure enough, when he was rehearsing in England for an American tour this spring, I was invited over.

I got the impression that Clapton still found the idea of an interview about as appealing as a trip to the dentist, and for a week he kept putting off our first meeting. When we finally sat down to talk, in a comfortable room down the hall from his manager's London office, I told him we could start anywhere he liked. "Let's start at the beginning," he said, and for most of the next week we met every afternoon for a three- or four-hour session. . . .

Clapton is still married to the former Patti Boyd, whom he wooed away from her first husband, Beatle George Harrison, more than a decade ago. At the time of the interview, however, their relationship was in a rocky phase. "The one thing I will not discuss," Clapton had announced before we began, "is my personal life." After several days of talking about Clapton's heroin addiction and period of alcoholism, openly and often in clinical detail, I risked asking him how things were with Patti. "She's the only woman I have ever really loved," he said deliberately. And that was that.

Clapton met every other subject unflinchingly, and we took a long, careful look at his major musical involvements. The man has always been his own toughest critic, and along the way we opened some old wounds and raised some formidable specters—guilt, fear, challenges that were not squarely faced. But when all was said and done, and despite Clapton's frequently harsh assessments of his own achievements and worth, he seemed to emerge from the grilling with a certain feeling of pride. "I think he's finally discovering," one of his associates said, "that his life hasn't been such a bloody waste after all."

Since we're starting at the beginning, why don't you tell me a bit about the town of Ripley, where you grew up.
It's only about thirty miles outside of London, but it's very country—Ripley is not even a town, it's a village with farms all around it. And very few people ever leave there. They usually stay, get jobs, get married.

What kind of music did you hear when you were growing up?
Pop music, first. Mostly songs that were still hanging over from wartime: "We'll Meet Again," that sort of thing, melodic pop music.

There was a funny Saturday-morning radio program for children, with this strange person, Uncle Mac. He was a very old man with one leg and a strange little penchant for children. He'd play things like "Mule Train," and then every week he'd slip in something like a Buddy Holly record or a Chuck Berry record. And the first blues I ever heard was on that program; it was a song by Sonny Terry and Brownie McGhee, with Sonny Terry howling and playing the harmonica. It blew me away. I was ten or eleven.

When was the first time you actually saw a guitar?
Hmmm . . . I remember the first rock & roll I ever saw on TV was Jerry Lee Lewis doing "Great Balls of Fire." And that threw me; it was like seeing someone from outer space. And I realized suddenly that here I was in this village that was never going to change, yet there on TV was something out of the future. And I wanted to go there! Actually, he didn't have a guitarist, but he had a bass player, playing a Fender Precision bass, and I said, "That's a guitar." I didn't know it was a bass guitar, I just knew it was a guitar, and again I thought, "That's the future. And that's what I want." After that I started to build one, tried to carve a Stratocaster out of a block of wood, but I didn't know what to do when I got to the neck and frets and things.

I was living with my grandparents, who raised me, and since I was the only child in the family, they used to spoil me something terrible. So I badgered them until they bought me a plastic Elvis Presley guitar. Of course, it could never stay in tune, but I could put on a Gene Vincent record, look in the mirror, and mime.

When I was fourteen or fifteen, they gave me a real guitar, an acoustic, but it was so hard to play. I actually didn't even try for a while. And pretty soon the neck began to warp. But I did invent chords. I invented E, and I invented A. I thought I had discovered something incredible. And then I put it down again, in my later teens, because I started to become interested in being an artist. The bohemian existence beckoned; actually, the good-life part of it beckoned more than the work. And at that point, when I was about sixteen, I started making weekend trips to London.

From hanging around in coffee bars and so on, I met a certain crowd of people, some of whom played guitar. One was Long John Baldry, who was then playing a twelve-string, doing folk and blues. Every Friday night, there would be a meeting at someone's house, and people would turn up with the latest important records from the States. And shortly, someone showed up with that Chess album, *The Best of Muddy Waters*, and something by Howlin' Wolf. And that was it for me. Then I sort of took a step back, discovered Robert Johnson, and made the connection to Muddy. For me, it was very serious, what I heard. And I began to realize that I could only listen to this music with people who were equally serious about it.

Did getting involved with this music send you back to the guitar?
Yeah, Baldry and these other people would just sit in a corner, playing folk and blues while everyone else was drinking and getting stoned. And I saw that it was possible to actually, if you like, get on with it—to just sit in the corner playing and not have everyone looking at you. I saw that it wasn't something to be frightened or shy in doing. So I started doing it myself.

Playing what, folk-blues?
Yeah, things by Big Bill Broonzy and Ramblin' Jack Elliott, "Railroad Bill," "Cocaine." But then I was drawn more and more toward electric blues, along with a few friends, a select few people. And, of course, then we had to be purists and seriously dislike other things.

When I was about seventeen, I got booted out of art school, and I did manual labor for about a year for pocket money. And during that time, I met up with a guy, Tom McGuinness, who was going to get involved with a band, and I knew just about enough to be able to play and keep up that end of it. So I got involved in that band, the Roosters, and that was a good feeling.

What kind of music did the Roosters play?
We did "Boom Boom" and a couple of other John Lee Hooker things, "Hoochie Coochie Man" and some others by Muddy, I think. We did whatever we could get on records, really, on up to rock & roll things like "Slow Down" by Larry Williams, because you had to have the odd rock & roll number in there.

Then Tom McGuinness brought in "Hideaway" by Freddie King, and the B-side was "I Love the Woman," which is still one of the greatest. And that's the first time I heard that electric lead-guitar style, with the bent notes — T-Bone Walker, B.B. and Freddie King, that style of playing. Hearing that Freddie King single was what started me on my path.

According to rock historian Pete Frame's family tree of your various bands, the Roosters only lasted from January to August 1963.
Yeah. . . . After the Roosters, I got a job with Tom McGuinness in another band, Casey Jones and the Engineers. That folded pretty soon, too, and then I heard the Yardbirds had started up.

The Stones had been playing at the Crawdaddy Club, and when they moved on, the next band in was the Yardbirds. I had met two guys from the Yardbirds at some bohemian parties, and at that time they were playing music by Django Reinhardt, "Nuages" and so on. We became friends. I went down to hear them at the Crawdaddy and was fairly critical of them, especially the guitarist they had. And I don't really remember how it came about, but I replaced him. . . .

At first, if we could get a good gig and make the crowd happy, that was enough. But then the Stones came out of that whole scene, and it sparked ambition in some members of the band. The Stones were getting on big package tours, they were on TV, they got a Chuck Berry song onto the charts. And some of the Yardbirds and Giorgio [Gomelsky, their manager] began to see a future in being internationally famous. I couldn't see what was so wonderful about competing with the Liverpool sound and all of that, trying to jump on the bandwagon; there was still a great part of me that was very much the blues purist, thinking, "Music is this, it's not that. . . ."

Were the Yardbirds' gigs with Sonny Boy Williamson the first chance you had to play with an American bluesman?

Yes, and I think that's when I first realized that we weren't really being true to the music—when Sonny Boy came over and we didn't know how to back him up. It was frightening, really, because this man was real and we weren't. He wasn't very tolerant, either. He did take a shine to us after a while, but before that he put us through some bloody hard paces. In the first place, he expected us to know his tunes. He'd say, "We're going to do 'Don't Start Me to Talkin' or 'Fattening Frogs for Snakes,'" and then he'd kick it off, and of course, some of the members of this particular band had never heard these songs.

There was a certain attitude in the band, a kind of pride in being English and white and being able to whip up a crowd on our own, and there was a sort of resistance toward what we were being asked to do— why should we have to study this man's records? Even I felt a little bit like that, because we were coming face-to-face with the reality of that thing, and it was a lot different from buying a record that you could take off when you felt like it. So we were all terrified of him, me most of all I think, because I was really making an attempt. Years later, Robbie Robertson of the Band told me that Sonny Boy had gone back to the South and hung out with them and had said he'd just been over playing with these white guys who didn't know how to play anything at all.

Yeah, Robertson once told me that Sonny Boy had said, "Those Englishmen want to play the blues so bad—and they play it so bad!"

Right. At the time, I thought we'd done pretty well. But by that time, the momentum of the band was toward becoming a pop group, and this man arrived and took it all back down to the basic blues. And I had to almost relearn how to play. It taught me a lot; it taught me the value of that music, which I still feel.

It's a very subtle language, blues. Much more than a matter of licks, it's a matter of sound, and how much you bend or flatten a note is directly related to the feeling you're trying to convey.

Yes. I got so obsessed with that that I forgot another essential, and I still do. And that is time—when you hit the note and when you stop. How you place it exactly. I thought I'd learned very early on all about sound, about how with one note, if it sounds right, you can create everything. But I kept forgetting about where you put the note. I discovered when I went back and listened to some of the live Cream records, a year or so after making them, that I sometimes turned the time around, played on the wrong beat, because I was so into the sound of it.

What caused you to leave the Yardbirds just when they were on the brink of success? You're supposed to have been grossed out by that first pop hit, "For Your Love."

Yeah. At a certain point we started getting package tours, with the Ronettes, Billy J. Kramer, the Kinks, the Small Faces, lots of others, and we lost our following in the clubs. We decided to get suits, and I actually designed suits for us all. Then we did the Beatles' Christmas show, and at that point we really began to feel the lack of a hit. We'd be on for twenty minutes or half an hour, and either you were very entertaining or you did your hits. . . . It became very clear that if the group was going to survive and make money, it would have to be on a popular basis. We couldn't go back to the clubs, because everyone had got that taste and seen what fun it would be to be famous.

So a lot of songs were bandied about, and Giorgio came up with a song by Otis Redding. I thought that would make a great single because it was still R&B and soul, and we could do it really funky. Then Paul got the "For Your Love" demo, and he heard it with harpsichord. Whoa, harpsichord. Where does that leave me? Twelve-string guitar, I suppose. So we went in the studio to do both songs, but we did "For Your Love" first. Everyone was so bowled over by the obvious commerciality of it that we didn't even get to do the Otis Redding song, and I was very disappointed, disillusioned by that. So my attitude within the group got really sour, and it was kind of hinted that it would be better for me to leave, 'cause they'd already been to see Jeff Beck play, and at the time he was far more adaptable than I was. I was withdrawing into myself, becoming intolerable, really, dogmatic. So they kind of asked me to leave, and I left and felt a lot better for it.

Is this the time when you did nothing but practice every day for a year? Or is that story apocryphal?

Well, it wasn't a year, it was only a few months. . . . I went up to Oxford to stay with Ben Palmer, who had played piano in the Roosters and was a close friend, and during that time I began to think seriously about playing blues. And then while I was there, I got a call from John Mayall, who'd heard I was serious, if you like, and not money orientated or popularity orientated, and he asked me to come and audition, or just come around and play. I got the job, and I actually got to feel like I was a key member of that band from the minute I walked in. Right away, I was choosing material for the band to do.

And Mayall went along with this? He has a reputation for being kind of autocratic.
Well, I think in me he met a soul mate who liked the same things. With the guitarist he'd had before, he hadn't been able to do certain numbers he wanted to do—the Otis Rush songs, for example, which I really wanted to do. We were really together on that.

"Double Trouble" and those other Otis Rush things were on Cobra, a really obscure label, and at that point I don't think they'd ever been reissued. I've always thought your playing had a lot in common with Otis's—you both really get off on minor-key blues. But where did you hear this stuff?
John was quite a collector. I went down to his house to audition and saw this record collection that was beyond my wildest dreams. It was almost all singles, and every one I put on, I would right away start saying, "We should do this."

Otis Rush is very intense. What did you think when you first heard him?
I always liked the wilder guys. I liked Buddy Guy, Freddie King, and Otis Rush because they sounded like they were really on the edge, like they were barely in control and at any time they could hit a really bad note and the whole thing would fall apart—but of course, they didn't: I liked that a lot more than B.B. I got into B.B. later, when I realized that polish was something, too.

You were with Mayall for a while and then, before making the *Bluesbreakers* album, you left to go to Greece. What was all that about?
I was living in a place with some pretty mad people, great people, really. We were just drinking wine all day long and listening to jazz and blues,

and we decided to pool our money, buy an estate wagon, and take off round the world. The job with Mayall had become a job, and I wanted to go have some fun as well. So we ended up in Greece, playing blues, a couple of Rolling Stones songs, anything to get by. We met this club proprietor who hired us to open for a Greek band that played Beatles songs. . . .

When I got back with Mayall, Jack Bruce was on bass, and we hit it off really well. Then he left to go with Manfred Mann, and Mayall got John McVie back. I decided that playing with Jack was more exciting. There was something creative there. Most of what we were doing with Mayall was imitating the records we got, but Jack had something else — he had no reverence for what we were doing, and so he was composing new parts as he went along playing. I literally had never heard that before, and it took me someplace else. I thought, well, if he could do that, and I could, and we could get a drummer . . . I could be Buddy Guy with a composing bass player. And that's how Cream came about. . . .

Were you already thinking about starting Cream, or at least starting a band with Jack Bruce?
Well, after I had the experience of meeting and playing with Jack, the next thing that happened was that Ginger Baker came to this John Mayall gig. We'd worked the same circuits as the band Ginger was in, the Graham Bond Organisation, and I'd liked their music, except it was too jazzy for me — the jazz side of Ray Charles, Cannonball Adderley, that's what they were playing. But then Ginger came backstage after this Mayall gig and said to me, "We're thinking of breaking up, and I like the way you play. Would you like to start a band?" I said, "Yeah, but I'd have to have Jack Bruce as well," and he kind of backed off that. It turned out that he and Jack were really chemically opposite, they were just polarized, always getting into fights. But we talked some more, and then we had a meeting at Ginger's house, where he and Jack immediately had an argument. I had no foresight whatsoever; I didn't think it was really serious. I left Mayall pretty soon after that.

What were your original ideas for Cream? You became known for those long jams, but on your first album, *Fresh Cream*, there was a lot of country blues and other songs, all of them pretty compact.

I think our ideas about what we were supposed to be were pretty abstract. At first I was throwing in Skip James and Robert Johnson songs, Jack was composing and Ginger was composing. The American thing with "flower power" was filtering over, and I started seeing us as the London version of all that. I had an idea of how we could look good as well as be a good band. We were just scrambling for the forefront, and we didn't get much feedback until we played in front of an audience. That was when we realized that they actually wanted to go off somewhere. And we had the power to take them.

I heard Cream play one night at the Café Au Go Go in Greenwich Village, on your first trip over to the U.S. It was really loud—big stacks of amps in this little room! And you'd go off into these twenty-minute jams. I wasn't really aware that Jack and Ginger had such strong jazz backgrounds, but it did seem like they were going off into a much freer thing and sort of playing around your blues, which was like the music's backbone. Were you comfortable in that role?
Very occasionally, when my purist side got the better of me, I might get a little insecure. But if you think about it, if I had formed a trio, say, with a blues drummer and a blues bass player, we would have gone on imitating, as I had been doing with John Mayall. I would never have learned how to play anything of my own. In Cream, I was forced to try and improvise; whether I made a good job of it a lot of the time is debatable.

The three of us were on the road all the time, trusting one another, living in one another's hearts, and I found I was giving, you know, more than I had ever done before, and having faith in them. Jack is such a musical genius, there was no way he could be wrong about anything. I had to trust these people, so I did, I went with it. Of course, when we got back to our hotel rooms, we would all be listening to something different. And then I would sometimes have doubts, because a part of me still wanted to duplicate. That's the fear, you know, of actually expressing and being naked.

There seems to have been a change in your listening tastes between the recording of *Fresh Cream* and the second album, *Disraeli Gears*. You started using some effects, like wah-wah, and you must have been

very impressed by Albert King, because your solos on "Strange Brew" and several other songs were really pure Albert.

The big change was that Hendrix had arrived. Cream was playing at London Polytechnic, a college, and a friend brought this guy who was dressed up really freaky. That was Jimi. He spent a lot of time combing his hair in the mirror. Very cute but at the same time very genuine and very shy. I took to him straightaway, just as a man. Then he asked if he could jam, and he came up and did "Killing Floor," the Howlin' Wolf tune. And it blew me away. I was floored by his technique and his choice of notes, of sounds. Ginger and Jack didn't take to it kindly. They thought he was trying to upstage me. But I fell in love, straightaway. He became a soul mate for me and, musically, what I wanted to hear.

We were hanging out in some London clubs not long after that, and we started listening to the singles Stax was putting out by Albert King. We were both very, very attracted by that.

Even after you'd been hanging out with Hendrix, your playing and his were still really different.

He was the leader of his band, and that was that. What I felt with Cream was that I owed it to the other two not to try and dominate too much, even though I did. Apart from that, I didn't—and still don't—like to rely on effects that I can't create myself. It's what you're going to play that matters.

This was the period when you ascended to godhood.

All during Cream I was riding high on the "Clapton is God" myth that had been started up. I was flying high on an ego trip; I was pretty sure I was the next best thing happening that was popular. Then we got our first kind of bad review, which, funnily enough, was in *Rolling Stone*. . . . The magazine ran an interview with us in which we were really praising ourselves, and it was followed by a review that said how boring and repetitious our performance had been. And it was true! The ring of truth just knocked me backward; I was in a restaurant and I fainted. And after I woke up, I immediately decided that that was the end of the band. . . .

We didn't really have a band with Cream. We rarely played as an ensemble; we were three virtuosos, all of us soloing all the time. . . .

You were also doing some sessions—"While My Guitar Gently Weeps" with the Beatles, for example. And you played that gig in Toronto with John Lennon and Yoko Ono and the Plastic Ono Band. What was that like?

I'd met John and would see him a lot around the London clubs. I got the impression that he was a very shy, slightly bitter, but also very sweet young man. There seemed to be a sort of game going on between John and George [Harrison], partly, I suppose, because John was a pretty good guitar player himself. When I was with Cream, George became interested in my playing, and I think he might have told John that he liked my work. So John assumed that if George liked me, I was probably better than George. So we got into these sessions.

John called me one Saturday morning and said, "Do you want to go to Toronto?" I said, "Sure. When?" And he said, "In a couple hours." I happened to have my equipment at home, so I met them at the airport, with [bassist] Klaus Voormann and [drummer] Alan White. We all got first-class seats on the plane and learned the repertoire on the way. There was a guy there who was a Gillette salesman—I'll never forget that—and he was trying to give us free razors, 'cause we all had beards.

I got slightly disillusioned when we landed at the other end and John and Yoko were whisked off in a limousine and all the band was left standing in the rain. We didn't know how we were going to get to the gig or anything, but that wasn't their problem. Then before the gig, we did so much coke that I actually threw up and passed out. They had to take me out and lay me on the ground. And at the last minute, we realized that we were going on between . . . I think it was Jerry Lee Lewis and Chuck Berry, and we were terrified. We were shaking. But it turned out to be a great experience.

You were getting involved with some heavyweight people.

Well, I'd been with Jack and Ginger, and those were heavy people. I remember one gig in the north of England where Jack had what appeared to be a semi-epileptic fit because of the adrenaline. He got in such a state that he actually passed out. Ginger and I played for about half an hour without any bass. And Ginger was using [heroin] pretty heavily; he would sometimes just throw up while he was playing a solo.

I know you haven't had much good to say about Blind Faith, but I actually think the album holds up really well.

Well, there was a lack of direction in Blind Faith, or a reticence to actually declare among ourselves where we were going. Because it seemed to be enough just to be making the money, and that wasn't good; the record company and the management had taken over. I felt that it was too soon for Steve [Winwood]. He was feeling uncomfortable, and since it had originally been my idea, I was uncomfortable. I started looking for somewhere else to go, an alternative, and I found that Delaney and Bonnie [Bramlett] were a godsend. After the Blind Faith tour, I lived with Delaney for a while.

The first night we met, we were in New York, and we went down to Steve Paul's club, the Scene, and we took acid. From there we went to see Mac Rebennack [Dr. John] and hung out in his hotel room, and then we went back to our hotel, to one of the rooms, his or mine. And Delaney looked straight into my eyes and told me I had a gift to sing and that if I didn't sing, God would take it away. I said, "No, man, I can't sing." But he said, "Yes you can. Hit this note: Ahhhh . . ." And it was suddenly like the most impossible thing I could do was to hit that note, because of the acid. So it quavered, but I did hit it, and I started to feel that if I was to gain his respect, I ought to really pursue this. That night we started talking about me making a solo album, with his band. . . .

Sounds like Delaney, being from Mississippi, got into a Baptist-preacher bit to get you singing again. So what happened after the Blind Faith tour? Did you start working on the solo album?

No, first of all we did a tour of England and Europe, as Delaney and Bonnie and Friends with Eric Clapton. And having got me to sing, Delaney started trying to get me to compose, as well. So we were writing a lot. And that was great. He'd start something off, and when I came up with the next bit, he'd say, "Look what you can do." Some of the time I think it was so he could get fifty percent of the songwriting, but it was also inspiring me. By the end of that tour, I was ready to make the album and felt very sure of myself. . . .

It's funny, because on the *Bluesbreakers* album, your vocal on the Robert Johnson tune ["Ramblin' on My Mind"] seems to me like better

blues singing than almost anybody coming out of England at the time, because you didn't just torture every syllable like just about everybody else. You must have lost confidence in your singing after that.

I felt a lot of insecurity about it in Blind Faith, because I felt that Steve was probably the finest singer in England. His range . . . see, my range isn't very good and he can really get up there.

Toward the end of the Bonnie and Delaney thing, I started to feel a lot of pressure, to feel trapped. Certain parts of the concert audiences had come to see me, and I'd do one solo number and they'd all applaud and say, "More Eric Clapton." That created a kind of tension inside the group, and I sort of felt I was spoiling it for them. At the same time, Delaney didn't want to let me go, because I had the popularity and the status to carry the whole thing a lot further. It was heartrending, but finally I extricated myself from it and came back home, without any kind of idea of what to do next. Then at that point, [drummer] Jim Gordon and [bassist] Carl Radle got in touch with me; they'd asked Delaney for a raise and he'd fired them all. And I thought, why not get 'em? I hired Jim and Carl and Bobby [Whitlock, a keyboard player]. And they came to England and we lived together at my house for a year, and we played night and day and took all kinds of dope. We did a club tour in England as Derek and the Dominos, which was funny because no one knew who we were. But the word spread very quickly, and we had good crowds most of the time.

Why did you go to Miami to record *Layla*?
The attraction was Tom Dowd. I'd worked with him in Cream, and he was to me—and still is—the ideal recording man.

Yeah, he engineered all those great early Atlantic R&B and soul sessions and practically invented stereo.
Right. And he can guide you in a very constructive way. So we got there, we were doing a lot of dope and drinking a lot and just partying. It was great times. After about a week of jamming, I wanted to go hear the Allman Brothers, who were playing nearby, because I'd heard Duane Allman on Wilson Pickett's "Hey Jude," and he blew me away with that. After the concert I invited him back to the studio, and he stayed. We fell in love, and the album took off from there.

The first time I saw you was during those sessions at Criteria Recording Studios. There was a lot of dope around, especially heroin, and when I showed up, everyone was just spread out on the carpet, nodded out. Then you appeared in the doorway in an old brown leather jacket, with your hair slicked back like a greaser's, looking like you hadn't slept in days. You just looked around at the wreckage and said, to nobody in particular, "The boy stood on the burning deck/Whence all but he had fled." And then you split.

Yeah, we were staying in this hotel on the beach, and whatever drug you wanted, you could get it at the newsstand, the girl would just take your orders. And we were on the up and the down, the girl and the boy, and the drink was usually Ripple or Gallo. Very heavy stuff. I remember Ahmet [Ertegun, chairman of Atlantic Records] arriving at some point, taking me aside and crying, saying he'd been through this shit with Ray [Charles], and he knew where this was gonna end, and could I stop now. I said, "I don't know what you're talking about, man. This is no problem." And, of course, he was dead right.

I guess you have to work that stuff out for yourself.
I don't know about that. When I started using [heroin], George [Harrison] and Leon [Russell] asked me, "What are you doing? What is your intention?" And I said, "I want to make a journey through the dark, on my own, to find out what it's like in there. And then come out the other end." But that was easy for me to say, because I had a craft, music, that I could turn to. For people who don't have that, there's a lot of danger; if you haven't got something to hold on to, you're gone. It's no good just saying, "Well, that person is gonna go through it, no matter what." You've actually got to stop them and try to make them think.

The music you and Duane got into on *Layla* was really special, a once-in-a-lifetime thing. Did you tour after you finished recording?
Not with Duane, of course, but the Dominos did a very big tour of America. We copped a lot of dope in Miami—a lot of dope—and that went with us. Then I met up with this preacher from New York who was married to one of the Ronettes, and he asked if he could come along on part of the tour. The spiritual part of me was attracted to this man, but he immediately started giving me a very hard time about the dope. I felt very

bad about this, and after the first week on the road I put everything I had in a sack and flushed it down the loo. Then, of course, I was going to the other guys, trying to score off them.

By the end of the tour, the band was getting very, very loaded, doing way too much. Then we went back to England, tried to make a second album, and it broke down halfway through because of the paranoia and the tension. And the band just . . . dissolved. I remember to this day being in my house, feeling totally lost and hearing Bobby Whitlock pull up in the driveway outside and scream for me to come out. He sat in his car outside all day, and I hid. And that's when I went on my journey into the smack. I basically stayed in the house with my girlfriend for about two and a half years, and although we weren't using any needles, we got very strung out. All that time, though, I was running a cassette machine and playing; I had that to hold on to. At the end of that period I found I had boxes full of playing, as if there was something struggling to survive.

I guess that's what kept you alive.
I had no care for the consequences; the idea of dying didn't bother me. Dying from drugs didn't seem to me then to be a terrible thing. When Jimi died, I cried all day because he'd left me behind. But as I grow older, as I live more, death becomes more of a reality, something I don't choose to step toward too soon.

So then, in January 1973, Pete Townshend organized a concert for you at the Rainbow in London, with Ron Wood, Steve Winwood, and others.
I did that very much against my will. I wasn't even really there. It was purely Townshend's idea, and I didn't know what I'd done to earn it. It's simply that he's a great humanitarian and cannot stand to see people throw their lives away. It didn't matter to him if I was willing or unwilling; he was making the effort so that I would realize, someday, that someone cared. I'm always indebted to him for that.

If that didn't draw you out, what did?
Carl Radle sent me a tape of him playing with Dick Sims and Jamie Oldaker in Tulsa. I listened to it and played along with it, and it was great. So I sent him a telegram saying, "Maintain loose posture, stay in touch." And at some point after that, I started to get straight.

Then you made *461 Ocean Boulevard*, your resurrection album. Are you happy with that record?

Yeah, very. I'd wanted to do "Willie and the Hand Jive" since my childhood, and the Robert Johnson song ["Steady Rollin' Man"] and "Motherless Children" for almost as long. George Terry was there [in Miami], and when we were hanging out before the band arrived from Tulsa, he played me this Bob Marley album, *Burnin'*, and "I Shot the Sheriff" was on there. I loved it, and we did it, but at the time, I didn't think it was fair to Bob Marley, and I thought we'd done it with too much of a white feel or something. Shows what I know. When I went to Jamaica after that, a lot of people were very friendly because of the light it had thrown on Bob Marley, and Marley himself was very friendly to me as well.

Your Tulsa band could play everything from reggae to blues to pop. What happened to the band?

Toward the end of that particular band, we were getting out of it again, and I was in the lead. I started to get straight, but I was drinking maybe two bottles a day of whatever hard stuff I could get my hands on. And there was real bad tension in the band that was aimed at me. Then I hired Albert Lee. We became friends, and there was a division between these two Englishmen and the Tulsa boys. And at the end of this particular tour, I think it was in '78, I fired everybody. Not only that, I didn't even tell them—I fired them by telegram. And I never saw Carl again. He'd saved me at one point, sending me that tape, and I turned my back on him. And Carl died. It was, I think, drugs, but I hold myself responsible for a lot of that. And I live with it. . . .

Your next band was all English. Had you become disenchanted with crazy Americans?

Yeah. The idea of being with English gentlemen was a break. They weren't ambitious. They just wanted to play good music, and that was really easy for a while. Unfortunately, there were some things they just couldn't do. And one was to play the blues.

I guess I was underachieving a little bit, putting a certain kind of playing to one side because I didn't think the band would be able to do it. But there were things they did bring out in me, especially a wish to be more of a composer of melodic tunes rather than just a player, which was very unpopular with a lot of people.

But if you're a blues player, which I am by my birthright, it seems, you can't face it all the time. Sometimes you need to hear some harmonic softeners, some quiet, some subtle, to kind of quench the fire and calm yourself. Don Williams's music and some of the other things I was into were very calming to me. When I got back to being me, it was almost a shock to realize how tough my stuff was in comparison.

When you were touring England in the late seventies with that band, you urged one audience to support Enoch Powell, a member of Parliament who had a decidedly racist bent. Somehow I had trouble picturing you as a racist.
I was drunk, and a drunk will blab off about anything to as many people as he can; you cannot believe anything a drunk says. The funny thing is that I was able to play through all that. The old survivor, the automatic pilot, still managed to help me play. But there were many occasions around that time when I had to be led offstage and given some black coffee or some oxygen. I was really on the edge of collapse, completely insane.

I remember you coming to America in 1981 for a tour and landing in the hospital about eight days into the tour. Was that when your drinking started to come to an end?
Not quite. But it was pointed out to me while I was in hospital that I had a drink problem, and I think that was the first time anyone had ever said something like that to me. But I was still happy drinking and actually quite terrified of not drinking. I had to go further down that road to complete insanity before I stopped. It wasn't until it finally hit me in the head that I was killing other people around me, as well as killing myself and going insane, that I decided to stop. . . .

Liner Notes for the *Led Zeppelin* Box Set

(Atlantic, 1990)

Separately, in recent conversations, Jimmy Page and John Paul Jones practically echoed each other's comments when pressed to define what it was about Led Zeppelin that made playing in the band such a special experience for them. "Musically," said Page, "we weren't afraid to go in any direction whatsoever. I guess that was the way we kept ourselves really alive as musicians. The band wouldn't have existed if it hadn't been like that." Jones put it this way: "The very thing that Zeppelin was about was that there were absolutely no limits. There was freedom to try anything, to experiment. We all had ideas, and we'd use everything we came across, whether it was folk, country music, blues, Indian, Arabic. All these bands that are now borrowing from Zeppelin haven't figured that out, and because of that, none of them have got it right. None of them have gotten close."

The preponderance of "Led Clones" on American FM radio, and continuing, frequent airplay of the original recordings, have kept the band's legacy alive. They have also done our memories of the band's music a great disservice by carrying on as if "Stairway to Heaven" and a few crunching, blues-based riff tunes—"Whole Lotta Love," "Black Dog"—represented the entire scope of the Led Zeppelin heritage. They don't. Zeppelin's stylistic and emotional range were as broad and encompassing as those of any other band in rock's history. The present set, programmed and digitally remastered by Page from the original master tapes, allows a new picture to emerge, the picture of a band whose only limits were the imaginations and resources of the musicians.

And the musicians had unusually rich and varied backgrounds to draw on. At a time when many British rock bands were still being started by purist record collectors and other semi-professional players, Zeppelin had a guitarist whose insatiable curiosity about different musics and prior career as a top session man had encouraged him to tackle everything from hard blues to acoustic folk stylings to Indian music. John Paul Jones had also served a long session apprenticeship, doing everything from Motown-style bass to keyboards to full orchestral arrangements. Robert Plant and John Bonham had been professional pub-wrecking provincial rockers who had tackled blues, soul, west coast psychedelia, and more. Any band willing to mix and match such a crazy quilt of experience and influences was bound to be different.

Despite the leadership Page exercised as the group's founder, producer in the studio, and *de facto* musical director, Led Zeppelin was definitely a *band*. It is instructive to compare *Led Zeppelin* and the much-anticipated debut album by the Jeff Beck Group, *Truth*, both released in 1969. Beck puts his own name first and seems to have conceived the group primarily as a vehicle for his own playing despite the stellar talent of sidemen Ron Wood and Rod Stewart. Since both guitarists had become "names" with the Yardbirds, Page was sensitive to comparisons between the two groups; he was distressed to find out, too late, that both albums included covers of Willie Dixon's "You Shook Me." But from the first, Zeppelin had something going for it that the Beck group, with its battling egos and moody, introverted leader, lacked—a real group spirit. In Zeppelin's music, the song was most important, followed by the ensemble arrangement, overall sound and mood, *then* the solo turns. This group spirit had a lot to do with Zeppelin developing so rapidly, playing so tightly, and lasting so long without a single personnel change. Each member was considered irreplaceable, which is the reason the band had to call it quits following John Bonham's death.

"When recording," Page recalled recently of the Zeppelin sessions, "I was extremely conscious of building and maintaining the atmospheric quality of the song from square one. No matter how many guitar parts I might layer on in the studio, I followed the tune's overall theme and ambiance in my mind. Sometimes I did get carried away a bit, but fortunately I always managed to catch myself. That's what it's all about, catching yourself."

John also emphasizes his role as a team player, a song player. "I suppose in my case it's an arranger's ear," he said while talking about the music in this set. "That was one of the very good things about the band, it wasn't just a bunch of musicians playing, we treated the songs as top priority. You would try to bring out the best in the song, rather than look at it as an excuse for a blinding solo."

Page describes his work in the studio as "a kind of construction in light and shade. Usually, we'd start with the framework, we'd lay down the tracks and Robert would do a guide vocal. I would then overlay lots of different guitars, and then Robert would come in and do a final vocal." Page experimented not only with combining the sounds of his Les Paul, Danelectro, and other guitars, but played them through various amps and miked them from different spots and from different distances, resulting in what can only be called in retrospect the beginnings of modern guitar orchestration in the studio.

Jones, also an inveterate experimenter, was always the heartbeat on bass, but gradually his keyboards became an increasingly important part of the sound. He tried everything from the reliable Hammond organ to an early EMS VCS3 synthesizer, hand-patched, which can be heard on "In the Light" and "No Quarter." He was adept at reproducing string sounds on his mellotron, but beware of generalizations. The strings on "Friends" are actually strings, played by Indian musicians in an Indian studio, arranged and conducted by Jones. On "The Ocean" he's playing an old Farfisa organ with a glide pedal that enabled him to slide notes up or down as much as an octave.

In the studio, as in their music, Zeppelin tried just about everything. "We had amps in toilets," recalls Jones, "mikes hanging down chimneys. Sometimes when we were renting these big old houses to write in, we'd experiment with the sound there. Very often the sound would suggest a tune, and we'd write or arrange with that in mind—'When the Levee Breaks' is a good example of that."

Led Zeppelin made its impact primarily with its hard rock, some of the hardest around. It was a new, savage sound in riff-based electric music, one Page had been conceiving and refining during his years with the Yardbirds. "I was always experimenting with riffs and things then," Page said, "and began to see during that period that playing such music with a highly inventive rhythm section could move the music into new dimensions." At the same time, on *Led Zeppelin* the band's range and ambition were already in evidence. "I always thought our mixing of the electric with acoustic music was one thing that really made us stand out as a band," Page said, "and it was there from the beginning. On the first album, between things like 'Babe I'm Gonna Leave You' and 'Communication Breakdown,' you've got something that's driving all the way and then something that's far more subtle, with changes and such. And everything just kept on moving from there." In fact, "Babe I'm Gonna Leave You" is a kind of initial blueprint for later songs that used multipart structures, complex arrangements, and constantly altering instrumental textures, culminating in opuses such as "Stairway to Heaven" and "Achilles Last Stand."

Zeppelin's relationship to the blues was complex. Jones was much more influenced by soul music and, especially, jazz; his keyboard idol in his early days was Ray Charles. He reports that on the Zeppelin tour plane, he and Bonham "were James Brown freaks and used to play his records all the time. It wasn't terribly cool to listen to James Brown then, especially around the FM underground stations, where they really didn't like black music at all, which was a real shame. But onstage, we'd get into funk grooves a lot. Bonzo, incidentally, had very broad listening tastes. When we weren't listening to James Brown or Otis Redding, he might be listening to Joni Mitchell or Crosby, Stills, Nash & Young. Bonzo was a great lover of songs."

Plant had started in folk and skiffle bands, put in his blues apprenticeship (with Bonham) in the Crawling Kingsnakes, and then turned toward west coast psychedelia before meeting Page. But it was the blues that taught him some of his most valuable lessons. He explains: "With the blues, you could actually express yourself rather than just copy, you could get your piece in there. Only when I began singing blues was I able to use the medium to express what was inside me, my hopes and my fears. I could use several blues lines, well-known blues lines, but they were all related to me that day. And that's because the blues is more elastic. It also encouraged me to be more flexible vocally, even at the risk of losing the melody. I could just sing *out*. Yet the blues is just one of the many sources I drew from. I mean, Ray Charles was as much of a contributor as anyone else, and he wasn't a blues shouter, he was testifying. It came from all angles: Ray Charles, Screamin' Jay 'Hawkins, Howlin' Wolf."

Although the young Jimmy Page was playing Chicago blues the night he was "discovered" at the Marquee Club (a gig that led him to the first of his many studio sessions), his first inspirations were fifties rock & roll singles. By the time he'd begun to delve heavily into blues, he was already a session musician, playing straight pop one day and ersatz Motown the next.

In other words, none of these musicians was a blues purist, or collector, like, say, members of the Rolling Stones. Zeppelin played the blues, but blues filtered through a very individual group sensibility. Perhaps the most familiar example is "Whole Lotta Love," which begins as a bluesy riff-cruncher but moves organically into psychedelic sound-collage territory on the break ("that was Page and Eddie Kramer just going crazy twisting knobs in the studio," an observer reported) without ever losing sight of the mood and intent of the original tune.

When Page took a blues guitar solo on record, his tendency was to simply play two or three takes, see what came out, and use the best take—often the most exciting rather than the most technically perfect, for as Page admits, there are plenty of "mistakes" in his Zeppelin solos. Yet they still thrill, and convince.

It isn't entirely surprising to learn that Page's blues influences weren't exactly conventional, compared to the preferences of his contemporaries. In 1966, after a Yardbirds concert, I approached him and asked him about his favorite blues listening, and he mentioned in particular the piano playing of country bluesman Skip James, some of the more eccentric works in the entire blues canon. When I recently reminded Page of this, he said, "Yeah, those records seemed so off-the-wall in their timing, yet so *right*. If you count them through, though, they're regular

4/4. Anything like that, that was sort of bizarre or sounded avant-garde, that was for me. But I'd have to say my main blues influences was Howlin' Wolf, and his stuff wasn't just straight groove, playing on the beat, either. I loved his voice and the sheer intensity of the music as well as the timing of it. I've often thought that in the way the Stones tried to be the sons of Chuck Berry, we tried to be the sons of Howlin' Wolf."

Country blues and early Howlin' Wolf sides with staggered, off-kilter rhythms had a lot to do with shaping Page's riff construction, and he passed on this approach to Jones and Bonham, who with their fondness for James Brown's rhythmic whiplash were more than ready to meet the challenge. All that, combined with Plant's highly personal vocal approach, resulted in a new kind of blues feel, miles away from the more imitative work of Zeppelin's British precursors and contemporaries; it was heavy, even ponderous-sounding, but it was always swinging. "That was very important to us," Jones noted. "We all always liked bands that really grooved."

Individually, the players also expressed their own personalities within blues forms. Page never played a solo that sounded like any other single blues guitarist, something that can't even be said of Eric Clapton, who went through his imitative Albert King and Freddie King phases on records before finding his own blues voice. And Plant simply cut loose. Former Zeppelin engineer Eddie Kramer described the Plant of Zeppelin days as "a wild man of the vocal cords, with tremendous range and highly charged emotional impact."

Zeppelin has frequently been charged with plagiarism for uncredited use of blues riffs and tunes. It's one thing to run afoul of Willie Dixon, a professional Chicago songwriter and session bassist who wrote and copyrighted the original "You Shook Me" and "I Can't Quit You Baby" and successfully sued after Zeppelin released their considerably altered versions of those songs. Yet several of Dixon's copyrights are of material from the folk-blues public domain—tunes like "My Babe" were current in the South long before he claimed them. It is the custom, in blues music, for a singer to borrow verses from contemporary sources, both oral and recorded, add his own tune and/or arrangement, and call the song his own.

The same sort of brouhaha might possibly emerge over Zeppelin's "Travelling Riverside Blues," heard here for the first time as preserved on a 1969 BBC broadcast. Is this the famous Robert Johnson "Traveling Riverside Blues"? The title and opening verse are the only evident borrowings from the Johnson recording, which was itself partly reassembled from traditional sources. Page's complex slide-guitar rhythms and the rhythm-section figures are miles away from Johnson's conception, and Plant strings together verses from a variety of sources, the way bluesmen of Johnson's generation so freely did. Our copyright laws were written to the specifications of Tin Pan Alley and are of little relevance here, it seems to me. You can copyright a melody or lyrics, but not styles or riffs or rhythm patterns. Thus Clapton can insert a solo whose vocabulary is pure Albert King into "Strange Brew" with impunity, but Zeppelin's more deeply assimilated and originally conceived reworkings of material like "Travelling Riverside Blues" are sources for debate.

I'm not arguing that Dixon didn't deserve royalties for songs he clearly wrote, but I am arguing that the whole issue is more complex than it seems on the surface. Meanwhile, Zeppelin progressed, moving further and further away from specific blues sources as they incorporated the blues language more organically into their own creative processes. There was always a lot more to Zeppelin's music than "heavy blues." Page says he had a sitar before the Beatles got one, but couldn't find out how to tune it! One of the first British musicians to develop serious interest in Indian music, he explains: "I saw a parallel between the bending strings of blues music and the emotional quality of that, with what was being done in Indian music—especially in the *alap* [the early, meditative, improvisational, and rhythmically free part of the raga] as well as in the timings or time sequencing of Indian music. Once I started to kind of digest the whole system of Indian music and learned what was involved, I realized it was far too complicated for someone who was really a rock & roll guitarist. But *ideas* from Indian music were well worth incorporating, tunings and such."

This Indian influence can be heard everywhere from the keyboard introduction to "In the Light," which was a Jones inspiration, to Page's "White Summer"/"Black Mountain Side" medley, recorded live by the BBC and heard here for the first time. But by no means is the medley "Indian" in form or execution. Its relationship to Indian music is roughly comparable to Zeppelin's relationship to the blues. In fact, Page calls it his "CIA connection—part Celtic, part Indian, part Arabic. That's played in a guitar tuning very close to the standard Indian sitar tuning," he noted, "but then again it's like a mishmash, really, because it's sort of pseudo-Indian and pseudo-Arabic as well, so that what comes out still has a sort of Western feel, in the combination, the fusion."

Page's and Jones's interest in Indian and Arabic music ran deep and was long-lasting. The latter recalls: "When I was a kid, my father had a big, old short-wave radio, and we could pick up North Africa, so I spent many hours listening to Arab music. I loved it—still do." Perhaps the best example of the ways in which these strains worked together in a band context is "Kashmir." Plant, an inveterate traveller who frequently visited Morocco in Zeppelin days and returns there periodically, remembers writing the lyric when he was driving, alone, across a desolate stretch of the Moroccan Sahara between Tantan and Goulimine. Page came up with the cascading, descending phrase for massed guitars that periodically punctuates or paces the tune. Then, he explains, "I had this idea to combine orchestra and mellotron and have them duplicate the guitar parts. Jonesey improvised whole sections with the mellotron and added the final ascending riff, whereby the song fades." The resulting mix of sounds, in which both guitars and brass lose their identities in a wholly unique sonority, is Zeppelin at its best.

Plant recalls that he, too, had benefited from early exposure to non-western musical forms: "When I was seventeen, I began dating the consequent mother of my children. She lived in an East Indian area, so I was constantly surrounded by Indian film music. To a conservative ear, the swirling strings and the way the vocals came out of the instrumental sections wouldn't have been attractive at all. But to me, it was all very sensual and alluring. And five blocks from that was the Jamaican neighborhood, where I used to hang out when I wasn't working, eating goat stew and listening to ska records. Then I later went to Morocco, which moved me into a totally different culture. The place, the smells, the colors were all very intoxicating, as was the music. On the radio you could hear a lot of Egyptian pop like Oum Kalsoum, and depending on where you were, Berber music. I never tried to write anything down or to play it, I was just developing a love affair. But I know it did something to me, to my vocal style. You can hear it in the longer sustained notes, the drops, the quarter tones. You hear that in 'Friends' or in 'In the Light' for instance, lots of other places too."

There are also strong British Isles folk and Celtic influences in Zeppelin. One good example is "Bron-Y-Aur Stomp," a kind of tribal highland fling. Another is "The Battle of Evermore," lyrically Plant's evocation of the long history of conflict between Celts and Saxons along the Welsh border, near his hometown. "You don't have to have too much of an imagination or a library full of books if you live there," he says. "It's still there. On a murky October evening, with the watery sun looking down on those hills over some old castle and into the river, you have to be a real bimbo not to flash occasionally. Remember, I wasn't living in London. There you can be a fashion victim, but you can't feel like your average working man's Celt." At another extreme, Plant and Page shared an affinity for the rockabilly of the fifties—Gene Vincent with guitarist Cliff Gallup was a big favorite. This influence has emerged even more clearly in Plant's solo work but is certainly present here, especially in "Candy Store Rock" and the psychobilly of "Ozone Baby."

One thing this set throws into sharp relief is how much new ground Zeppelin broke, and how little credit they've received for it. The "world beat" phenomenon that has captured the attention of Peter Gabriel, Paul Simon, and other eighties pop stars has accustomed us to hearing music heavily influenced from other cultures. When Zeppelin started, there was no "world beat," and rock groups' borrowings from other cultures were largely window dressing. (Did "Norwegian Wood" really *need* that sitar? Did it have anything to do with the song?)

Zeppelin's interest in world music, sparked by Page's and Jones's early curiosity, really began to pay off artistically when Plant blossomed as a lyricist. His travels through some of the more remote regions of the planet gave him plenty to think and write about, and many of his songs display a healthy (and, at the time, very rare) cultural relativism. Perhaps the apex of this aspect of Zeppelin was "Kashmir," about as perfect a blend of lyric, of music, tradition, and innovation as one could imagine.

Zeppelin also showed us many a new way of swinging. To ears accustomed to lighter drummers than Bonham and to riffs less chiseled-in-stone than Page's, early Zeppelin didn't sound very swinging. Now that rap and pop producers have been sampling beats and drum licks from Zeppelin records for several years, often using them as the rhythmic basis for a new dance single, the lurching beats and staggered rhythms sound a lot different: they swing like mad.

Perhaps Zeppelin's greatest legacy is a quality that is now in short supply: They showed that four individuals, from varied backgrounds and with diverse personalities and imaginations, could chart their own adventurous musical course, make their own records just the way they wanted to without intrusion from corporate execs hoping for a hit single, innovate with every album, and *keep on doing it*, long after many another band would have grown creatively slack from the excesses that come with fame and fortune. Luckily for us, they persevered.

This collection is among other things a showcase for Page's radically recombinant approach to programming. His intricately plotted sequences of often startling juxtapositions reveal unexpected angles in even the most familiar Zeppelin works. This gives us a chance we rarely get with a rock band of this stature—the chance to share their own mature reconsideration of how much of what they did was built to last.

JOHN LENNON AND YOKO ONO: "NOW THE MUSIC'S COMING *THROUGH* ME AGAIN."

John Lennon: Must an Artist Self-Destruct?

THE NEW YORK TIMES | NOVEMBER 9, 1980

"Is it possible to have a life centered around a family and a child and still be an artist?" asked John Lennon. For Mr. Lennon, widely regarded as the most thoughtful and outspoken of the four Beatles during their heyday in the sixties, the question is far from rhetorical. Together with his wife, Yoko Ono, and their five-year-old son, Sean, the forty-year-old Lennon has been engrossed in a settled family life since dropping out of the music business five years ago. Now, with Miss Ono, he is reentering the pop mainstream with a new album, *Double Fantasy*, which will be in stores this week.

In a series of candid conversations that took place in a recording studio during the making of the album, and at the Lennons' New York apartment after its completion, both artists talked at length about the demands of making music versus the demands of a family. "In a way,"

Mr. Lennon said, "we're involved in a kind of experiment. Could the family be the inspiration of art, instead of drinking or drugs or whatever? I'm interested in finding that out."

At the door of the family's apartment in the Dakota, Mr. Lennon greeted me, smiling broadly, one hand on his heart, the other arm out-stretched, like a thirties crooner. "Pardon me," he sang, "if I'm sentimen-tal . . ." The Warner Bros.–distributed Geffen label had just released a single, "Starting Over," backed with Miss Ono's "Kiss Kiss Kiss," from the album. I'd written the previous week that while Mr. Lennon's pop craftsmanship was intact, the song's lyrics seemed a bit obvious and senti-mental. Since then I'd heard the complete album and been struck by the contrast between Mr. Lennon's generally adoring and plainspoken songs (though his crunching, bluesy "I'm Losing You" is considerably more potent) and the mystery and bitterness in several of Miss Ono's pieces. The latter sound remarkably like the music of certain new wave rockers, many of whom (the B-52's, for instance, and surely Lene Lovich) were inspired by her experimental vocal techniques of the late sixties and early seventies.

We sat down at a plain wooden table in the middle of a spacious kitchen that had a stereo, a large video screen, and a couch and lounging area at one end. There were Italian cookies and pastries on the table, and Mr. Lennon brewed a pot of coffee. "I've heard 'Starting Over' hundreds of times now," Miss Ono said, "but I still get choked up and cry sometimes when I hear it, because . . . well, in the sixties we went through this thing with everybody feeling that we were going to be free. And it turned into a big orgy; in the end, the women realized that all the sexual liberation was really just for men. And now here's a guy, John, saying to a woman, let's start over again, let's try. These are times when women are still bitter about these things, and I think men have to make that first move."

"The sixties," Mr. Lennon said with a smile, sitting down with the coffee. "When I met Yoko, we were two poets in velvet cloaks—almost literally—both full of positive ideas for the world, but for ourselves those ideas didn't count. We were both self-destructive; I'd come up thinking of myself not so much as a musician, you know, but as a writer, and big examples in England were Dylan Thomas and Brendan Behan. I'd just naïvely accepted the idea that an artist had to self-destruct in order to create. And we both came out of that through the gift of having the baby.

"By 1975 I wasn't really enjoying what I was doing anyway. I was a machine that was supposed to produce so much creative something and give it out periodically for approval or to justify my existence on earth. But I don't think I would have been able to just withdraw from the whole music business if it hadn't been for Sean. I gave him five years, taking care of him while Yoko ran our business affairs, but it's going on, and I feel it should go on. When I look at the relative importance of what life is about, I can't quite convince myself that making a record or having a career is more important or even as important as my child, or any child."

Mr. Lennon lit a cigarette and pushed a tempting chocolate cake to the far end of the table. "Another thing those five years did for me," he said, "was to move a lot of intellectual garbage out of the way and allow whatever it is in me that wants to express itself to do it naturally. This is a digression, but going back to the beginning of rock & roll, Elvis and Jerry Lee Lewis and so on were working-class entertainment; they were working-class. The Beatles were slightly less working-class; for Paul McCartney and me, at least, going to university was a possibility. I had all this artsy stuff in me anyway, so we put a little more intellect in our music, just because of what we were. And gradually, expectations for the Beatles became educated, middle-class expectations. And I tended to get too intellectual about pop music. I had this sort of critic John Lennon sitting over me saying, 'You did that already, you can't do it again. You can't say it that simply.' Now the music's coming *through* me again."

The *Double Fantasy* album, subtitled *A Heart Play*, isn't going to be accused of being overly intellectual. Mr. Lennon's songs are direct and, in their celebrations of enduring love and the pleasures of home and hearth, they will undoubtedly strike some listeners as simplistic, finely crafted though they are. Miss Ono's songs tend to have more bite, though "I'm Your Angel," a piece of thirties-style whimsy, wouldn't find itself out of place in a Walt Disney movie. "For me," Mr. Lennon said, "a lot of the so-called avant-garde in pop is pseudo-intellectual—which is something I contributed to. Basically, you just want a good record, right? You can enjoy it no matter what level it's on, whether it makes you want to dance or makes you want to lie down and think about the universe."

"I'm not impressed by pop that plays a lot of intellectual games," Miss Ono added. "The more you intellectualize, the more you get lost."

At work at a recording console in New York's Hit Factory, bracing himself with a strong cup of coffee, Mr. Lennon looked trimmer than he had in the late sixties and early seventies, and in his black jeans, black work shirt, and wire-rimmed glasses, he seemed more like John Lennon, pop star, than like a "house husband," as he's taken to calling himself. Miss Ono, a founding member of the sixties performance-art vanguard known as the Fluxus movement (other participants included John Cage, La Monte Young, and Nam June Paik), was sitting at the console too, and they were both listening to Mr. Lennon's song "Starting Over," which was to be the first selection and the first single from their new album. "I don't think you should put another voice on it, John," she said as she lit a cigarette. The song already boasted a rich mesh of voices, some provided by backup singers and some by Mr. Lennon, whose reedy tenor and personal inflection are still immediately recognizable.

"Mother," he said in measured tones—he often calls Miss Ono "Mother," apparently with a great deal of respect—"I don't want to double the same part, I'm hearing another harmony that I want to try." Mr. Lennon turned to explain. "Back when we were doing Beatles records, I used to want to double-track my voice on everything, mostly to make it stronger. Now"—he waved his arm to indicate the expanse of blinking, whirring equipment, some of it computerized—"you don't have to do that." He downed the rest of his coffee and walked out into the studio, glancing on the way at the large color photograph of Sean that hung from a monitor speaker. "I'll bet," he mused aloud, "that I miss him a lot more than he misses me."

Recording studios have changed a great deal since the Beatles recorded *Sgt. Pepper's Lonely Hearts Club Band* on a four-track machine—for that matter, they've changed since 1975. Helping the Lennons explore the possibilities of new technology were Jack Douglas, who had worked for them as an engineer in the early seventies and now produced popular rock groups like Cheap Trick, and the engineer Lee DeCarlo, a burly Vietnam veteran with a dreamy, bearish smile. "They've been a big help," Miss Ono said as the two busily adjusted settings and Mr. Lennon cleared his throat into a microphone. "But the two of us are very headstrong. For the final word on my songs I always look to John, and the final word on his comes from me."

Mr. Lennon practiced singing along with the track, which had been recorded in an intensive series of sessions that began on August 8. It was a melodious, loping tune with a fifties backbeat, and the more he ran over it, the more scraps of Beatles songs he was able to insert, just for fun. "Why don't we do it in the road," he sang, echoing the title line from one of [the] songs on the Beatles' *White Album* when he should have been singing "why don't we take off alone." But soon he turned serious and was able to perfect his harmony part after only a few tries. It made the song sound uncannily like a Beatles record, though the backing band was composed of New York studio professionals.

Miss Ono had been taking care of business details while Mr. Lennon sang. Periodically, a Japanese assistant would bring her hot tea and a pad with telephone messages in Japanese characters—from photographers, journalists asking for interviews, record-company representatives (the album, and the Lennons' immediate future as recording artists, hadn't yet been assigned to any company, and the bidding was intense). She'd gone into a room adjoining the studio to return the most important calls. "Well, Mother," Mr. Lennon said, plainly elated that his work was going so well, "I'm done for now. Time to work on one of your songs." He stretched out on a nearby couch and went to sleep.

After hearing Mr. Lennon's melodious pop, Miss Ono's song "Give Me Something" was a little startling. Propelled by a serpentine chromatic guitar figure from the former David Bowie sidekick Earl Slick and clocking in at a brisk one minute and thirty-eight seconds, it offered a vision that was considerably bleaker than Mr. Lennon's reassuring "Starting Over." "The food is cold," Miss Ono sang, tunefully but piercingly, "your eyes are cold/the window's cold/the bed's cold." There was a screaming solo from Earl Slick and the song abruptly crashed to a halt.

"You know what I listened to for the last five years?" Mr. Lennon asked after his nap. "Muzak! For the chores I was doing around the house, it was perfect. I know people are going to say, 'Oh, that's because he's got to be forty and got soft.' Well, it might be that; it's irrelevant to me. The attitude is that when you change when you get older, there's something wrong with that, but the world is stupid enough as it is; if the young were running it, it would be really dumb. Whatever changes I'm going through because I'm forty I'm thankful for, because they give me some insight into the madness I've been living in all my life."

The Real Way to Remember Lennon

THE NEW YORK TIMES | DECEMBER 9, 1981

"Everybody loves you when you're six foot in the ground," John Lennon sang in 1974 on his album *Walls and Bridges*. As usual, he was being trenchant, and as usual, he was right. He was loved by millions when he was alive, but in the year that has passed since last December 8, when he was shot down outside the Dakota, it seems he has been loved by just about everybody, indiscriminately.

Books about Mr. Lennon were hastily thrown together and rushed into print within a few weeks of his death. They were all "tributes," "remembrances," testimonials to what a wonderful artist and all-round wonderful guy he was. The anniversary of the shooting has brought forth a torrent of radio and television "tributes," many exercises in nostalgia-by-the-book: film clips from A *Hard Day's Night*, snatches of Beatles songs, glimpses of John F. Kennedy and other early-sixties icons and newsreel voices lamenting the passing of an era.

The Cincinnati Pops Orchestra, the hammy belter David Clayton Thomas, and the pop singer Roberta Flack, none of whom have the remotest relationship to rock & roll as Lennon perceived and created it, will take A *Tribute to John Lennon: A Concert in His Memory* into Radio City Music Hall tomorrow night. If Lennon could somehow comment on all these outpourings of love, his response would undoubtedly be unprintable.

"I'm sick and tired of hearing things from uptight short-sighted narrow-minded hypocritics," Lennon practically shrieked on his second post-Beatles album, *Imagine.* Now that was Lennon—opinionated, outspoken, engaged, and combative. The major fallacy of the majority of "tributes" is that they are tributes to Beatle John.

Lennon was justly proud of his work with the Beatles, but he did his best to torpedo the Beatles myth, beginning with his first post-Beatles album, *John Lennon/Plastic Ono Band,* released in 1970.

"I don't believe in Beatles," he announced on that album in a song called "God": "I just believe in me, in Yoko and me. The dream is over."

In retrospect, it's evident that Lennon was chipping away at the Beatles' four-lovable-moptops image early on. In the mid-sixties, when the Beatles should have been on top of the world, he wrote and sang "Help!"—and he meant it. When Paul McCartney was writing "Yesterday," Lennon was writing "Norwegian Wood," a thinly veiled account of an extramarital affair.

And once he was freed from the constraints he had felt as a member of the Fab Four, he no longer felt the need to thinly veil anything. In 1969, he wrote and recorded "Cold Turkey," a graphic account of his first brush with heroin addiction and the torment of withdrawal. On his *Plastic Ono Band* album, he sang about his mother's death, his early insecurity, and his continuing feelings of isolation and paranoia. And on his next album, *Imagine,* he posed some of the most difficult questions and confronted some of the most bitter realizations that a pop singer has ever grappled with.

"How can I give love when I just don't know how to give?" he asked. "How can I give love when love is something I ain't never had?" In order to "be somebody," he counseled, "you got to shove." And he warned that while "you can hide your face behind a smile, one thing you can't hide is when you're crippled inside."

These aren't the Lennon songs one hears on the radio, and they aren't the Lennon songs pop singers work into their "tribute" medleys. But to many of Lennon's longtime admirers, they are *the* Lennon songs, the true measure of the man.

At the same time, they are not the whole story. Lennon somehow managed to be both an acerbic, hardheaded analyst of himself and his times and a cockeyed optimist. And most of the tributes that have been lavished on him since his death have failed to grapple with either of these extremes.

A recent review of *The Playboy Interviews with John Lennon and Yoko Ono* is typical. Lennon's soul-searching candor, it says, is "often rather embarrassing." His optimism is dismissed as "the requisite shoveling of cosmic gumdrops, the gratuitous harping on Peace and Love and Living in the Now."

How Lennon would have hated being patronized in this manner! "As if love and peace were invented in the sixties," he snorted when this writer interviewed him a month before his death. "As if Gandhi didn't exist or Christ didn't exist. Naïveté is something the media attributed to the sixties, by saying: 'We told you they were all stupid, those hippies. They were so naïve. The reality is disco and drugs and A *Clockwork Orange*, you see.'

"But the naïveté is to buy the idea that the sixties were naïve. The musicians weren't naïve; they were playing the music for the sake of the music. And look at the things that have come out of the sixties—health food, therapies, meditation, all these things have become mainstream."

Those who choose to love Lennon by attempting to sanitize his memory can point to the domestic sweetness of *Double Fantasy*, the "comeback" album he made with his wife, Miss Ono, in the months before his death. Lennon finally seemed to be at peace with himself in those final months, and his songs reflected that peace truthfully; the album's tougher, more questioning songs were by Miss Ono.

But *Double Fantasy* was not Lennon's final piece of work. The night of his death he had finished work on Miss Ono's "Walking on Thin Ice," a profoundly disturbing song, shot full of foreboding.

Encouraged by favorable reviews of Miss Ono's contributions to *Dou-*

ble Fantasy, Lennon pulled out the stops on "Thin Ice." He helped Miss Ono craft an arrangement that was as abrasively up-to-the-minute as any new-wave disk, and he contributed one of the most violent, wrenching guitar solos in the history of rock & roll.

According to Miss Ono and to the Lennons' coproducer, Jack Douglas, Lennon saw "Walking on Thin Ice" as the beginning of a new phase in his music, a phase more in line with the provocative lyrics and astringent musical textures of albums like *Plastic Ono Band* and *Imagine.*

One night shortly before his death, Lennon talked at some length and with considerable pride about the dissonant, howling feedback solos he had contributed to some of Miss Ono's most extreme disks in the early seventies. He expressed the desire to indulge in such brinksmanship again, and he and Miss Ono said they intended to follow up *Double Fantasy* with records that would grow more and more experimental, more and more challenging.

Lennon enjoyed stirring things up. There was something almost anarchic in his quick, unrestrained laughter, something that wanted to test the limits of the situation behind his most relaxed smile. It's the wildness of the laughter, the challenge behind the smile that I'll remember, and love. Beatle John belongs to an era that is gone now, but honest, ornery John Lennon belongs to the ages.

John and Paul

THE NEW YORK TIMES | NOVEMBER 7, 1985

The media attention recently given a four-year-old interview in which Paul McCartney calls John Lennon, his Beatles songwriting partner, insecure, jealous, and a "maneuvering swine," is curious indeed. The rivalry that existed between the two has been explored exhaustively for years in books and articles on the Fab Four.

My own brief encounters with the two former Beatles may shed a glimmer of light on their differences and on a fragile but long-lasting mutual affection. I have interviewed Mr. McCartney twice. In one of our talks, he attributed differences between the two to their upbringing. Mr. Lennon, he said, had had an unstable home life and, consequently, an insecure childhood, which left him with a chip on his shoulder. Mr. McCartney's family was extended and perhaps unusually sociable. When Mom or Dad weren't around to bounce the children on their knees, there were always grandparents, aunts, uncles, and other relatives to fill in. But the atmosphere around Mr. McCartney during the interview—tight security, a strict time allotment—showed little of this warmth.

I first met John Lennon and Yoko Ono when they invited me to one of their recording sessions. When I arrived in the control room, Mr. Lennon was in the studio adding vocal harmonies to "(Just Like) Starting Over." When he sidled in to join us, he said to me: "I figured you were the guy from *The New York Times*. It made me really nervous." The remark dissolved my own nervousness. After the session, we went to the Dakota, where we sat around the kitchen table most of the night, talking music and indulging ourselves with brownies, milk, and a cheesecake that must have been sent from heaven.

There were more visits in the two months before Mr. Lennon was murdered, and the talk was always fast, intense, mercurial. Mr. Lennon told Beatle stories from the early days, but had little to say on the subject of Paul McCartney. Basically, he said, their temperaments were very different, and while the clash added juice to their early songwriting collaborations, it was inevitable that they would drift apart. He did not pretend that he cared for Mr. McCartney's post-Beatles music, but he didn't go out of his way to excoriate it, either.

One man, Paul McCartney, living in self-imposed isolation, and perhaps providing for his children the close family life he had enjoyed as a child. The other, John Lennon, verbally brilliant, cosmic one moment and deftly cutting the next, a rocker until the day he died. No matter how much distance developed between them, they never showed signs of intense hatred—only a kind of puzzled acceptance of the way things had turned out for them, and a low, guttering, but never wholly extinguished flame of something very much like love.

On Thin Ice: The Music of Yoko Ono

From the liner notes for *Onobox* (Rykodisc, 1992)

The Loft

One chill, brittle October day in 1960, a small young Japanese woman stood at the bottom of an endless flight of stairs. Though not truly endless, the stairs led to what is referred to in New York City as a "fifth-floor walkup," and in New York you can't get to a fifth-floor walkup by climbing five flights of stairs. Ten flights is the norm in buildings like this one, fifteen not uncommon. How could stairs following such an apparently leisurely gradient be so broad, so solid, and still be so steep? Five, ten, fifteen, the stairs were, for all practical purposes, endless.

But they did end, on the top floor, in front of an industrial-strength door. Inside was one big bare room. "It was a cold water flat, there was no electricity, the ceiling wasn't very high, it was just a very long room,"

says Yoko Ono, the woman who had bounded up the stairs as if they were a path through the woods. "It had something for bringing heavy things up, not an elevator, you hooked this huge hook onto what you wanted and pulled it up. The windows in the back were hopeless, nothing but grime and soot. But there were windows facing the front, those old kind of windows that have wire in the panes, and they aren't transparent. And there was a skylight. You could look up and almost feel more connected to the sky than to the city. I liked the place, and the man who owned the store on the ground floor said I could get it. The price was $50.50 a month. Getting that together to pay him every month was hard . . . he ran a kind of sports store, not like the kind you see now. They sold hiking equipment."

The loft was 112 Chambers Street, in a rapidly changing area of downtown in Manhattan, a jumble of former loft-building sweatshops and storage warehouses, disintegrating ethnic neighborhoods, fish and produce markets. It was just what Yoko was looking for: an ample space in which to build her art and her life. The daughter of a Westernized Japanese banker and his traditionally Japanese wife, Yoko had dropped out of Sarah Lawrence College, where she was studying composition, and decamped to New York to become an artist in 1957. In the next two years, she met a large number of artists, especially musicians. All of them had been drawn to New York, where something new was about to happen.

Yoko had a theory about all these radical young music makers showing up in downtown Manhattan just as the sixties were dawning: Disparate as they were, they shared dissatisfaction with the impossibility of notation on musical staff paper of the sounds they heard in their heads. "You can't translate the more complex sounds into traditional notation," says Yoko. "The minute you do notate it and someone plays what you've written, the sound becomes totally different. I wanted to capture the sounds I'd heard of birds singing in the woods, things like that. And I think the reason all these artists came to New York and got together at this time was that all of them had this dissatisfaction about just writing musical notes. They were venturing into a different area and that's why we all got together." (Another kind of music that cannot be notated with any significant fidelity or accuracy is rock & roll.)

John Cage was the oldest and most celebrated of a group that included

La Monte Young (founding minimalist composer, whose first performing group left to join Lou Reed in the original Velvet Underground), Henry Flynt (composer, violinist, and the theorist who coined the term "concept art"), and a brilliant but now little-known electronic composer, Richard Maxfield. All of these artists were shunned by the uptown classical-music world. The lines were drawn somewhere around Fourteenth Street. "In those days," Yoko recalls, "when you said 'concert,' it meant Town Hall, Carnegie Recital Hall, that was it."

Only a few painters had hazarded the urban pioneering required to turn a downtown industrial or storage loft into a combination art studio and place to live when Yoko found her loft late in 1960. The experimental loft music scene that would help make artists such as Laurie Anderson and Philip Glass into stars and SoHo real estate some of the most expensive in New York was still some twenty years in the future. When she was looking for her loft, Yoko had finding a performance space in mind. It had also not escaped Yoko's notice that none of her friends had suitable venues for giving concerts in New York City.

Yoko decided to initiate a series—New York's first loft concerts. Then one day, Richard Maxfield called her and asked if "they" could join her, since he and La Monte Young were trying to put together some evenings of the new music. The initial event was set for December. "Everybody had advised me not to do this," Yoko recalls. "They said, nobody's going to go all the way downtown to listen to this, it's just a total waste. But I had an electricity line run in from the hall, and an old gas stove that had a fan to sort of spread the heat around the room. And I had empty orange crates for chairs. At other times, I would put all the crates together to make a large table, and at night I just collected them and made a bed out of them."

"The day of the first concert, it snowed pretty heavily, and you know how it is, when it snows you don't get a crowd. Twenty-five people came, most of them from Stony Point—John Cage, David Tudor, people like that." People hadn't come all the way from uptown after all; but they had driven down from the wooded area north of the city where Cage, Tudor, and several of their friends and collaborators lived. Cage had created the first effective, deep-structured blends of Western and Eastern musical traditions and pioneered electronic music before there were electronic instruments, using radios and similar hardware as sound

sources. Somehow he seemed to *belong* there, listening intently, head cocked in that sage way of his, sitting on an orange crate. The concert may not have been a smashing success, but for Yoko Ono it was an auspicious beginning.

Fear and Stuttering

It is quite likely that having John Lennon fall in love with her was the worst thing that could have happened to Yoko Ono's career as an artist. By the time she met the then-Beatle, at her one-woman show in London's prestigious Indica Gallery in 1966, she was controversial but internationally known and recognized for her work in music, film, and the sort of conceptual presentations a later generation would dub "performance art." By the mid-sixties, she had given performances at New York's Village Gate, the Bridge Theater, and, yes, far above Fourteenth Street at the Carnegie Recital Hall. Her first one-woman art exhibition had been presented by George Maciunas, the same gallery owner who had given Yoko and her loose band of confederates a name, the kind of name you give an art movement: Fluxus. There were further exhibitions at American universities and galleries and in Europe and Japan.

The Carnegie Recital Hall concert of 1961 must have been particularly memorable. There were electronic sounds, complete darkness, performers with contact microphones taped to their bodies hauling heavy objects across the pitch-black stage. "There was a point," Yoko told *Rolling Stone*'s Jonathan Cott, "where two men were tied up together with lots of empty cans and bottles around them, and they had to move from one end of the stage to the other very quietly and slowly without making any sounds. What I was trying to attain was a sound that almost doesn't come out. Before I speak I stutter in my mind, and then my cultured self tries to correct that stuttering into a clean sentence . . . and I wanted to deal with those sounds of people's fears and stuttering . . . and of darkness, like a child's fear that someone is behind him, but he can't speak and communicate like this. And so I asked one guy to stand behind the audience for the duration of the concert."

Does this sound like punk rock, in intent if not in execution? The sound of Yoko singing original songs like "What a Bastard the World Is,"

"I Felt Like Smashing My Face in a Clear Glass Window," "Woman of Salem," "Coffin Car," "Hell in Paradise," and "Walking on Thin Ice" is innovative, dangerous rock & roll that seems to want to grab your soul by the throat. There is great beauty in Yoko's music as well. But there can be no doubt that the woman who wrote this music has known fear and darkness. The man who wrote, in one of his own more celebrated songs, "I know what it's like to be dead" fell in with a perfect match.

One of the things art is uniquely suited to is confrontations with the fear, the darkness. Some people find art that deals with such themes "depressing," presumably because thinking about their own mortality gives them the willies. For most, probably all artists, confronting this kind of material takes courage. And Yoko Ono and John Lennon hadn't just read about or imagined dark, fearful things: They had lived them. John's first four years coincided with World War II. One night in 1945 when Yoko was a child, she huddled with her mother and two siblings in an underground bunker while the largest number of American B-29s to attack a single Japanese city rained incendiary bombs on Tokyo by the thousands. Eighty-three thousand people died; a quarter of the city burned. Yoko's mother, Isoko, and the three children joined many of their neighbors in a headlong flight away from the burning city, out into open country. But the farmers in the countryside were starving and unenthusiastic about sharing whatever food they had hoarded with this tide of urban refugees.

Yoko's father was missing and possibly dead in Hanoi. The Onos were reduced to foraging from farm to farm for food, which they pulled along, with a few belongings, in an ancient-style wheeled cart.

Yoko's father survived the war and when Yoko was nineteen she joined her family in Scarsdale, New York. The contrast between war-torn Japan and Red-spooked America—as well as the "never the twain shall meet" cultural mentality that had made Eastern and Western art and thought seem as foreign as their respective languages—had been looming, unavoidable perplexities for Yoko since early childhood. The twentieth century, with its industrialization of the East and the attendant influence of materialism played off against the steadily Eastward drift of Western culture, art, and even theoretical physics, was a century of drastic reversals and the constant, unsettling tectonic-plate rumble of cultural schizophrenia. Yoko's family embodied it perfectly. Their musical values alone adequately tell the tale. Her father's passion was Western classical music. Bach, Brahms, and Beethoven were as central to his musical values as they were for any European. He saw to it that Yoko had lessons in piano, music theory, harmony, all from the Euro-classic rulebook. But he didn't believe a woman would ever be an exceptional composer. Her mother played a number of traditional Japanese instruments and knew several archaic vocal styles, and these she imparted to Yoko. There must have been some skull-rattling cognitive dissonance along the way, but looking back at it, what a musical education! Especially for an artist whose most important music would encourage and embody the emergence of the first truly global popular music, jump-started by rockers.

A Night at the Dakota

I was writing for *The New York Times* in 1980, when Yoko Ono and John Lennon returned to songwriting and recording for the first time since the birth of their son Sean in 1975. When I learned the Lennons were back in the studio, I wrote a news item about it, and the next day I was surprised to receive a call from Yoko. I had never met her, or John, and friends had told me, "Don't even try to get an interview. They don't see anybody." Over the phone, Yoko said, "Well, do you want to come by the studio tonight?"

When I walked in the only people in the control room were an engineer, Yoko, and her coproducer Jack Douglas. Yoko was absorbed in making production notes on one of her ubiquitous yellow legal pads. Over the speakers came the immediately accessible sounds of "(Just Like) Starting Over." I looked out into the studio, and there was John, singing vocal overdubs on the song, layering his voice over and over again on the chorus. Yoko briefly introduced herself and offered me a seat. I watched, I listened.

When he was finished singing, John came into the control room. "You must be the guy from *The New York Times*," he said. "I figured because when you walked in, I got nervous." I stood and shook hands and those penetrating Black and Decker eyes drilled right into mine. I said something about being a little nervous myself, maybe it was contagious? John looked into my eyes one more fraction of a second, and then we all relaxed and laughed. "You were right about this one," he said to Yoko. They invited me back to their apartment after the session.

A compact station wagon, kind of an econo-limo, deposited us on the street outside the Dakota's dark, forbidding entrance tunnel around two A.M. and we walked in, unnoticed, unmolested. Over the next few months, I would walk down it with John and Yoko many times. In December, John would die in that tunnel.

Upstairs, on that first night, we drank coffee, gorged on chocolate cake, and talked music and art. There was nonstop conversation. John and Yoko shared the wit that had been John's trademark at the Beatles' press conferences. John and Yoko were surprised and pleased to meet someone who knew Yoko's art and many of her early associates in the Fluxus movement, as well as rock & roll. I had a passion for both, but as we talked, and the conversation turned to their work together, I began to get nervous all over again. Yoko's records hadn't exactly been pushed by Apple. And when the two were working together so prolifically, in the late sixties and early seventies, I was playing in a band myself, too broke to buy many records anyway. The fact was, I didn't know John's solo albums intimately, and Yoko's hardly at all. John wanted to know what I thought of his guitar playing on Yoko's records, his favorite subject. "Have you heard the guitar on 'Why?' " he asked. "And 'O' Wind' and 'Midsummer New York' off of *Fly*?" Should I tell these people that I really wasn't familiar with the music? These people? Would they throw me out?

John had sized me up in about sixty seconds of eye contact, and both he and Yoko had been open, friendly, down-to-it with me. I figured I owed them the same honesty and trust. Not without fear and stuttering, I told them that I had heard the records they were talking about—their records—quite long ago or not at all. I waited for a response. John and Yoko looked at each other. They looked at me. Silence.

I was considering melting into the carpet when they suddenly broke into howls of celebratory laughter. "He hasn't heard it yet!" they were shouting at each other. They jumped up and began scanning shelves, searching cabinets. The search soon spilled over into adjoining rooms. "John, I found a copy of *Fly*," Yoko would call from one room. "Great," said John from high atop a stepladder. "I've just finally got *Feeling the Space* and *Live Peace in Toronto*."

The search took nearly half an hour. Closets were ransacked, and a copy of *Approximately Infinite Universe* was finally found on a high shelf near the ceiling. Smiling broadly, out of breath, they presented me with the records: all of Yoko's solo albums, most of John's. "Here's your homework," John told me, mock-stern but with a glimmer in his eyes. "Listen to Yoko's first. We'll be expecting a report. And . . ." He went into a list of songs from Yoko's albums that he knew I would find highly unconventional in sound and execution and as fresh sounding as the 1980's downtown New York postpunk scene. "We want to get your reactions," John explained, "you know, this is me favorite stuff of anything I've done."

As he showed me out into the gray light of morning, he told me, "It really stretched me, playin' with Yoko, just improvising, opened me up. Give a listen and tell us what you think."

Music in a Jam

The sixties were a period of feverish experimentation and exploratory mixing of media in all the arts. In pop music, cutting-edge records—by the Beatles, the Yardbirds, Jimi Hendrix, and many others—often topped the charts, a situation that has not really been duplicated before or since. The audience for rock & roll was willing to sit still while artists searched, groped, and noodled their way toward the occasional epiphany, especially if well-known and much-loved musicians were doing the searching. "Revolution No. 9," for example, did not seem to affect sales of *The Beatles*, better known as *The White Album*. Some listeners may have skipped over it after the first few listens; for many others, it was simply "far out, man." But—and this is a big *but*—"Revolution No. 9" was on a Beatles album. In fact, it was the first John + Yoko music to reach the public, but nobody let it out of the bag at the time, and even the cognoscenti took it as "John being far-out."

Nobody, including John and Yoko, seems to have comprehended the vastly different contexts in which this music was made and received. Both were acutely aware of, and well informed about, the experimentation that was going on in all the arts at the time. Yoko had played an important part in creating a receptive climate for this experimentation through her work in the avant-garde. John had been aware of at least some vanguard art as early as the Beatles' Hamburg days, when bohemian art students formed an important part of the band's coterie.

The tape loop/sound collage mania that struck with "Revolution No. 9" and other early work on *Unfinished Music Nos. 1 and 2* wasn't just a by-product of LSD trips; it was explicitly inspired by the work Karlheinz Stockhausen and other "classical" composers were doing at the time. The most intensely abrasive of Yoko's vocal improvisations had as its own wider context the "free jazz" or "energy playing" that was then widespread (and controversial) in the jazz world. Indeed, Yoko had initially given such vocal performances in the company of free jazz innovators like Ornette Coleman. Hostile jazz critics charge Coleman, Albert Ayler, John Coltrane, and the other leading lights of free jazz with simply "screaming," an accusation Yoko found herself contending with.

The important thing is that the music Yoko was making at this time was part of a musical revolution already sweeping both classical music and jazz. It was not conceived in a vacuum, nor was it intended as willful provocation. It had a context, and it built on an already existing tradition, or more precisely, on several traditions: Varese, Stockhausen, Coleman and Coltrane, Little Richard and Bo Diddley. The mass audience for pop music was largely unaware of these traditions. Rock criticism was in its infancy and was no help at all; the press attention Yoko got was largely sensational in nature. The rock audience seemed to be tolerant concerning the eccentricities of a few cherished performers who were virtually brand names in the context of the pop marketplace. This tolerance had its limits; Yoko exceeded those limits.

But the controversy concerning Yoko's early recordings should be long past. *Onobox* gives us the chance to hear this music afresh, as a body of work that has been winnowed and resequenced by Yoko herself. On the first disc of *Onobox*, *London Jam*, she has passed over the "concept art" of *Unfinished Music No. 1*, retained only two minutes of "No Bed for Beatle John" from *Unfinished Music No. 2*, taken nothing from *Wedding Album* or from the very different *Live Peace in Toronto 1969*, which is strong enough to stand on its own, and reprogrammed almost everything from her landmark albums *Yoko Ono/Plastic Ono Band* and *Fly*. The result plays like a suite, or a continuous densely woven tapestry of sounds. Listening to it, one gains a new appreciation of just how acutely Yoko anticipated subsequent developments in rock and free improvisation. To me, this music sounds as contemporary in 1991 as it did when Yoko and John proudly presented it to me at the Dakota in 1980. . . .

As *Onobox* goes into the final stages of production, Yoko Ono continues to move on. If her later recordings brought her full circle musically, she is now moving in this direction on a broader artistic front as well. Her recent one-woman art exhibits in museums and galleries around the world have been reminiscent of some of the extramusical work she was doing before she met John Lennon—in a sense. In another, deeper sense, all her work has been of a piece. One suspects her visual art has benefited from the compression and specificity she acquired as a writer and performer of pop/rock songs.

Yoko has spent her adult life making art in a variety of mediums— sculpture, painting, drawing, performance art, avant-garde and popular music. Whatever the medium, her work displays a finely honed whimsy and dryly devastating wit while addressing concerns that strike to the roots of the human condition in the late twentieth century—the need for world peace, the constant struggle between creative and destructive impulses, the importance of communication and tolerance between individual humans, between their varying cultures and values. These are serious issues indeed, and Yoko Ono makes a fundamentally serious kind of art. No matter what, she seems to be telling us, keep creating; to borrow a phrase from British author Valerie Wilmer, art can be "as serious as your life."

PUNK ROCK AND BEYOND: "FEAR AND NOTHING"

Walk on the Wild Side

(excerpt from *Rock & Roll: An Unruly History*)

ROLLING STONE | OCTOBER 5, 1995

Rock should rock in every conceivable way. It should have heart, it should have a beat and move you, and it should be done well enough so you can listen to it twenty years down the road, and it will still have its force and power like a good short story you go back to. At the time people thought the Velvet Underground were being very negative and bleak and dark and anti, whereas I thought we were an accurate reflection of things that were happening and were going to happen on a larger scale. I thought I was being very realistic and compassionate. I think one of the things people forget about the songs is how compassionate they are.

LOU REED, THE VELVET UNDERGROUND

The sound of the Velvet Underground really comes from the work that was done with La Monte Young in the Theater of Eternal Music. . . . We found out what a great orchestral noise we could get out of bowing a guitar. We applied it to viola and the violin, and then I filed the bridge of the viola down and played on three strings. . . . It made a great noise; it sounded pretty much like there was an aircraft in the room with you. . . . Lou and I had an almost religious fervor about what we were doing—like trying to figure ways to integrate some of La Monte Young's or Andy Warhol's concepts into rock & roll.

JOHN CALE, THE VELVET UNDERGROUND

What our band did was basically make a big noise and create some movement with that noise. Slowly I came up with a kind of concept. A lot of it was based on the attitude of juvenile delinquency and general mental grievance that I'd gotten from these dropouts I was hanging out with, mixed in with the sort of music that I like: hard R&B, hard rock & roll, and the exciting elements of jazz, 'cause I was starting to listen to John Coltrane and the unpredictability of that. And then an added element was to find something simple, monolithic, metallic, like a big machine—like the drill presses at the Ford plant stamping out fenders. I'd listen to that and think, "God, those are impressive sounds, big sounds." And they're so regular and simple, I thought, "Those are sounds that even we could master."

IGGY POP, THE STOOGES

In suburbia you're given the impression that nothing culturally belongs to you, that you are in this wasteland. I think most people who have an iota of curiosity about them develop a passion to escape, to get away from our desperation and exhaustion with the blandness of where we grew up and try and find who one is and find some kind of roots.

DAVID BOWIE

There are two kinds of "success," two ways of "making it" in rock & roll. One is pretty much your standard all-American success story: Seize the time, ride the zeitgeist, hit the nail on the head, take the money and run. This is the way of hit records and mass adulation, the way of Elvis and the Beatles—the way of "pop." The alternative doesn't sound like nearly as much fun: Be an innovator, march to the beat of your own drum, go against the grain of the times, make your statement, sit back and starve, and hope you become a legend before you die of old age (or malnutrition). This is the way of "art." From a pop point of view, art means nothing. This is one of the ways we can tell the difference between pop music and rock & roll, for in rock the way of art is very much a viable alternative if not an invitingly lucrative one. It even has its rewards, provided you live long enough to enjoy them.

Just as yesterday's sleazy sex-and-violence B movies have a way of becoming today's classic film noir, some of the rock that sixties listeners and critics ignored and/or reviled has proved at least as influential as the work of the period's commercial and critical icons and arguably more so. Ever since the epochal arrival of punk in the mid-seventies, the music of sixties punk precursors—suburban garage bands like the Seeds, the Standells, Count Five, and ? and the Mysterians (all of whom at least scored one or two hit singles each) and the more artistically ambitious Velvet Underground, Stooges, and MC5 (none of whom ever even made *Billboard*'s Hot 100)—has enjoyed an ever-increasing influence and esteem. But make no mistake: Back in the day, these groups were generally and heartily despised. The Velvets and the Stooges were variously described as decadent, crude, dark, negative, abrasive, nihilistic, and incompetent. "The only thing this will replace," predicted Cher when the Velvets first visited Los Angeles, in 1966, "is suicide." Still, this was recognition of a sort. The garage bands weren't even taken seriously enough to dismiss.

Then there was the makeup-wearing, fishnet-hose-and-spandex-sporting "glam" movement, spearheaded by the likes of Pink Floyd founder, singer, and guitarist Syd Barrett in his frilly lace cuffs and eye shadow; T. Rex's main man Marc Bolan, with his fey androgyny; and the early David Bowie warbling "Space Oddity" and posing for the cover of his album *The Man Who Sold the World* in a dress. It is no accident that these early glam rockers were British; in America cross-dressing was considered as threatening and out of bounds as the Velvet Underground's songs about hard drugs, sadomasochism, and leather.

"Radio stations in mainstream America would not touch that kind of stuff," recalls Danny Fields, who signed the Stooges and the MC5 to their first recording contracts and later managed the Ramones. "It's a very conservative industry; the promoters were conservative, the radio stations were and are very conservative. Sexual ambiguity was more acceptable in England, where there's always been this camp tradition. In America, it was all horrifying, deep-seated righteousness and biblical homophobia.

It was an atrocious sensibility that's rampant in America to this day, and people rebelled against it. But there was no way to break through on musical merit once you put on lipstick."

The early glam exponents, the garage rockers, and the more "artistic" protopunks had at least this much in common: They were all outsiders, not just in society at large but in the pecking order of rock & roll itself. If the mainstream of rock seemed rebellious to those on the outside looking in, the sixties "losers" were rebelling against the rebellion. In the long run their stance made them heroes. In the short run they were scum.

In many cases they were *self-made scum*: Lou Reed with his BA in literature from Syracuse University, fellow Velvet John Cale with his prestigious classical-music background, ex-suburbanite art student David Bowie, not to mention the musical progeny of America's suburban garages.

"These were middle-class, spoiled, creative young people, and they took the record companies by surprise," says Fields. "Suddenly the record execs were dealing with people who were as spoiled, demanding, and obnoxious as their own children. These were not some people out of the projects that they could herd in and out of the studio and pay disgraceful royalties to—they were people who knew about art and who *knew about lawyers*. The record companies had to adjust very quickly."

In 1965, two of the Velvet Underground's founding members, Lou Reed and original percussionist Angus MacLise, described their band as "the Western equivalent to the cosmic dance of Shiva. Playing as Babylon goes up in flames." Reed had already written many of the songs the group would record for its first album, *The Velvet Underground & Nico*, which was finally released in March 1967, almost a year after it was completed. In fact, Reed had written "Heroin" while still in college, under the influence of cutting-edge literature such as Hubert Selby Jr.'s *Last Exit to Brooklyn*, William Burroughs's *Naked Lunch*, and the work of his college mentor, the poet Delmore Schwartz, whose advice and example Reed took to heart. "In the unpredictable and fearful future that awaits civilization," Schwartz had written, "the poet must be prepared to be alienated and indestructible." Especially when the poet spins his tales of drugs, kinks, and hincty high jinks in the first person, backed by bracingly intense, in-your-face music that fairly snarls, as Johnny Rotten would snarl a decade hence, "We really *mean* it, man."

"I had no intention of letting the music be anything other than troublesome to people," says the Velvets' John Cale. "We really wanted to go out there and annoy people." Lou Reed recalls that pop artist Andy Warhol, the VU's early sponsor and the nominal producer of their first album, "pulled me aside when we were going to record, and his only advice to me was, 'Everything's really great, just make sure you keep the dirty words in.' And I knew what he meant: Keep it rough. Don't let them tame it down so it doesn't disturb anyone. Andy wanted it to disturb people and shake 'em up—so did we."

Before long, armed with a "punk" attitude that lavished "hatred and derision" (Cale's words) on the West Coast hippie bands and considered making audiences "uptight" a valid artistic goal, the Velvets were soon shaking *themselves* up. Nico, their ice-blond German chanteuse, had been Warhol's addition to the Velvets' lineup and was never entirely accepted into the band. After the VU's first album, her position was no longer ambiguous: She was out. She went on to record *Chelsea Girl* with Reed, Cale, and VU guitarist Sterling Morrison, and four subsequent albums arranged and partly composed by Cale, beginning with the hypnotic, autumnal *The Marble Index*.

The somber lyricism of Nico's work with Cale and the others did not carry over to the second VU album, *White Light/White Heat*, which had all the grinding, lurching momentum of the intravenous amphetamine rush hymned in Reed's title song. In the studio minus Warhol, the Velvets turned their amps up to eleven and fought each other for sonic supremacy throughout the seventeen minutes and twenty-five seconds of "Sister Ray." Partway through, Cale's organ took off with a tremendous surge of power amid the guitarists' howling feedback. He was the clear winner of the volume battle but lost the war a few months later when Reed, over the protests of Sterling Morrison and drummer Maureen Tucker, asked Cale to leave the band. Two subsequent Velvet Underground albums, with the mercurial, multitalented Cale replaced by bassist Doug Yule, were quieter, more intimate affairs, the playing and songwriting reflecting a kinder, gentler Lou Reed.

Cale's restless nature and avant-garde classical sensibilities led him to a variety of recording situations after he left the Velvets. He made an album with fellow La Monte Young associate Terry Riley, whose own late-sixties LPs for Columbia Masterworks had introduced the new mini-

malist classical music to the world at large. As it developed, Cale's solo
career proved as eclectic and unpredictable as the man himself, ranging
from the neo-classical *Paris 1919* to the hard-edge, abrasively rocking
mid-seventies albums *Fear* and *Guts*. But perhaps Cale's greatest impact
on rock & roll was as a producer. In time he would produce debut albums
for two of the most important punk-rock precursors: Jonathan Richman
and the Modern Lovers and Patti Smith. But already in the late sixties he
was anticipating the shape of punk to come with his production for a new
band out of Detroit: Iggy (Pop) and the Stooges.

Raised in a Michigan trailer park, James Osterberg acquired his Iggy
nickname when he played drums for an R&B–oriented garage band, the
Iguanas. The groups and songs that came clambering out of America's
suburban garages in the wake of the British Invasion were an inspiration
during Iggy's high school years: "The Kingsmen's 'Louie Louie,' Can-
nibal and the Headhunters, who were an East L.A. street gang, 'Farmer
John,' by the Premieres—I just flipped when I heard those things," Iggy
says. "It was a transcendental experience. These songs sounded like they
were recorded in gymnasiums, they had such a big, ringing sound. What
I loved was the distortion, the overtones, the sound of the universe that
I was hearing in these little records. Phil Spector records, too, and the
Motown stuff, which always had a big, powerful sound to it. And there
was always a friction in the beat, something that rubs against you like a
little itch that you have to scratch: the sexual thing."

Having heard the "sound of the universe," Iggy was determined
to make that sound his own. He did not find it an insurmountable
problem that the musicians he was able to infect with his vision were
high school dropouts who were barely competent on their instruments,
"juvenile delinquent kids who were running wild in America, basically
supported by their parents but completely out of control. They'd sleep
all day and then party all night, and they just wanted to be rock stars."
Bassist Dave Alexander was the most experienced player in the band;
the brothers Ron and Scott Asheton (guitar and drums, respectively)
had a bit more woodshedding to do, but at least they were able to do it
at home while their mother was away at work. Iggy would show up with
their daily ration of marijuana: "Every day I would wake 'em up and get
'em stoned, and then I would play them the following records: I'd play
'em Ravi Shankar; John Coltrane; some Harry Partch, the American

avant-garde composer; and then maybe a little Stones, Hendrix, Who, that sort of thing. But then I'd play 'em some Lebanese belly-dance music or one record that I particularly liked called *Bedouin Music of the Southern Sinai*. And then we'd go down in the basement where we played and just go wild. By the time we got kicked out of rehearsing at their mother's house, we had a band." Having learned to appreciate everything from Arabic and avant-garde music to jazz to hard rock while they were still working out how to play their instruments, with all of their influences filtered through "the attitude of juvenile delinquency and general mental grievance," the Stooges were bound to be different.

The Stooges were signed to Elektra Records in 1968 largely because the company had sent Danny Fields to check out the burgeoning "underground" scene in Detroit and nearby Ann Arbor, Michigan. Elektra, a company originally identified with the coffeehouse folk-music boom, had become perhaps America's hippest rock label. Among Elektra's mid-sixties signings were the Paul Butterfield Blues Band, featuring the incendiary guitarist Michael Bloomfield.

In 1967, Elektra released the debut album by a band from Los Angeles, the Doors. Fronted by former UCLA film student and self-styled poet Jim Morrison, the Doors opposed the "peace, love, and flowers" strain of sixties solipsism with darkly droning tales of death and transcendence, murky Freudian freak-outs ("Father, I want to kill you. Mother, I want to . . . *aaargggh!*"), and ecstatic derangement of the senses: "Let's swim to the moon/Let's climb through the tide/Penetrate the evening that the city sleeps to hide." The Doors spoke to the shadow side of rock & roll's Dionysian impulse, reveling in a psychosexual theatricality and an aesthetic of direct audience confrontation at least partly inspired by the in-your-face revolutionary fervor of Julian Beck and Judith Malina's Living Theater troupe. Fired from the Whisky a Go Go for performing their ten-minute-plus Oedipal epic "The End," the Doors found more sympathetic ears at Elektra. To almost everyone's surprise, their 1967 debut album, *The Doors*, included a song that became one of the year's biggest hits and an enduring rock anthem: "Light My Fire." If the Doors could be dark, weird, and commercially successful, perhaps other "revolutionary rock" would fare as well.

So Elektra had Fields go to Michigan, not to hear the Stooges, whom he hadn't yet heard of, but to attend a show by the MC5. Detroit was and remains a hard-rock town, having nurtured the likes of Mitch Ryder and the Detroit Wheels and Alice Cooper. The Motor City Five, already shortened to MC5 when the band played its earliest gigs, were a supremely tight and hard-hitting example of this Detroit sensibility, but like the Stooges, they kept their ears wide open. Poet and activist John Sinclair, who wrote about the free jazz of John Coltrane, Sun Ra, Ornette Coleman, and their cohorts for *Downbeat*, encouraged the MC5's jazz listening and became their manager. He also enlisted their services for the revolution; his White Panther party was a yippie-like association of radicals and artists whose program called for "revolution, dope, and fucking in the streets."

The MC5 initially attracted media attention when they played in Chicago's Grant Park for the demonstrators protesting the nearby 1968 Democratic National Convention, volleying their huge twin-guitar sound against the tear gas and billy clubs of Mayor Richard Daley's police. The venue was rough—their fellow rockers stayed home, perhaps to write protest songs—but it was not entirely unsuitable to the 5's volatile rhetoric and high-energy performing style. When Fields saw them whip a capacity crowd at Detroit's Grande Ballroom into near hysteria, they were opening their show with the invitation—or was it a command?—to "kick out the jams, motherfuckers."

It was the MC5 who convinced Fields to attend a show by the scene's other musical radicals, the Stooges. The band Fields saw was nowhere near as technically accomplished as the MC5, who boasted two distinctive guitar stylists in Wayne Kramer and Fred "Sonic" Smith, as well as a flexible, jazz-aware rhythm section. But if anything, the Stooges were more rabidly confrontational. "You had rowdy elements in the audiences in Michigan and also resistant elements," says Iggy Pop. "So I started mixing it up with the crowds, and if they wouldn't give me what I wanted, I would go out and take the show to them."

Elektra signed the MC5 forthwith, but Fields found the Stooges even more fascinating and made sure they got a recording contract as well. "In those days," he says, "Iggy was scary. I became his manager, and I was terrified every time he went out onstage that he would cause death and/or mayhem, that he would smash someone over the head with a bench, say, or eviscerate himself onstage. It was very, very powerful; I never saw anything like it. And for me, the Stooges were by far the most musically interesting band since the Velvet Underground."

John Cale was an appropriate choice to produce their first album, *The Stooges* (1969). When he added his minimalist one-note piano to the immortal "I Wanna Be Your Dog" and a sawing electric viola drone to the ten-minute free-improv workout "We Will Fall," it fit right in with the corrosive churning of Ron Asheton's wah-wah guitar and the whacking, trudge-tempo grooves of bassist Dave Alexander and drummer Scott Asheton.

The second Stooges album, *Fun House* (1970), was even better, with Steven Mackay's Albert Ayler–ish tenor saxophone thickening the already sludgy grooves and bringing the improvisational freak-outs to a frothing pitch of intensity. "T.V. Eye" and "Down in the Street" provided prototypes for much subsequent punk songwriting. "L.A. Blues" prefigured the noisy No Wave of the early 1980s. And the heavy, hulking crawl tempo and hypnotic plagal cadences of "Dirt" offered a virtually complete blueprint for the Goth rock/death rock stylings of postpunk icons such as Bauhaus, the Birthday Party, and Joy Division.

Without the Velvet Underground and the Stooges (and to a lesser extent the Doors and the MC5), one has to wonder where the first wave of American punk rockers would have found its inspiration. In 1972 to '73, however, New York's immediate punk precursors, the New York Dolls, were just getting started. The Stooges had broken up in June 1971, with the MC5 calling it quits some six months later. The standard-bearer for Detroit hard rock was now Alice Cooper, né Vincent Furnier, who had (predictably) streamlined the Stooges' grungier style while becoming the first successful American rocker to adopt a glam look.

Cooper also had a penchant for cheesy horror-movie imagery, expressed in songs like "Dead Babies" and in an ever-more-elaborate stage show, featuring at various junctures live snakes and a working guillotine. "Alice Cooper had to stop wearing ladies' sling-back shoes and dresses and get more into horror," asserts former Warhol "creature" and punk band leader Wayne (now Jayne) County, "because people in America could understand horror and blood and dead babies, but they couldn't understand male-female sexuality, androgyny, or . . . as little American boys would say, fag music."

One listener who did appreciate the likes of the Velvets and the

Stooges was Britain's David Bowie, finally hitting his commercial stride in early 1972 in the guise of the possibly hermaphroditic extraterrestrial Ziggy Stardust, backed by a diamond-hard, stripped-down guitar band, the Spiders from Mars. "The Velvet Underground became very important to me," says Bowie. "There was this mixture of Cale's avant-garde influence and Lou Reed's very fine pop tunesmithism, and the combination was so brutal. For me, Lou and Iggy Pop represented the wild side of existentialist America; they were the personification of the next generation after Kerouac and Ferlinghetti and Ginsberg. It was that side of the underbelly of American culture that they represented, everything I thought we should have in England. At that time one was borrowing heavily from the American influence, but, of course, being filtered through the British system, it came out more vaudeville than the MC5."

In 1972, Bowie met Reed and Iggy Pop amid the fabled rock-star excess in the "back room" at Max's Kansas City, the New York club, restaurant, and hangout. It didn't take long for Bowie to realize that both his friends were seriously in need of a career boost and that he now had it in his power to do something about it. Subsequently, he coproduced Reed's breakthrough solo album, *Transformer* (1972), which contains what is still Reed's best-known song, "Walk on the Wild Side," a chronicle of Andy Warhol's Factory crew.

By Reed's previous standards, the album was slickly produced, but the songwriting sparkled, and there were indelible guitar riffs from coproducer Mick Ronson, Bowie's onstage foil in the Spiders from Mars. "The whole glam thing was great for me," says Reed, who toured with a new androgynous look and a Detroit-style hard-rock band built around the road-tested guitar team of Dick Wagner and Steve Hunter. "This was something I had already seen with Warhol, but I hadn't *done* that thing. The seventies was a chance for me to get in on it, and since no one knew me from Adam, I could say I was anything. I had learned that from Andy: Nobody knows. You could be anything."

Bowie also helped Iggy Pop reassemble the Stooges (who now featured a more technically accomplished hard-rock guitarist, James Williamson) and produced their 1973 album, *Raw Power*. This time the Bowie touch resulted in an album that was simply more conventional than *The Stooges* and *Fun House*, though some hard-rock fans preferred it to the band's more anarchic earlier work. In any event the album failed to spark the sort of Pygmalion-like rebirth Bowie had helped engineer for Lou Reed.

Between 1972 and 1976, Bowie went through a dizzying series of personas like so many suits of clothes. Ziggy Stardust and the Spiders from Mars became a sensation, especially in Britain; after Ziggy's memorable farewell concert, Bowie made *Aladdin Sane* (1973), whose title character had a streak of lightning painted down half his face. *Diamond Dogs* (1974) was an attempt to write a stage musical around themes from George Orwell's *1984* and the William Burroughs oeuvre; in the cover painting, Bowie was both ambisexual and half-canine. His most elaborately mounted tour followed. Then came the "plastic soul" of *Young Americans* (1975), cut at Philadelphia's legendary Sigma Sound with some of the same session musicians who backed the O'Jays and Harold Melvin and the Blue Notes. John Lennon limbered up his rarely displayed chops as an R&B–oriented rhythm guitarist on a funky tune he wrote with Bowie, "Fame." There was altogether too much of that around.

Finally, on the *Station to Station* album and tour, Bowie rejected the sheer theatrical spectacle of his earlier shows, appearing on an almost bare stage in stark expressionist-noir lighting as "the Thin White Duke, throwing darts in lovers' eyes." Another name for the Duke was cocaine, which was as omnipresent as fame in Bowie's world. Cruising the L.A. freeways late at night in a limo, wired and paranoid, Bowie asked himself the same question the critics had been asking all along: Who is David Bowie? *Is* there a David Bowie behind the glitz and the glamour and the passing parade of disposable identities?

"In Los Angeles at the time, I knew nobody but bad people, and I was doing nothing but bad stuff," Bowie says. "I think you would only have to take fifteen seconds from 'Cracked Actor' to see the state of mind that I was in. So I changed location and put myself in a very anonymous situation in a quiet working-class part of Berlin, a Turkish area, just to distance myself."

Iggy Pop, who'd been hanging out for much of Bowie's last tour, joined him in Berlin. "We were excited to be there even before we got there," Iggy remembers. "Both of us had been living in L.A., where everybody wants to kiss your ass for the wrong reasons, and Berlin was directly the opposite of that. This is a no-man's-land, a very egalitarian city and mentally tough. . . . We got tougher minded, and the music got tougher minded and much more daring, and it had more to say—his music, I think, as well as mine."

In Berlin, Bowie and Iggy Pop claimed for themselves something few rock & roll musicians are able to achieve once they get on the album-tour-album-tour treadmill: the opportunity to rethink their act from top to bottom and start afresh. Bowie, working with the composer, producer, and Roxy Music alumnus Brian Eno on Bowie's 1977 albums *Low* and *Heroes*, was finally able to incorporate the avant-garde minimalism that had earlier inspired the Velvets into a musical idiom that was indisputably his own. He also found the time to produce Iggy Pop's most gripping and original albums since 1970's *Fun House*—*The Idiot* (1976) and *Lust for Life* (1977). When Iggy returned to the U.S. to tour, Bowie joined the group as an "anonymous" sideman in form-fitting black leather, playing basic, workmanlike electric piano. For the first time in a long time, he looked like he was having fun.

As the punk era dawned, every sensational new band seemed to be affirming its debt to the Velvet Underground, the Stooges, and the garage-band credo: "Keep it simple, stupid." The punks were trashing sixties icons right and left, but David Bowie, Iggy Pop, and Lou Reed continued to hold their attention and to earn their (often grudging) respect. The "trash" of the sixties was back with a vengeance, just in time to help save rock & roll from its big, bad, bloated self.

The Velvet Underground: *Peel Slowly and See* (Polydor)

ROLLING STONE | NOVEMBER 30, 1995

Peel Slowly and See, the long-awaited five-disc Velvet Underground box set, offers fresh perspectives and some hidden truths, even for longtime Velvets fans. None is brought home more vividly than this simple proposition: The Velvets were a band.

It wasn't singer-songwriter Lou Reed plus backing musicians, and it wasn't just a laboratory for volatile interactions between Reed's literary and street sensibilities and John Cale's classical pedigree and avant-garde proclivities. It was a true unit. The synergy of Reed, Cale, Sterling Morrison's incisive R&B–driven lead and rhythm guitars, and Maureen Tucker's Olatunji-via–Bo Diddley tribal stomp was the "genius" of the Velvet Underground.

Ignored or reviled during their time together, VU have proved themselves over the long haul to be arguably the most admired and influential American rock band. Musically they've been important not just for their sonic minimalist aesthetic but for their all-around grasp of rock's roots, vocabulary, and resources, from lyrical ballads to machine-shop clamor, modal droning to crafty pop, folk rock to country rock, raga to music-hall soft-shoe.

In the beginning, recording without drums or percussion, the Velvets played an eccentric sort of folk rock. Their '65 demos—the first of *Peel's* five discs—are reminiscent of New York folk hipsters like the Holy Modal Rounders. The early demos generally make for archival, rather than pleasurable, listening. While Reed was already an extraordinarily gifted songwriter, it was often the other Velvets' contributions that made the music truly special. It's only when Cale cuts loose on the viola that "I'm Waiting for the Man" begins to surge with power, and "Heroin" would not find its ultimate levels of intensity and drama until Mo Tucker's nervous tom-tom pulses entered the picture.

The four Velvets studio albums are included in their entirety; Album 3, *The Velvet Underground*, is represented by Reed's preferred, now oddly alternative-sounding "closet mix." The sound throughout is breathtaking in its clarity; lyrics one could never disentangle become easily audible. And it's no longer difficult to follow the individual instruments through the densest collective mashups, even on the heretofore impenetrable "Sister Ray."

Discs two and three, which include the first two albums and some welcome extras, document VU before the sacking of John Cale. They're as transcendent as rock & roll gets. Among the extras are live workouts that display the band's often-obscured R&B roots ("Booker T.," "Temptation Inside Your Heart") as well as two group improvisations with Nico. There are also some demos intended for Album 2 (*White Light/White Heat*)—the stunning "Here She Comes Now" is all swirling, droning, shifting tone colors.

After the bracing, take-no-prisoners barrage of the first two albums, the later group, with bassist Doug Yule replacing multi-instrumentalist Cale, emphasized the more tuneful songwriting of Reed. He seems somehow more appealing when yelping, "Whip it on me, Jim," in the middle of "Sister Ray" than he does crooning the creepy "Jesus." . . .

Nevertheless, there's a great deal to enjoy on the last two discs. We get Tucker's splendid vocal features on "After Hours," "I'm Sticking with You," and "The Murder Mystery." And we get more of Morrison's subtle, special magic: the wailing, guitar-driven "Foggy Notion" and "I Can't Stand It"; roaring live runs through "It's Just Too Much" and "Some Kinda Love." There are also early studio run-throughs of songs Reed would record for later solo albums — like the haunting "Satellite of Love."

This is some of the most inspirational and ultimately timeless music you'll ever hear, reproduced with brilliant sonic verisimilitude. The selections that reveal these musicians to have been ordinary mortals just make masterworks like *The Velvet Underground & Nico* all the more impressive. When the VU synergy triumphed over individual foibles and failings, it triumphed so spectacularly that personal limitations and hang-ups seemed to melt away in its white-hot glare. It's as though the participants had been somehow alchemized by this "band spirit" into functioning as highly idealized versions of their everyday selves, and we are all the richer for it.

Richard Hell and Tom Verlaine: Visions of Hell

PENTHOUSE | NOVEMBER 1982

Back when Richard Hell was a teenager named Richard Meyers, he filled his head with French nihilist literature, trashy American garage-rock, and reckless mixtures of intoxicants. His favorite literary work was Lautréamont's "Les Chants de Maldoror," a novel-length prose-poem described by its author as a "desolate morass of . . . gloomy and poisonous pages," chock-full of hallucinatory images, celebrations of evil, and unbridled loathing for everything human. ("With a head in my hand, gnawing the skull, I betook myself to the place where stand the posts that support the guillotine. I placed the smooth grace of the necks of three young girls beneath the blade. . . .") Compared with that, Meyers's favorite bands were pretty tame. Most of them were one-hit wonders, or psychedelic pioneers who were still attempting to compress their firsthand reports on sensory derangement into three-minute pop-song forms. Ah, but if garage bands could speak the language of Lautréamont . . .

In the early 1970s, Richard Meyers and a school friend named Tom Miller moved to New York City, where they found work selling postcards of dead movie stars and tomes on film noir at a Greenwich Village bookshop called Cinemabilia. They read more French lit—J. K. Huysmans's diabolist *Là-Bas*, Arthur Rimbaud's *Une Saison en Enfer*—and wrote their own visionary poetry, but nobody read it, so they started a band called the Neon Boys. By this time, Richard was calling himself Richard Hell and Tom was calling himself Tom Verlaine. The Neon Boys metamorphosed into Television, but two visionaries was one visionary too many; before long Hell had left, only to resurface a couple of years later leading his own band, the Voidoids. By that time, the Bowery bar where Richard and Tom had first unleashed their music had attracted a whole slew of newer bands—the Ramones, Patti Smith's group, Blondie, the Talking Heads. Something new was happening, people were calling it punk rock, and Richard and Tom had more or less invented it.

Two of the most exciting and most durable albums to come out of that initial New York punk rock explosion were Television's *Marquee Moon* and Richard Hell and the Voidoids' *Blank Generation*, both released in 1977. But neither album was a spectacular seller, and both Tom Verlaine and Richard Hell were too ambitious (Hell now says he was too arrogant) to settle comfortably into what rapidly became the "new wave" scene. The poppier Blondie and the preppier Talking Heads were the scene's commercial successes. Verlaine disbanded Television after being disappointed in the performance of a second album. Hell wrote prose and poetry, acted in a few underground films, and released only a smattering of singles and an EP. But recently he came up with his own second album, *Destiny Street* (Red Star). Verlaine has also been active. Last year he emerged from hibernation with a solo album called *Dreamtime* (Warner Bros.) and this year followed it up with another album, a kind of surreal memoir of a war fought only in his imagination, *Words from the Front* (Warner Bros.).

In a sense, both Hell and Verlaine have revived the literary spirit that inspired surrealism (and changed their own lives) by making their dream visions and warped perceptions into rock & roll. But in terms of both craft and temperament, they are polar opposites. Hell and his Voidoids make crazed, careening rock & roll that roars hell-bent toward the precipice of his imagination and then takes a dive. If you like rockers who sing in tune and band arrangements that are orderly and restrained, Hell and the Voidoids will not be your cup of tea. Verlaine has become one of rock's most accomplished and daring guitarists. His music *is* tuneful and ordered, and while it's true to the spirit of the literature Verlaine and Hell both admired as teenagers, it's particularly reminiscent of the refined symbolist poetry written by the man whose name Tom Miller adopted, Paul Verlaine. Richard Hell and *his* music are more reminiscent of Arthur Rimbaud, who insisted that one could become a true poet only by practicing "the disordering of all the senses."

There is a kind of luminous austerity to Tom Verlaine's music that makes it particularly attractive and particularly elusive. In the studio, Verlaine lays down interlocking guitar parts that mesh with an almost uncanny accuracy. In a way, they're too perfect; their clarity is the clarity of vivid dreams, the sort of clarity that you can never quite get a grip on even though its edges appear to be sharply defined. The harder you listen to this crystalline music, the more its outlines seem to shimmer and bend, like images refracted through summer haze. This odd quality is particularly appropriate to the songs Verlaine wrote for his most recent album, *Words from the Front*. In "Days on the Mountain," he compares a time in his life to "walking around the ring of a bell." That's a pretty succinct description of the sort of moods the album evokes.

But Richard Hell and the Voidoids have made the most passionate and vital rock album of the year. Verlaine may project a certain visionary intensity, but his sensibility is basically cool. Richard Hell is hot; he's a soul singer. On *Destiny Street* he takes songs by the Kinks, Them, and Bob Dylan and pushes them as far as they'll go. Dylan's "Going Going Gone" is particularly revelatory. Dylan, even at his best, tends to whine. Hell simply sings from his guts; he may be singing Dylan's nothing-left-to-lose lyric, but he pours his own emotions into it and finally claims it for himself. The album's other ballad, a Hell original called "Time," is about writing songs and about honesty. He sets out to "write a song that's really, really real" but concludes that "the most a man can do is say the way its playing feels/And know he only knows as much as time to him reveals."

But most of *Destiny Street* roars along at a breakneck clip, propelled by Fred Maher's crisp, fastidious drumming, Hell's own tumbling bass lines, and the screaming guitars of Naux and Robert Quine. It's Quine, lead guitarist in the original Voidoids and this year's new guitar star following his brilliant performance on Lou Reed's recent *The Blue Mask*, who backs Hell to the hilt. His solos on songs like "Ignore That Door" and the very spooky "Staring in Her Eyes" sound like they're going to ignite your turntable; if they aren't the most committed, most imaginative, most *dangerous* rock guitar solos since Eric Clapton and Duane Allman pushed each other to the limit on "Layla," they're certainly in the same ballpark.

Unless you listen to a college radio station or happen to live in a town that still has a progressive radio station, you will never hear Richard Hell and the Voidoids on the air. Hell, the band, the album, and the label it's on (previously a vehicle for New York extremist bands like Suicide) are all genuinely underground. When the garage bands Richard and Tom used to like in the 1960s burgeoned into that decade's "underground rock scene," the major record companies moved in immediately—remember the Columbia records ads that began, "The Man Can't Bust Our Music"? These are very different times. America's major record companies aren't rushing to sign serious fanatics like Hell; even Verlaine's Warner Bros. contract is something of an anomaly. One result of this state of affairs is that Hell's *Destiny Street* has to be sought out; they just might not have it at your neighborhood record store. But it's often the case that the best things are among the hardest to find. After all, Richard Meyers didn't just pluck a copy of Lautréamont's "Les Chants de Maldoror" from the paperback rack at his local supermarket.

Elvis Costello—Is He Pop's Top?

THE NEW YORK TIMES | JUNE 27, 1982

Is Elvis Costello, the original angry young man of rock's new wave, going to turn out to be the Cole Porter of the 1980s? His most devoted admirers are convinced that he is exactly that—and Mr. Costello himself says that's just what he is aiming for. "That kind of songwriting—Porter, Kern, Rodgers and Hart—is something I'm very fond of and aspire to," he admitted recently. "When people ask me to name a great song, I mention something like 'Love for Sale' or 'Someone to Watch Over Me.' In the last twenty years or so, very few people have been up to that standard of lyric writing."

In any event, it seems reasonably certain that the twenty-seven-year-old Mr. Costello is the most talented pop tunesmith of his generation. His new album, *Imperial Bedroom* (Columbia), is his seventh album of original songs since 1977, when he first burst upon an unsuspecting world with *My Aim Is True*. He has been prolific (one album, *Get Happy!!*, included twenty songs, eighteen of them Costello originals), yet the quality of his work has been remarkably consistent. Moreover, unlike most of his new wave contemporaries, he hasn't stopped changing—and maturing.

Most of the songs on Mr. Costello's earlier albums were in a melodic pop-rock vein. "Alison" was a hit for Linda Ronstadt, and Dave Edmunds also scored a hit with a Costello song, "Girls Talk" ("Though you may not be an old-fashioned girl, you're still going to get dated"). But as early as his second album, *This Year's Model*, Mr. Costello and his superb backing trio, the Attractions, began to expand their range. The lyricism and rhythmic thrust of songs like "Pump It Up," "Radio, Radio," and "Accidents Will Happen" made them staples of American FM radio programming.

But other songs examined the ups and downs of romance in a wryly epigrammatic style that was unflinchingly adult. "You lack lust; you're so lackluster," he complained in "Possession." In "New Amsterdam" he announced that he was going to "step on the brake to get out of her clutches." In a lilting waltz, "Motel Matches," he transformed a one-night stand into pure poetry: "Boys everywhere fumbling with the catches, I struck lucky with motel matches/Falling for you without a second look, falling out of your open pocketbook, giving you away like motel matches." And while he was learning to say more and more in fewer words, he was mastering more musical idioms, from country and western stomps to soul ballads to jazzy jump tunes to harmonically sophisticated torch songs.

Nevertheless, *Imperial Bedroom* is a decisive step forward. The album seems to be a conscious attempt to get away from rock entirely, to write pop songs worthy of a Sinatra or an Ella Fitzgerald—the sort of pop songs that become standards. The lyrics retain their aggressive edge, but his range of subjects and musical styles is much broader. The subjects include a marriage's unraveling ("It's been a long honeymoon/ She thought too late and spoke too soon"), a family's disapproval of a thuggish son ("Don't get smart or sarcastic, he snaps back just like elastic/ Spare us the theatrics and the verbal gymnastics, we break wise guys just like matchsticks"), and corruption in the English aristocracy ("He's got a mind like a sewer and a heart like a fridge/He stands to be insulted and he pays for the privilege"). The music ranges from sultry supper-club balladry to brightly baroque counterpoint for strings and french horns to restaurant-table serenades featuring accordion and gut-string guitar. Mr. Costello's singing has never sounded better, but above all *Imperial Bedroom* is a songwriter's tour de force.

Mr. Costello is a very ambitious young man, and he is an enigma. He has given few interviews. Some of the songs on that first album, "Alison" for example, were tenderly lyrical, but others were charged with vitriolic anger, and Mr. Costello's early performances were aggressive, even arrogant. On a number of occasions he played very short sets, refused to do encores, and drove away fans who refused to leave with unendurable, high-frequency electronic feedback.

This sort of behavior was bound to cause trouble, and it did. One night in 1979, after a concert in Columbus, Ohio, Mr. Costello got into a drunken argument with several American rock musicians who had made their reputations in the 1960s and represented everything Mr. Costello in particular and the new wave in general was a reaction against. The argument grew more heated, and more personal, and Mr. Costello responded to the taunt that no Englishman would ever match the artistry or emotional depth of black American singers like Ray Charles with a racial epithet he hoped would outrage and silence his opponents. His outburst had the desired effect, but the next day the musicians he had been arguing with reported his comments to members of the press, and the result was a major scandal. Mr. Costello flew into New York for a press conference that began on an apologetic note but ended as a shouting match. He did not tour the United States again until 1981.

"Obviously, that was the most horrific incident of my whole career," Mr. Costello said last week, "and I've never been able to sit down in an unemotional atmosphere and say I'm very sorry. It was a drunken brawl, and I wanted to say whatever would outrage those people the most, but that's no excuse. A lot of people were very angry, and rightfully so. Those words I used certainly don't represent my view of the world, I had always just assumed that people would recognize my allegiance to R&B, to black music, but it wasn't obvious enough. I suppose if you allow uncontrolled anger to run away with you, and if you make a career out of contriving anger, up onstage, whether you're feeling angry or not, sooner or later you'll find yourself saying things, using words you don't mean. It'll all come back at you. But I don't want to sound like I'm making excuses. There aren't any excuses for saying things like that."

Mr. Costello said the Columbus incident "colored everything I've done since. The next album I made after that, *Get Happy!!*, I set out, subconsciously at least, to make a soul record. Not just in terms of style, but a record that was warmer, more emotional. And I think all the records I've made since then are more directly emotional, more personal, I've been trying to cut back on the clever wordplay and write songs with more heart."

Imperial Bedroom isn't short on clever wordplay. One song, "Shabby Doll," begins with the line, "Giving you more of what-for always worked for me before," and Mr. Costello's ear for internal rhymes and alliteration has always been one of the things that made his work special. But the songs on *Imperial Bedroom* do reflect an emotional maturity that wasn't always evident on his earlier albums. Musically, the new record is more self-consciously "adult." It's a far cry from the spare, functional new wave modernism of albums like *This Year's Model*, from 1978.

"I don't think of the new album as a rock & roll record," Mr. Costello noted. "I was making a conscious effort to remove the dominance of the beat. The important things to me are the melody, the words, the way you sing them, all the little innuendos you can get into them. And above all, the feeling behind them. I don't want to be just yelling and screaming; I'm not a wild man as such. I'm in pop music. Now Jerry Lee Lewis, Little Richard, those are rock & roll singers. There aren't that many of them. There are a lot of pretenders—bozos dressed in silly clothes."

The British critic Allan Jones wrote in 1977 that Mr. Costello's songs were often "fiercely detailed accounts of romantic encounters and failures—but he introduces a ruthless honesty to these themes." A number of Mr. Costello's more recent songs have been about sex and power. Some have compared the way people allow themselves to be used by lovers to the way people allow themselves to be used by unscrupulous politicians. And the English class system figures in some of these songs— "Man Out of Time" on the new album, for example. "I do tend to think there's a lot of decadence and moral weakness among people in positions of power," Mr. Costello said. "Traditionally, the aristocracy in England has been decadent and immoral. There's always a lot of intrigue, government scandals, like the Profumo affair. None of my songs are literally about that or any other particular event, but some of them have that flavor. The more personal songs are either imaginary scenarios, observations of other people, or observations of myself. Most of the really vitriolic songs I've written have been observations of myself."

Although Mr. Costello's songs have been recorded by Linda Ronstadt and other artists, most of these versions have left him unimpressed. "I'd really like to hear one of my songs recorded by Frank Sinatra or Aretha Franklin," he said. "Those are two of my favorite singers, along with Chet Baker, Billie Holiday, Stevie Wonder, and Jerry Lee Lewis." Coming from a musician who seemed only a few years ago to be an angry new wave avatar, full of contempt for earlier pop music, this was a revealing list. "I always thought it was a real mistake to toss around that expression 'new wave' in connection with my records," Mr. Costello maintained. "Why does everything have to be pigeonholed? Why can't you hear Hank Williams and then Billie Holiday on the radio?"

Cole Porter and the other songwriters Mr. Costello is beginning to be compared to frequently wrote for the stage, but Mr. Costello said he had no such ambitions. "What am I going to do, write a rock opera?" he laughed. "Rock musicals, rock films, they're pathetic, a joke. So there's really just continuing the songwriting, honing that, doing it better. If you write pop songs, you do hope they'll be important in people's lives. I'd love for one of my songs to be as important to someone as 'I'm Gonna Make You Love Me' by the Temptations was to me. But I hate this precious idea that every song has to be the Sermon on the Mount. The songs I write for my next album will be about whatever happens to me between now and when we start recording again, and that's what it's about, really. It's about life."

Truly Compelling Rock & Roll

THE NEW YORK TIMES | AUGUST 10, 1980

The most compelling rock & roll performers have often been those who were able to walk a tightrope between private obsessions and public role-playing on the one hand, and musical conservatism and innovation on the other. Elvis Presley practiced his music and cultivated his image in front of a bedroom mirror until he made his first records, and a number of seminal rockers began similarly; without private obsessions, rock & roll as we know it probably wouldn't exist.

Likewise, even rock's most innovative artists have necessarily retained a basic musical conservatism; if you add too much to rock's basic rhythms, harmonies, song forms, and instrumentation, you haven't got rock & roll anymore, you've got hyphenated rock—jazz-rock, classical-rock, and so on. But even performers who are gripped by private obsessions have to relate those obsessions to their audience if they're going to play for an audience, and musical conservatives who avoid anything that smacks of experimentation tend to turn into archivists. It's the balance, or the tension, between these opposing tendencies that makes for compelling rock & roll.

Competence and cleverness are not in short supply in contemporary rock, but music that's genuinely compelling is. People who buy a few albums every year and play them over and over probably find those albums more or less compelling, but the more records one has access to, the more one tends to play certain records, even good records, only a few times before moving on to something else. Records that keep revealing new dimensions every time they're played and that simply demand to be played again and again, records that pull the listener into the orbit of the performer's obsessions—these are the records that people who listen to a lot of rock & roll really prize.

The Feelies and Joy Division, two rock quartets from Haledon, New Jersey, and Manchester, England, respectively, have made recent albums that are genuinely compelling. Both groups build on a foundation of traditional rock & roll song forms and instrumentation, and both groups have managed to find fresh musical possibilities within these self-imposed limitations. More importantly, each band has a private, unique vision and manages to make this vision matter to the listener. It won't matter to every listener, of course, but once one enters willingly into the worlds the Feelies and Joy Division have created, one becomes a part of those worlds, and not just when the records are playing.

The Feelies' *Crazy Rhythms* is a delightful anomaly. Glenn Mercer and Bill Million, the two guitarists and songwriters who provide the band's material and conceptual direction, have created a quirky style and a handful of painstakingly crafted songs that they rarely display in public. The Feelies, it seems, perform infrequently and almost always on national holidays. Their most recent New York appearance, a Fourth of July show at Danceteria, found Mr. Mercer and Mr. Million bounding around the stage in an apparent frenzy while the bassist Keith Clayton, the drummer Anton Fier, and an anonymous additional percussionist trumped out the music's tribal rhythms. There's definitely something tribal about the Feelies' music, and something intensely white and suburban, too. They seem to look at suburbia as an anthropologist might, to see it as a self-contained little world with its own curious rites and taboos. But this understanding comes across more in the group's musical stance and cultivated boys-next-door image than it does in the songs' lyrics.

In fact, the Feelies' lyrics often seem to be appendages or afterthoughts. Mr. Mercer and Mr. Million rarely stray beyond the most traditional and basic rock & roll harmonies, and their playing is a virtual catalog of the lead and rhythm guitar styles that have developed over the past twenty-five years or so, but the structure of most Feelies songs is anything but traditional. "Loveless Love" begins with a rousing twin-guitar rave-up that builds to a breathless climax and then abruptly segues into the "song"—that is, the part with the lyrics. But the lyrics, which are a pithy exposition of emotional distance in an interpersonal relationship, simply serve as a kind of transition into the song's third section, a chromatic roller coaster of interlocking guitar lines that finally subsides into a single, luminous chord. Most of the other songs on the album have similarly inventive structures, but because the band's basic materials are so traditional, the music still sounds like rock & roll.

Ian Curtis's lyrics are much more central to the impact of Joy Division, a group that has yet to have an album released in the U.S. (though their two albums are available as imports and will soon be issued here by Rough Trade) and that broke into the English bestseller charts with a single, "Love Will Tear Us Apart," only after Mr. Curtis hanged himself on the eve of what was to have been Joy Division's first American tour. Like Glenn Mercer and Bill Million, Mr. Curtis has written tellingly about estrangement and alienation within love relationships, especially in several of the songs on the first Joy Division album, *Unknown Pleasures*. But if the album has a single unifying theme, it's the willful obliteration of limits.

Several of the songs on *Unknown Pleasures* involve images of travel through time and space, of experiencing the sensations of other beings, of wandering frantically through the streets of Interzone (the endless, hallucinatory city described in the novels of William S. Burroughs), of losing control of one's thoughts and actions. But Mr. Curtis doesn't seem to be writing science fiction; he seems to be dramatizing (or perhaps describing as best he can) mental events. (The album's cover is a chart of a few seconds of brain-wave activity.) The music drives Mr. Curtis's personal vision home with economy and power. Bernard Albrecht, Joy

Division's guitarist and occasional synthesizer player, chords sparingly. In "Disorder," the exhilarating "Shadowplay," and several other songs, his guitar parts consist of ringing melody lines that move along at oblique angles to Peter Hook's equally melodic bass figures and Stephen Morris's terse drumming.

After *Unknown Pleasures*, Joy Division released two singles, the second of which, "Love Will Tear Us Apart," seems to have signaled the end of the interpersonal crises that flicker like brush fires throughout *Unknown Pleasures*. The conflicts delineated in the group's second album, *Closer*, which was completed shortly before Mr. Curtis's death last May 18, are internal conflicts. "This is the crisis I knew had to come, destroying the balance I'd kept," he sings wearily at the beginning of a harrowing song called "Passover," and when he does touch on love relationships, in "A Means to an End," he imagines the ultimate consequences: "A house somewhere on foreign soil/where aging lovers quarrel."

If *Unknown Pleasures* is about the obliteration of limits, *Closer* is about the consequences of that obliteration, and the air of recklessness that pervades the music on the first album has given way to a richer, more synthesizer-dominated sound. "The Eternal," a kind of dream vision that mixes images of a funeral with images of childhood in a manner that suggests the two might be stages in a cyclical process, is swathed in mournful, synthesized string sounds, and the album's last song, "Decades," finds Mr. Albrecht consciously imitating the sound of a classical orchestra, but with a motivic simplicity and rhythmic vigor that mark the music as rock.

There's darkness in the Feelies' music, despite its ebullient surface and stomping tribal rhythms, but not the sort of darkness that lurks at the heart of Joy Division's music and even in the group's name (a Joy Division was the prostitutes' wing of a concentration camp). Nevertheless, listening to both groups can leave one feeling refreshed, cleansed. The Feelies offer a vision of community that's bright and inviting, even if the community exists primarily in the minds of Glenn Mercer and Bill Million. Joy Division's albums confront some difficult questions unflinchingly. Is the pleasure one derives from love worth the pain that always seems to intrude sooner or later? Does one struggle to overcome despair or depression for a valid reason or simply as a sort of reflex action? Is life really worth living?

Hopefully one will emerge from this sort of self-examination with a renewed commitment to living. Ian Curtis made another choice, but he didn't proselytize for it, and as a group that also included three exceptional musicians who should soon be heard from again, Joy Division created an extraordinarily vivid, moving, and original body of work. This compelling music is a desperately needed antidote to the competent, clever rock "product" that gluts our airwaves and record stores; it's a welcome confirmation that rock & roll is still worth caring about and believing in.

X: End of the World?

PENTHOUSE | JULY 1981

A police helicopter was buzzing like an angry fly just above a darkened Hollywood hardware store. On the sidewalk two squad cars and several motorcycles were huddled together like a circle of covered wagons, and helmeted policemen swarmed nervously around the front of the building. Across the street, members of X, a rock band a number of critics have called America's best, stood in the open door of a small recording studio, watching the show. "The cops here always seem to travel in packs," drummer D. J. Bonebrake remarked, "and they have these loudspeakers. You'll be crossing the street against the light or something, and all of a sudden you'll hear this voice saying, 'All right, you, back on the sidewalk!' " Inside the studio, over a pummeling rhythm and a driving, metallic guitar, X's John Doe and Exene were chanting the chorus to one of their new songs: "We're desperate/Get used to it."

Los Angeles, known for its balmy weather, celluloid fantasies, and laid-back soft rock, is mutating. The crime rate is soaring, and many law-abiding citizens are afraid to go out at night. If they do, they're apt to run into crowds of teenagers with shaved heads or blue hair on their way to a punk-rock show, because Los Angeles rock is mutating, too. The city that gave the world the Eagles, Linda Ronstadt, and Jackson Browne is now breeding bands with names like Fear, the Circle Jerks, Agent Orange, and Black Flag, bands that play hard, fast, and loud and that sing "I don't care about you/Fuck you" (Fear), "We're tired of getting screwed" (Black Flag), and "The world's a mess/It's in my kiss" (X).

The neighborhoods around several Los Angeles clubs that feature punk rock have become war zones. The Starwood's entertainment license was revoked last spring after area residents complained of teenagers throwing bottles, fighting in the streets, using front yards for toilets, and noisily fornicating in the shrubbery. At press time the club was open again and appealing its case to the California State Supreme Court. On a recent, typical Saturday night, police patrols went screaming by at regular intervals, scattering the pedestrians while the leather-jacket-and-Mohawk-haircut brigade that congregated in the club's parking lot pretended not to notice. Two other Los Angeles rock clubs were facing similar neighborhood complaints. But punk rock keeps popping up in unlikely places—recently, the Flesheaters and the Gun Club performed in the basement of a Chinese restaurant just off Hollywood Boulevard.

Punk rock originally flared up in the mid-seventies as a response to the smugness and solemnity that seemed to have infested so much big-time rock. Its centers were London, where genuine working-class anger fueled the movement, and New York, where bands like the Ramones, Blondie, and the Talking Heads worked their way out of seedy Bowery bars and into the limelight. But in these cities punk's moment has passed. Of the original English punks, the Clash are trying their hand at everything from reggae to soul, and Johnny Rotten is making inventive art-rock with Public Image Ltd. A few inferior bands continue to play pure, go-for-the-jugular punk for a relatively small audience. In New York, punk as it was in 1976–77 has virtually vanished. But the music and its related styles of dress and behavior have flourished in Los Angeles, and while much L.A. punk is derivative and doctrinaire, the city's punk scene has produced a vivid, compelling film documentary complete with soundtrack album

(*The Decline of Western Civilization*, album on Slash) and at least one world-class rock & roll band, X.

Many of the city's punk musicians are against anything that smacks of tradition ("If it's been standing for too long, it's evil," says bassist Gary McDaniel of Black Flag), but X has consciously allied itself to traditional rock & roll values. Billy Zoom, the quartet's blond-haired, blue-eyed guitarist, has been playing the instrument since he was a child and seems to know every fifties rockabilly riff. His attack is hard and modern, but his ideas come from such rock fountainheads as Chuck Berry and Carl Perkins. Bassist John Doe and vocalist Exene write lyrics that are often poetic and elliptical, and drummer Don Bonebrake drives the band with a jacked-up rock & roll momentum that's timeless. The group's records are produced by Ray Manzarek, who was the organist in L.A.'s seminal sixties band, the Doors, an X favorite. *Los Angeles* (Slash), the band's first album, included organ solos by Manzarek and a double-tempo version of the Doors' "Soul Kitchen." The group's second LP, *Wild Gift*, dispenses with the organ and concentrates on tough, terse originals. It successfully captures X's explosive but cannily controlled live sound and will probably turn out to be one of the year's most satisfying rock & roll LP's.

Most of America's major record companies have headquarters in Los Angeles, but none of these companies has shown much interest in the city's punk bands. Slash Records, which began as an offshoot of the now defunct punk fan magazine *Slash*, has filled the gap with ingenuity and considerable commercial success. X's *Los Angeles* has sold more than fifty thousand copies a year after its release, an impressive showing for a tiny independent label like Slash; more important, the album is still selling steadily. At the end of 1980, a nationwide pop critics' poll conducted by the *Village Voice* named the album one of the year's twenty best and voted X the country's finest "local band"—that is, the finest band without a major-label recording contract.

The Los Angeles punk scene hasn't produced another band with X's relatively broad appeal, but several groups have distinguished themselves in one way or another. The Germs were an inept but cocky quartet fronted by Darby Crash, whose thrashing, drunken performances and snarled, unintelligible vocals tended to disguise his considerable talents as a lyricist. Crash died of a heroin overdose last December, becoming the L.A. punk scene's first martyr. The Circle Jerks recently released an intelligent, witty first album, *Group Sex* (Frontier Records). Keith Morris, the Jerks' lyricist, warns his young fans that antisocial actions are ultimately self-defeating. "You can cuss, spit, throw bottles, broken glass," he chides, "but it ends up with a swift kick to your ass." The Jerks' "Group Sex," written with the Gun Club's Jeffrey Pierce, satirizes Southern California's hot-tub culture; "Beverly Hills" rants about people in "Spandex pants and cowboy boots" and concludes, "Maybe I'll have to even move."

Other punk bands lack the Circle Jerks' wit and are considerably more virulent. Fear's lead singer, Lee Ving, who has been dubbed "the Don Rickles of punk," insults the band's audiences ("You're a bunch of queers. . . . Next time don't bite so hard when I come, okay?") and writes songs that deal in calculated outrage. Punk audiences are aggressive to begin with, and more than one show featuring Fear and various other groups has turned into a pitched battle between bands and listeners or between punks and police. Even the latest mode of punk dancing— "slamming," in which stoned celebrants hurl themselves at each other across the dance floor, frequently knocking hapless onlookers off their feet—is a form of aggression.

The Decline of Western Civilization, which is presently being shown at art theaters around the country, captures the brilliance of X and the ugly venom that's also endemic to the L.A. punk scene. In a series of disquieting interviews, young punk fans chat noncommittally about beating each other up, talk about how much they hate cops and would like to kill hippies, and, in interview after interview, remark that they rarely see their parents or don't know where or who they are.

One suspects these extremely disaffected fans make up a minority of the punk audience, and the punk audience itself is a small part of California's rock fandom. But it's an exceptionally volatile audience, and the only thing holding it together is a handful of kamikaze bands. X, which has appeared on television's *Midnight Special* and undertaken several successful national tours, seems destined for stardom, and a few other L.A. bands may follow it to the top. But most of the town's punk groups play anarchic, sociopathic rock & roll noise for an anarchic, sociopathic youth subculture. In context, the music is chillingly specific. The decline of Western civilization? Could be, could be.

Lou Reed Hits Top Form and Knows It

THE NEW YORK TIMES | MARCH 10, 1982

Lou Reed's new album *The Blue Mask* is stark, harrowing, and ultimately uplifting rock & roll. It is the most powerful and the most consistent album Mr. Reed has made since his 1967 recording debut with the Velvet Underground—and he knows it.

"I'm not above appreciating my own work," Mr. Reed said the other day as he sat in a conference room at RCA. "And I don't think *The Blue Mask* is just a good album. It's way better than that."

Just when it seemed that large-scale ambitions had all but vanished from rock & roll, Lou Reed has suddenly decided to make his bid. "I've always liked trash, and I hear some trash records these days that are cute," Mr. Reed said. "But I don't hear anybody trying to do a Lear, or a Hamlet soliloquy, in rock & roll. Who says you can't do that? People say rock & roll is constricting, but you can do anything you want, any way you want.

And my goal has been to make an album that would speak to people the way Shakespeare speaks to me, the way Joyce speaks to me. Something with that kind of power; something with bite to it."

Lou Reed, a forty-year-old New Yorker, has always aimed high. *The Velvet Underground & Nico*, the first album to feature his songs, his singing, and his wildly inventive guitar playing, took aim at the "All You Need Is Love" philosophy that was so prevalent in 1967. Compared to the Beatles' *Sgt. Pepper's Lonely Hearts Club Band*, released the same year, *The Velvet Underground & Nico* seemed darkly demented.

The Beatles said they'd "love to turn you on," but Lou Reed sang "Heroin" and "Waiting for the Man," the ultimate hard-drug songs, both cautionary tales, both almost unbearably vivid. He sang about love, but he sang about sadomasochism, too. And in "The Black Angel's Death Song" he unleashed [a] feedback-laced electric guitar solo that is legendary for sheer abrasive energy.

There were several more Velvet Underground albums, and they revealed the sensitivity and heart behind Mr. Reed's tough facade. Songs like "Sweet Jane," "Beginning to See the Light," "Pale Blue Eyes," and "Rock & Roll" became rock & roll standards and got extensive radio airplay, unlike most of the music on *The Velvet Underground & Nico* and its follow-up, *White Light/White Heat*, which were too explosive for all but a handful of particularly daring radio programmers. In August 1970, Mr. Reed left the Velvet Underground and went to England to launch a solo career. After a somewhat disappointing first solo album, he hired David Bowie to produce *Transformer*, and that record was a milestone for him. It also yielded a hit single, "Walk on the Wild Side."

Onstage, Mr. Reed seemed to be borrowing David Bowie's sexually ambiguous stance, and "Walk on the Wild Side" became a kind of anthem in homosexual circles. But Mr. Reed said, "I didn't write anybody's national anthem when I wrote 'Walk on the Wild Side.'

"I wrote a character study of four people who hung around Andy Warhol's studio. My past is my past, and it's my business."

Mr. Reed married two years ago, and he says that his wife, Sylvia, "helped me so much in bringing things together and getting rid of certain things that were bad for me, certain people. I don't know what I would have done without her. She's very, very smart, so I have a realistic person I can ask about things: 'Hey, what do you think of this song?' I've got help, for the first time in my life. And I'm surrounded by good, caring, honest business people. In my life, that's a real change."

The ups and downs of Mr. Reed's career during the 1970s are chronicled on *Rock and Roll Diary*, a compilation album released by Arista in 1980. He made the brooding, enormously influential *Berlin* in the mid-1970s, and he also made *Metal Machine Music*, a barrage of electronic noise that was inspired in part by the avant-garde composer La Monte Young's music. Later in the 1970s, Mr. Reed looked back at his New York roots in the nostalgic *Coney Island Baby*, and he met the challenge of the punk-rock explosion head-on with the musically adventurous *Street Hassle*.

Mr. Reed's music, with the Velvet Underground and on his own, has probably been the single most pervasive influence on punk and new wave rock. But while Mr. Reed's songs have continued to be outspokenly personal, the music he has made in recent years has been uneven, for reasons he is not afraid to analyze. "For the last few years," he said, "I was working with musicians who were into funk and jazz. I wasn't playing the guitar on my records because I couldn't really play with those guys, being a simple rock & roll player. I thought it would be interesting to explore that direction, but there was a gap between me and them. You can hear it on the records. I heard it one day when some radio station was being brave and played one of my albums. And I said, 'You've carried this experiment far enough. It's not working. The ideas are there and then they disappear, the music isn't consistent, you seem isolated, there's a certain confidence that's not there because you're not really in control.' So I dissolved the band."

Mr. Reed played guitar again on *The Blue Mask*, and for the first time in years he worked with a basic, no-frills rock band, with Robert Quine on second guitar, Fernando Saunders on electric bass, and Doane Perry on drums. These four musicians interact like a seasoned combo; there are no ego contests, no power plays. The two guitars blend into a delicate, shimmering latticework, and Mr. Saunders plays melodically as well as holding down the bottom. Mr. Perry's drumming is spare and telling; he doesn't play a single gratuitous accent. When he was asked why the *The Blue Mask* succeeds so brilliantly where his other recent albums have been uneven, Mr. Reed laughed and said, "You mean, has there been a tremendous personal change in me that made possible this clarity of vision? No, it's mostly working with the right musicians."

The musicians were undoubtedly very important, but every song on

The Blue Mask scans and sounds as if it has been written and rewritten. There is more evidence of careful, deliberate planning in the sequencing of the songs. The album begins charmingly with "My House," a portrait of Mr. and Mrs. Reed at home, continues with a tribute to "Women," then abruptly goes for the jugular with songs about an alcoholic, a mugger and rapist, and a masochist that Mr. Reed calls "a very twisted individual." The album's second side begins with another light tune, "Average Guy," but the song that follows, "The Heroine," is a meditation on human needs, sexual roles, heroism, and other weighty topics and may be, line for line, the most brilliantly complex and sustained song that Mr. Reed has ever written. Its mood of near-panic is sustained by "Waves of Fear" and a touchingly personal reminiscence of "The Day John Kennedy Died" before the album finally cascades into a transcendent paean to heterosexual love and the possibility of ultimate salvation, "Heavenly Arms."

"I spent a lot of time on the song order," Mr. Reed said. "These things are important. If you can get a feeling of continuity from the album, a feeling of somebody trying to speak to you, well then, that's the difference between a 'good album' and something that's much finer."

There have been a number of public Lou Reeds over the years, and one suspects there have been a number of private Lou Reeds as well. His personality seems both complex and mutable; attitudes and ideas flicker across his face like so many shadows. "Some people like to think I'm just this black-leather-clad person in sunglasses," he noted with some amusement. "And there's certainly that side of me; I wouldn't want to deny my heritage. But while I have my share of street smarts, I'm not a rat from the streets by any means. I always wanted to be a writer, and I went to college to prepare myself for it.

"I took a major in English and a minor in philosophy; I was very into Hegel, Sartre, Kierkegaard. After you finish reading Kierkegaard, you feel like something horrible has happened to you—Fear and Nothing. See, that's where I'm coming from. If you have my interests and my kind of academic background, then what I'm doing is not really an unlikely thing to do. And now that I've made this album, I'm very, very happy. I'm not going to tour to promote this album; maybe I'll play a club in New York. Touring is just too hard on my body and spirit, and I don't want to subject myself to that now. I feel like I'm just starting to peak, and I want to feel like I've got plenty of time."

Patti Smith's Sweet Dream

ROLLING STONE | AUGUST 25, 1988

Dream of Life (Arista)
Patti Smith

For all its surface fury, punk rock has always had a surprising metaphysical aspect. In New York in the mid-seventies, when Tom Verlaine and Patti Smith were friends struggling to remake themselves as artists—Verlaine with his band Television, Smith as a poet—their shared tastes in reading, from Rimbaud to Paul Bowles, helped shape a unified aesthetic with definite spiritual aims. The flowering of "sonic punk" in the last few years, in the guise of bands such as Sonic Youth, has been part of the same process, a sort of philosophy of sound.

Dream of Life is Patti Smith's first record in some nine years, and the first fruit of her artistic collaboration with her husband, Fred "Sonic"

Smith. Playing in the late sixties with the MC5, Fred Smith crafted a resonating sonic architecture: a soaring Gothic cathedral of electric-guitar harmonics, constructed on a foundation of gut-level rock & roll throb, which could induce listeners to surrender as in some ancient tribal rite. Together the Smiths began recording *Dream of Life* after spending years in a kind of retreat, raising a family. It can be understood as an ambitiously visionary (and at the same time eminently practical) attempt to recharge the ideal of punk.

After nine years, you would expect Patti Smith to have grown as an artist, and she has. The imagery of her new lyrics reveals a high order of compression and heat. And if you thought she would never be much of a singer, think again. The old force and urgency are still abundantly present, especially in "People Have the Power" and in the alchemical intensity of "Up There Down There." But at the same time, the singing is liquid, full-bodied, musicianly. The rockers at the album's heart, "People Have the Power," "Up There Down There," "Where Duty Calls," and "Looking for You," and quieter moments like the eloquent ballad "Paths That Cross" are as vital and challenging as today's major-label rock & roll is likely to get.

Jimmy Iovine, who coproduced with Fred Smith, is inevitably going to incur the wrath of punk diehards, who may feel that the album's sonorous, rounded guitar sound should have had a more abrasive edge. But the majestic "People Have the Power" and "Up There Down There" have an exhilarating drive and punch. On these tunes, Fred Smith comes off like the psychic offspring of Keith Richards and Tom Verlaine. He has Richards's implacable rhythmic concision and earthy authority, and he uses heavily amplified guitar harmonics and interference patterns as a kind of cosmic metaphor à la Verlaine. The humming harmonic-sustain guitar on "Looking for You," the whacking momentum of "People Have the Power," and the meta–"Gimme Shelter" tropes he unleashes on "Up There Down There" create a highly charged sonic space.

"People Have the Power," with its arcing high-frequency droning, thunderous bottom, and fevered lyricism, is one of the most effective attempts at populist anthem making rock has seen. The power it packs and praises is both explicitly political and explicitly visionary, a power that pulses with the promise of imminent combustion. "Where Duty Calls" is the anthem's flip side, reminding us how easily power can be twisted.

The last song on *Dream of Life*, a hymn to home and family called "The Jackson Song," is the least satisfying. Musically, it's blandly inoffensive, something that cannot be said about the rest of this extraordinary record.

With Patti Smith's confident singing and incandescent lyrics, Fred Smith's persuasive riff craft and expressive sonic palette, and Jimmy Iovine's sense of definition and clarity going for it, *Dream of Life* couldn't really miss. And the inspired contributions of Jay Dee Daugherty and Richard Sohl, former members of the Patti Smith Group, cannot be overlooked. The thought and care that evidently went into the creation of this album should be a lesson to certain rock icons who have been churning out dreary product on schedule, rather than taking the time to create a music, and a vision, worthy of their talents. What may be most striking about *Dream of Life* is that there is no product here at all, only music.

WORLD MUSIC: "THE WORLD IS CHANGING AND SO IS OUR MUSIC."

The Resounding Impact of Third-World Music

THE NEW YORK TIMES | APRIL 15, 1979

The Mongolians started it, and now it's all over town. No, it isn't a new strain of influenza, it's a peculiar singing technique, developed by Mongolian nomads, that allows a vocalist to sing a duet with himself. The vocalist sings a primary tone, then tenses his throat and adjusts the shape of his mouth cavity, thus producing a delicate, flutelike overtone high above the original tone. On a recent weekend, one could hear the Harmonics Choir using this technique in concert at the La Mama theater, the Natural Sound Workshop using it in a loft concert on Eighth Avenue, and the composer and choreographer Meredith Monk using it in one of her *Songs from the Hill* in a performance at the Kitchen.

An avant-garde thrives on new techniques and new source materials, but the American and European avant-garde aren't the only musical sectors that have been heavily influenced in recent years by what used to be called "primitive" cultures. Our popular music, especially disco, our jazz and our concert music are increasingly drawing their inspiration from Africa and Asia; traditional Western modes of playing, writing, and perceiving music are being challenged and in many cases supplanted, and the trend is accelerating.

Skeptics will argue that, after all, one hears plenty of new concert music that is no more exotic than Webern or Stravinsky, that our pop singers still sing traditionally structured pop songs in recognizably Western styles, that our mainstream jazz musicians still play the blues and "Body and Soul." Quite true. On the other hand, when younger composers name their influences these days, they are as likely to say "Indian music" or "West African drumming" as they are to mention John Cage or Karlheinz Stockhausen (composers who were themselves profoundly influenced by non-Western music). Indeed, the number-one pop hit at any given moment is likely to be a pulsing, repetitive chant, with conspicuous African or Afro-Latin rhythms—overlaid in polyrhythmic counterpoint and played on African or Afro-Latin percussion instruments.

And the kind of jazz improvising popularized by the saxophonist John Coltrane and his pianist McCoy Tyner, perhaps the most influential jazzmen of the past twenty years, has been institutionalized in high school and college jazz programs, which continue to turn out hundreds, and perhaps thousands of Coltrane and Tyner imitators. It is a kind of improvising based on modes or scale patterns rather than traditional harmony; on short, repeating base figures rather than on a continuous moving bass line and on polyrhythms, particularly superimpositions of duple and triple meter. All these developments run against the grain of traditional jazz practice and are a direct result of Mr. Coltrane's studies (with Ravi Shankar and others) of Indian, Middle Eastern, and African music.

Non-Western influences are sometimes present even where they are not immediately discernible. Recently I had a brief backstage conversation with Leonard Bernstein and was surprised to hear him say how very profoundly he had been influenced, beginning in his student days, by the classical music of India. Several years ago, the subject of the African and Asian-influenced American composer Steve Reich came up during a conversation with Karlheinz Stockhausen, the celebrated German composer, who suggested that "any composer who is trying to do something new in this day and age had better know what's been done, and not just within his own tradition. The people in Europe who think Reich's music is so new have not heard the music from . . . that former Portuguese colony." Mr. Stockhausen was referring to the African nation of Mozambique, where traditional orchestras of mallet instruments play complex suites that do have a great deal in common with some of Mr. Reich's pieces.

Mr. Stockhausen is a cagey man, but from the rest of the conversation it was evident that he has listened to much African traditional and tribal music. His influential choral composition "Stimmung" would not have been possible without Indian music, and his most recent recording, a piece for a mixed ensemble of acoustic and electronic instruments called "Bird of Paradise," was directly inspired by music he heard in Ceylon.

Just what are these non-Western musics that suddenly seem to be exercising a subtle and not-so-subtle influence on so many different strata of our musical life? There are too many of them to permit really comfortable generalization, but for the purposes of this discussion we can isolate five major traditions that are having a demonstrable impact in the West.

1. *Indian* classical music, an ancient and refined tradition that was already being heard in Western concert halls during the first decades of this century, has had its greatest effect since the late 1950s, when recordings of Ravi Shankar and Ali Akbar Khan began to appear on American labels and these artists began to tour widely here and in Europe. The emphasis in Indian music is on melody, just as so much Western classical music emphasizes harmony. There is no harmony as such in Indian music, just very refined melodic exposition and improvisation over a single held tone or drone. These melodic expositions, which can be rendered on instruments like the sitar or sarod or by a wind instrument or the human voice, are often accompanied by virtuosic drumming that makes use of additive principles (two beats plus two beats plus three beats and then repeat, for example). These modular rhythmic structures have had a profound influence on certain Western concert music — the compositions of Olivier Messiaen and Philip Glass, to name two

disparate examples. But the influence of Indian melodic improvisation over a drone has been much more pervasive; it has been felt in the jazz of John Coltrane and his many disciples, in rock music, especially rock guitar playing, and in the avant-garde music of composer-performers such as Terry Riley and La Monte Young.

2. *Southeast Asian* music is many-faceted, but one tradition, that of the gamelans, or orchestras of mallet instruments found in Java and Bali, has been widely influential. The composer Colin McPhee's book *Music in Java* inspired a generation of American composers, including John Cage, whose early and widely influential "Sonatas and Interludes" (1946–48) bears more than a passing resemblance to gamelan music, especially in the sonorities of Mr. Cage's specially prepared pianos.

3. *African* music is especially complex, since it consists of an almost infinite number of tribal and traditional musics that sometimes do not have very much in common. But in general, rhythm is as important in African music as harmony is in European music and melody is in Indian. Certain well-established African traditions — the ceremonial and recreational music of the peoples who inhabit the West African coast, for example — include polyrhythmic music of remarkable complexity and density. This music is reflected in the West, and especially in America, on many levels, from concert music and jazz to disco.

4. *Middle Eastern* music, or the traditional music of the Islamic world, profoundly influenced Indian classical music (especially in North India, where Ravi Shankar and most of the Indian musicians who have been heard here come from). It has also had considerable impact in Islamic Africa. It uses additive rhythmic cycles, like Indian music, and it features improvisation over a static or drone backdrop. But the improvisations tend to be much more rhythmic and to be based on complex families of modes or melodic structures, and Middle Eastern vocalists like the late Oum Khalsoum of Egypt project a wailing intensity and a sophisticated use of rococo vocal ornamentation. The use of modes and the vocal style are reflected in John Coltrane's soprano saxophone style (and by extension, the style of practi-

cally every jazz and rock saxophonist since Mr. Coltrane), and in the work of certain composers, most notably Terry Riley.

5. *American Indian* music has been fascinating certain American composers for decades. It has not given rise to major styles or schools, but it has been reflected in numerous isolated compositions and in the work of some experimental composers who are particularly interested in chanting.

Where do we hear these traditions? Let's begin with disco, the popular music one is most likely to hear whenever people get together to dance. Of course, disco is not the whole of pop music, and a case can certainly be made for non-Western influence in rock, from the Beatles' Shankar-inspired use of the sitar, to Led Zeppelin's "Kashmir," to the Indian raga influence in the work of almost every major rock guitarist, right on up to the use of Afro-Latin rhythms by most contemporary jazz-rock fusion groups. But disco seems to be a more widely popular music now than all but the most successful rock (which has grown quite conservative, as the styles of Linda Ronstadt or Foreigner or Fleetwood Mac attest). Even established rock stars are embracing disco rhythms—the Rolling Stones with "Miss You," Rod Stewart with "Da Ya Think I'm Sexy," which at this writing is the nation's number-one pop single.

On the surface, disco is simply a revival of the old Tin Pan Alley glitter, and certainly a number of straight pop artists are jumping on the disco bandwagon. But rhythmically and often structurally, disco music represents a rejection of Western musical values. As we've noted, the lyrics are often little more than a chant or a repeating catchphrase. The real meat of disco records is their mesh of interlocking rhythm patterns, played percussively on Fender bass, synthesizer, choked electric guitars, and African and Afro-Latin instruments such as the conga and bongo drums, the West African double iron bell (which figures prominently, almost as a lead instrument, in Tasha Thomas's current disco hit "Shoot Me"), and the Afro-Brazilian friction drum that makes a moaning, whooping noise like a wild animal. The interlocking polyrhythms produced by these instruments are reproduced in discos at numbing volume and reinforced by rhythmic lighting effects (as well as by the tactile stimulation involved in dancing).

Theoretically, the disco dancer is supposed to be carried away in a kind of ecstatic experience. In this regard, it's interesting that poly-rhythms, played on batteries of very loud drums in enclosed spaces for dancers, figure in religious rituals throughout Africa, Latin America, the Middle East, and Asia, where they are associated with spirit possession or trance.

Afro-American music has often emphasized rhythm, or "the groove," over melody and harmony, and in doing so it reflected its African roots. The rediscovery of traditional African music by young black American musicians, which began around the same time that Dizzy Gillespie and other jazzmen began using Afro-Cuban rhythms and percussionists in their bands, meant that polyrhythm, as opposed to the hard, insistent beat of earlier black American popular music, could flourish here as it has in Africa. The polyrhythmic density of much disco music, and the rejection of Western melodic and harmonic norms that often seems to accompany it, are the result of this historical process. It may be that in the future the conscious employment of repeating polyrhythms to pro-duce hypnotic or trancelike effects will become even more sophisticated and overt.

We have already mentioned the saxophonist John Coltrane, who studied various non-Western systems and incorporated them into the far-reaching changes he effected in jazz. The modal improvising he popu-larized derived from his studies of Indian and Middle Eastern music, while his use of syncopated ostinato bass figures was directly inspired by albums of African field recordings. The rhythms his band played also reflected African practices, especially the loping 6/8 rhythm of his hit recording of "My Favorite Things" (a pop song he characteristically altered by reducing the chord changes to a bare minimum).

We have also noted the influence of various non-Western idioms on jazz-rock or fusion music. Sometimes one hears not just influence but out-right appropriation. For example, one of the most successful and widely imitated fusion hits of recent years was a mid-seventies album by Herbie Hancock, *Head Hunters,* and one of the most widely played selections from that album was a rearrangement of Mr. Hancock's mid-sixties hit "Watermelon Man," with a catchy new introduction. At least the introduction was new to most people; African music aficionados recognized it as a more or less exact reproduction of an African pygmy whistle song. It turned out that Mr. Hancock's percussionist, Bill Summers, who now leads his own fusion band, was trained as an ethnomusicologist and had played a field recording of pygmy music for Mr. Hancock. Unfortunately, the pygmies did not hold a copyright.

The wing of contemporary jazz that seems to owe relatively little to non-Western music is the acoustic avant-garde, but even here non-Western influences are evident. In a group like the Art Ensemble of Chicago, which uses a number of exotic percussion instruments, these influences are relatively close to the surface. But what about an artist like Anthony Braxton, the jazz saxophonist and composer whose albums have been among the more important statements of new jazz currents in the seventies? Mr. Braxton is often taken to task in the jazz press because of his admitted fondness for the work of certain European and white American composers, and in fact his most recent album, a three-record boxed set on Arista, is an entirely written composition for four orchestras that has little apparent jazz content. But according to Mr. Braxton, all this has to be viewed in context.

"I love some of Stockhausen's music," he says, "but I can take a piece like Stockhausen's 'Momente' and play you a recording of a direct African corollary. There's a Luciano Berio piece that's an African ritual. A number of factors have affected what we know as Western art music. You have to deal with the Moorish influence in Spain. If you look at the instrumentation of Western music, you find that only three or four instruments cannot be traced back to Africa. Then you read about the ancient connections between Greece and India, India and Africa. These transformations have been happening on many different levels. So I'm not just attracted to one form of music; I'm attracted to checking out music on a world level."

Mr. Braxton says that "creative music from the black aesthetic has been bringing Western music back into the world music arena." What he means is that Western concert music, which turned its back on improvisation several centuries ago, has been moving to embrace improvising again, a move he sees as a kind of rapprochement with the great world musical systems that have always emphasized improvisation—Indian, Middle Eastern, African—and which he attributes to the impact of jazz.

Some students of contemporary musical thought might argue that John Cage's readings in Eastern philosophy and his romance with the indeterminacy of the ancient Chinese oracle I Ching were an important factor in this swing back toward improvisation, but jazz, an improvisational art music that developed within Western culture and began fascinating European and white American composers as early as the turn of the century, has undoubtedly had a more telling and long-term effect.

John Cage does deserve mention here, for his early, Asian-influenced compositions and for his example as a challenger of convention. It was Mr. Cage who proposed in 1952 that even four minutes and thirty-three seconds of silence could be listened to and evaluated as music; the field has been wide-open ever since. In 1960 La Monte Young premiered a new composition that consisted of turning loose a jar full of butterflies. These composers and others who came along a little later effectively annihilated traditional modes of perceiving music, creating a kind of vacuum. For a while there was considerable improvisation in the more avant-garde sectors of contemporary concert music, but it rapidly became evident that new forms were needed. (Improvisation is not a very satisfactory incubator of new forms unless the improvisers happen to be well versed in a developed improvisational tradition, as American jazz musicians are and most other Western musicians and composers are not.) And it was at just this point that recordings of Indian and African music—Ravi Shankar's first American disks, Folkways recordings of African pygmy music—began to become available and to be heard. A number of important composers, among them Olivier Messiaen, Lou Harrison, Alan Hovhaness, and Pierre Boulez, had been using certain non-Western ideas, particularly rhythmic ideas, since the 1940s. Their music paved the way for the widespread acceptance of the new Indian classical and field recordings.

At the same time, the discipline of ethnomusicology—basically the study of non-Western musics—began to develop, in the United States at least, a marked performing orientation. By the end of the sixties, world-music programs at Wesleyan University and UCLA regularly employed Western African master drummers, gamelan musicians, and so on. These programs have spawned a number of composers who more or less "went native"—such as David Reck, who composes and plays original music on the Indian vina, or Barbara Benary, who has led a gamelan orchestra of instruments made from cans and hubcaps, the cast-off junk of the industrial West.

But the most important and influential American composers to have emerged from the era of the global village are La Monte Young, Terry Riley, Philip Glass, and Steve Reich. All of them arrived at their working methods more or less independently, and for all of them, becoming involved in non-Western music was the turning point in their careers.

After his early theatrical pieces, La Monte Young delved deeper into static, or very slowly changing, music, an interest that had surfaced in his early compositions when he was still in college. Eventually this interest led him to Indian music, and to studying with an Indian classical vocalist, Pandit Pran Nath. Now Mr. Young has two careers. He composes and performs his own music, and he sings Indian classical music as second vocalist when Pandit Pran Nath is performing.

Terry Riley's albums *In C* and *A Rainbow in Curved Air*, released by Columbia Masterworks in the late sixties, were the first important recordings to come from any of these new composers. "I feel like I got into these areas," he says, "partly through my association with La Monte, partly through my travels in Morocco and elsewhere, and partly through my own temperament."

Philip Glass, whose score for *Einstein on the Beach* has made him the most visible of the new composers, wrote in the conventional contemporary post-serialist idiom until he went to Paris in the mid-sixties. There he met and began studying with Allah Rakha, the Indian hand-drum virtuoso, and landed a job helping Ravi Shankar score a film. "My ideas wouldn't have developed the way they did if I hadn't started in that place," he says. "Also, I traveled, first in Morocco, where I had my first contact with non-Western music and was influenced by the geometric repetitions in Islamic art, then in Asia. Later I became interested in South Indian music and in West African drumming."

Steve Reich, whose *Drumming* was recorded by Deutsche Grammophon and whose *Music for 18 Musicians* was recently performed at the Bottom Line, traveled to Ghana to study with a master drummer and has also studied other non-Western musics in depth. Many of the musicians who have played in his ensembles came from the world music programs at Wesleyan. And recent concert programs at the Guggenheim Museum, sponsored by the Reich Music Foundation and featuring new works by young composers, suggested that Mr. Reich is going to play an important role encouraging a new generation of global village composers.

These four composers have considerable influence. After all, Mr. Glass's *Einstein on the Beach* was performed at the Metropolitan Opera, and all four of them, along with a number of other composers who work in comparable idioms, are widely appreciated in classical circles in Europe. Their work is also being reflected in progressive rock. Brian Eno and David Bowie were in the audience at some of Mr. Glass's first European concerts, and, as two of the most influential musicians in rock, they have spread far and wide certain ideas developed by Mr. Glass and his peers. German rock groups have also made use of some of the innovations of Mr. Young, Mr. Riley, Mr. Glass, and Mr. Reich, and their music is reflected in much of New York's punk or new-wave rock as well.

It is tempting to make too much of the increasing internationalization of our music, to make it out to be a revolution when it is really an evolutionary process. But it would be shortsighted to dismiss it as a fringe movement or a passing fancy. Fifty years ago, what little non-Western influence one heard in Western concert, jazz, and popular music was mostly Chinoiserie, or fake exoticism. Today non-Western music has colored various strata of our popular music, deeply and decisively affected the structure and substance of modern jazz, and become the single most important influence on several of our most widely admired and imitated composers. And this trend has not even begun to peak.

Some people will fret that in accepting musical internationalization, we are accepting the decline of the West, that we are rushing to embrace the "primitive" because we are not so sure that "civilization" is necessarily a good thing. But we should do more than accept this internationalization; we should welcome it. It indicates that Western culture is finally shaking off the aesthetic arrogance that was such a persistent and crippling legacy of the colonial period. The world is changing and so is our music, and in welcoming fruitful new ideas, whatever their source, we can only be enriched.

Voices Transport the Ear to Another Realm

THE NEW YORK TIMES | JULY 27, 1986

Pandit Pran Nath, the Indian classical vocalist, sat singing phrases from a raga amid a clutter of electronic equipment at the downtown loft of the composer La Monte Young on a sunny afternoon. Some of the equipment had been set up for recording purposes, but just now Pran Nath was singing to the sustained drone of an electronic tone generator, while Mr. Young tracked his most minute fluctuations in pitch on the screen of an oscilloscope. "This way," Mr. Young said, "you can see the difference between what we think of in the West as being 'in tune,' and what the greatest Indian musicians can do."

Pran Nath's voice rose until he was singing in unison with the electronic tone; on the screen of the oscilloscope, one saw two waveforms of apparently identical amplitude, pulsing only slightly out of phase with each other. To the ear, it was difficult to distinguish Pran Nath's tone from that of the generator—they sounded perfectly in tune. "Just about any Western musician would tell you that they are perfectly in tune," Mr. Young said. "But watch." Pran Nath, who was sustaining a steady, continuous tone without resorting to the vibrato so many Western singers and instrumentalists use to stabilize their intonation, made a tiny, barely perceptible adjustment in pitch. On the screen, the two waveforms slowly pulled together into a single wave. And at the moment they merged, one heard . . . something. It was something beyond what we think of as being "in tune," something deeper.

Until the recent release of Pandit Pran Nath's *Ragas of Morning & Night* (Gramavision), American listeners were able to experience the singer's work only in a difficult-to-find French album and at occasional concerts in New York and a few other cities. One did encounter vocal effects that partly depended on painstaking intonation, for example, in the work of the American composer David Hykes and his Harmonic Choir, whose third album, *Harmonic Meetings* (Celestial Harmonies), has just been released. But a student of acoustics, the science of sound, would say that different acoustical effects are responsible for the intriguing sounds one hears when Mr. Hykes sings three distinct sounds at once. One hears a fundamental tone, a deep subtone below it, and a silvery countermelody high above it.

Mr. Hykes and the singers in his Harmonic Choir primarily use muscle control to shape their mouths into resonating chambers. Other effects having to do with reverberation and echo are obtained when the group records its material in a medieval abbey in France, as on *Harmonic Meetings*. But for the listener who has been inculcated with the musical values of the Western classical tradition, the phenomena that help make both Pran Nath's and David Hykes's music special take place in the same sort of twilight zone, a place where music, the science of acoustics, and the experience of the mystical all intersect.

Our very vocabulary places such phenomena beyond the pale of conventional musical discourse; we have no words to describe the realm of in-tune-ness that lies beyond being in tune. Yet we can measure the phenomenon with electronic equipment, and, perhaps with a bit of practice, we can hear it, too. It is not a psycho-acoustic chimera (or will-o'-the-wisp). Something does happen, and it can be quite enthralling.

Phenomena of such subtlety are best appreciated in the intimacy of a live performance. But the new albums by Pandit Pran Nath and David Hykes's Harmonic Choir offer the armchair listener the same sort of experiences, and the opportunity for some perceptual fine-tuning. Pran Nath's *Ragas of Morning & Night* captures two extended performances of exceptional depth and nuance. And on *Harmonic Meetings*, the singers David and Michelle Hykes and Timothy Hill utilize demanding vocal techniques from Indian, Tibetan, and Mongolian traditions in a suite of devotional music.

The casual listener will find these disks pleasantly melodious, like much of the currently popular "new age" music. But unlike the gentle sounds marketed by labels such as Windham Hill, this music offers more attentive listeners a great deal more—an active, participatory listening experience that can refine, and intensify, one's conception and perception of beauty.

In his insightful notes to Pandit Pran Nath's album, La Monte Young, the first American minimalist composer and a longtime Pran Nath student, speaks of the singer's "uncompromising adherence to the authentic rendering of the traditional ragas and his unwillingness to change his style to meet modern tastes for rhythmic and popular elements." Over a period of development that may well have lasted thousands of years, Indian sages refined a unique musical system, bequeathing their successors a body of knowledge that identified every melodic blueprint, or raga, with a time of day, season of the year, emotional attitude, and overall mood. It is said of the sixteenth-century Indian court musician Mian Tansen that when he sang a raga for the rainy season on a sunny day, clouds would gather, the skies would darken, and rain would fall. In the lore of Indian music, such tales are commonplace.

Today, many popular Indian musicians observe the tradition of singing each raga at its proper time and season in a loose manner or ignore the tradition altogether. But Pandit Pran Nath, who gave the first concert of morning ragas in the United States at Town Hall one Sunday morning in 1971, scrupulously observes the traditional strictures. Only by performing each raga in its proper time and season, he believes, can the musician transcend mere entertainment and, as La Monte Young says, "resonate the nervous system of the listener."

Pran Nath often says that "raga is created in between the tones." Even when two ragas use the same scale structure, the deft employment of microtonal shadings, melodic ornamentation and filigree, sliding and vibrating tones, and other traditionally prescribed techniques gives each raga, and each performance of it, a distinct character of its own. The evening raga on the new album, "Raga Darbari," intended to create a mood of "late night inner prayer, the yearning of the soul for peace and fulfillment," works its magic with the help of minutely flattened intervals recalling the harmonic ambience of the blues. It is a deeply moving, emotionally intense performance, with enough detail and nuance to repay repeated listening.

On the first album by David Hykes and the Harmonic Choir, *Hearing Solar Winds*, techniques adapted from Tibetan Buddhist chanting and a peculiar style of Mongolian solo singing enabled a small group of American singers to achieve the textural density of an orchestra, with each singer producing two or three intervals simultaneously. The basic melodic structures of Mr. Hykes's compositions emphasized the eerie, floating, high harmonics of the Mongolian singing and the deeply resonant bass tones produced by the Tibetan techniques. The sounds themselves were enchanting enough to render more complex structural development superfluous.

Harmonic Meetings, a double album consisting of an extended composition and some shorter pieces, expands the music's range by adding substantial Indian elements, and by focusing on individual singers, particularly Mr. Hykes and a virtuoso of the Tibetan chanting technique, Timothy Hill. The music, underlined here and there by the droning of an Indian tamboura or the tolling of a bass drum, attains an impressive richness of texture despite the fact that there are never more than three people singing at one time. Indeed, much of the music consists of improvised vocal solos which expand on simple melodic motifs both linearly and texturally. And for the first time on a record by the Harmonic Choir, words are used, mostly simple devotional texts from the Christian, Islamic, and Judaic traditions.

The Pandit Pran Nath and Harmonic Choir albums would be valuable if all they did was dramatically expand the range of vocal techniques available to contemporary solo and group singers. But the use of devotional texts on both albums is no coincidence. The mood, shape, and substance of the performances conspire to draw the willing listener into an experience that is moving in a spiritual rather than a primarily emotional manner. And the deeper one dives into the music's depths, the more one finds to marvel at.

Journeying into a World of Arab Music

THE NEW YORK TIMES | DECEMBER 17, 1989

Any listener whose interest in Western classical music extends beyond superficial "music appreciation" to a concern with origins, formal principles, and stylistic evolution must sooner or later come to grips with the rich musical heritage of the Arab world.

During the ninth and tenth centuries, Europe was in its dark ages. Christian plainchant, troubadour ballads, and dance music were dominant; art music was in its infancy. But in the great cities of the Islamic world, from Spain and North Africa to India, composers and instrumentalists who enjoyed royal patronage were already creating orchestral compositions of symphonic complexity.

Forms such as the nouba of Andalusia (Moslem Spain) and the Syrian wasla left room for improvisation but were rigorously structured and preserved through a form of alphabetic notation. A single nouba or wasla consisted of five or more highly organized, distinct movements. These compositions were performed by orchestras of stringed and wind instruments, percussion, and voices.

This music would be of interest to students of Western classical music if only because so many of the instruments of the European orchestra were derived from Arab models. As Jean Jenkins remarks, in liner notes for the exemplary six-record series *Music in the World of Islam*, issued some years ago, "Our oboes, trumpets, viols, violins, lutes and guitars, harps, dulcimer and psaltery, kettledrums, tambourines, castanets and triangles all originated in Islamic instruments."

But the Arab influence on European music extends far beyond instrumentation, as some recently released and reissued recordings make clear. The concept of long-form orchestral compositions, designed not as ritual or incidental music but as art music for serious listening, seems to have passed into European culture from the Arabs during the eight centuries of Moorish rule in Spain. The organizing principles of this early Arab classical music were also influential.

Paul Bowles, the American author and composer who recorded the double LP collection *Music of Morocco* some years ago (Library of Congress Archive of Folksong L63–L64), believes he has found in certain Moroccan traditions the roots of the sonata form. And certainly the early Arab composers were adept at the development of melodic material through theme-and-variation techniques. It seems likely that without the impact of Arabic musical thought and practice, European classical music as we now know it simply would not exist.

The term "Arab" in this context is somewhat misleading. The music that emerged from the opulent courts of Baghdad, Damascus, Aleppo, Cairo, Cordoba, and other urban centers between the ninth and thirteenth centuries mixed traditions from the Arabian peninsula with influences originating in Persia, Syria, Byzantium, and Central Asia. In addition, Arab rulers instituted ambitious translation projects, giving their court musicians and composers access to ancient musical treatises.

But what did this early Arab classical music actually sound like? Although many early works have been preserved and are studied and performed in musical conservatories throughout the Islamic world, they have remained the province of a select group of scholars and devotees, and have rarely been recorded.

Even the examples that have been issued on record, such as the splendid excerpt from an Andalusian nouba in *Music of Morocco*, have been fragmentary. One could get a sense of the sound of the music and of performing styles. But the "anthology" approach common to album releases of ethnomusicological field recordings tends to mix classical, folk, and popular selections on one disk; it was impossible to hear an Andalus nouba or a Syrian wasla in its entirety.

Recently, with the advent of the compact disk and the dedication of a small group of French scholars, this situation has been changing. In 1985, the French Ocora label issued a recording of two complete Andalusian noubas on CD, performed by the orchestra of Abdelkrim Rais of Fez, Morocco (*Maroc: Musique Classique Andalou-Maghrebine*, Ocora C559016). This disk, enchanting as it is, documents Andalusian music as it is performed today, almost five hundred years after its transplantation to North Africa following the Christian reconquest of Spain.

A new companion CD, *Ustad Massano Tazi: Musique Classique on Andalouse de Fes* (Ocora C559035) is a recording of a different sort. Here, a group of performers who are also Sufi mystics and have preserved early musical traditions for metaphysical as well as aesthetic reasons, set out to re-create as accurately as possible the sound and performing style of Ciryab, the celebrated court musician who left Baghdad in the ninth century to found the first Spanish musical conservatory, at Granada.

Ciryab's musical theories were linked with alchemical studies; the balance of timbres within the orchestra was thought to be crucial to the music's spiritual effect. Mr. Tazi and his ensemble here perform two complete noubas (one runs almost fifty-three minutes) on copies of instruments in use in Ciryab's time, with the gut strings of that era replacing the steel strings introduced into the music during the eighteenth century. This is an endlessly fascinating recording, with frequent shifts in rhythm and complex routines alternating solo and group vocals with perpetually shifting groupings of stringed and percussion instruments.

Wasla D'Alep: Chants Traditionnels de Syrie, by Sabri Moudallal and the Traditional Music Ensemble of Aleppo (Inedit MCM 26007), again presents a complete performance of a long-form orchestral composition from Arab music's golden age, a wasla being roughly equivalent to the Andalus nouba in terms of both antiquity and formal structure. These nouba and wasla recordings are a singular event in modern musical scholarship. For the first time, nonspecialist Western listeners can hear complete performances of highly developed orchestral—one is tempted to say symphonic—compositions from the Arab world of a thousand years ago.

Archives de la Musique Arabe, Vol. 1 (Ocora 558678) is the first release in a new series in which some of the earliest recordings of Arabic music are being reissued. The selections on this disk were transferred from cylinders recorded between 1908 and 1920; some of the performers were already professional musicians as early as the 1870s. Because cylinders did not impose time strictures quite as stringent as the later 78-rpm disk, some of these performances run as long as fifteen minutes.

The performers include Sufi sheiks, former muezzins (religious cantors) who left their mosques to go on the road with secular theater troupes, and a remarkable dervish flutist whose angular phrasing and novel tonal effects suggest that in the Arab world as in the West there were idiosyncratic progressives as well as traditionalists. Considering the age of the recordings, they are astonishingly clear, with only minimal distortion.

There is no better introductory sampler to the classical, folk, and popular idioms of the Islamic world than *Music in the World of Islam*, a series of six LPs devoted, respectively, to "The Human Voice," "Lutes," "Strings," "Flutes and Trumpets," "Reeds and Bagpipes," and "Drums and Rhythms" (Tangent TGS 131 through 136). Another welcome event for students of non-Western music is the recent reissue of many of the original UNESCO World Music recordings compiled by Alain Danielou in the 1960s.

The outstanding *Turkey I* (Barenreiter Musicaphon BM 30L2019) is devoted to the ritual music of the Mezlevi or whirling dervishes, the Sufi order founded by the poet Rumi. Additional volumes relating to Arab music are devoted to Turkey and other parts of the Islamic world. In addition, several of the later UNESCO recordings that were originally issued by EMI/Odeon are beginning to be reissued on CD by the French Auvidis label. Among the highlights are *North Yemen* (Auvidis D8004) and *Syria: Islamic Ritual Zikr in Aleppo* (D8013).

Two reliable mail-order sources for these and other recordings of non-Western music are the World Music Institute (109 West 27th

Street, New York, NY 10001) and Down Home Music (10341 San Pablo Avenue, El Cerrito, California 94530). Robert Browning of the World Music Institute has edited and published *Maqam: Music of the Islamic World and Its Influences,* a collection of essays by various authorities that includes both broad historical surveys and specialized studies of local traditions.

MOROCCO: "WE FELL THROUGH EACH OTHER, WEIGHTLESS, INTO THE SKY."

Behind the Story of "Up the Mountain"

Like any budding beatnik growing up in the twilight zone between *On the Road* and Woodstock, I always made it a point to read anything by William Burroughs. I kept noticing cryptic allusions in Burroughs's work to Jajouka, a mountain village somewhere in Morocco, home of the Master Musicians (who were they?) and their mysterious Rites of Pan (what was *that*?).

Being a Stones fanatic, I was intrigued when I heard that Brian Jones had visited the village with Burroughs's longtime friend and frequent collaborator Brion Gysin. Then Gysin published a novel called *The Process*, which described Jajouka, its music, and the lifestyle of the Master Musicians. They were the sons of sons of musicians, and apparently they sat around all day playing music and smoking kif when they weren't driving possessed tribesmen into mass Dionysian frenzies. It sounded like my kind of scene.

I reviewed *The Process* in *Rolling Stone* and mailed a copy to Gysin, care of his publisher. He wrote back from Tangier, saying, "Drop in any time." Meanwhile, Rolling Stones Records announced plans to release an album called *Brian Jones Presents the Pipes of Pan at Jajouka*. I contacted label honcho Marshall Chess, and he showed me footage of Jajouka on Robert Frank's Moviola. The place looked like Paradise. One night Marshall and I listened to Jones's tape. I don't think we ever figured out whether we were playing the tape backward or forward, but we had a lot of fun trying. Later, I learned Jones had subjected some of the music to studio processing, including overdubs involving tracks running backward *and* forward.

In 1969 and 1970, Ed Ward had written glowing *Rolling Stone* reviews of two albums by the band I played with, Insect Trust. We met after a show, and when he became the magazine's record editor and found himself in a jam for a jazz reviewer, he remembered me. I had a journalism background, played sax and clarinet, claimed to know something about jazz, had long hair, and was under thirty. Obviously, I could be trusted. I began writing reviews, but Jajouka was still on my mind.

By 1971, I was living in Manhattan, and among my friends was Michael Herr, recently returned from Southeast Asia and in the early stages of writing the best book on Vietnam, bar none, *Dispatches*. One night Michael called and insisted that I be at his apartment no later than ten the next morning. We were both cheapo-horror-trash-movie buffs, and some New York channel was showing the cult classic *Carnival of Souls* at that ridiculous hour. I'm glad I went. I saw a truly outstanding movie, listened to a bunch of Stones records for about the billionth time, and met Jann Wenner.

Naturally, Jann wanted to get Michael into *Rolling Stone*. But since I was already writing reviews for the magazine, he also asked me if I had any feature ideas. By this time we were strolling down Seventh Avenue South, and a shop selling Oriental rugs captured our attention. It reminded me of my imaginary Morocco, and I started barraging Jann with secondhand Jajouka lore. When I told him about hearing the Brian Jones recordings, Jann said: "I'll tell you what. You go over there and get that story, and I'll pay you five hundred dollars for it."

That was about five times as much as I'd ever been paid for a story. I agreed instantly, right before Jann shelled out several thou for a Persian rug without batting an eye. It didn't occur to me that travel expenses hadn't been mentioned. The deal was five hundred dollars, period. But even though it was the seventies, it was still the sixties, if you know what I mean. This was going to be an adventure.

I booked passage on a Yugoslav freighter. My fellow passengers fell into two groups: hippies running away to Morocco and parents going to Morocco in search of their runaway sons and daughters. This state of affairs made the communal meals somewhat tense, and the freighter's five-ways-to-cook-potatoes cuisine did little to soothe frayed nerves. On the other hand, you could sit right up in the bow of the boat, party all night, and watch the sun come up out of the Atlantic. It was, like, spectacular.

Instead of looking up Gysin and going after the story, I ended up traveling south with some hippies from Kansas City. I soon found myself in the walled city of Essaouira, ravaged by dysentery, with a spider bite on my arm that swelled to baseball size. The local doctor, a Foreign Legion veteran who had survived the carnage at Dien Bien Phu, checked my vital signs, lunged for his bag, and shot me up with digitalis. "Since there is nothing in your system to counteract the poison, it is making your heart beat quite irregularly," he said cheerfully. "You could die at any moment. If you stay in this hotel, I cannot assume responsibility; I suggest you check into the hospital."

The expatriates around town all told true-life horror stories about the hospital. My companion asked the doctor, "If your wife was in this condition, would you check *her* into the local hospital?" The doctor huffed: "Certainly not! I would put her into my car and drive her to Casablanca." I elected to take my stand amid the echoing stone halls of the Atlantic Hotel. After two weeks of spider venom and no food or drink other than water, I noticed I was still alive and caught the train for Tangier.

This was the fabled *Marrakech Express*, but it wasn't exactly what it was cracked up to be. It stopped in every outpost and often, for no apparent reason, in the middle of nowhere. My first night on the train I awoke from a fever dream to find the car I was in deserted. The train was sitting—somewhere. All I could see outside was a single halogen light set too far up on a pole to illuminate anything at ground level. All else was darkness. Thinking absently about trying to find something to eat, I stepped off the train, without seeing or hearing a soul. I walked a few yards into the pitch-black night; as I neared the light pole, I noticed what looked like a dozen pairs of demon eyes coming my way. Before I could decide if I was dreaming, the demon eyes resolved into a pack of wild dogs, all snarling, salivating, and bearing down fast. There was something to eat out there after all: me. I made it back to the train, but only just.

In the middle of the second night, the local from hell finally wheezed into Tangier. I got a taxi and headed straight for Gysin's. He was hospitable and charming and lived conveniently near the city's all-night pharmacy. Before long I was back on my feet and listening to Gysin's own unadulterated tapes of the Master Musicians. The double-reed horns set up a buzzing field of harmonics, and the drumming sounded like an earthquake. Before long, I was ready to go.

The article excerpted here, filed from Tangier, gave me a feeling of accomplishment and, eventually, the five hundred dollars. But my involvement with the Master Musicians was just beginning. The ancient moon-goddess/horned-god religion of the Mediterranean basin wasn't just *celebrated* in Jajouka, it was *alive*, and it drew me. I returned a few months later and spent some time studying the traditional music and the magic of the old souls there. In 1973, I returned again in the company of saxophonist Ornette Coleman. We recorded a so-far unreleased album at the height of the Pan festival, with the screaming and shrilling of hundreds of hill tribesmen in trance overlaying the elemental ritual music.

After a 1988 visit I wrote "Into the Mystic" (RS 548), an article recounting trance experiences, light visions, strange nights in high-mountain Phoenician temple ruins, and running with Bou Jeloud—the village's Pan—through the mad riot of the Rites. "You sent them *that?*" my friends asked incredulously after reading the manuscript. "Nobody will ever believe this stuff. You think they're going to *publish* this?" To my surprise, the editors told me they loved it; they paid me more than five hundred dollars for it, too.

It does seem curious—though not by Jajouka standards—that this article is resurfacing now [in 1992]. Bill Laswell recently released *Apocalypse Across the Sky*, a splendid album featuring the Master Musicians, on his Axiom label. Bachir Attar, son of Chief Jnuin, who taught me much in the seventies, led a Jajouka contingent on "Continental Drift," a track on the Stones' *Steel Wheels*; a fanfare from the track introduced shows on the *Steel Wheels* tour. The Tangier expatriate scene has inspired a number of recent movies (*The Sheltering Sky, Naked Lunch*) and books (Michelle Green's *Dream at the End of the World*, Stephen Davis's *Jajouka Rolling Stone*). You can call this synchronicity or happenstance; I call it that old Jajouka magic. I have only one question: When do I get to go back?

Up the Mountain (excerpt)

ROLLING STONE | OCTOBER 14, 1971

Hamri, the painter, went up the mountain to the village of Jajouka because he had family there. Hamri took Brion Gysin up the mountain and Gysin wrote about it in *The Process*. Gysin took William Burroughs up the mountain, and Burroughs described it in *The Ticket That Exploded*. Brian Jones heard Gysin's tapes of the Master Musicians of Jajouka and went up the mountain with a Uher and a recording engineer. He heard half the music and made a tape that is now a record; but that isn't half the story.

We went bouncing up the mountain in a VW with Sanche and Nancy Gramont and their son Gabriel, out of the Tangier afternoon and south along Morocco's Atlantic coast, where cattle and sheep graze down to the ocean's edge and cork forests crowd the roadside. Turned inland at Larache, blank bungalow siestas, dusty streets with children and dogs, and left the paved road at Ksar-el Kebir, squatting on a hill, white-walled and old with Coca-Cola signs.

From there the narrow cowpath of a road climbs steeply into dramatic green hills and broad expanses of tall grass, past lean-to settlements walled with dried reeds and sudden vistas opening off into the beginnings of the Rif. Nearing the end of the road, the crown of a great hill, we came to the outskirts of Jajouka; houses of mud, plaster, and polished dung; roofs made of thatching and corrugated tin; tents pitched among the houses and, off to one side, the red-and-white carcass of a freshly killed cow being hacked to pieces a few yards from the tomb of the saint.

The remains of Saint Sidi Hamid Sherk, who introduced Islam to the region sometime around the year 800, give Jajouka a moral authority unquestioned, until recently, by the people of the neighboring villages. This authority is expressed, and sustained, by Jajouka's Master Musicians, the sons of sons of sons of musicians, who play to exorcise the illnesses of pilgrims, to reaffirm the identity of villagers and visitors at festival and feast times, and to entertain and instruct their listeners and themselves, wafting their time-seasoned melodies and handed-down rhythms out across the Jebel on clouds of kif smoke. Hamri says the musicians "want all time play and smoke kif, smoke kif and play," but the sound we drove into our first afternoon in Jajouka was the buzz of hill families gathered for Miloud, amid the smoky smell of sizzling mutton and calves' liver.

So we downshifted through the haphazard houses and tents, into laughing curious crowds and up across the wide, grassy summit of the hill. Just below the summit, we stopped before a lone, white building, two big rooms and a long, tin-roofed front porch: the "school," lodge and living quarters for the musicians. Took a few tentative steps out of the car and spun around in a circle, open space and open sky rushing away into all the degrees of distance, elliptical mountains, rolling fields, valley villages, and enormous trees; nothing flat, only heights and depths.

Hamri welcomed us and we went walking across the green and down into the village, attended by a hundred children, wide-eyed at my red beard, too excited to keep a respectful distance. The adults studied us with welcoming eyes as we walked among the tents, past baskets of almonds, currants, and spun sugar confections until finally, overwhelmed, we sat on a rock in the middle of the surge and the sunlight, utter strangers utterly at home.

"The Mother Ship," was all I could say, "the Mother Ship."

Back at the "school," Hamri was holding court, attended by the coming and going of musicians, a few of them young, most of them old, all identifiable by the brown djellabas and white turbans that serve as all-purpose clothing and uniforms. Some of the musicians were preparing mint tea, cleaning up scraps from lunch, or helping Hamri hang a goat's carcass from the eaves. The rest sat in groups, talking softly and smoking their long sebsis, which they filled from pouches made of sheep's bladders, while Hamri set to work stripping off the goat's meat with his bare hands. We eased into a corner and looked off into the approaching evening while I played back, in my mind's ear, selections from the background Brian Gysin had given us the night before:

"The musicians have papers from the Alaouite Sultans, who came to power about the same time as Louis XIV in France and Charles II in England. The text of these, written by a royal chamberlain or official scribe, addresses them with extraordinary respect, and acknowledges that they have rights over the sultan: the right to play him to bed, to play him to the mosque on Fridays, rights for a group to live in the Palace, and so forth. Two musicians who are still alive remember being at the court of the Sultan Moulay Hafid, who was sultan in Marrakech when his brother was sultan in Fez.

"This all broke up with the French occupation in 1912. A pirate called Raisouli, who set himself up as a would-be sultan, treated the musicians of Jajouka royally while he lasted; it was very good for his publicity to have them. In the twenties he paid them a hundred dollars a month apiece, which was a huge sum of money in those days. But then Raisouli was busted by the Spaniards.

"The Spaniards looked after these things in some ways better than the French did; they had much more understanding of it, because it's so mixed up with their own music, their own cultural history. What the music is, in fact, is the popularization of the classical music that was written around the ninth, tenth century in Andalusia, court music at the courts of Cordova and Seville. Around 1492, there was a big expulsion of the Moors from southern Spain, and a great many of these people settled back in the hills at that time. The Spaniards were fairly good to those up in Jajouka; they were allowed to collect a tithe on all of the neighboring villages, who acknowledged the moral authority of the saint buried in

Jajouka. The musicians would simply travel around to the fields at harvesttime, and people would give them a measure of whatever it was they were harvesting.

"Now the political development of the music in all the countries has been that, as soon as a nationalistic revolution is successful, they immediately want to put down their own music; to get out of their old clothes, and get into Levi's. Here, at the moment of independence in 1956, there were enormous parades with the entire population streaming through the streets for several weeks on end. They were beating up any Moroccan musicians who even dared to make a squeak and started huge samba lines shouting, 'The samba and the rhumba are the national music of New Morocco.'

"All musicians who were caught were taken away and put in concentration camps, along with all the whores who were caught; they were going to be settled down and taught useful handicrafts. Music came back because of the tourist boom, but still . . . last August, September at harvesttime the musicians from Jajouka had fights with people, who stoned them when they came to the fields to ask for their tithe.

"Hamri's been most anxious to try and get these things reestablished by the government, but the government just doesn't want to hear about such things anymore. In fact, the really shocking thing is that every one of the musicians up in Jajouka is taxed for his instrument, something like six dollars a year, and his total yearly income isn't more than ten dollars in cash. There was no future at all visible a couple of years ago, when Hamri really rooted around and gave them money for what he calls the 'school.' They have a place to hang out and meet regularly, and they have a group of young kids who come and learn all the drumming rhythms. So something is going on. Still, it's a terrible scramble."

I awoke from a nap in the darkened school. A bonfire was beginning to crackle outside. "Get the Uher quick," Sanche said. A gigantic sound rent the air. Lining the rock wall that runs across the hill's summit were fifteen rhaita players—rhaita is a kind of oboe, a double reed horn with a flared bell—playing a ringing fanfare in outlandish harmony. At right angles to the farthest rhaita player a line of five drummers beat an incantatory counterpoint. The sound of the band, as I set up the taping equipment in the firelight, was an intense presence louder than any amplifier, filling the hilltop like an amphitheater. The rhaitas shrilled simultaneously into a shrieking falsetto register that seemed to trail off into dog-whistle frequencies and sounded like thousands of Arab women screaming, "yuyuyuyuyu."

The musicians call this opening piece the "Kaimonos." It begins as a slow processional march, with the horns phrasing freely over an almost quizzical rhythm, and then accelerates, the rhaitas building kinetic phrases to a pitch of hysteria that signals the arrival of Bou Jeloud. Bou Jeloud means "the Father of Skins"; Gysin has identified him further as "the Father of Fear"; he is none other than a continuing survival of the Horned God of antiquity, the goat-god, Pan.

When Marc Antony, dressed in animal skin, ran the race of the Lupercal in Rome, Caesar asked him to strike his barren wife Calpurnia as he ran. Bou Jeloud dances in Jajouka today sewn naked into the skin of a freshly slaughtered goat, a huge straw hat tied over his ears, his hands, face, and feet blackened with charcoal, and it is said that the women he flails with his two leafy switches become pregnant within a year.

"Bou Jeloud is always taboo," says Gysin. "The boy who dances Bou Jeloud just automatically never comes and sits down and shares the kif pipe with other people, or when they're sitting around the tray of tea, he's always sitting ten feet away. Slimou, the boy who's been dancing him these last few years, is a very wild creature. He never comes into a house, not even the musicians' house, he just comes under the porch, sits on the very edge of the circle of people."

When Slimou isn't dancing, he often seems to vanish; occasionally you can spot him, far off down the hillside, meandering along with a herd of goats. He appeared out of darkness, one night in Jajouka, while I was rummaging in the backseat of the VW, and in halting French bummed a cigarette, disappearing with it into the blackness outside the perimeter of firelight.

When he leaps into the circle of celebrants, half-man and half-goat in the half-light, Slimou is no longer Slimou; he is Bou Jeloud. He stands before the row of rhaita players, his entire body vibrating with the energy of their music, drinking up the concentrated force of ancient pandemonium and feeding it back into a pyramiding intensity that wants to send the hilltop spinning off into space. The musicians respond with a new propulsive phrase that catapults him across the grass and through the bonfire, attacking men, women, and children with his sapling arms. The crowd scatters before his lunges, screaming their own counterpoint to the antiphonal interplay of drums and rhaitas.

The head piper leads the horns into a blaring announcement of Aisha Hamouka, "Crazy Aisha," a personage so powerful she must be danced by a crowd of little boys dressed as women. The villagers say that Bou Jeloud was enticed to Jajouka by promises of prolific sex, but that Crazy Aisha was always there, dancing in the trees.

"Sounds a lot like the Bacchae and other such ladies who danced around an oak tree," says Gysin. "Hamouka, that's the same word as *amok*. It's thought that in Punic maybe Aisha is Asharat, or Astarte." Whoever she is, Bou Jeloud flails her into frightened parts; we can hear the saplings connecting with their bodies from across the field.

The musicians have been wailing nonstop for an hour and a half with a controlled abandon that raises questions about the limits and force of human breath. At any given moment two of the horn players are laying out, drawing on their sebsis. When they finish the pipe, they spit the coal onto the ground and roar back into the melee, giving two others the chance to lay out for a smoke. They phrase together in section, trade patterns between sections, and then rise together into that piercing, high-mountain unison, fingers sliding up and down the horns quicker than the eye can follow.

The chief drummer, unable to contain himself, dances into the circle, strutting and prancing and whirling around and around without missing a beat on his drum. Both he and Bou Jeloud make rushing approaches at our little enclave on the porch, the drummer smiling and inviting us to the dance, Bou Jeloud growling and grimacing, a wild-animal battering ram storming the doors of our Europeanness.

Suddenly, the pipers fall into a single held tone and the drums rumble and roar to the climax; they stop on a dime, seconds before the end of my reel of tape. Gabriel de Gramont, age seven, has been looking from the dancers to the musicians to the Uher and back again. "The tape recorder has a very good memory," he says, as the musicians drift down to the house and the temporarily spent crowd disperses. "It remembers everything it hears and tells it back to you whenever you want. But it's too bad it doesn't have any eyes."

There is something special about the chief drummer, who teaches the rhythms to dancers and drummers alike, some extra-linguistic communication line that is reading me loud and clear. After the evening meal, when most of the musicians have left to play Bou Jeloud out into the thickets and between the cottages in the village proper, the head drummer, the head piper, and two of the other musicians stay behind to play for Hamri and for us at the house, with cane flutes, taut skins, and a dancing boy. Some part of my mind is wondering, as they play, how the pipers can hold tones for so long, since they aren't doing the cheek-puffing, Roland Kirk–style circular breathing routine I've seen many players in Marrakech using, but my body is far from any such considerations. I'm weaving and bobbing to the music, the flutes floating free over a piledriver 6/8 rhythm straight down from remotest Near Eastern antiquity, and the drummers shouting "Aiwa"—"Everything's groovy."

The chief drummer suddenly drops his drum, jumps into our little circle, and dances right over to the space I am shaking, smiling broad as a river and flashing deep eye contact, vibrating saucer sightings back to Elijah's Air Force: the Mother Ship. After the music he says to me through Hamri, "Sometimes the musicians cannot play together, all playing and going high, high. . . . Tonight I see you with the music, I see you in the rhythm. I know you are a musician." I am found out, I am recognized, and I can see that putting away the tape recorder and getting out my horn is the only way I am going to get *this* show on the road.

Whatever vibrations Brian Jones may have felt his one night in Jajouka, we know that he spent the next few weeks in Tangier, listening and relistening to his tapes, finding his way to the music. He heard it running forward, he heard it running backward, he heard it overlaid upon itself, and he re-created his multicultural hearing with considerable expertise in a London studio. Since he visited Jajouka at an off-time, between festivals and full moons, he heard only a few pieces which a small group of musicians played especially for him: parts of the "Kaimonos"; parts of Bou Jeloud's music and none of Crazy Aisha's; plus some of the interplanetary after-dinner music performed with flutes and one or two drums. He added to what he heard with a backward drum track here, a backward melody there, an electric undercurrent that suggests the menace of the darkness outside the circle of firelight. The basis of the unusual stereo effects achieved was the positioning of the recording engineer, who stood with his Uher 4400 in the center of the musicians, crossing his two microphones in one hand while they marched around him in a revolving figure 8.

Jajouka, the first commercial recording of the Master Musicians (to be released by Rolling Stones Records), thus emerges as a kind of hybrid, a mélange of funky hill music and sophisticated studio techniques. A note from Brian Jones on his reasons for making the album is included in the package, which an anecdote from Brion Gysin may help clarify:

"We were sitting on the ground with Brian, under the very low eaves of this thatched farmhouse, and the musicians were working just four or five feet away, ahead of us in the courtyard where the animals usually are. It was getting to be time to eat, and suddenly two musicians came along with a snow-white goat. The goat disappeared off into the shadows with the two musicians, one of whom was holding a long knife which Brian suddenly caught the glitter of, and he started to get up, making a sort of funny noise, and he said, 'That's me!' And everybody picked up on it right at once and said, Yeah right, it looks just like you. It was perfectly true, he had this fringe of blond hair hanging down in front of his eyes, and we said, of course that's you. Then about twenty minutes later we were eating this goat's liver on shish kebab sticks."

Hamri, who contributed a cover painting to the *Jajouka* LP, hoped it would help the musicians out of their present dilemma, but so far this has not been the case. (Trevor Churchill, of Rolling Stones Records, contacted by telephone late in May, said, "We probably wouldn't be paying royalties directly to the musicians because the LP came to us through Brian Jones's estate.")

Meanwhile, many of Jajouka's finest young musicians have already left to work at industrial jobs in the cities. The musicians have always been an aristocratic group—Arabic rather than Berber-speaking, set apart from a majority of the villagers. They share the family surname Attar, which means "the perfume maker." The name belonged to a well-known Persian poet of the thirteenth century, and is a password in Sufism implying the divine essence. According to Gysin, "at certain moments of mystical experience induced by music, instead of hearing you smell this divine perfume."

Only the son of a Master Musician can become a Master Musician, and considerable esoteric knowledge is doubtless passed on along with musical secrets, but mystic masters are rarely breadwinners in the

American Century, and though Hamri, Gysin, and other friends of the community have ideas for survival procedures, ranging from sending the musicians on concert tours to turning Jajouka into a sort of overnight theater, the practical choices are limited.

With more and more pop musicians wandering about Morocco, the irresistible rhythms and sounds of the cannabis culture bid fair to become a major musical influence during the next few years, but no one is sure how this will affect Moroccan musicians.

The Moroccan government's belated recognition of the wealth and diversity of native musical folklore has resulted in their sponsorship of an annual Moroccan Folklore Festival, a mixed blessing. Held in Marrakesh, the festival attracts a number of tourists and music lovers and gives numerous groups a week's work, but each group is allowed only five minutes onstage. In this competitive atmosphere, with only the best-received groups coming back night after night, the crowd-pleasing techniques of the most popular performers are quickly adopted by groups from other regions. Consequently, the power and depth of the music and dancing, its intimate connection with the earth and the local culture is being plasticized into a sort of Ed Sullivan common denominator.

Whether because of a long-standing north-south rivalry or religious-political reservations, the musicians of Jajouka have yet to appear in the festival, now in its tenth year. Interested parties in Tangier are plotting a rival festival using northern groups who haven't been invited to Marrakech, but even half a dozen festivals will scarcely support the countless musicians who are being replaced by radio and television programming aimed at an urban, essentially rootless, and "Europeanized" population.

The Jamaa-el-F'na, the great public square of Marrakech, offers musicians and dancers a stage of sorts the year round, and troupes of drummers and dancing boys, rhaita virtuosos, and small bands made up of gimbris, violins, rebabs, and hand drums are playing strong, exciting music there almost any sunny day, competing for the crowd's attention with tricksters, clowns, whores, short-change artists, magicians, and beggars, some broadcasting their spiels through portable PAs powered by auto batteries. Lined with merchants in tiny stalls selling everything from clothes to household utensils to endless piles of sebsis and hookahs, the Jamaa-el-F'na is the tourist's Mecca, but admission is free and only the most determined dancing boy can squeeze enough pennies out of a besieged crowd to pay for a trip down from the hills and back.

Many groups that were once towers of power fold up under the barrage, splintering and then disbanding as the players marry Europeans, take menial jobs, drift back to the country, or drown in the shark-infested hustle. New groups come to take their place, the tourists disappear, replaced by ragged hippies left over from the summer influx, and the cycle repeats itself.

Many of the groups that are holding together are connected with one or another of Morocco's musical brotherhoods, mysterious organizations whose origins, rituals, and other secrets are as inaccessible to outsiders as the sources of power that lie just under the surface in Jajouka. All anyone seems to know about these brotherhoods is that each has its own peculiar rhythm, and that each of these rhythms produces trance.

Many members of brotherhoods think of themselves as doctors who happen to be using music rather than pills to effect their cures, and devotees say they awake the morning after a night of trance-dancing refreshed and rested in body and soul. A person in a trance may do almost anything: jump ten feet in the air, speak in animal languages, walk on red-hot coals, cut or otherwise mutilate himself. An extreme case is the devotees of the Hamadcha brotherhood, centering in the region around Meknes, who chop fissures into their own skulls with small axes, but these and other trance-induced wounds heal with a rapidity that baffles European physicians.

Why do certain rhythms produce trance states? There are no real answers, only clues. In a rural, tribal life, babies are liable to hear the rhythms, and sense their parents' reactions, even in a prenatal state. A Moroccan from Tafraouet told us that those who fall into trance most easily often were cured of a childhood fever by musicians from the local brotherhood. Still, there are a growing number of new converts, many of whom were never exposed to the music during childhood. These new devotees join a particular brotherhood by ear; according to Gysin, "One day you hear the music and you start to dance, and then you know that you belong to that brotherhood. You dance until you can't stop and then, when you've passed out and been brought around again, you realize that you've established a contract with them for life." Paul Bowles notes that all trance rhythms are polyrhythmic and/or polymetric, and Gysin has suggested that these rhythms play back and forth on the alpha-wave rhythms of the brain. No clear-cut conclusions are possible.

The most public, and currently popular, of the musical brotherhoods is the G'naoua. G'naoua musicians are usually black, as opposed to the lighter Arab and Berber people who make up the plurality of Morocco's population. Their following is largest because their rhythm is both irresistible and easily accessible to native and Westerner alike.

One G'naoua troupe toured the United States several years ago and this troupe, composed of drummers and of dancers who play qarqaba (dumbbell-shaped pieces of iron that maintain a clacking, metallic rhythm), tears up the Marrakech Festival every year, storming onstage for five minutes of sheer ecstatic insanity, sandwiched between elaborately costumed static professionals and abstractly folksy courtship dances. Other G'naoua groups sometimes employ the gimbri (a three-stringed lute, often with a tortoise-shell resonator) for more intimate gatherings, and these groups often work "G'naoua parties," given by visiting freaks or hippies-in-residence in towns like Essaouira, Marrakech, or even Tangier.

We attended our G'naoua party, in the tiled courtyard of an old Portuguese house in Essaouira. A young gimbri player, two drummers, and several hand-clapping devotees made up the G'naoua contingent, together with a thirteen-year-old dancing boy high on LSD. Pipes passed around the circle, the conversation welled up and subsided, and then the gimbri player hit a handful of notes, establishing an eternal-sounding pattern like the bass riffs that introduce a Pharoah Sanders record.

The drummers and handclappers locked into the pattern, and they were off for an hour or more with the dancing boy gliding around the room, his hand gestures turning into animals and birds on the candlelit walls. The music had no melody, no harmony, neither theme nor variation, no beginning and no ending. It traveled down a straight, narrow, infinitely continuous road, and we traveled with it, spacing into the drone and out of time. The "monotony" established a hypnotic effect, as it does in much Moroccan music, so that each slight shift in emphasis, and each change in the drum and gimbri patterns, caused parallel shifts in planes of consciousness, amplified by the absence of distracting surface decoration. The devotees fell to their knees, rolling their heads about wildly at the feet of the drummers, the dancing boy whirled around the circle, his feet barely touching the floor, and while nobody went into trance (a definite experiential state that takes hours to complete and must be played on through to unconsciousness, at the risk of psychic damage to the ecstatic should the music end prematurely), a good time was had by all.

Tangier, of course, is an old hand at trance-dancing parties and stoned-out cultural interchanges, moody old whore of a Scorpio city with as many psychic ups and downs as hills. The city's expatriate colony includes several Americans whose vast, though largely unpublished, knowledge of Moroccan music comes from years of firsthand experience. There is Randy Weston, genial giant jazz pianist with numerous African musical acquaintances, whose African Rhythms Club is a sort of Tangier equivalent to the Village Vanguard. There is Paul Bowles, author of *The Sheltering Sky, A Hundred Camels in the Courtyard*, and numerous other books, and a trained composer/musician as well. Bowles recorded the Library of Congress collection of Moroccan music, and his tape library, which lines the walls of his apartment near the U.S. Consulate three reels deep, contains extensive samplings of music from every corner of North Africa. He was generous with musical information, recorded examples, and explanations shot through with his remarkable, intuitive intelligence, but Brion Gysin, who first came to North Africa with Bowles in 1937, was our one-man crash course, filling our heads with sounds from his own tape library and telescoping his twenty years of field recording and speculation into a few intensive weeks of talking and listening.

The tragedy of the Tangier scene is that its comprehensive collective knowledge sits, for the most part, on shelves or in drawers, wrapped in layers of plastic to ward off dampness and decay. Gysin and Bowles played us samplings of the hill music of the Jebel, with its gimbris, lutes, flutes, and violins; of the rebab players of the south, who saw at their banjolike instruments with a short bow; of the wailing, nasal vocal music, accompanied by gimbri or lute and common to all Islam; of monastic choirs from the high Atlas, overpowering drumming cadres from the Sahara, and the drum-dominated trance music of each of the Moroccan brotherhoods. These are the twisting, winding rhythms of the Aissaoua, who subjectively become snakes when far into the trance state; the Hadaoua, who spice their kinetic drumming with a dash of theater and smoke enormous amounts of kif; the D'kaoua, who dance and breathe together in the Sufi way, stomping and repeatedly shouting *Allah! Allah!* until they fall unconscious; and the previously mentioned G'naoua and Hamadcha.

Of all the brotherhoods, only Jilala, who are numerous in and around Tangier, have been commercially recorded. The album *Jilala*, issued a few years ago in a limited pressing under the Trance Records logo, is poorly balanced, and the group included a G'naoua infiltrator whose qarqaba is foreign to Jilala music and works at cross purposes to the predominating rhythmic thrust. The album cover confounds the confusion; it depicts a group of Hamadcha screaming down a hillside.

The tapes painstakingly recorded over the years by collectors like Bowles, Gysin, Christopher Wanklyn, and others are more valuable than ever today, with the continuing dearth of commercially available recordings, the breaking up of traditional Moroccan cultural patterns, and the concurrent splintering and adulterating of music groups and styles. The earliest of these tapes are already beginning to decompose, but the painters, writers, musicians, and other artists who recorded them are neither equipped for nor inclined toward the kind of painstaking study, systematization, and preservation that is necessary if the Moroccan musical legacy is to survive intact.

Meanwhile, far off in the hills that ring Tangier from the coastline to the bay, the Master Musicians of Jajouka play their rhaitas, flutes, and drums, smoke their kif, guard their chain of secret knowledge unbroken since pagan times, and wonder about their luck and their future. Change is in the air, as more and more outsiders step through their space-time doorway and their legend grows, but their friends wonder, while they think and talk and work toward the community's survival, whether concert tours or tourist invasions will undermine the music's roots in the hill country, whether culture shock will paralyze the music's strength and growth as surely as the starvation that seems to be the only other alternative.

I am wondering now, on the road back down the mountain, what part, if any, I am playing in this karmic cycle. Sunlight is pouring down, like the energy that poured into me when the musicians played and I played and we fell through each other, weightless, into the sky. Our VW passes groups of villagers, returning homeward from the feast and stopping here and there along the road to look off into the hills.

The music lingers in their bodies and in each synapse of their minds, spreading its ripples across the meanest particles of matter, and each ripple vibrates the shape of the Mother Ship that landed on the mountain ages ago, disgorging Bou Jeloud and the first of the Master Musicians, shutting down its motors and waiting, overgrown with foliage and trees and layers of dung and earth, losing its shape in the gentle rising oval of the hilltop. When the last of the Master Musicians dies and the last Musician's son moves on to find work in new industries or to hustle new jungle streets, that Mother Ship is going to come to life with a low, barely perceptible hum, increasing in volume and in force until she roars off into the void with Crazy Aisha dancing like mad around the deck and Bou Jeloud at the controls.

Into the Mystic

ROLLING STONE | MARCH 23, 1989

Muhammad says, "I come before dawn to chain you and drag you off." It's amazing, and funny, that you have to be pulled away from being tortured, pulled out into this spring garden, but that's the way it is.

JALAL AL-DIN RUMI, *The Masnavi*, TRANSLATED BY COLEMAN BARKS

The open window of my Tangier hotel room faces this ancient city's newest mosque, named for the late king Mohammed V and built, in the classical style, since my last Moroccan sojourn fifteen years ago. The facade is a delicate lattice of entwining vines, curves, and planes, abstractly but meaningfully patterned in the age-old Arab manner. The dun-and-white-tiled spire is surmounted by dual antennae. The taller of these supports three dish-shaped loudspeakers, ranging in size from a large, moonlike bottom speaker to a tiny disk at the top. The second antenna, possibly some kind of transducer, is a stark needle, pointing heavenward and encircled by a curling spiral of metal, like a stretched spring or a Tesla coil.

I sit in my room, a little after three A.M., waiting for the early-morning call to prayer and reading about Tangier's misty origins in Elisa Chimenti's *Tales and Legends of Morocco*. "The origin of Tangier harks back to remote antiquity," she writes. "Its existence is acknowledged in the myths of Hercules and Atlas. . . . A Moroccan tale assures us that it was founded by Noah at the beginning of the earth's existence." If the ancient Greek geographer Strabo is to be believed, the white-walled city, perched on its rolling hills across the straits from the Rock of Gibraltar, had been held by the Hindus, Persians, or Phoenicians for thousands of years before Strabo's era, the first century B.C.

More recently, before Moroccan independence arrived in the 1950s, Tangier was a free port, a haven for smugglers and international scams of every description, the inspiration for the archetypal world city of Interzone in William Burroughs's novel *Naked Lunch*. At night the streets of the old casbah narrow into dark, sinister alleys, and even the broad avenues of the new town, perched high above the old port, are dappled by concealing shadows. From my hotel window, I hear the dogs—Tangier is known for having more, and louder, dogs than any other city—barking across the distances. The late Brion Gysin—painter, poet, visionary, patron of the Master Musicians who live in the mountain village of Jajouka, and influence on artists ranging from Burroughs to Paul Bowles, the Rolling Stones to David Bowie, Iggy Pop to Patti Smith—taught me to listen to the dogs when I lived here in the early seventies. He claimed he had cracked the dogs' code and used to provide a running translation: "Everything okay there? Enough food? People good?" And from miles away in the suburbs the responses would come back: "Good food here, but people beat us." "Out here we're hungry."

Now the enormous speakers of the Mosque Mohammed V crackle, and the honey-voiced muezzin's cantillation of verses from the Koran ricochets off the white walls of the city, quieting the dogs. The chanting forms a sonic grid that focuses, or perhaps completes, the City as Ideal Form: The community of the faithful is being irradiated by harmonics of degree and distance. Tangier's cunningly balanced architecture of surfaces, arches, and crenelated towers serves as a kind of transformer for the spiritual electricity of the muezzin's call. In Morocco there are different kinds of electricity. This kind is called *baraka,* a kind of psychic current that certain holy places, sounds, and people absorb and hold like storage batteries. The receptive can plug into these power sources—without getting fried, one hopes.

After spending fifteen years watching New York City deteriorate into Calcutta, I have gotten a different kind of jolt from finding Tangier not merely preserved but actually winning the tug of war with entropy I had assumed the entire planet was losing. The streets are cleaner, the buildings in better repair. The people smile more and seem to have more money. From the curbside café near the fountain of the old Place de France, you can watch European and American tourists mingle with sailors on shore leave from Qaddafi's navy, with no apparent friction. The café habitués, and even the hustlers down in the twisting alleys of the casbah, seem to agree that the long, long reign of King Hassan II has been a blessing. He has steered a difficult middle course between Muslim extremism and American xenophobia and saber rattling. The advantages of the modern world—speaker dishes on the mosques, for example—are being gradually, harmoniously integrated into the patterned circuitry of the traditional ways.

Accompanied by a film crew jointly organized by French and Spanish television, I returned to Morocco to provide English-language narration for a documentary on the great American jazz pianist and composer Randy Weston. Fifteen years ago I spent many nights hanging out in Weston's African Rhythms Club, a combination disco and jazz boîte a couple of blocks away from my own Tangier pension. In a series of groundbreaking collaborations with members of Tangier's dervish brotherhoods and with the Master Musicians of Jajouka, Weston was then transforming the jabbing, percussive blues abstractions he learned running with Thelonious Monk in the fifties. Weston had come back to rekindle those associations and to preserve on film and videotape the remarkable musical conflagrations ignited fifteen years earlier.

My first night back in Tangier, I found myself near the city's original Portuguese ramparts, down in the ancient open space known as the Plaza de Kasbah. A motley crew of natives and expatriates was in attendance. Among them was American author and composer Paul Bowles, a resident of Tangier since the forties. Down in the dark, dingy basement rooms of the old Portuguese fort, members of two dervish brotherhoods were warming up for an outdoor concert. The Jilala, who trace their lineage back to the Qaddiriya order, one of the oldest secret fraternities in Islam, were blowing into long flutes and heating the skins of their shallow, tambourine-like *bendir* drums over crackling fires that threw dancing shadows along the grimy walls. A group of black musicians— members of the G'naoua brotherhood and the descendants of slaves who were brought from the same West African regions that provided American plantations with forced labor—tuned three-stringed, guitarlike gimbris to their drums and iron castanets.

Weston's handpicked jazz band—which included saxophonist Billy Harper, one-time Count Basie trombonist Benny Powell, and former Blue Note house drummer Al Harewood—was warming up, too. Weston paced through the dank, decaying rooms, his face lighted by a smile that seemed almost as broad as his six-foot-seven-inch frame is tall, murmuring over and over, as if he couldn't quite believe it himself, "Tangier— down with the cats."

I hadn't quite recovered from the overseas flight, and as the trance rhythms beat against one another and against the walls and low ceilings, I began to feel disoriented. The chief of one of the dervish brotherhoods noticed my unease, caught my eye, and filled his pipe for me with the traditional mixture of kif and tobacco. The stuff doesn't lay you out on the floor like American designer pot, but after one pipe I found my sea legs. Now I could go out, face the cameras, and announce the concert.

It was a spectacular evening, there under the floodlights and the stars, surrounded on all sides by the venerable, crumbling ramparts with the Mediterranean just beyond. When the Jilala, resplendent in their orange robes and turbans, stormed onstage and brought their swirling rhythms in sync with the Weston band's Afro-blues, the whole plaza seemed ready to levitate. The Jilala end-blown flutes, intricately constructed from copper, tin, and brass, cut through the other sounds with their keening undertow. The G'naoua entered, their castanets adding a rhythmic layer that sounded like an iron foundry, their gimbri lutes playing riffs that might have generated the blues. The last thing I remember, before the jet lag caught up with me, was Benny Powell shedding his fifteen years as Basie's lead trombonist and flashing back to his New Orleans roots, dancing, waving his slide from side to side, and stitching a riff from "When the Saints Go Marching In" into the seamless pancultural boogie.

Back in my hotel room, I found I couldn't sleep after all, and so I sat awake, waiting to plug into the *baraka* through the three A.M. prayer call. In the morning we were all going up into the mountains, to Jajouka, and I knew I was going to need all the strength I could muster.

In Moroccan folklore, and especially in the mountain fastnesses around Jajouka, the old gods and goddesses—Pan or Dionysus and Astarte or Ishtar—live on, not only in folk tales but in potent rituals and in what we Westerners so casually call real life. Jajouka is only a couple of hours from Tangier by automobile and burro, but effectively it is several thousand years away. When Brion Gysin was first taken there in the 1950s by the Moroccan painter Hamri, Gysin's knowledge of antiquity enabled him to identify the musical rituals celebrated there as a survival, perhaps *the* survival, of the Rites of Pan, which were already very old when they were first enshrined by the Romans in their calendar as the Lupercalia.

The ancient Pan music, and the magic that crackles around it, have been responsible for drawing the tiny village's small but distinguished list of Western visitors. Gysin brought William Burroughs, Timothy Leary, and Brian Jones of the Rolling Stones, whose recordings of Jajouka music were issued by his band several years after his death. Ornette Coleman recorded with the Master Musicians in the early seventies, and the unreleased sessions have been a decisive influence on the development of harmolodic electric jazz. Recordings of Jajouka music, issued on a few obscure albums and passed around on private tapes, were the hidden source of much that was weird and wonderful in Patti Smith's music, especially *Radio Ethiopia*. And Robert Plant has made use of his own Moroccan experiences both in Led Zeppelin's music and his later solo work.

During the early seventies, I made three trips to Jajouka, and on two of my visits I was drawn into their Rites of Pan, which are prudently celebrated on Islamic holy days. Jaouka crowns the summit of one of the jebels, or little hills, which are really mountains, little only in comparison with the Rif Massif, which towers beyond. At festival time the village vibrated all night to the thunder of fifteen drums and fifteen piercing double-reed horns, or rhaitas, which made a sound like a hundred electric-guitar bands with a hundred rhythm sections, all resonating one vast open chord. Bonfires blazed from dusk to dawn, and hundreds, perhaps thousands of volatile tribesmen from the surrounding mountains pitched their tents among Jajouka's huts and compounds. When the music and energy were at their height, the tribesmen and their women milled in ecstatic trances, their eyes rolled back in their heads, screaming like a great rending of the heavens, firing their flintlocks into the air in volleys that only occasionally matched the thunder of the drums.

Pan himself was there. Several times I witnessed the instant when the current began to surge in earnest and coursed through the quivering frame of a local shepherd, who was naked except for the skins of a freshly sacrificed goat and a broad-brimmed straw bonnet that hid his face in shadows, but not his eyes. When the power came down, Abdeslam the shepherd suddenly wasn't there, and Someone Else was looking out of eyes that abruptly began to glow like ruby lasers. He would run like the wind through the frantically milling throngs, and one night he came and jerked me out of the crowd, and I ran with him.

He leaped through a bonfire, and then I was in the bonfire, surrounded by flames but unharmed. Then I was spinning like a top, spinning into darkness. I woke up to total silence and impenetrable blackness, lying on the ground far down the mountain. It took me twenty minutes to climb back up to the village, but I was uninjured after my apparent fall. In fact, I never felt better in my life. When I finally stumbled into the center of the village, I noticed there was still a light on in the musicians' house. The stern-faced chief, Jnuin—whose given name comes from the same Arabic root as the word *jinn*, or "elemental spirits"—was waiting for me, along with other elders and a sherif, or lineal descendant of Muhammad. "We have seen you through the music," they told me. "Now you are one of us."

And now, after fifteen years, I was going back. The film crew was coming later in the day with Weston and his musicians, and they were all planning to leave early the next morning. They wanted me to return to Tangier with them, but I wanted a couple of days in Jajouka on my own. I figured I had some unfinished business there.

I am bouncing along on my faithful burro up a steep rock track, sunlit greens and browns and blues spattering the hills that stretch away into immense, hazy distances. An occasional gust of lightly stinging rain blows past on mountain winds. At first the burro's deliberate pace makes me impatient. But then my sense of the passing of time slows down; I begin to balance the burro's bumps and jolts confidently, instinctively, from my solar plexus.

We meander up the trail, over corrugations of earth and rock, and then the lane narrows to a dirt track between walls of man-high cactuses. The houses of the village, painted the purest white or the most diaphanous blue under their roofs of thatching and tin, are ranked behind and among the cactuses in an arrangement that seems at first to be a jumble but soon manifests an Apollonian balance.

The burro, absolutely impervious to my gees and haws, ambles past the village well, a centuries-old stone cistern, like a long trough with a wider, deeper shaft at the end nearest the mountain's summit. We seem to be moving in slow motion toward a head-on collision with an imposing, gnarled tree whose branches fan out over a sheer precipice. The burro comes to a stop, and I experience a shock of recognition. This is Jajouka's sacred tree, whose branches become flails in the hands of the dancer possessed by the spirit of Pan, who here is called Bou Jeloud, the Father of Skins. I have time to grab a handful of fronds and inhale their perfume as we finally make the crest and trot into a wild but subtly ordered garden of flowers and shrubs facing the long, rectangular house of the Master Musicians.

The house was built in the sixties, with money from Brion Gysin. In those days, the musicians, who had been accustomed to royal patronage since the days of the medieval Alaouite sultans, were reeling from the fall of France's last puppet sultan and the uncertain climate of independence. But the Master Musicians, a kind of extended clan presided over by the family of Attar, have weathered more than one difficult period during the centuries of their history.

They trace their descent back to Farid al-Din Attar, the thirteenth-century Persian Sufi sage and poet whose *Parliament of the Birds* is counted among the enduring masterpieces of world literature. The Jajouka branch of the Attar family seems to have settled in what is now Syria. When they sensed they were about to be charged with diverse heresies by the fundamentalist mullahs of their day, they packed their musical instruments and other belongings and headed to Andalusia, or Muslim Spain, which rivaled Baghdad as a center of Arab culture and learning. Andalusian savants knew far more about such things as astronomy, physics, mathematics, and the Pythagorean number theory at the root of the Attar family's music and magic than any of their contemporaries in pre-Renaissance Europe. Even so, by 1492, when Ferdinand and Isabella conquered the last of Spain's Islamic provinces and still found time to see Columbus off on his fateful voyage, the Attar family had found its way to Jajouka (the name translates from the Arabic as "something good will come to you").

Jajouka has been a hot spot in the world's spiritual geography since earliest antiquity; the hills round about are dotted with Phoenician temple ruins. In a sense, the Master Musicians were reconnecting with some of their deepest roots. Bou Jeloud, local tales say, came with them. But Aisha Hamouka, or Astarte, had always haunted these mountains. The rites practiced in Jajouka have to do with fine-tuning or equalizing the male-female polarities of the Old Earth's spiritual charge. The whole mountaintop is said to be one great storage cell for *baraka*.

Jnuin, the old chief, is dead, and it is his son, twenty-seven-year-old Bachir Attar, who greets me as I slide off the burro. Half the musicians, including the wise old master drummer Berdous, are away, playing a government-sponsored folklore festival in Marrakech, but seven are here, and they have been waiting for me. "My father always told me that before when you came, there was magic," says Bachir, who spent much of his youth in Paris. "So here you are at home. Anything you want in Jajouka is yours."

The film crew arrives in fits and starts, some of the crewmen and jazz musicians comically hanging on to their burros for dear life. Just as the cameras and recording equipment are in position for a night of filming, it begins to rain. There are glum looks among the crew, but as soon as the musicians start playing their flutes and drums, the rain stops. I've seen this before. During one Pan festival, on a morning when low, black cloud cover blanketed the mountains as far as the eye could see, the Master Musicians retreated into the tomb of Saint Sidi Hamid Sherk, who brought Islam and the cultivation of wheat to these mountains around A.D. 800. They played some music I hadn't heard before.

The skies abruptly cleared, but only over the village. The rest of the day, while rain clouds covered the other mountains, Jajouka's mountaintop was bathed in a perfectly stable spotlight of sunshine.

After the musicians play dutifully through several retakes, the film shooting wraps, and everyone parties into the dawn. Just before first light, the rhaitas and drums are wailing Bou Jeloud's music, and though Pan himself is nowhere to be seen, things are getting pretty intense. Eric Assiente, an Ashanti drummer from Ghana who is the percussionist in Randy Weston's band, drums for a while, then prances out into the circle around the bonfire to dance. First he stamps repeatedly, making his connections with the earth and its power. Then he looks skyward and begins miming, pulling down something like a long, long chain out of the heavens. I can almost see it—a chain of light.

It's impossible for me to sleep. I sit on a cliff's edge and watch the sun come up, then put in a full day—climbing the mountains up to a cave that was a neolithic cult center, where Bachir and I plumb the spooky acoustics with a pair of cane flutes, returning to the village to jam with Mohammed el-Bakkari (who plays intricately soulful music on the gimbri), to feast in Jnuin's old house, and to dance around a bonfire to wailing pipes and drums and, during an intermission, to tapes of Patti Smith's *Dream of Life*. I wouldn't have thought of playing rock & roll tapes in Jajouka fifteen years ago. Now people have boom boxes, and certain pop music harmonizes with the village's age-old ambience. There's still no electricity, no running water, no real road in or out, but Jajouka is no longer floating in some other century. It is ancient *and* modern.

Walking around the village with Bachir the next morning, after another sleepless night, I broach a delicate question. "Before," I say, "the jinn were everywhere. Gysin said you could see them hovering about your father Jnuin's head, like an eddying disturbance in the air. I saw them myself. Are they still around?"

Talking about elemental spirits, the jinn, is not something mountain people like to do, but I am, after all, an honored guest. "I will tell you what my father told me," Bachir says gravely. "Back in the time when there were Spanish in this part of the country, there was a man named Bou Haza living in a nearby village. This man, he was a sherif—he was the law. But he married this devil woman, and she would bring the jinn from all the countries of their world when she and Bou Haza wanted to listen to music. And many times Bou Haza came to hear Jnuin, my father, play. They were good friends.

"One night," Bachir continues, "it is very cloudy, too much rain, and about three o'clock in the morning Bou Haza come to Jajouka and bring with him one horse. And he says to my father, 'Come with me. All the jinn are waiting for you to come and play the music, waiting for *only you*. There is a big party in the world of the jinn, and the king of all the jinn is there.'

"And my father says to him, 'Ohhh, my friend Bou Haza. I have the family, the children. If I go there with you, maybe I see other things, not like here, and maybe if I stay with the jinn, I get crazy.' Then Bou Haza showed him the horse, and its saddlebags, and they were full of gold. And he said to my father, 'This is gold money for you if you come. If you don't want gold, what can I give you to come with me?' And my father says, 'Oh, my friend, I don't need nothing.'

"So Bou Haza, he leave, but first he tells my father, 'When you play your music in Jajouka, when your family play, when your sons play, the jinn come to listen to all the parties, but nobody can know them.' And he shake his head then and lead the horse away, and my father see the horse clearly for the first time, and he whistle. He says to himself, 'There is so much rain, nothing but rain, rain, rain. But this horse is perfectly dry.'

"So, Bob, I know you see many things in those days. Now, today, what do you want from Jajouka?"

The question catches me off guard. "I would like," I hear myself saying, "to visit the shrine, the tomb of Saint Sidi Hamid Sherk." Everyone in Jajouka knows that the shrine is the village's power center, the pulsing core of the *baraka*. Fifteen years ago the musicians played secret music inside the shrine to cure the mentally ill. Today, according to Bachir, the music no longer sounds in there, but the pilgrims still come, and the power is undiminished. Fifteen years ago no infidel was allowed inside the whitewashed walls of the sacred compound. Bachir nods his assent; we stop for candles, and I allocate some money as an offering for the old man who lives in the compound as its guardian.

"Say, '*Bismillah*,'" says Bachir as we walk through the outer courtyard and pause under the arch that leads to the inner sanctum. I hear myself say, "*Bismillah, er-Raman, er-Rahim*" ("In the name of God, the Merciful, the Compassionate") in a deep, resonant voice that sounds nothing like my own. Inside the courtyard, I see a stooped, desiccated, apparently lightning-blasted tree. Hanging from it are links of iron chain that look as old as the mountains themselves. "When the crazy people come here to be cured," whispers Bachir, "some of them would be violent, so they chained them to the tree. Then the musicians would play for them until they returned to their senses. If you want to feel the *baraka*, you wrap yourself in those chains."

At this, I have to roll my eyes heavenward. The entry into the village on a donkey, carrying fronds from the sacred tree . . . the chains . . . the suspiciously cruciform tree in the shrine . . . I can't resist zinging a one-liner at the Man Upstairs: "Isn't this just getting a little bit too *symbolic*?" But then, as I approach the chains, I pick up on the current. The chains seem to be blurring before my eyes, sounding an intense vibratory hum. I pick them up and wrap them around me. For an instant. I think that maybe I am dreaming; then I don't think, or hear, or see, anything at all. And then I am returning to consciousness from the Place of No Words, Bachir leading me out of the shrine. "I think," I manage to croak, "that I had better lie down."

Then I am in a room built onto the musicians' house, on a cot, staring at the red-tiled ceiling. And suddenly the tiles aren't red anymore; instead, the ceiling is purest white and very, very high. Hanging from it, lazily turning in some otherworldly breeze, are ceiling fans. Instead of blades, the fans are the shapes of Arabic letters, representing one of the names of God. Which one, I don't know. A week later I find the one I saw in a book. The translation of this name reads, "Light upon light. Allah guides to his light whom he pleases" (Koran 24:35).

Next I see garlanded chains of the brightest of white lights, with threads of incandescent violet interwoven among them. And this is just the beginning. Back in Tangier, I am seeing lights everywhere. One night I walk into my room and turn out the lamp, and before I can hit the bed, I am frozen standing in my tracks. A radiance begins to suffuse the room, and I notice that it is not my room at all but some ancient, white-walled grotto, lighted from above. Slowly, I rotate my eyes heavenward, and I see that the room has no roof; above me is a field of stars, glittering like diamonds. Then the floor starts to throb, the stars start to move, and I feel like I'm in an elevator, going up, up through constellations and galaxies into realms of light that are luminously white, emerald green, then blacker than black. Something explodes in my head, and I find myself back in the *real* room, shaking, traumatized, feeling a little like the survivor of some astral auto wreck, or as though I have been mugged by Allah.

Under these circumstances, delivering my narration for the movie becomes a difficult task. And on my last afternoon in Tangier, hours before I am due to get on a plane to fly back to America, Luc, the film's patient director, is coaching me through my last scene. I'm sitting on some old stone steps in the garden of the Musée de Kasbah, and the sun is glinting off my glasses. Luc wants me to take them off, but what he says is, "Bob, would you please take off your light?"

I give him a curious look, then shake my head. "No," I tell him. "I'll take off my glasses, but I don't think I'm ever going to take off my light."

ON THE EDGE: "LISTEN, AS IF A NEW WORLD HAD SUDDENLY OPENED UP."

William Burroughs: The *Rolling Stone* Interview (excerpt)

ROLLING STONE | MAY 11, 1972

William Burroughs lives in a sparsely furnished flat near Piccadilly, in London. The neighborhood is comfortable, but Burroughs works and lives with a minimum of encumbrances: typewriter, table, plain chairs, bed, books, a cassette machine. Brion Gysin, Burroughs's friend and longtime collaborator, lives upstairs in surroundings that include Moroccan rugs, a few of Brion's paintings of Marrakech and the desert, a stereo, two Uhers, and an extensive library of sounds which Brian recorded in Morocco. It's a quiet place for a man who has made some of the biggest waves in contemporary literature: from the early autobiographical *Junkie* through the influential *Naked Lunch* and early experimentation with psychedelics, lightshows, and the surreal cut-up writing technique.

The interview took place in Brion's flat, which he recently occupied after an extended residence in Tangier. Tapes of trance music, fifties rock & roll, Sun Ra, and Coltrane furnished by Brion, Charlie Gillett, and myself played in the background and various young people, many of whom Burroughs met while teaching at the University of the New World in Switzerland, were in and out. . . .

The first question I asked Burroughs concerned infrasound, air vibrations that oscillate at less than ten hertz, or ten vibrations a second, below the range of human hearing. Professor Vladimir Gavreau of Marseilles has developed and patented a "Death Ray" using these inaudible sounds, but Burroughs has suggested other uses for them. He gave me, as explanation, a clipping from the *National Observer*; he had underlined the following passages:

". . . the team built a giant whistle, hooked to a compressed air hose. Then they turned on the air.

"'That first test nearly cost us our lives,' Professor Gavreau says. 'Luckily, we were able to turn it off fast. All of us were sick for hours. Everything in us was vibrating—stomach, heart, lungs. All the people in the other laboratories were sick too.'"

You've mentioned the possibility of using this infrasound in music. Could you expand on that?
The point is that here it has been developed as a weapon. Now there are possibilities, say at the borderline of infrasound, experimenting with very slow sounds, that you could produce rhythmic vibrations that would not necessarily be fatal or unpleasant; they might be quite the contrary. In other words, it would be another step toward producing—as all music, all writing, all art is really attempting to do—is to produce very definite psycho-physiological effects in the audience, reader, viewer, as the case may be. Of course they've never been completely successful in that. If they had they would have taken over years ago. But if they were successful, presumably you could kill a whole Shea Stadium full of people in their seats.

There's been a great deal of work done recently in autonomic shaping and brain waves—people now being able to reproduce brain waves and to learn to control heartbeats, etc. That is, people can now learn in ten hours what it takes a yogi twenty years to learn, if they want to. They have a battery now that they can plug people into which records brain waves, blood pressure, heartbeat, resistance, tension, etc. As far as I know, no experiments have been done along these lines while listening to certain music to see what the actual physiological and psychological correlates of that music are and what happens when someone listens to it.

So I wanted to suggest the possibility of very precise musical experiments.

How would that relate to Moroccan music? How precise do you think Moroccan trance music is at producing definite states?
Certainly Brion knows a good deal more about that than I do, but I would suggest the same experiments be carried out. If you knew what a state of trance was, what the brain waves, blood pressure, heartbeat, and so forth was, then you'd have some idea as to how to go about producing it, and also you'd know when you are producing it and when you're getting close.

What about your experiments with projections?
I've said quite a lot about that in *The Job*. Antony Balch and I did an experiment with his face projected onto mine and mine onto his. Now if your face is projected onto someone else's in color, it looks like the other person. You can't tell the difference; it's a real mask of light. Brion was the first to do this at the rue Dragon in Paris, and no one would believe how it was done. They thought it was all a film.

Jan Herman was here with his little video camera outfit and we did quite a precise experiment, which was: Antony brought up the Bill and Tony film, I sat there, and he projected it onto my face, which was rephotographed on the video camera, but that faded in and out so that it would be that face, then fade back to the now face, so that you got a real-time section. We wanted to project it onto the television screen from the camera, but we couldn't because the cycles were different; Antony and Jan Herman were fooling around and they managed to fuck up the television. But even seeing it on a little view screen, it was something quite extraordinary.

Another experiment that Antony and I did was to take the two faces and alternate them twenty-four frames per second, but it's such a hassle to cut those and resplice them, even to put one minute of alternations of twenty-four frames per second on a screen, but it is quite extraordinary. An experiment I always wanted to make was to record and photograph very friendly and very unfriendly faces and words and then alternate them twenty-four frames per second. That should have quite an upsetting effect, I think; you don't know until you actually do it.

What about your story in *The Job* about the Buful Peoples projecting baby faces on their audiences and making them run out and shit in the streets? Is that your idea of what the effects of such an experiment might be?
They could be. It's a question of getting a sufficient degree of precision. If I really knew how to write, I could write something that someone would read and it would kill them. The same way with music, or any effect you want could be produced if you were precise enough in your knowledge or technique.

How would that work with writing?
Exactly the same way. What is a writer trying to do? He's trying to reproduce in the reader's mind a certain experience, and if he were completely successful in that, the reproduction of the experience would be complete. Perhaps fortunately, they're not that successful.

Can words actually be that successful?
I think so. I think words possibly above all.

Back to music: Do you feel that a pop group's dependence on costly equipment and establishment media makes it difficult for these groups to disseminate an anti-establishment, anti-control message?
I think the dividing line between establishment and non-establishment is breaking down. People tend to say that if an underground paper succeeds and makes money, that it is now part of the establishment, or if pop singers make a lot of money and their records make a great deal of money for big companies that they are now part of the establishment, but the underground or any movement is not going to succeed by not succeeding. If you publish an underground paper that nobody reads or produce music that nobody listens to, there's no point.

And if people do read your paper or listen to your music, then you are subject to make money.

Do you think the force and amplitude of rock can make it a force for liberation, regardless of the lyric content?
I would say so, very definitely. And potentially a tremendous force, in view of the experiments that I have suggested.

It's hard to say how much it has to do with the words and the lyrics.
Very difficult to say. I usually can't hear the words.

Well, some groups, like the Rolling Stones, purposely mix the words down in the track.
[The semanticist Alfred] Korzybski pointed out that one of the basic errors of Western thought is the either/or proposition, which is implicit in our language. "Are they broadcasting an anti-establishment message or are they . . ." Well, they might be doing both at the same time quite well. Or all sorts of variations. Really it's not an either/or proposition.

And it might affect each listener differently.
Right. But the mere fact of the number of people reached and the fact that these people are young people and therefore the most subject to revolutionary ideas makes them a terrific force.

Do you think a group that's operating its own record company has a freer hand than a group that must operate through a conglomerate?
I do not know enough about the music business to answer that question, but a similar question: Do you think that writers would have more effect if they published their own work? Definitely no. Because the publisher is set up to distribute just as the record company is. If you're going to try to do all that yourself—for one thing it's going to take up all your time, and you're not going to do it as well. If you regard a record company simply as a means of distributing or selling your records, as I regard a publishing company . . . now that doesn't mean that record companies and publishing companies may not have all sorts of establishment preconceptions about what they distribute, and how hard they push it, but the question of taking over their function, for, say, pop

stars to do all that themselves, they wouldn't have time. Any more than writers should take over publishing, although they've talked about it, but nothing has ever come of it.

The media are really accessible to everyone. People talk about establishment media, but the establishment itself would like to suppress the media altogether. There was a program on television the other night where they came right out and said that showing wars and riots on television can produce wars and riots. There's never been a comparable situation, where whatever is happening anywhere people can switch on their televisions and see it. I recall in Chicago, the riot pictures were shown in the convention hall live as they were happening, and then all sorts of similar incidents broke out in the convention hall. Cops blackjacked delegates. . . .

You'd say, then, that pop music is not a part of what you've called "the control machine"?
No; it might overlap with it, but it's not a part of it.

Bob Dylan has mentioned his interest in and indebtedness to your work, and several of your phrases have popped up in Rolling Stones songs—like in "Memo from Turner" from *Performance*. Have they been into your work from reading, or from talking with you?
In both cases, definitely from reading. I have only met Bob Dylan on one occasion, and Mick Jagger about four or five times, occasions when there were other people around. There was no discussion of the books. So it must be from reading.

Do you have anything to say about the music of Soft Machine and the Insect Trust, groups which took their names from your work?
Not really. I've listened to the music. It's interesting. It's certainly very fancy music, very sophisticated music.

Do you think their music relates to your work in any way?
It's my feeling, none whatever, and I can say that with a clear conscience because they have never underlined the connection. I mean many people don't know that *The Soft Machine* is actually one of my titles, and they haven't mentioned it in their interviews.

What about the many references to popular songs in your books, especially some of the sequences in *The Soft Machine* which are made up of song titles and lines?

In writing, I see it as a whole set. It's got a script, it's got pictures, and it has a sound track. And very often the sound track is musical. I've used quite a bit of these techniques actually—that is, a sentence to be sung to a certain tune.

Do remembered tunes call up stronger and more specific associations than images that aren't related to tunes?

Very definitely, yes. That's what tunes are all about. I think it's pretty well established pragmatically that music is more precise in evoking a scene, particularly a past scene, than, shall we say, a neutral sound track of words. But I notice that they are tending, at least in the Jajouka record [*Brian Jones Presents the Pipes of Pan at Jajouka*, Rolling Stones Records], toward deliberately using some of the background noise: shouts, dogs barking in Jajouka, the chauffeur snoring in another reference. That's something I think that has to be done with a very precise hand. In practice, the music is played on a location so that there will be background noise as well.

Would you like eventually to put out books with accompanying records? Having the musical and sound references along with the writing?

I had not thought of that. I think that is a very brilliant idea, because people have put out books with a record. I even did that, but the record simply consisted of a spoken tape of the book, which in this case was a short book. But to me, spoken tapes, you can just take so much. It's a different operation than reading. The idea of spoken books is completely unworkable. But I hadn't thought of a sound track, which could actually be quite carefully prepared, have some of the dialogue, etc., but be principally musical. Or some of the sound effects that people haven't heard, for example, like howler monkeys, the noise that howler monkeys make. It's like wind in the trees, but not quite, because there's nothing quite like it. And listening to it for a few seconds is much more precise than talking about it.

Giant Black Centipedes, So Why Worry

You wrote in *The Job*, "It is now possible to decondition man from the whole punishment-reward cycle."
I simply mean that if we had sufficient knowledge we could—any neurosis, any hang-up resulting from past conditioning must express itself in actual physiological reaction patterns. Now recent experiments have indicated the possibility of simply reprogramming reaction patterns, as you would reprogram a computer. Scientists have attached an ape's brain to a computer, so that the electrical impulses from the ape's brain were giving orders to the computer—that is, setting programs which could then be fed back the other way. Now undoubtedly they could get to the point of simply reprogramming, and they might be able to do that in a matter of hours. We don't know because it has never occurred in history what a completely deconditioned human being would look like, or act like.

Or whether he would exist at all.
Right. But as Korzybski always used to say, I don't know, let's see.

What about the giant black centipede the deanxietized man turned into in *Naked Lunch*?
I have no reason to think that the result would be . . . of that nature. [Laughter] And if it is, what the hell, I mean we're all black centipedes at heart, so why worry about it.

Isn't it going to be very dangerous if, as seems likely, the people who control these techniques are the people most opposed to deconditioning?
That argument is always raised with any new discovery or any piece of equipment, but this equipment is not all that expensive, or difficult. Anybody can do it. It is simply a very small electrical charge in a certain brain area. Now Scientology processing on the E-Meter—the E-Meter passes about a half a volt through the brain and body—is really sort of a sloppy form of electrical brain stimulation, because it consists of repetitive questions like, "What are you willing to talk to me about? What would you like to tell me about that? Repeat it and repeat

it and repeat it." So the current is going through there, and they are directing that current toward a certain area. It seems to me that the best insurance that the discovery is not used for control purposes is people knowing about it. The more people that know about it, the less chance there is to monopolize it, particularly such very simple techniques as these, which consist simply of electrodes in certain areas, which anyone can learn.

Now the E-Meter is in fact a lie detector and a mind-reading machine. You can read anyone's mind with it—but not the content, only the reactions. But if I ask a specific question, say if I ask someone, "Did you fuck your mother? Did you ever fuck your mother?" I'll get a read. That's a protest read, maybe dreams, fantasies. But if after going through all that, it still reads, by God, he did. I mean there's no beating a lie detector on a direct question like that.

How does the machine read the subject's reactions?
It is a read on the needle. Takes quite a while to know how to work it, because you have all sorts of reads. You have protest reads. All sorts of things that can happen. You can have a stuck needle—very rare—where the needle doesn't move at all—that usually means you have a mental defective or something wrong with the apparatus.

Now there are many actions that you can get on this needle, but the commonest is a fall, which indicates a read, which indicates a reaction. A fall is only one reaction, there are others. There's a rise, which means boredom, inattention. There's also a floating needle, which is a point of release, which the Scientology processing aims for. The needle floats back and forth, quite free.

What kind of effect is achieved on a personal level after you've learned to get a floating needle on very highly charged questions?
It's a very handy thing. If you've got a business associate and you get a strong read on his name, you're much more suspicious of him than you may realize, and usually with good reason. Any incident that disturbs you, if you run it to a floating needle, it sort of evaporates. I use it sometimes for that, not very much anymore, but it works, very well. If some disturbing incident has just happened, you run it on there until you get a floating needle. It may take varying lengths of time, usually not more

than ten or fifteen minutes at the most. A floating needle means that it's gone for now. It may come back; it may disturb you tomorrow.

Now there's every evidence that a floating needle here would correspond to alpha waves. Joe Kamiya in San Francisco has done an awful lot of work with this autonomic shaping. He found that the way to inhibit alpha waves is to make anything very solid in your mind. All you have to do is to get a very clear picture of something, and that knocks out the alpha waves, which exactly corresponds to what happens here, there's something solid in your mind. So this could be cross-checked with those machines.

Aside from the value of the E-Meter, are your feelings on Scientology pretty much what they were when you wrote *The Job*?
No. I've written another little article since then where I criticize their reactionary policies. And some of the old Scientologists have defected and set up a new organization, protesting what they consider the fascist policies of Hubbard and his organization.

A New Mayan Comic Book

You've talked about hieroglyphic or picture writing. Do you feel that we're living out the end of the age of literacy, that people are going to be reading more and more picture books?
Well, that is not at all certain, because the actual picture magazines are all going out of business, *Life, Newsweek*, and all of them. There are ideas that I had which have not been borne out. Like when I said in the Academy Series, "recommend that the daily press be discontinued." Remember that the Academy Series was all predicated as occurring in 1899, and it was my feeling that if certain measures had been taken then, the present mess might have been avoided, that being an arbitrary date when it might have been possible. But that is 1899, and this is 1972. I would certainly not recommend it now.

You're working on a comic book?
Yes. It is a comic book in that it has whole sequences of action in pictures. But there are also about sixty pages of text, so it's something between a comic book and an illustrated book.

Malcolm MacNeil is doing the artwork. It is most closely similar to the actual format of the Mayan Codices, which was an early comic book. There'll be pictures in the Codices, and sometimes there'll be three pages of text in writing that we can't read. We can read some of it, and we can read the dates. A great deal of it was dates. The story concerns someone who has discovered the control secrets of the Mayan books.

Is the fact that the Mayan books were a control system, able to control the people very precisely by having the calendar dates and knowing what stimuli were going to be applied on any one day, your main interest in the Mayan civilization?
Yes. It was a control system that required no police, working on psychological controls. The priests were only about one percent of the population. Priests and artisans would certainly not come out to more than five percent. And how did they keep them working?

A good question.
Yes, come to think about it. [Laughter]

Any ideas how they might have done it?
Oh, very precise ideas, which I developed in the books.

Have you looked at the Mayan books here in London?
I've seen them all, but there were only three. You see, Bishop Landa burned a stack of them as big as that rug. Somebody who was there grabbed three out of the fire. They're burned around the edges. Those were the Dresden, the Paris, and the Madrid Codices, named for the places where they now are, in the respective museums. These turned up, I think, in the seventeenth century, in some old bookshop somewhere. There are copies of those available. They have them over there at the British Museum, and I went over and looked at the copies with Malcolm, and then we had photostats made, but of course those are not colored, and the originals are colored.

So there's no way of knowing what the others consisted of. I mean a whole civilization there went up in flames. It's as if you piled all our physics books, Shakespeare, and everything else into a pile and burnt the whole lot, and there was nothing left. We don't know what is left, you understand. The books that we now have, we assume, but perhaps not with good reason, were of a similar nature to the others.

Are you using any of the simplified hieroglyphic script which you gave samples and explanations of in *The Job* in this new book?
No. That is something that will have to be worked out, because there are all sorts of problems. I started trying to learn how to use Egyptian hieroglyphs, but picture writing at a certain point becomes incredibly cumbersome. The grammar is very complicated. To get around this and get something people could write, the scribes must have started at a very early age, I suppose like the Chinese, and I presume they each had a different style.

So you don't feel, as McLuhan does, that print is on the way out?
Well, no. What does he think is going to take its place? We know that physics and mathematics have whole nonverbal communication systems.

Apparently he thought electronic media, spoken words, and pictures were going to take the place of print.
Well, you still have the problem of the actual prose. Now I see that in this book I'm doing with Malcolm, there are lots of sections which go just like film. But the text is really still essential. There are sixty pages of text; we're already having problems with translating that into images—not the problem that we can't do it, but the problem that it would take three hundred pages to do it all. If we took every sentence and translated it into pictures, we'd have a huge book that would be way out of our budget. And there are things really that there's no point in translating into pictures, since they are much clearer in prose. There's another point where a page of prose can't do what a picture can.

Well, when you said, "Rub out the word," was that another way of saying, "Learn to use words instead of being used by them"?
That's one I will have to think about, because I've been thinking about a whole field theory of words. I don't think when I said that I had any clear idea as to what it would involve, or even what words were. I have a much clearer idea now, as to what would be involved, but it's something pretty drastic. Of course it was Brion's suggestion originally. . . . Let us say you would have to first have some idea of what the word is and how it

operates. I predicate that the word is an actual virus, and a virus that has achieved equilibrium with the host, and therefore is not recognized as a virus. I have a number of technical books on that subject, and there are other viruses that have achieved this. That is, they replicate themselves within the cells but they don't harm the cells.

Are you thinking of something like the proliferation of responses to Mailer's one article about Women's Lib?
Not precisely. I mean that a phrase can replicate itself and jump all over the world. It usually is a pretty simple formula. An example: Years ago I found out that a cure for the common cold was Vitamin A in massive doses. I've used it for years, and it definitely does work. Well, someone seems to have a vested interest in the common cold, because Vitamin A was completely ignored and they started this Vitamin C bit. And Vitamin C is absolutely worthless for a cold. Now time and time again I've told people about Vitamin A and they immediately say, in exactly the same tone, "You mean Vitamin C." No, I don't mean Vitamin C, I mean Vitamin A. I got exactly the same tone of voice from a number of people that I spoke to about this Vitamin A. It's a turnoff on Vitamin A.

Where do you think that turnoff originated? Has it been implanted by some of these vested interests you spoke of?
I would say so, yes. Because at the time I made this discovery, I was working for an advertising agency in New York, and I said, "We'll put it on the market as a patent medicine, put a little something else in it." Absolutely, the company didn't want to know, and they said, quite frankly, because it might work. They said, "The AMA is very down on self-medications." They don't care if you take a little pill with quinine and this and that in it that doesn't do a thing, but if you take something that actually does something, so that you wouldn't need them . . . for years the doctors have been afraid of any really effective panacea, or effective medicines that anyone could use, which are also harmless, and so that they wouldn't have any necessity for a doctor's prescription.

Is this similar to the fear of apomorphine?
Yes, I would say so, because apomorphine and the possibility of synthetic derivatives which would have a much stronger action—and they could

probably eliminate the nausea altogether—could be just such a general panacea against conditions of anxiety and intoxication: a metabolic regulator. Well, a drug with such general application is something that they would regard with considerable misgivings. It is not a dangerous drug actually, and if it were widely used, that would become apparent; there really isn't any necessity for a prescription.

Do you have any information on the introduction of white heroin into Harlem and into the ghettos during the forties, which seems to have been the beginning of the current problem?
I don't. You see, I was there in the late forties and early fifties, and the agents then were just beginning to bother addicts. Before that they'd been more interested in pushers.

Why did they start bothering addicts rather than pushers?
In order to spread it. That kept the pushers continually looking for new markets.

Do you see that as a very conscious attempt to spread it for certain, say political ends, or as a tendency of bureaucracies to perpetuate themselves?
Both. The tendency of bureaucracies is to increase personnel, of course. If you've got one person who isn't doing anything, then he gets five or six subordinates in, and so it goes. They tend to make themselves necessary.

Well, they're really cracking down on grass and psychedelics now, and causing lots of kids to turn to downers. They called last year the year of the downers, and none of my friends who used to take acid, say, once or twice a week, have had any in the last year and a half.
Brion Gysin: Did you get uncomfortable physical side effects from acid?

No. Some uncomfortable psychological effects occasionally, but never a bad trip or anything like that.
Gysin: Well, I had two bad trips, and I would never touch it again. So really my considerations on acid are pretty personal. I think it's horrible stuff.

Why do you think it's horrible stuff?
Gysin: So far as I'm concerned, it has absolutely nightmare reactions—symptoms of an extreme and depressing nature. I felt as if I was on fire. Maybe someone didn't get all the ergot out of it. But I just don't want to know about acid.

Do you think it can have value for some people?
Burroughs: It seems to, but then it's very dubious, because lots of people that take it all the time, they think they're benefiting, but I don't, as an observer.
Gysin: Oh, but I think everybody should have taken it at least once. I don't think that anybody has to take it more, in fact. Essentially very square people have taken it just once, and it's made an astounding difference in their lives and their outlook.
Burroughs: But couldn't they have done the same with majoun [a preparation of hashish]?
Gysin: I don't think so. It doesn't take you quite as far out.
Burroughs: Not quite as far, but at least there I'm in an area that I can control. . . .
Gysin: No, but the experience is to get into an area that you can't control and realize that you can go there and come back again.
Burroughs: I find both mescaline and yage, which has never been circulated, though it could be—it's just a question of chemical analysis—much more interesting. Peyote made me terribly sick, so sick I couldn't get any enjoyment out of it.

Do you have any ideas why many of the popular rock groups today are those that put out a wall of noise for people who come in with a wine-and-Seconal head?
I don't know. I'm not really in touch with the situation in the States at all. I was there two years ago for six weeks, and before that I left in 1965. So since '65, I have only been back for the Chicago Convention and a brief stay in New York . . . it seems that alcohol is on the increase, as opposed to pot, I hear that from a number of sources.

"Ripple and reds . . ."
Oh my God, that is absolutely terrible. You really get some terrible effects from that. I've always hated barbiturates. I hate the sensation,

and the most unpleasant hangover in the world is the barbiturate hangover. Worse than alcohol, and of course in combination . . . Also it's very dangerous. You know, alcohol ups the toxicity by about thirty percent.

Of the drugs people take to get high—say, barbiturates, speed, cannabis, psychedelics—which ones do you think have some value?
Cannabis, I think, has the most value. Amphetamines, absolutely none. Barbiturates, absolutely none. I just can't see anything that could possibly result from either barbiturates or amphetamines that could be considered desirable from any point of view. . . .

Do you foresee a situation of cannabis being legalized in the West any time in the near future?
I don't know. It would seem to me to be a concession that they could not afford to make. "Grant too many concessions and they'll ask for more and more and more." It seems doubtful that they could risk making that concession. . . .

Cut-ups & Dream Machines at the Old Beat Hotel

Let's delve into the past a little. Where and what was the "Beat Hotel"?
Gysin: The Beat Hotel was in Paris at 9 rue Git le Coeur, just off the Place Saint Michel in the Latin Quarter. For a lot of young people in Paris it was more than a home. That's where the Beat scene in Paris was born. A Dutch painter turned Allen Ginsberg on to it in 1956, I am told. I didn't get there myself until 1958 when I ran into Burroughs on the street, and he told me he lived in room 15.

The hotel was run by a wonderful Frenchwoman named Madame Rachou, who might have made herself rich and famous if she had laid away just a few of the manuscripts of what was written under her roof or collected some of the pictures painted in her hotel. She was a funny mixture of peasant shrewdness and hardness along with the most disinterested generosity. She would do anything to help anyone just coming out of jail, no matter who they were or what they had been in for. She had her own ideas about who she wanted in her so-called hotel and some people waited forever, buying drinks at her little zinc-covered bar. I remember her telling an American that there would be a room ready in ten minutes. From behind her bar, she could see the municipal undertakers going up the stairs to take out a poor old French pauper who'd died in his rent-controlled room. Americans pay more, even beatniks. On the other hand, the better-off anyone looked, the more likely she was to turn them away, and she certainly preferred young people—even troublesome young people—to old.

Were you working on the *Naked Lunch* materials at that time?
Burroughs: I wasn't doing all that much at that time, actually. Girodias of Olympia Press, the eventual publishers, had turned the manuscript down the first time, around two years before that, and I just wasn't doing much work.

Had you written *Naked Lunch* in Tangier, then?
Burroughs: Right.
Gysin: In a hotel we called the Villa Delirium, which was another great spot, near the beach in Tangier. It had a garden and . . .
Burroughs: Another memorable Madame . . .
Gysin: The lady from Saigon. The number of people who revolved through those two hotels is really remarkable. All the Beats . . .
Burroughs: . . . and so many people who have really gone places since then. That young filmmaker, for example . . .
Gysin: Oh, Mel Van Peebles.
Burroughs: Terry Southern, Mason Hoffenberg . . .
Gysin: The list is really endless. An enormous number of musicians. The place was always bubbling with music, whether being produced on instruments or being played on tapes or records. Mezzrow's son lived there . . . Mezz Mezzrow! My God, he was a fantastic cat. He was around the hotel quite a lot. I remember one day in winter. It was very, very cold, and I opened the door, and here was this big, fat, black woman complaining about something. She really put on such a scene that I just told her, "I don't know, I don't know," and I slammed the door, and she went banging on the next door, which was Gregory Corso's, across the hall. And I think it was Gregory who cracked up and said, "But, Mezz, what are you doing?" The old man had got himself into drag, put some

kind of makeup on his face, and he went through the entire hotel until somebody just said, "What is that you're doing?"

Was it during this time that you discovered the cut-up technique?
Gysin: I had a big table on which I worked very often with a Stanley blade, and I had cut up a number of newspapers accidentally. They had been underneath something else that I was cutting. The pieces sort of fell together, and I started matching them up, and I thought, Wo-o-o-ow, it's really very funny. And I took some of them and arranged them in a pattern which was visually pleasing to me and then typed up the results, and I have never laughed so heartily in my entire life.

The first time around, doing your own cut-ups and seeing the results, there's a sort of feeling of hilarity. . . . But it doesn't happen again. It's a oner, a single sensation that happens just that one first time, it seems to me. But I was really socked by that. And it had exactly the same effect on him. But I must say that I had thought of it as a rather superior amusement, and was very impressed by William's immediate recognition that here was something extremely important to him, that he could put to use right away, and did.

With great excitement we put together a book, and the title was really pulled right out of the air. It seems to me we were standing in the doorway to my room, 25, when someone said, "Hurry, hurry, there's only minutes to go!" and I said Wow, that's the title obviously.

What was it you saw in the cut-ups initially, after you stopped laughing?
Burroughs: Well, I saw the possibility of permutations, particularly of images, which is the area in which it has worked best over a period of time. A book of Rimbaud's poetry or any extremely visual text will cut up and give you new combinations that are quite valid new images. In other words, you are drawing a whole series of images out of this page of text.

Does this technique relate to twentieth-century painting?
Gysin: A whole lot. Look at it like this: Twentieth-century painting ceased being representational, gave up storytelling, and became abstract. Today, only squares can stand in front of a work of art whining: "But what does it mean?" Confronted with a piece of writing, that is the only question that readers still do ask. Perhaps there could be abstract

literature, as abstract as is what we call abstract painting. Why not? We wanted to see.

We began to find out a whole lot of things about the real nature of words and writing when we began to cut them up. What are words and what are they doing? Where are they going? The cut-up method treats words as the painter treats his paint, raw material with rules and reasons of its own. Representational painters fucked over their paint until they made it tell a tale. Abstract painters found that the real hero of the picture is the paint. Painters and writers of the kind I respect want to be heroes, challenging fate in their lives and in their art. What is fate? Fate is written: "Mektoub," in the Arab world, where art has always been nothing but abstract. "Mektoub" means "It is written." So . . . if you want to challenge and change fate . . . cut up the words. Make them make a new world.

Within weeks of stumbling on the cut-ups, I came across the Divine Tautology in Huxley's *Heaven and Hell*. I AM THAT I AM. I took a long look at it and found that the design of the phrase did not please me at all. I decided to make it more symmetrical by displacing the words. The biggest block was THAT, so I decided to leave it in the middle. My first move was to put at each end the word I. It read: I AM THAT AM I. That sounded more like a question. What had been one of the most affirmative statements of all time had become a question, and a poignant one, simply by changing the word order around.

As I began to run through some of the other one hundred and twenty simple permutations of these five words, I heard the words running away by themselves. THAT I AM I AM, AM I THAT I AM? etc. They went on asking and answering themselves like the links of a chain, jingling against each other as they fell apart and changed places musically. I heard them. I actually heard the words falling apart. I fell back on my bed in room 25, hearing this strange distant ringing in my ears like Newton said he heard the music of the spheres when he stumbled on the laws of gravitation. I was as high as that. All that period in the Beat Hotel was one enormous intellectual high, wasn't it, William? I have a whole book of permutated poems I've never been able to get published. Ian Somerville put them through the computer for me. In 1960, I gave a program of them on the BBC and they have come out on records issued by Henri Chopin for his review, *Ou*.

William, would you encourage people to read *Minutes to Go* before reading your subsequent books? Is it important for people who want to understand what you're doing?
I think it's quite an important book, and it does give a much clearer indication as to what I'm doing and the whole theory and development of cut-ups.

Where do you feel you've used cut-ups to greatest advantage?
I would say in sections of *The Soft Machine*, *The Ticket That Exploded*, and in *Nova Express* as well. In certain sections it has worked. I feel that in all those books there was too much rather undifferentiated cut-up material, which I eliminated in *The Wild Boys*. The cut-up technique has very specific uses.

Brion, what about your Dream Machine? You've both used it?
Gysin: Yes. It's a stroboscope, in one word. But regulated to produce interruptions of light at between eight and thirteen flashes a second, complementing the alpha rhythms in the brain, or eventually bringing the two into phase, and at that moment, immediately, one begins with sensations of extraordinary, bright color and infinite pattern which is quickly elaborating itself into fields that appear at 180 degrees to begin with and eventually seem to be occurring around 360 degrees. There are several different areas of color, of intensity and changes of pattern, which follow each other in apparent random order, and then give way, at a certain point, to things recognized as dream images, imaginary events occurring at a certain speed, much like a speeded-up movie. But depending on one's own state, or the length of time one watches, they become like the most elaborate, highly structured sort of dreams. I've had science fiction dreams, I've imagined that I was swimming over what seemed to be an ocean bottom and that big mollusks at the bottom opened up and through them appeared swimmers in Leonardo da Vinci–type helmets, and a lot of dreams about fights between them, or flights of them.

There seems to be no end to it. I've watched for literally hundreds of hours, and things never repeat themselves. Patterns do. Apparently they can eventually be learned and recognized. Some of the people who've investigated them, including a group in Germany, have identified a great many of the elements of design all over the world, found in weaving or in pottery or in archaeological objects, elements of these patterns. All of them have been related to the sort of visions that one has with the Dream Machine. But there just haven't been many of these machines around; it's never been possible to have them made. We struggled along for years and years to try to get someone to manufacture them, and nothing has ever come of it. . . .

Are the technologically equipped homosexual warrior packs of *The Wild Boys* projections of yours, or a prediction . . . ?
Is the book a projection? Yes. It's all simply a personal projection. A prediction? I hope so. Would I consider events similar to the *Wild Boys* scenario desirable? Yes, desirable to me.

Do you think things might get to the point of there being guerrilla armies of young people throughout the world, marching on the citadels of authority?
There is a presupposition in the *Wild Boys* book of some disaster or plague which has reduced the population of the world by about three quarters. All these empty streets, etc. So they are in a set that is already quite depopulated. Of course, under the present circumstances, any such thing is impossible, there simply isn't room, there's no place to go. Well, South America . . .

You're assuming that this plague would've killed off mostly older people—that the younger people, being stronger, would have survived?
Yes, definitely. Bore down kinda heavy on the whites, too. I think it was ninety-nine percent fatal in South Africa and the Bible Belt.

Brion has talked about a decay of services—canceled mail deliveries, unsafe streets—before the fall of the Roman Empire. In *The Wild Boys*, civilization is reduced to holding enclaves, and the suburbs are no-man's-land. Were you thinking of historical parallels?
Well, that is the set that I presupposed in *The Wild Boys* as already existing, which means that communications have broken down, there's very little gasoline, people are going back to signal drums or other primitive communications systems.

Why aren't women involved in these bands of wild boy guerrillas?
I have a number of things to say on that subject. . . . Because women
are trouble. It is another organism with interests perhaps basically
irreconcilable with the male interests—which has installed itself as
indispensable. Well, they may be indispensable to some people, but
they're not necessarily indispensable to me. So I was merely proposing this as one experimental line that I would be most interested
to follow, in the direction of mutations from the present humanoid
form. That is, boys who had never had contact with women would
be quite a different animal. We can't imagine what they would be
like. I certainly have no objections if lesbians would like to do the
same. . . .

**Women who had never had contact with men would be a pretty dif-
ferent animal too.**
Indeed they would. They could be given female babies to raise from
birth.

Have you got any ideas on what that might lead to?
I don't know. They could mutate into birds, perhaps. But what I was
proposing on an overall scale is that the present human product seems to
have gotten itself into a real bind. And what we need is variety, in other
words, mutations. Now, at one time there may have been many human-
oids, but only one strain survived. Have you read *African Genesis*? Well,
there was the aggressive southern ape, who survived because he was a
killer, and has really in a sense forced his way of life on the whole species.
There is only one game and that game is war.

**Do you feel that that game is genetically built into the species as it
exists now?**
Yes.

**Have you seen any signs of mutations such as you're looking for begin-
ning to occur?**
Well, occasionally you do see really quite extraordinary people that look
like they might be mutating. I've seen rather more lately.

What kind of characteristics do they have that are different?
Well, I don't know whether a genetic mutation would be necessary for this, but, if people were simply actually in control over their bodies, they would appear superhuman. That is, if they never dropped anything, spilled anything, fumbled anything. Which, obviously, they're quite capable of doing. The only problem is that after thousands of years they've never learned to operate their own machine. It's a quite complicated machine, but still, they should learn over a period of time. They go on trying to do the same things that just don't work. And that's what no politician can ever admit. You can't get up there and say, "Boys, the whole thing just won't work."

Does the writing technique in *The Wild Boys* differ from that of the previous four novels?
Yes, I think that in *The Wild Boys* I was really quite deliberately returning to older styles of writing. Quite a bit of it is really nineteenth century. It's a different style of writing.

Did you use cut-ups in *The Wild Boys*?
Yes, but sparingly, and very carefully selecting the phrases from the cut-ups, sifting through them many, many times. I didn't use it to the extent it was used in *The Ticket That Exploded* and *The Soft Machine* and *Nova Express*, nowhere near.

Has there been a progression in your writing to using them more sparingly and with more precision and control?
Yes. And also there are literary situations in which they are useful, and others in which they are not. Now, in re-creating a delirium, they're very good, because that is what is happening. In high fever the images cut in, quite arbitrarily. So I used that in the dream section where the Boy is dying in the jungle.

Is *The Wild Boys* closely connected to your previous novels, or does it stand by itself?
I think it stands by itself. There's no carryover of characters as there are in the other books. *Naked Lunch, The Soft Machine*, and to some extent

The Ticket That Exploded and *Nova Express* even, were all part of about a thousand pages of manuscript. And then I had to get together one book for Girodias in two weeks. And I did. That is how it happened. I thought, which chapter goes where is going to be very complicated, but it came back from the printers, and Sinclair Beilles took one look and said, "Why don't you leave it like this?" And we did. That's just pure chance, as the chapters were going in as we typed them out.

That was *Naked Lunch*. Then I had lots of material left over, and I started writing *The Soft Machine* after that, from this material. But there were no cut-ups as such used in *Naked Lunch* at all.

How far does that material go back?
The actual notes for *Naked Lunch* started, I think, around 1955, or '54. They piled up over a period of years, and I sent one version to Maurice Girodias, who didn't want it at that time. A few years later I was in Paris, and he sent Sinclair Beilles over to say that he wanted to publish it within two weeks. And a month later, a month from his saying that he wanted it, it was out on the bookstands.

Eric Mottram calls your first four novels "The Tetralogy." Is a similar grouping emerging from your new work?
Yes, everything I'm doing now is connected with *The Wild Boys*. The comic strip is using one of the same characters, as well as the other book. . . .

What does this other book have to do with?
It concerns an incestuous family of father, mother, two brothers, and two sisters—completely interchangeable sexual combinations. And they succeed because they are incestuous, liberated from all their inhibitions.

Succeed at what?
Well, by selling short during the Depression, they're able to fill a swimming pool with gold dollars.

Is that the last or the next Depression?
The last one; it's set back. What they do, in a sense, is make capitalism work. That is, they buy up the dust bowl, so they keep people there on

the land and turn them all into incestuous family groups in completely interchangeable sexual combinations. So not only are they happier, but they're much more efficient, and nobody could compete with these families.

So this is a very different scenario sexually from _The Wild Boys_, but it's approached in the same way?
Yes. I thought it might have more popular appeal. . . . And that of course brings them into conflict with the sinister forces of Big Money; they're subverting the whole meaning of money. . . .

You've often pointed out attitudes and styles shared by young people all over the world—they dress similarly, use cannabis and other consciousness-expanding drugs, hear the same music. Are these generational ties more binding than national, cultural, family ties?
Yes, I would say so, very definitely. And one reason that they are is of course media.

Do you foresee these ties eventually unifying the world's youth to the point where they can destroy the control machine being perpetuated by their elders?
Certainly. They will become their elders, and therefore make the changes. Now in twenty or thirty years all the Wallace folks etc. will have died. Well, who's going to take their place? Occupying all the positions that are now occupied by their elders, either occupying all those positions or nullifying them, you're bound to have a whole different picture. I mean, if they've got some cool, pot-smoking cat as president, he's not going to make the same kind of decisions or impose the same policies. Now the question of whether the control machine, as you said earlier, would impose certain necessities on anybody that used it—that's another consideration, and to some extent it would. But they certainly would be more willing to listen to the idea of basic alterations, and perhaps change it.

The control machine is simply the machinery—police, education, etc.—used by a group in power to keep itself in power and extend its power. For example: In a hunting society, which can only number about thirty, there's nothing that could be called a control machine in operation. They must function effectively as a hunting party in order to survive, so leadership is casual and you have no control machine. Now as soon as you get an agricultural society, particularly in rich land, you will tend to get inequality. That is, the advantage of slave labor then becomes apparent and you may have, as with the Mayans and Egyptians, workers and priests—in other words, stratification, repression, and you have a control machine. As I said, the ancient Mayans had almost a model control machine through which about one or two percent of the population controlled the others, without police, without heavy weapons. The workers all had such weapons as were available, stone axes, spears, etc. So it was pure psychological control.

Is the modern control machine's dependence on heavy weapons a sign that psychological control is breaking down?
Yes. Of course, the whole concept of revolution has undergone a basic change with the introduction of heavy weapons. Now anybody can go down into his basement and make a sword or a spear, and they can make some approximation of small arms. But they can't make automatic weapons, tanks, machine guns, planes, and so on. So with heavy weapons five percent can keep down ninety-five percent by just sheer force, if they have to. Of course no government has ever survived for any length of time anywhere by sheer force, because of the personnel that they would have to have. They would have to have constant surveillance, unless they used some form of psychological control like electric brain stimulation. But the problem that you see in all guerrilla warfare of occupying a territory where the governed are hostile, or even a good percentage of them, of course is terrific and ultimately insoluble. The French had to get out of Algeria; they'll all have to get out of Vietnam.

Now, as to the effectiveness of street fighting in a revolutionary context, you must remember that America is not in a state of revolution. It is not even in a state of pre-revolution, and any guerrilla movement, in order to survive, must have supplies from outside. The liberals in the Colombian civil war had seized an area that bordered on Venezuela, so they were getting their arms in through Venezuela. In Vietnam they're getting their arms from the North. Without something comparable to that, no guerrilla movement is ever going to be able to survive. They may talk about guerrilla movements in the large cities, but they're just not talking in realistic terms. In Algeria the rebels occupied the mountains, and therefore they could supply their guerrillas in the cities. And also an underground army must have popular support. They don't have the potential for much support in America.

So that would not seem to be a viable tactic at present. I don't take back what I said in *The Job*, that there should be more riots and more violence, because at that time—May 1968—they were indicated. They accomplished something, there's no doubt about it. If there had been no riots, no violence, they wouldn't pay nearly as much attention to militants or their demands as they are paying now.

You also wrote in *The Job*, "once a problem has reached the political-military stage, it is already insoluble."
Yes, because it's not meant to be solved. This is a game universe. Basically there's only one game and that game is war, and we just have to keep it going, if we're to have political/military units at all.

But a new generation just might not be interested in such things. They've got all those countries on the west coast of South America, countries like Colombia and Peru—they all have armies and they all consider that Peruvians are bad people, or Ecuadorians are bad people. And that, of course, is kept going by the military and by the very wealthy people. Otherwise, there'd be no reason for their existence. Now if a generation took over that just wasn't interested in maintaining these states, there'd be no reason for these countries to have any boundaries, or armies, at all.

What would you say to young people who want to change things through street fighting?
The only context in which street fighting would become important would be in the wake of some catastrophe, possibly an atomic war. In the chaos following an atomic attack on America, street fighting is a very important factor. I've already pointed out that I don't think street fighting is at all a viable tactic, or a revolutionary tactic in the States. It is not in any country once it reaches a certain technological stage.

There are, of course, weapons that anyone can make in their basement, if they know how, and those are biological and chemical weapons. I have a reference, commenting on the discovery of the synthetic gene, from the science representative of one of America's major embassies: "This is the beginning of the end. Any small country with good biochemists can now make the virus for which there is no cure. Someone will do it." That means, of course, any small country or any private group with a good biochemist and a small laboratory. It could be done in a place as small as this room. If they can make life particles, they can make death particles. They can make a virus to order, a virus that will do what you want it to do.

But how do you protect yourself from it if there's no cure?
No cure for the attack. Usually they develop antitoxins at the same time. It would be quite possible, for example, to develop a plague that would attack only whites. And incidentally, any college physics major, with that much technical knowledge and about three hundred thousand dollars, can turn out a low-yield nuclear device and take out New York from Times Square to Central Park. Nothing big, you understand. . . .

The thing about virus weapons is that they need not be recognized as such. It could just come on as a paralyzing depression. Everyone just feels a little worse and a little worse until they can't get out of bed, and the whole thing founders.

Do you think any particular dissatisfied group in the society might be most inclined to use this kind of weapon? Say, the right wing?
I think the right wing more than the left. The left is still back there with Che Guevara and barricades and bullets. But to hesitate to use them I think would definitely be foolish.

This Is a Game Universe & There's Only One Game

. . . Brion, what did you mean when you said "Rub out the word"?
Gysin: "Rub out the word" was essentially to do with the fact that all the religions of the "peoples of the book," that is the Jews, the Christians, and the Muslims, all these three religions are based on the idea that in the beginning was the word. Everything seems to be wrong with what was produced from those beginnings, and so let's rub out the word and start afresh and see what really is going on. The methods were first of all a disruption of the time sequence, as William said a few minutes ago,

produced by the cut-ups, and one had the idea of rubbing out the word itself, not simply disrupting its sequential order and finding out some other way. There are other ways of communication, so an attempt at finding them would begin by rubbing out the word. If the whole thing began with the word, well then, if we don't like what was produced, and we don't, let's get right to the root of the matter and radically alter it. . . .

What precisely is the desirability of not verbalizing?
Gysin: Well, verbalization has got us precisely where we are: War is a word. The whole war universe is a verbal universe, which means they've got us in an impasse. And in order to break out of that impasse it would seem desirable to explore alternative methods of communication.

How would you compare exploring these avenues to exploring more and more precise manipulation of words?
Gysin: Well, it would certainly be a step in the same direction. The more precise your manipulation or use of words is, the more you know what you're actually dealing with, what the word actually is. And by knowing what it actually is, you can supersede it. Or use it when you want to use it. Most people never stop talking—"talking to themselves," as they call it. But who are they actually talking to, and why? Why can't they simply lapse into silence?

La Monte Young: Lost in the Drone Zone

ROLLING STONE | FEBRUARY 13, 1975

When La Monte Young Says Take It from the Top, He Means Last Wednesday

Here's how composer/instrumentalist La Monte Young plays the blues. He finds a space in a museum or gallery, moves in slide projectors, electronic sine-wave generators, microphones, as many Altec Voice of the Theater speakers as possible, and two or more instrumentalists. He tunes one of the generators to 180 cycles per second, hooks it up to a bank of speakers, and turns it on. "Three times sixty is 180 cycles," explains Young. "And on the North American continent sixty cycles is the standard frequency of wall current. That frequency runs this country: If you're walking around on the streets, a large percentage of the hum that you hear from electrical and electronic installations is sixty cycles and it's harmonics. Since the listener is already tuned into it I decided to use it in my music rather than fight it and create some kind of spurious vibration."

Once the generator is humming away at a *pure* 180 cycles per second—the point of using sine waves is that they have only one frequency component and are thus the cleanest, simplest sort of sound vibration—chords can be built up with the help of additional generators, other instruments, and amplified voices. *And*—pay attention, now—the result can be a form of blues "in which each chord change is played for a day or two days. In other words, a day can represent a bar so that it takes twelve days to play a twelve-bar blues. With electronic tones, I'm able to set up this really large-scale rhythmic structure, where you can have the concept of a chord going for a few months and switching to another chord for a few weeks, coming to some little short note for a day and dropping off into something else for the weekend and then coming back Monday morning for a full week of another chord."

This slowly changing sound environment, which is being amplified through the bank of speakers, is complemented by slowly focusing and defocusing calligraphic slides superimposed from four projectors by Young's wife, artist Marian Zazeela. Both of them sing through the speakers along with the sine-wave frequencies for varying periods of time each day the installation is operating. The entire presentation is called a Dream House. The music performed therein will be a snippet from a theoretically eternal composition titled *Map of 49's Dream the Two Systems of Galactic Intervals Ornamental Lightyears Tracery.*

No, La Monte Young is not some callow SoHo madman. He's thirty-nine years of age and "his role as father figure for the younger avant-garde is surpassed only by John Cage," according to *The New York Times*'s John Rockwell. His round Midwestern face is framed by a long, involved black beard and usually crowned by a brightly colored knit cap. He pads around his loft, where incense burns and time stands still, in slippers and loose-fitting Indian garments while his visiting musical guru, the Indian singing master Pandit Pran Nath, intones resonant *hare oms* behind a partition. A tamboura, the gourd-bodied Indian drone instrument, is being tuned by Marian in a corner. But this is not your typical urban ashram. On the walls are scientific charts of frequency makeup, and oscilloscopes and other gear divide the loft's work area into passageways, little rest areas, private nooks. Not too long ago Young kept a constant sine-wave drone going in the loft twenty-four hours a day, for weeks and months at a time, boosted to a volume most visitors found decidedly uncomfortable. Verbal communication had to take the form of shouting, but this drawback was compensated for by the opportunity the drone afforded to study high- and low-pressure areas in the loft. When the Youngs sang, or some of their musicians came by for a rehearsal, they were all able to slide into tune with a drone which had been going for a very long time.

Drones, introduced via Indian music, were big during the sixties. John Coltrane's improvisations took advantage of these one-note or one-chord continuums, as did Canned Heat's boogie. Young took them even more seriously. "What a drone gives you in the world of pitch is a constant, something you can count on," he says. "Because it's there, you can have a much more precise relationship between your other pitches. So you can have better tuning, and at the same time you can do much more imaginative things in the tuning, because you have a point of reference. Also, you can get into a *drone state of mind*. The mind can have and enjoy the same advantages in *its* improvisation that a musician can enjoy if he has a frequency which is constant." With the drone going day and night, mental improvisations reached dizzying heights.

Now the drone is silent and other projects occupy La Monte's attention. Since 1970 he has been studying the difficult Kirana style of Indian singing with Pran Nath. He accompanies his teacher on the tamboura. He prepares presentations of his own compositions. In order to make time for these activities he and Marian get up before sunrise, practice their singing, perform their other musical and spiritual exercises. Afternoons are for business and conversation. Marian manages to work on tambouras, execute some of her delicate calligraphy, and make spiced tea while La Monte takes telephone calls, looks after Pran Nath, and answers questions about his life and work.

He was born in a log cabin in Bern, Idaho. As a child he enjoyed singing along with power lines and transformers. Later he harmonized with lathes and drill presses. He attended Los Angeles City College with jazz saxophonist Eric Dolphy, led jazz groups during the fifties which included drummer Billy Higgins and trumpeter Don Cherry, the nucleus of Ornette Coleman's original quartet, and then moved to New York. Throughout the sixties he was an important organizer of the Fluxus movement which included Cage, Yoko Ono, Nan June Paik, George Maciunas, Henry Flint, and others and involved happenings, chance procedures, and generally stretching art to its limits. The static quality of his 1958 Trio for Strings, which takes five minutes to present four notes, gave way temporarily to verbal scores in which various performers were instructed to draw a straight line and follow it, to build a fire onstage, to turn a butterfly loose in the performance area, to try and coax a grand piano into eating a bale of hay and drinking from a bucket of water.

In addition to his Fluxus activities Young was a formidable saxophone soloist and was playing regularly with a group of gifted young musicians which included Angus MacLise and John Cale, who went on to apply some of Young's methods to his work with the Velvet Underground and Nico. By 1963 La Monte was performing quicksilver sopranino saxophone improvisations over a drone supplied by Tony Conrad's bowed guitar, Cale's viola, and Marian's voice. Then, around 1965, he became attracted to the 120-cycle hum (twice sixty) of an aquarium motor. He amplified it with a contact microphone: "I wanted to see what it would mean for our sense of pitch and for the intonation of the music we were all practicing to play against a drone that fixed. I liked it so much that I immediately added a sine-wave generator to play a harmonically related interval." This was the beginning of the end of music as a series of events, as a body of works in which things happen, and the beginning of a new, timeless kind of music in which "the sine waves are just the resonators," the principal instruments being the listener's ear, basilar membrane, auditory neurons, and cerebral cortex. Stockhausen had experimented with similar ideas, but it was Young who directly inspired the static forms popularized by Steve Reich, Philip Glass, and especially Terry Riley, who played in Young's group and was himself one of the most influential composer/performers of the sixties.

By 1970 Young had given up the saxophone for singing, and two broad areas had emerged which were of crucial significance to his music. One was Indian music, which extends back thousands of years through an unbroken chain of guru/disciple relationships. "Indian music has the highest performance standards of any system in the world," he says. "And the frequency relationships are all associated with psychological states. The mere fact that they have the means to classify the moods of the different ragas, in whatever poetic way, means they have something that has almost totally disappeared from Western music. Sure, you had a few romantics who talked about the moods of various scales or chords. But for every romantic you had a hundred imperialists who were just writing notes."

The other important area is the physics and psychophysics of sound, with special reference to the science of acoustics. The Indian system predicts which sequence of notes will be most pleasing and harmonious at specific times of day, but it does not offer a technical exegesis of just how these sequences interact with biological and psychological systems. Current "models" of hearing theory explain how, for example, the strictly sequential repetition of tones in an Indian raga can lull the mind by setting up a pattern which plays across the surface of the basilar membrane in the inner ear. Since different tones stimulate different areas of that surface, the membrane will be rhythmically "massaged" by the repeating tones, causing neurons to fire messages toward the cerebral cortex in the same hypnotically repeating pattern. Using sine waves instead of tamboura for the drone should reduce the number of neurons firing at a given time. But by amplifying his sound through large speakers Young increases the firing rate of each neuron, thus creating a listening experience that is both specific and intense.

The fact that each frequency makes a different part of the basilar membrane oscillate and sets a distinctive reaction going in the nervous system goes a long way toward explaining Young's fascination with single-frequency tones or sine waves. "What is a sine wave?" he muses. "It's a pulse in one direction which rebounds the same distance in the opposite direction. In the case of light, it's a laser. In the case of sound, it sets the air molecules vibrating forward and back, forward and back. What does that remind you of? Plus and minus, night and day, positive and negative, mother and father? I mean, it's really very basic and very profound. And once you get two or more sine waves together, it becomes fantastically interesting."

The timbre of any sound can be represented by some combination of sine waves. When a string is plucked or bowed, a horn blown into, a drum struck, or a syllable said or sung by the human voice, a multitude of waves occurs. These waves or vibrations, each with its own particular frequency, array themselves according to known physical laws into patterns. Each pattern can be represented schematically as an overtone series of sine waves that begins with a fundamental vibration. When the overtones are "in tune"—when their frequencies represent integral (or whole-number) multiples of their fundamental—they are called harmonics. Many primitive tribes in the world, including the pygmies and bushmen of Africa, sing and play only intervals of the harmonic series which, according to Indian legend, is a gift from the gods. And La Monte enthuses, "The harmonic series is everywhere. It's in this room, in the harmonies of our vocal cords, in our ears, in the electronics we use. It's throughout our knowledge of universal structure."

Young's "Drift Studies" dramatize the profundity of harmonic sound vibrations. He tunes two or more sine-wave oscillators to resonate a certain interval or series of intervals from the harmonic series and leaves them on for an indefinite period. Walk around the room where the waves or a recording of them are playing and you hear pitch changes according to high- and low-pressure areas. Surprisingly, they change even when you sit still. They are drifting slowly in and out of phase, so that "the composite wave form of the combination tones of the two sine waves gradually, internally and organically, shifts. And, your whole concentration being locked in with these frequencies, you get very subtle changes. The body intuitively recognizes that information having to do with basic universal structure is coming in as sound."

Scales extracted from a harmonic series can be used to construct unusually affecting melodies. Even the sound of a single interval between two harmonically related tones is naturally pleasing to the ear, which explains why virtually all European music prior to the sixteenth century was sung and played according to the tunings based on the harmonic series. Then J. S. Bach, one of our first keyboard-oriented (as opposed to voice-oriented) composers, hit on well-tempered tuning as an aid in modulating from key to key. This tuning developed into meantone and eventually into equal temperament, the standard Western tuning for the past 150 years. In equal temperament the acoustically perfect octave (perfect because high C, for example, represents exactly twice the vibrations per second of middle C) is divided into twelve equidistant tones that approximate but do not conform to the overtones of the natural harmonic series. The mathematical intricacy of the harmonic series does not coincide with rigid subdivision of the octave. Without equal temperament European music as we know it, with its distinctive harmonic language, would have been impossible to achieve. But with it, as even Arnold Schoenberg admitted, having a musical ear means "to have an ear in the *musical* sense, not in the *natural* sense."

La Monte prefers the mathematical perfection of the overtone series to the acoustically imperfect compromise of equal temperament. In his Dream House he starts with basic sine waves—simple frequencies without overtones—and then builds the harmonic series back up component by component, emphasizing various elements as he sees fit. In his *The Well-Tuned Piano*—obviously a jibe at Bach's *The Well-Tempered Clavier*—he retunes the piano so that it conforms to the harmonic series. He then plays a series of partially improvised rhythmic and melodic variations, using what he calls "permutation combinations between the individual fingers, which I situate over particular combinations of notes." First realized in 1964 and first performed before an audience ten years later, *The Well-Tuned Piano* is without a doubt La Monte Young's masterpiece.

The work lasts three hours without breaks, but there is no fidgeting when it's performed. Once in a while Young gathers a few people who are interested in hearing it—they are likely to include critics, gallery owners, and various friends and musicians—and puts on a recording of the piece's world premiere in Rome. The first thing that strikes you is that the sound is not that of a piano at all. It seems to change from one instant to the next, from zither to lyre to sitar to orchestra of mandolins to choir. The listeners simply sit on the floor and . . . listen, as if a new world had suddenly opened up. By changing the piano's tuning, Young has radically altered the nature of the instrument.

He will be recording *The Well-Tuned Piano* soon, and a new LP consisting of a Drift Study and a forty-minute Dream House sequence is available on the French Shandar label. You probably won't find it or any of his earlier recordings and published writings in your local book or record store. "It's very hard for a commercial record company to work with me," he explains, "because I'm absolutely uncompromising. I have to have complete say over what goes on every record and what the cover is going to be, how it's going to be promoted, everything. No really big commercial record company will have anything to do with that approach: They're all afraid they're taking a big chance on me to begin with."

La Monte laughs and pulls gently at his beard. "Not that I'm unfriendly and not nice and illogical. None of that. It's just that if I can't put out something that really represents me, I don't want my name on it."

On this point Young will not be moved, which leaves him in the position of being an unheard major composer. His formative influence on an entire generation of composers is unquestioned and he already occupies an honored place in history books such as Peter Yates's definitive *Twentieth Century Music*. He performs frequently in European and American museums and galleries, and he admits that he would rather enjoy singing with his sine-wave drones and performing his piano piece than dealing with the details involved in making commercial recordings. A remark he made in the course of a 1960 lecture sums up his involvement in experiencing the essence of the here and now. "Once I tried lots of mustard on a raw turnip," he said. "I liked it better than any Beethoven I had ever heard."

Terry Riley: Doctor of Improvised Surgery

DOWN BEAT | NOVEMBER 20, 1975

Terry Riley's "In C" has proved to be the single most influential post-1960 composition by an American. George Crumb and the other American post-serialists have their corps of adherents; Ornette Coleman, Cecil Taylor, and other composers of Black Classical Music have had a profound, worldwide impact, but their improvisational procedures have been more influential than any one of their compositions. "In C," on the other hand, has inspired a unique range of responses from artists working in a variety of areas. Some of the better-known American composers whose work would be much different had Riley not written "In C" include Philip Glass, Steve Reich, and Frederic Rzewski. Several pop groups and figures, including Soft Machine, John Cale, and Eno, have borrowed heavily from Riley. Echoes of his structural ideas and keyboard sonorities are evident in some contemporary jazz.

"In C" consists of fifty-three melodic/rhythmic motives, most of them as short and simple as a whole note or a group of six or eight sixteenths. It can be played by an ensemble of any composition and size. The musicians begin by playing the figures consecutively, but each one proceeds at his own speed, so that the melodic kernels soon begin to overlap in wild profusion, forming constantly shifting prismatic relationships with each other. Within the apparent stasis of a single key signature and the repetition of simple figures, a sound universe of infinite variety emerges, a universe whose content will be quite different each time the piece is performed.

In other words, "In C" is not just a score; it is a template or blueprint for collective improvisation. For this reason, Riley's work has often been compared to jazz, and, indeed, his career has touched and responded to developments in jazz in several illuminating ways. He worked his way through college playing ragtime piano in the Gold Street Saloon on San Francisco's Barbary Coast. His first major composition involved a collaboration with trumpeter Chet Baker, and he was inspired to use the soprano saxophone by hearing John Coltrane. So, although Eastern music has had a considerable impact on him, Riley is a truly American musician. He is now a self-contained composer/improviser. When he performs his "Rising Moonshine Dervishes" on Yamaha organ with tape delay, the music shimmers like light rays bending in a haze. Compact melodic kernels shift in relationship to each other over a series of kinetic ostinato bass lines; the musical processes expounded in "In C" have been refined and condensed into a framework for solo improvisations which are mesmerizing and breathtakingly lyrical.

This interview occurred in New York, where Terry had been performing his *Dervishes* improvisations for a week as part of a two-month-long "Dream Festival" sponsored by the Dia Art Foundation.

Tell me about your earliest musical experiences.
OK, I'll see what I can remember. I was born in Colfax, California, in 1935, and grew up in Redding. My mother and father were not musicians, but I was always doing music; almost before I could talk I could sing all the songs on the radio. Most of my youth I spent growing up in the sticks, away from cultural centers, and the music I heard was mainly popular and country and western. I had a few classical piano teachers when I was little, but I didn't go to any big cities or get serious about my piano studies

until I went to San Francisco State, when I was eighteen. Then I started doing recitals and composing music for piano and for chamber groups, influenced mainly by French music: Debussy, Ravel, Milhaud. Poulenc. And by Bartok. And then I got exposed to Schoenberg and Webern and I began to write chromatic pieces, imitating their sound. But twelve-tone music just didn't feel good. It was too full of anxiety, too dark; it had such a narrow range.

Then you met La Monte Young? [Young is the founding father of the so-called static or hypnotic school of American composers. He now lives in New York and directs the Theater of Eternal Music.]
I met La Monte around 1960; we were in a composition seminar at UC-Berkeley together and we became very close. I heard his *String Trio* (a work which takes five minutes to present four notes), and the long tones and general feeling had a profound influence on me. He used to talk in those days about getting inside a note, inside the sound. I felt very sympathetic toward what he was trying to do and we started working together, as musical directors for Ann Halprin, the dancer. There wasn't much electronic music around; we made sounds by resonating floors and windows, scraping wood and metal, Zen-type things, and she danced to them.

Then La Monte came to New York and I stayed on in California, finishing up my degree. I got some cheap Wollensak tape recorders and began working with tape loops. Then when I went to Europe after getting my MA the idea of the loops, the repetition, and the different cycles all came together, stayed in my mind, even though I had no equipment. While I was traveling around Europe, playing piano, making happenings, I had only two records with me. One was a French BAM recording of Moroccan music, dervish-type stuff from the Atlas mountains, very repetitious and hypnotic. The other one was *Cookin' with the Miles Davis Quintet.*

So you were already into the idea of slow changes within repeating cycles, and into improvisation.
Yes, I feel like I got into those areas partially through my association with La Monte, partially through my travels, and partially through my own temperament. I visited Morocco and was very impressed with the music,

but I think the main reason I started doing this kind of music was that my own spirit felt happy with it. I could do it for a long time and still feel good, still feel balanced and centered.

In 1963, just before I left Europe, I did a piece by taping Chet Baker's band playing and then cutting the parts up. In other words, I recorded all the instruments separately and then re-formed the parts. They were playing Miles's "So What" with that bass figure, and I took the bass part and stacked it up so that I had six layers of bass, and then I looped it, put it through delays, things like that, so that by the time I had finished putting the piece together there were like twenty trumpets, fifteen basses. That's when I started really working with long-term tape delay and with loops, and after I started on my way back to the States I decided I'd like to try the same ideas purely with instruments, no tapes. I started making sketches and then one night after I was back in California I started hearing the whole first line of "In C." It just sort of came into my ear and I wrote it down and then started working it out from there, using the techniques I'd developed in Paris. The next fall, '64, it was premiered at the San Francisco Tape Music Center.

I wanted to go back to Europe and Morocco after that. I was going to get a boat from New York and instead I ended up staying here four or five years. For a while I played with the Theater of Eternal Music, La Monte's group, and then I decided there was a sound I wanted to get with the soprano saxophone. I'd been listening to Coltrane a lot and was very much in love with his soprano sound, so I got one and started teaching myself to play it and combined that with the ideas I'd worked on with the Chet Baker group. I got a couple of tape recorders and started playing through them with delay. That piece "Poppy Nogood" which I recorded for Columbia is something I used to play in various forms at concerts for four or five years. ["Poppy Nogood and the Phantom Band" is on Riley's *A Rainbow in Curved Air*. It was released in 1968 as his second Columbia Masterworks LP, the first having been *In C*, released a year earlier.]

"Poppy Nogood" reminds me of festival music from cities in Morocco, when you hear double-reed horns that sound like your soprano, playing from the minarets of mosques and echoing off the buildings, but A *Rainbow in Curved Air* sounds more like what you're doing now with the *Der-*

vishes series. But while you were doing these improvisational concerts, "In C" was getting a lot of attention. *Glamour* called it "the global village's first ritual symphonic piece." Wasn't there a certain amount of pressure on you to come up with the global village's *second* ritual symphony?

Well, I saw at the time that the opportunity was open to me to go on and do "In A" and "In B♭" and make each one more and more elaborate. But I felt that "In C" was really complete, that it's the beginning and the end of an idea. A lot of people have tried to rewrite it, but I haven't. In fact, I never wrote any more music after that; I started improvising. For me, improvisation has become the important element in the music, the real thing that breathes inspiration and life into it.

When did you start doing the *Dervishes* pieces? Was "Persian Surgery Dervishes" the first?
Yes. I started working on that before *A Rainbow in Curved Air*, but I didn't record it then. The first germ of the idea was an earlier piece called "The Keyboard Studies," which I started around 1965.

How would you describe the structure of the *Dervishes* improvisations?
Well, the pieces started with just a four-note motive, which started to define a mode. I used to play a very simple version of just permutations on the four notes F, B, A♭, and D. Then, a long time later, I . . . added C. (Laughter) As I kept playing it, I tried to tie it together into an overall rhythmic structure; that slow, underlying beat you hear in the left hand is a 16-beat basic pattern. I use the tape recorder to give me an echo, one delay after the original signal, and I integrate that into the melodies and patterns that I'm playing. I work out a series of inter-related patterns within the mode that are varied with constantly shifting alignments. That is, I move the patterns against themselves, and sometimes I do the same thing with one hand playing double speed. One of the patterns in "Persian Surgery Dervishes" is forty beats long, and when you start moving that one around against itself it becomes pretty difficult. Actually, a lot of the devices I use are just contrapuntal devices that have been with us for centuries, but the application is different from what anyone did before. I think that's the thing in my music that's been most interesting to people writing music now. It's given them a new tool to work with.

If the mode and the patterns are fixed, to what degree are the performances improvisational?

I almost hate to talk about it, you know? I feel so metaphysical about music that I almost hate to talk about it in any kind of way. To a certain degree I work everything out, right? I work out many fixed, set patterns, but as I'm playing along, I never know what's going to happen next. Suddenly I'll bring in themes that I never imagined, or I'll start accenting in different ways or recombining patterns differently. You can hear the structure going by, you can hear one idea evolving into another, transformations taking place, but it's very difficult to say what the structure is in words. Every time I play it seems to happen differently, and that's the magic of improvising, for any improvising musician.

When I heard you do "Rising Moonshine Dervishes" last night, I kept thinking of "moonshine" in terms of mountain stills. I was getting this mountain music, Louisiana hayride imagery.

That's true, the harmonic structure of that piece has a lot of mountain-type chords in it, I and IV are the predominant chords which are worked into the modal fabric of the music. I was thinking of calling it mountain something. But titles are just icing on the cake. Sometimes a title will happen, like *A Rainbow In Curved Air* gave an image of space and so on to the music. But on the other hand, you can just throw a title on something that you called something else the week before, just to satisfy people who have to call it something.

What's the significance of the *Dervishes* titles?

The reason I use the word "dervishes" is that I really admire the saints and dervishes. They have all forms, just like God, who has every form and shape, so the titles are just my imagination, images of saints taking their ethereal forms.

What about your equipment? The organ you use seems to have some of the capabilities of a synthesizer.

The Yamaha organ I use has a touch-sensitive keyboard. There's a stop that allows the tones to rise and fall about a quarter tone above and below the pitch by moving your finger to the left or right. Also, there's a touch-sensitive harmonic shaper so that you can increase or decrease the harmonics by using the key laterally. And I had variable resistors added, so each oscillator is variable up to about a tone and a half.

Do you tune to harmonic relationships outside tempered pitch?
Yes. When you get them, the organs are tuned to equal temperament, and in modal music that's really a hindrance. You'd have to have something like fifty-three notes to the octave to be able to modulate easily in just intonation [a tuning system in which intervals are "spread" to conform to the harmonic overtones of a single tone, rather than "pinched" to produce twelve equidistant semi-tones as in equal temperament, the tuning system used in Western concert music]. But you don't have to modulate in modal music. You have only a few tones and you want to hear them clearly in tune, so they all have to be adjusted separately. That's why I had the oscillators put on.

This is another area where I owe a lot to La Monte. He's done a lot of work in tuning, as you know from hearing "The Well-Tuned Piano" [a Young composition for piano retuned into just intonation]. I learned a lot from working in his group during the mid-sixties, and from his studies in Indian music, in regard to tuning. It allows you to slow down your pace and really savor each note that you're playing, which is something I could never do when I was playing tempered instruments. On an equal-tempered piano you hold down a chord as it goes wahwahwah, you know, beating. It feels very unstable. That may be one of the reasons why Western music in general is so jumpy; because of the instability of the tuning you just want to get it on and create a lot of movement, so that you don't notice the beats between the notes. It's especially true of music dominated by the piano.

One thing I'm doing with the Yamaha is tuning two sets of tonics and dominants, so that a beat that's about a second and a half in duration separates the two tonics and the two dominants. When you press them down together you get a kind of phasing effect, because the beats actually make a separation in the sound. You hear that a lot in Southeast Asian music; they consider the beats within the music, that shimmering effect, to be a holy feeling, and they use them very precisely to create effects. In the case of the organ, it makes it sound more orchestral.

What was your knowledge of Indian music when you began working in these areas?

I had hardly any. I had heard Ravi Shankar and Ali Akbar Khan play a couple of times, there were a few recordings, but even later, after I'd heard Indian music a lot, I still didn't consider seriously studying it. I found it interesting, but I wasn't that strongly influenced by it. But then this tape came over of [Indian vocalist] Pandit Pran Nath, and there was a different feeling in his music, certainly. There's no question in my mind that he's the greatest musician walking around today.

I know that La Monte has been studying with him for a long time. When did you start?

In 1970. I stayed with him in India for about six months to get a good start on it. One of the possibilities in music that I couldn't see before I started studying with him is in the area of the tone itself, which is something that isn't considered too strongly in Western music. There's a great science in India having to do with this study, because, since they have only a melody over a drone, the melody has to be quite sophisticated. So they have an incredible sophistication relating to the notes themselves, all the different shadings that are involved to color the ragas. This has helped me adjust the organ for the tones that I really want to hear, not just the ones from the factory. But it's more than that. Working with him is like tuning up the whole being. You can't isolate it to the ear or the throat. It's like as a person you become more finely tuned, because you live a little bit differently to try to do everything a little bit more consciously.

Actually, I've had a lot of criticism because of my studies with Pandit Pran Nath. People seem to be afraid of a cultural invasion, afraid their artists are going to lose their integrity and go scampering off after some charlatan. It has something to do with the idea that's so common here that you have to get bigger, do more, going back to what you were saying about writing the second global symphony or whatever. It's the Madison Avenue sell. Whereas, what studying with Pandit Pran Nath has done is made me go deeper into the thing I was already doing in order to try to make it more and more profound. The goal is to deepen the effect of the music, not just to do cosmetic work on it.

What kind of effect do you expect your music to have? Do you want to create specific moods and emotions in the way that specific ragas do in Indian music? Are you after a hypnotic effect?

I guess I don't think of it in quite that way. You do try to have an effect on your listeners, but first of all you have to create the effect on yourself. To me a musician really has a chance to create magic whenever he's playing, and I find it really rare and inspiring to play for people. Sure I want to create a kind of hypnotic effect on the public. I want to create a kind of concentration on a musical idea so that people can go inside themselves and comfortably follow the development, until they slowly rise up and disappear into the clouds.

Liner Notes for *Einstein on the Beach* by Philip Glass

(Tomato, 1979)

"I remember reading a letter of Mozart's," Philip Glass mused. He was sitting at the kitchen table in the corner of a friend's loft in lower Manhattan, taking a break from rehearsing his ensemble of electric organs and woodwinds. He looked comfortable—craggy, engaging face, checkered shirt, jeans, white socks, and battered loafers—and the music, part of his score for *Einstein on the Beach*, felt comfortable, even though following its whirlwind of repetitions and pattern shifts required stamina and absolute attention from his musicians. The players—Dickie Landry, Jon Gibson, Richard Peck, Michael Riesman, Iris Hiskey, and Kurt Munkacsi—were scattered around the loft talking music, jazz, and what have you. And here was Glass, thinking out loud about the eighteenth century.

"In this letter," he continued, "Mozart commented that in every coffee shop, people were singing arias from *The Marriage of Figaro*. There was a time when there wasn't this tremendous distance between the popular audience and concert music, and I think we're approaching that stage again. For a long while we had this very small band of practitioners of modern music who described themselves as mathematicians, doing theoretical work that would someday be understood. I don't think anyone takes that very seriously anymore. There was a time, too, when Paganini, Liszt, Berlioz made their living playing. I would like to think that we're entering a period again when concert musicians, people who are concerned in a progressive way with musical ideas, are involved in that."

If the interest of popular musicians is any indication, the era of the serious composer as performing musician and pop hero is already upon us. Ever since he performed at the Royal College of Art in London, in 1970, Glass has numbered David Bowie and Brian Eno among his fans. His kind of music—it has been called solid state, minimalist, and trance music, images from the world of electronic circuitry, the visual arts, and non-Western ritual music that may help illuminate what he does but do not quite define it—is a worldwide influence in progressive rock. You can hear some Glass, some Terry Riley, some Steve Reich, and some La Monte Young in Tangerine Dream, Pink Floyd, and dozens of other rock bands. But as talk at the kitchen table veered from Mozart to rock, Glass insisted, "There's one important distinction between pop and concert music; I think it's the only important distinction."

He shifted in his chair, running a hand through his short but tangled hair. "When you talk about concert musicians, you're talking about people who actually invent language. They create values, a value being a unit of meaning that is new and different. Pop musicians package language. I don't think there's anything wrong with packaging languages; some of that can be very good music. I realized long ago that people were going to make money off my ideas in a way that I'm not capable of or interested in doing. It doesn't bother me; the two kinds of music are just different. One thing these English and German groups *have* done, though, they've taken the language of our music and made it much more accessible. It's been helpful. If people had only heard Fleetwood Mac this music would sound like music from outer space."

Ever since the Philip Glass–Robert Wilson opera *Einstein on the Beach* was given two sold-out performances at New York's Metropolitan

Opera House, ever since a progressive rock label released Glass's album *North Star*, ever since he gave a concert at Carnegie Hall and sold the place out, critics have been saying that he is a "crossover" phenomenon (music-business jargon for a minority-appeal artist who suddenly connects with a mass audience).

Glass insists that this is not quite true. "The record companies are crossing over," he said, "the audience is crossing over, but I'm not. I began writing a certain way because I've always been interested in the grammar of music, in the way it fits together. I'm a serious composer, but I'm working at a time when audiences no longer assume strong and exclusive allegiances to one musical style. The significant thing isn't what's happening to me, it's what's happening to audiences."

What's happening is an important shift in the way Western concert music is composed, performed, and appreciated. The roots of this shift can be traced back to John Cage, who turned the thoughts of American composers in an eastward direction and helped create an atmosphere in which anything that was possible might possibly be called music. But it began in earnest in the mid-sixties. Glass was studying with Allah Rakha, the Indian virtuoso of the tabla drums. Through this association he became involved with the Indian sitarist Ravi Shankar; who hired him to help in the scoring of a film. "My ideas wouldn't have developed the way they did if I hadn't started in that place," Glass says. "Also, I traveled in Morocco, where I had my first contact with non-Western music and was influenced by the geometric repetitions in Islamic art. Then in Asia I would stay in Himalayan villages for two or three weeks without seeing another Westerner. Later I became interested in South Indian music and in West African drumming."

By 1966 Glass was composing music in a nascent version of the style that flowers in *Einstein on the Beach*. He didn't know it at the time, but at least three composers who were then living in California were working on similarly influenced music. La Monte Young had developed earlier and was already well along on a personal path, more involved with the perception of harmonic resonances than with the repetition of rhythm. Nevertheless, he would emerge as something of a father figure to the movement. Terry Riley, an early associate of Young's, had composed "In C," the first orchestral work in the new idiom, in 1964, and he attracted more attention than any of the other young composers working in the field later in the sixties, when Columbia Masterworks recorded both *In C* and his *A Rainbow in Curved Air*. The third composer, Steve Reich, played in Glass's ensemble in New York from 1968 until 1970, when he first put together his own ensemble of pianos, mallet instruments, winds, and voices. He now records for the ECM label.

In retrospect, it seems inevitable that some of the brightest young minds in American music would have been profoundly affected by the cultural currents of the mid-sixties. After all, superficial influences from Indian music were already creeping into pop through the Beatles' experiments, and Cage and a number of artists working in other media had been saying for some time that so-called primitivism often proves highly sophisticated while Western complexity often masks banality or simplemindedness. But at the time, the development of a trance or minimalist or solid state school of American composers did not seem to be a foregone conclusion at all. In fact, it was unimaginable. Classical music changes at a glacial pace compared to pop music and jazz, and in the mid-sixties its progressive wing fell rather neatly into two opposing camps. On the one hand, the serialists were in the process of reducing every element in music—melody, harmony, rhythm, timbre, and so on—to a series of mathematical formulae. On the other hand, Cage and his followers and successors were championing indeterminacy, happenstance, improvisation. And never the twain did meet.

Glass could easily have ended up in one camp or the other. Certainly he started conventionally enough. He was a precocious student, beginning his studies at the Peabody Conservatory in his native Baltimore when he was eight and entering the University of Chicago at fifteen. Between 1957 and 1961 he was a composition student at Juilliard, and after graduation he received a grant from the Ford Foundation to be composer-in-residence with the Pittsburgh public school system. His grant was renewed in 1963–64, and by this time he was writing pieces in the accepted academic serialist manner that found ready publishers in America and Europe. In 1964 Glass was awarded a Fulbright grant for study in Paris with Boulanger.

But Allah Rakha, who taught Glass the additive principles of Indian rhythmic structure that he has drawn on in his subsequent compositions, and Ravi Shankar had more effect on the budding composer than Boulanger, and when he returned to New York in 1967 Glass began performing his new music of hypnotically repeating rhythmic modules and cool, spare textures. In the fall of 1968 he formed his first ensemble of amplified keyboards and winds, with Jon Gibson and Dickie Landry as early members along with Steve Reich and Arthur Murphy. Unfortunately, the foundations that had helped when he was composing conventional music were profoundly uninterested in these new developments. The support he had enjoyed dried up, but he stuck to his guns, working days and rehearsing in lofts in downtown Manhattan at night. The word that he was making a mesmerizing new music spread, but it spread slowly. He formed his own record company, Chatham Square Productions, in 1971, issuing two albums of his own music and several others by the members of his group, most of whom are accomplished and individual composers as well as performers. It wasn't until 1974 that a "real" record company, Virgin Records of England, developed an interest in his work. Eventually, Virgin released parts one and two of his *Music in Twelve Parts* and an album of short pieces for a film about the sculptor Mark di Suvero, *North Star.*

Glass and his ensemble have toured Europe a dozen times since 1970; this goes a long way toward explaining his influence on European progressive rock. Recognition has not been as rapid in the U.S. For a long time Glass's supporters were mainly allied with the visual arts, and it is easy enough to find similarities between his music and, say, the painting of Kenneth Noland. But Glass's music is not at all difficult to listen to or to comprehend, quite the opposite in fact. "It's a music that has consciously reduced its means harmonically and melodically in favor of a structural clarity," he says, "a music that tends to be fairly consistent in terms of meter and tempo." Its harmonies are simpler than the harmonies used by your average pop songwriter. The music does seem to repeat a few ideas for a very long time, but as Andrew Porter noted in a review of *Einstein on the Beach* that appeared in *The New Yorker*, "Glass's score may be incantatory, but it is not lulling. . . . A listener to his music usually reaches a point, quite early on, of rebellion at the needle-stuck-in-the-groove quality, but a minute or two later he realizes that the needle has not stuck; something has happened. Once that point has passed, Glass's music—or so I find—becomes easy to listen to for hours on end. The mind may wander now and again, but it wanders within a new sound world that the composer has created."

With a few word changes, Porter's observations will serve as an introduction to the world of Robert Wilson, whose theatrical spectacles seem on the surface to be as repetitious as Glass's music and which one ends up wandering within rather than watching. Of course, it is Glass's music one hears on these records, but *Einstein on the Beach* as experienced on the stage is a true collaboration between Glass and the man Eugene Ionesco recently called America's most important dramatist. Like Glass, Wilson developed his methods during the middle and late sixties. Like Glass, Wilson is concerned with apparent motionlessness and endless durations during which dreams are dreamed and significant matters are understood. Like Glass, Wilson has found a group of dedicated performers to help him bring his vision to life.

Robert Wilson's pre-theatrical background was in painting and architecture, and as *The New York Times*'s John Rockwell has observed, "his stage works are massive, hypnotic theatrical pictures." The first of Wilson's major pieces, *The King of Spain*, began its life in 1969 at New York's Anderson Theatre. It was absorbed into a longer work, *The Life and Times of Sigmund Freud*, and Wilson went on to explore extremely long durations. *The Life and Times of Joseph Stalin*, which was presented at the Brooklyn Academy of Music in 1974, ran for twelve hours, and *Ka Mountain and Guardenia Terrace: A Story about Family and Some People Changing* ran continuously for seven days and nights at the 1972 Shiraz festival in Iran.

Wilson's other works have included *A Letter to Queen Victoria*, *The $ Value of Man*, and the celebrated *Deafman's Glance*, but his examinations of seminal twentieth-century figures—Freud, Stalin, and Einstein—have seemed to cluster in a class by themselves. Actually, they are not historical nor even particularly analytical. "Wilson's Einstein," wrote Jack Kroll in *Newsweek*, "is, like his Freud and Stalin, not so much a historical figure as a resonator, a magnetic catalyst creating a new gravitational field in human experience." Another way of looking at Wilson's operas is as meditations, with their central figures serving as mantras. However one conceives them, the event is only partly onstage. Part of it, perhaps the most significant part, is triggered by Wilson's images but takes place in the viewer's mind.

Einstein on the Beach is the tightest and most visually striking of Wilson's operas. (It may strike some readers that calling them operas is stretching the point, but this is what Wilson calls them, and technically, *opera* simply means "work.") It revolves around three recurring visual images, each of which has its corresponding music. There are trains, recalling the toy trains Einstein played with as a child and the trains he later used as analogies to illustrate his theory of relativity. A trial scene that includes a bed seems to resonate with the awesome implications of Einstein's discoveries. Did he ponder, while in bed at night, the threat of atomic catastrophe that his work had helped unleash? Might he have imagined himself, or modern science, on trial? The third image, representing, perhaps, the potential for liberation and transcendence that Einstein also unleashed, is a spaceship. But all the images are really more complex than these descriptions indicate, as dreams tend to be. The trial bogs down in the banalities muttered by a senile judge, and the spaceship is linked in some way to the nuclear apocalypse suggested by the opera's title—a reference to Nevil Shute's novel of nuclear holocaust, *On the Beach*. And then there is a fourth image, Einstein himself. The real Einstein often played the violin for relaxation, and in Wilson's opera he is seen periodically, standing apart from the action, observing it while fiddling like a thoughtful, tousle-headed Nero.

"*Einstein*," wrote Andrew Porter, "is precisely organized, tautly patterned, economical in its forces, and austere in its decor." The organization, the patterning, the decor, along with the images themselves, make up the content of Wilson's work, serving the functions that plot, characterization, and narrative exposition serve in more conventional operas. This nondidactic approach means that Wilson's staging, direction, and design and Glass's music can fuse into a single experience, an experience in which structure and substance are one and the same and the "picture" is completed by the listener/viewer.

Glass indicates in his notes to *Einstein on the Beach* that the music grew out of a series of works called *Another Look at Harmony* which he began composing in 1975. "In my earlier work," he explained one afternoon shortly before his first Carnegie Hall concert, "I took rhythmic structure and made it more or less the subject of the work. In *Music in Twelve Parts*, for example, each part is almost a catalog of rhythmic techniques that create overall structure. But in *Another Look at Harmony*, I tried to find a way of linking rhythmic structure with harmonic structures and rhythmic 'interest.'" In other words, the music is still "about" its own structure but the language is richer than in Glass's earlier work. Using relatively austere means, the composer has created a music of remarkable color and depth.

The New York Times's John Rockwell hears in this music a "mixture of mathematical clarity and mystical allure," and this mixture is the source of its great fascination and power. Any music that ignores the principles of order and simply expresses raw emotions must seem inadequate for this scientific age, and yet the contemplation of the transcendent probably plays a greater part in our lives than at any time since the dawn of the age of rationalism. So one listens to the music, just as one watches Wilson's shifting tableaux, and somehow, without quite knowing it, one crosses the line from being puzzled or irritated to being absolutely bewitched. The experience is inexplicable but utterly satisfying, and one could not ask for anything more than that.

Dream Music: Jon Hassell and Anthony Davis

PENTHOUSE | APRIL 1982

In 1935, in the remote highlands of central Malaya, an anthropologist named Kilton Stewart discovered a tribe of twelve thousand aborigines that had not experienced a single violent crime or instance of mental disease in several hundred years. The Senoi, as they were called, had no equivalents of police or jails, their society operating in a smoothly democratic manner with a striking absence of even minor frictions. They were ruled not by elders or royalty but by dream interpreters, seers who shared their detailed knowledge of dream symbolism and trance states with everyone in the community. These seers had developed a complex science of dream analysis that, according to Stewart, was "on a level with our attainments in such areas as television and nuclear physics."

Children everywhere dream disturbing dreams of falling. But among the Senoi, each family discusses the dreams of all its members over breakfast each morning, and children who have had falling dreams are told by their parents that the dreams are about learning to fly. This positive reinforcement is repeated each time the child dreams of falling, and before long fearful dreams of falling are replaced by pleasurable dreams of flying. Adolescent and adult dreamers receive detailed instructions on how to deal with sex dreams; it's very important, for example, to carry a sexual encounter in the dream state through to orgasm. Stewart reported that this communal focus on dream interpretation and dream lore produced well-balanced individuals and a well-integrated society.

Jon Hassell's latest album, *Dream Theory in Malaya* (Editions E.G.), is a musical portrait of the Senoi and their dream culture, inspired by Kilton Stewart's anthropological paper of the same name. Hassell is uniquely qualified for the task. He grew up in Memphis, where he played the trumpet in roadhouses, and after taking several university degrees he left for Europe to study with the pioneering electronic music composer Karlheinz Stockhausen. Back in the United States, he played his trumpet with La Monte Young and Terry Riley, the two creators of the minimal, repetition-oriented new classical music of the sixties and seventies. In 1972 he began studying the classical vocal music of northern India with a master singer, but instead of reproducing Indian music's swoops, glides, and curlicues with his voice, he found ways of reproducing them on the trumpet. His playing began sounding like a kind of hollow, disembodied spirit voice, and within a few years he was feeding it through a variety of electronics systems, getting unearthly sounds that had never been imagined. He called this synthesis of the ancient and the futuristic "fourth-world music," and an album he made in collaboration with the rock producer and electronics whiz Brian Eno, *Fourth World Volume One/Possible Musics* (Editions E.G.), became a surprising success in 1980. It won him a loyal audience and ended up on a number of music critics' year-end ten-best lists.

Dream Theory in Malaya is the eagerly awaited follow-up to *Possible Musics*. The earlier album had a more even, trancelike flow and an ethereal texture. Its principal ethnic influences were Indian and African. *Dream Theory* is a different sort of trance music, rooted in Southeast Asia, where trance rituals tend to be communal and dramatic. The rhythmic underpinnings of the music are provided by bowl gongs and pottery drums, and Hassell's remarkable trumpet playing, which can sound like a baby uttering its first words or like an angel choir bursting into song, has been filtered through some of the most sophisticated effects systems modern electronics can provide. Tapes of frogs in a bog and of Malayan tribesmen beating out rhythms in the flowing waters of a stream are woven into the music like shimmering threads, lending it an almost subliminal aliveness that warmly tempers the potentially cold electronics. The result is sheer magic. *Dream Theory in Malaya* is an invitation to step into another reality, a trip you don't need drugs to take.

Hassell isn't the only American musician whose work has been heavily influenced by the dream culture of Southeast Asia. Anthony Davis, widely recognized as the most gifted young jazz pianist to have emerged in the last decade, is busy making a new music inspired by the music of Bali, especially the floating, repetitious gong-and-xylophone music that accompanies the island's shadow puppet plays. *Episteme* (Gramavision Records, 260 West Broadway, New York, NY 10013) is light-years removed from Jon Hassell's fourth-world concepts. It uses no electronics, as Davis prefers to work with an entirely acoustic ensemble of vibraphone, marimba, percussion, strings, and horns.

But Davis, recently turned thirty, is already a masterful composer, able to extract shimmering, sleepwalking moods and textures from his ten-piece ensemble. Melodic figures repeat, fall against each other in shifting overlay patterns, seem to bend as if refracted through a haze, and eventually break down into thoughtful improvisations that sustain and amplify the written music. This isn't jazz, although a marvelous jazz drummer, Pheeroan Ak Laff, kicks it along. It isn't exactly new classical music either; there's too much swing and too much improvisation. It's another kind of fourth-world music, a fruitful melding of East and West. "I have made no attempt to imitate Balinese music," Davis insists in his liner notes. "The music has inspired me to look at my own musical tradition in a different way."

Why has the music of Southeast Asia had such a profound effect on two of America's most resourceful young musicians? The most obvious answer is that in Malaya, Bali, and Java, music is a means of bringing on and regulating altered states of consciousness or trance; in the words of folklorist E. D. Robertson: "This is a people amongst whom inspiration is still a very living thing." Robertson made a series of recordings in central Malaya of songs "given" to the Temiar people in dreams, by spirit guides.

He reported that during one session, a seer "went into a trance, for some minutes remaining in a kneeling position; he then leapt up, rushed to one of the fires, and picked up glowing embers, which he put into his mouth; he then rejoined the dancers, and danced around for some minutes with the red-hot embers between his lips."

Robertson's recordings can be heard on the Folkways album *Temiar Dream Songs from Malaya*. But heard out of their cultural context, these dream songs do not sound half as enchanting as the fourth-world dream music of Hassell and Davis. By combining the trance-inducing properties of Southeast Asian music with the latest advances in electronic music and jazz, they have come up with a new music that transcends all its sources, a music that carries the listener away to realms where inspiration is truly "a very living thing."

SONIC GUITAR MAELSTROM: "ALL HAIL THE OVERDRIVEN AMP."

To Otis Rush, the Guitar Is a Second Voice for the Blues

THE NEW YORK TIMES | FEBRUARY 26, 1982

Blues guitarists speak a language all their own. The broad outlines of the language are the same whether the guitarist plays screaming electric lead guitar or carries on an almost private conversation with himself on a battered acoustic instrument. But each guitarist has his own special way of using the language and it identifies him as unmistakably as a fingerprint.

Otis Rush, who is appearing at Tramps, can attack a note a certain way or press a guitar string just so hard and say precisely what he wants to say. When he is inspired, he bends and twists each note in a phrase so delicate that his instrument seems to be forming actual words. And perhaps it is. Blues guitarists have been "making the guitar talk" since the shadowy beginnings of the blues, sometime around the turn of the century. A guitarist of Mr. Rush's caliber can communicate so tellingly with his instrument that the words to the songs he sings are reduced to a kind of subtext. Mr. Rush sings a lot of familiar, tradition-encrusted blues standards anyway. It is the quality and feeling of his guitar playing, the fine points of the way he uses the language, that let the listener know how he is feeling and what he is thinking about on a particular night.

Although he grew up on a farm near Philadelphia, Mississippi, where he was born on April 29, 1934, Mr. Rush learned to sing and play the blues by listening to phonograph records. Philadelphia is in Mississippi's hill country, and when Mr. Rush was growing up, the state's live blues was concentrated in the Delta farmland to the west. When he was fourteen, Mr. Rush moved with his family to Chicago, where he was able to catch club performances by Muddy Waters and B. B. King, who were from the Mississippi Delta, and the influential Texas-born guitarist T-Bone Walker. These were his principal influences.

Mr. Rush was a powerful singer with a lot of gospel influence and a rudimentary guitarist when he began performing in low-rent Chicago blues bars in the mid-1950s. On several of his earliest recordings, most notably the classic slow blues "Double Trouble" from 1956, he let a more accomplished guitarist, Ike Turner, take the lead. But he worked at his guitar playing, studying the recordings of jazz guitarists like Kenny Burrell and taking lessons from a successful Chicago studio musician, Reggie Boyd. By 1965, when Mr. Rush recorded several numbers for a Vanguard Records anthology called *Chicago/The Blues/Today*, he was a formidable guitarist. That recording, along with the singles he cut for Chicago's Cobra and Chess labels in the late fifties and early sixties, made him a favorite with an entire generation of young white blues and rock guitarists, including Eric Clapton, Duane Allman, and Michael Bloomfield.

Blues guitarists, from Blind Lemon Jefferson in the 1920s through Otis Rush and a few other musicians who matured in the 1960s, decisively influenced the way the instrument is used in rock. And rock in turn has influenced most of the blues guitarists of Otis Rush's generation. They tend to take longer guitar solos and to play more rocking, up-tempo material than they did in the 1950s, when they were just starting out and rock & roll was in its infancy.

But in a deeper sense, blues guitar and rock guitar are fundamentally different. The idea of "making the guitar talk" is integral to the black blues tradition. It is rooted in the pitch-tone languages and "talking drums" of West Africa and in the earliest Afro-American vocal and instrumental music, and it retained its importance in the primarily oral black culture of the South and Southwest, the original home of virtually every important bluesman. The great blues guitarists are gifted with an acute sensitivity to the finest nuances of pitch, the subtlest differences in the attack and tone and decay of every note. In most cases, they learned when they were children to listen carefully, to size up a stranger in a few seconds by the timbre and inflection in his voice. And they play the guitar the way they listen, with an ear for the minutest details of phrasing and touch and meaning. They are great guitarists not because they can play more notes per minute than lesser musicians or because of their ability to fashion fancy, flashing phrases, but because they have a surer command of the blues language.

Some rock guitarists seem to have understood and worked at mastering this linguistic aspect of the blues guitar tradition—Jimi Hendrix readily springs to mind. But for the most part, the techniques blues guitarists use to approximate vocal inflections function in rock as ornaments, or as what Hollywood calls "special effects." The finest rock improvisers understand that a solo can "tell a story." But in rock, the story tends to be a kind of rough outline, expressed through the overall shape and direction of the solo. There is little sense of the sort of painstakingly detailed, note-by-note storytelling one hears in the blues.

The quality of Otis Rush's storytelling on a given night depends partly on his mood and partly on how comfortable he is with his backup band. At Tramps, he has put together a tightly knit outfit that is powered by the superb drummer Charles Otis. Mr. Otis grew up in New Orleans and honed his art playing behind the seminal blues pianist Professor Longhair.

"Rush loves the band," said Terry Dunne, who books talent into Tramps and is a knowledgeable blues aficionado. "He was rehearsing them here for hours the other day, working up some new songs he's written, sounding just great."

Like so many of the most gifted bluesmen, Mr. Rush likes to travel alone, sometimes works with inexperienced backup bands, and rarely rehearses before an engagement, being content to teach new musicians

the fine points of his tunes in actual performances. And he seldom performs new, original material. The indications are that Mr. Rush will be at
or near his best in his current engagement at Tramps. And when he is in
peak form, he has a surer command of the blues language than probably
any other guitarist around today.

Noisy Rock Returns

THE NEW YORK TIMES | APRIL 21, 1985

"Turn off that racket," a generation of exasperated American parents demanded when rock & roll first invaded their living rooms in the mid-1950s. And to listeners who had been brought up on classical music, swing, and pop balladry, early rock & roll *was* a racket—howling distortion and feedback from the electric guitars, singing that sounded uncannily like the growls and chattering of wild animals, and, dominating everything else, the brutal pounding of the drums, the "big beat."

Fifties rock & roll no longer seems to pose a challenge to authority. Instrumental versions of songs that raised hackles thirty years ago are being piped into offices and elevators. But rock that has been as thoroughly domesticated as most fifties "oldies" has lost something essential to its nature—its shock value. Rock that is intended to be more than mere entertainment *thrives* on controversy and opposition, as performers on the music's cutting edge have always understood, from Little Richard to the Rolling Stones to the Sex Pistols. It is abrasive by birthright.

A few contemporary rock bands and performers are deliberately putting the racket back in rock & roll. For the most part, they record for independent labels and play in small clubs. Their music is a deliberate antidote to the burbling synthesizers, polite crooning, and polished studio gloss of today's well-fed pop mainstream. In fact, New York's Sonic Youth, Swans, and Live Skull (along with Australia's Nick Cave, the Fall in Britain, Einstürzende Neubaten in Germany, and others) are making the sort of music rock's early opponents must have feared most, the music of their nightmares. Guitarists wrench hair-raising screams and sputtering distortion from their instruments, drums and metal percussion clang and hammer like steam drills, vocalists growl and bellow.

Noise-music is at least as old as the Dada and Futurist movements of the early twentieth century and the pioneering electronic experiments of composers like Edgard Varèse. Punk rock at its most extreme was decidedly noisy, and in the late seventies and early eighties New York "no wave" bands like DNA and Mars took brutal, bone-shivering sonic assault to extremes. But extremes, like limits, pose a challenge that will sooner or later be tested, and right now a four-man band called Swans is making the most abrasive, viscerally unsettling music around.

The Swans songs on the recent album *Cop* and the new four-song EP *I Crawled* . . . plod along at funereal tempos. The guitarist Norman Westberg overlays a pounding backbeat with droning feedback and crackling distortion, and the vocalist Mike Gira groans and growls his tales of rampant violence and brutality. At first, Swans records sound like gorillas beating on pots and pans and muttering incoherently, accompanied by the clamor of a machine shop. Closer listening reveals differences in verse structure, texture, and mood that distinguish one song from another. The sounds may be radical, but they are being made by the traditional rock-group instrumentation of singer, guitar, bass, and drums, and poured into more or less conventional rock song structures.

Some listeners who are appalled by the way Swans sound (and even fans of other noise bands often find them tough going) are also bothered by the images of dominance and submission in Mike Gira's lyrics. But in the tradition of spiritually corrosive literature exemplified by Lautré-amont, Jean Genet, and Charles Bukowski, Mr. Gira's lyrics probe basic human cravings. Their message is that power of any kind ultimately brutalizes and dehumanizes those who wield it as well as those who submit to it. This isn't a pretty message, and Swans don't make pretty music. But music that aims to be an antidote to fear—"you degrade yourself when you hide your fear," Mr. Gira sings—has to be strong stuff. For some listeners, this one included, Swans provide a bracing jolt that no other music can deliver.

Sonic Youth's new album, *Bad Moon Rising*, also kicks up a fearsome noise, but its palette of sounds and colors is considerably more varied. The group's two guitarists, Thurston Moore and Lee Ranaldo, participated in some of the experimental guitar orchestras assembled by the minimalist composers Glenn Branca and Rhys Chatham, though their own music is closer to rock tradition in its use of song forms and backbeat. What the guitar minimalists and Sonic Youth share is an interest in the broadest possible range of sounds and textures that can be wrung from electric guitars. And underlying this exploratory bent is an interest in the basic parameters of sound itself, recalling the explorations of acoustical phenomena such as interference patterns and sum-and-difference tones by the innovative downtown composers La Monte Young and Phill Niblock.

When two sine waves are sounded at equal volume but at slightly different pitches, the result is a fluttering effect called acoustical beating. This sound, the most fundamental form of distortion, introduces the second side of *Bad Moon Rising* and reappears at the end, having been woven into and around the differing textures of four diversely patterned songs. The album's first side is also linked into a kind of suite, but here the unifying element is a harmonious droning of overtones, a basic consonance to match the second side's equally basic dissonance. These compositional ploys, and some rather arch lyrics, run the risk of seeming self-consciously arty. But the music's edgy intensity never lets up, and the players' precise control over their arsenal of textures and effects makes for consistently absorbing listening. Sonic Youth is making progressive rock in the best sense—music that's smart, daring, and transcendent.

The Sharrock Way of Knowledge

ROLLING STONE | SEPTEMBER 19, 1991

Ask the Ages (Axiom)
Sonny Sharrock

Faith Moves (CMP)
Sonny Sharrock and Nicky Skopelitis

If you think you've heard everything an electric guitar can do but the name Sonny Sharrock doesn't ring any bells, it's time for you to think again. Back in the days before jazz guitarists were cranking their amps up to eleven and before rock guitarists began acquiring jazz-based chops—before Hendrix, before Cream—the R&B–seasoned guitarist Sonny Sharrock was whipping up sonic thunderstorms in the company of Pharoah Sanders and other seminal free-jazz players.

One minute Sharrock would be quietly, rhythmically chording, like the doo-wop vocal-group guitarist he once was. Then, without warning, he'd burst into a paroxysm of six-string mayhem—thumb-picked bass runs rumbling like subways, seething distortion, glass-shattering tone clusters that sounded like someone was ripping the pickups out of the guitar without having bothered to unplug it from its overdriven amplifier. In the days when the Yardbirds' "Shapes of Things" seemed to be the cutting edge of electric-guitar music, Sharrock was a true visionary, in a class with nobody but himself.

Sharrock wasn't just "ahead of his time." Like a freight train roaring through a darkened station not just hours but *weeks* ahead of schedule, Sharrock was here and gone before anybody even knew he was coming. After a memorable series of albums with Pharoah Sanders and other jazzers and some powerful but quickly deleted solo albums on the French Byg label and Atlantic's short-lived Vortex subsidiary, Sharrock seemed to fade from view. Musicians talked about him, keeping his legend alive, but Sharrock himself was back home in upstate New York, playing local gigs and waiting for music to catch up with him.

During the early-eighties New York No Wave fracas, punk and noise guitarists—ranging from certain Captain Beefheart axemen to Richard Hell/Lou Reed sideman Robert Quine—began exploring some of the areas Sharrock had mapped out. With bands like the Voidoids, the Contortions, and Sonic Youth breaking down boundaries, Sharrock's time drew nearer. When bassist Bill Laswell emerged from that same downtown scene as a producer and bandleader to be reckoned with, one of his first priorities was finding Sonny Sharrock. Laswell and Sharrock first collaborated on records by Material, Laswell's floating stock company of a band. In 1985 a Laswell-produced solo album, *Guitar*, announced that Sharrock was back and burning. Last Exit—a Laswell-organized electronic free-noise band featuring Sharrock—recorded and toured Europe around the same time.

But these events were mere preludes to the one-two punch of *Ask the Ages* and *Faith Moves*, which display Sharrock's wild and wily wisdom in all its tumultuous glory. Of course, a player as stubbornly original as Sharrock would never have been content to remain static while the rest of the world caught up with him; his playing has evolved enormously. The bursts of wall-rattling shiver and clang have been augmented by an equally intense concentration on the purest, most liquid guitar tone and by a simple, stirring lyricism.

Ask the Ages, the first album released by producer Bill Laswell's Axiom label through a new distribution deal with Island, is a quartet record with minimal guitar overdubs. It finds Sharrock reunited with Pharoah Sanders, whose tongues-of-fire saxophone assaults have also been tempered with maturity. The rhythm section—young bassist Charnett Moffett and drum titan Elvin Jones—couldn't be better. If some classic free-flowing jazz album from the sixties had been recorded with the clarity and punch of today's rock, the result might have sounded something like this. But *Ask the Ages* sounds even more like four indestructible veterans getting together to raise the old spirits of rebellion while collectively lifting the music to a new plateau.

Faith Moves, Sharrock's collaboration with Laswell house guitarist and all-around stringed-instrument maven Nicky Skopelitis, is even better. The music is all made by Sharrock's Les Paul and Skopelitis's battery of guitars, basses, and other Western and non-Western instruments, with up to ten overdubs per track. The versatile Skopelitis mostly provides multilayered settings for Sharrock's free-spirited leads. Some of the music leans east, some leans west. One tune, "In the Flesh," takes a gut-simple metal-guitar riff and wrests more sheer music from it than the likes of AC/DC ever dreamed of (I *like* AC/DC, but genius is genius). "Venus" is a deeply felt reworking of a Pharoah Sanders tune Sharrock got his first crack at on Sanders's 1967 album *Tauhid*.

Ask the Ages ranges from sinuous guitar-and-sax chants to metal-twisting sonic collisions. But while nobody actually sings on *Faith Moves*, the entire *album* sings, its six-string overtones chiming harmoniously with the richness and emotional immediacy of a gospel choir. *Faith Moves* is the ideal introduction to Sonny Sharrock's idiosyncratic style and bedrock soul.

Sharrock's auspicious reemergence ought to have a nation of aspiring guitarists taking another look at their methods and means. Who wants to play faster than Eddie Van Halen or Steve Vai when you can say as much as they say in an entire solo with just one perfectly inflected note? Welcome back, Sonny. It's been a long time, but maybe that doesn't matter; *this* music is timeless.

Band of Susans: *Veil*

(Restless)

ROLLING STONE | SEPTEMBER 2, 1993

All hail the overdriven amp, the feedback-saturated guitar pickup, the hum of harmonic sustain, the clamorous collision of power chords in the heart of the sonic maelstrom. Let us bow our heads in the direction of New York City and pray for deliverance from mindless metal riffs and warmed-over grunge. Let us now praise Band of Susans.

BOS are a different kind of guitar band. Instead of locking themselves into lead and rhythm role-playing, the group's three guitarists collaborate in the shaping of a soaring sonic architecture, subsuming individual identities in a volatile but highly focused group aesthetic. As conceived by founding guitarist/singer/songwriter Robert Poss, the BOS sound involves equal parts guitar formalism and Stonesy swagger. But Poss and bassist/singer/songwriter Susan Stenger, despite their avant-garde backgrounds, seem to value group chemistry more than concept. In other words, this is a rock & roll band.

On *Veil*, their fifth album, Band of Susans deliver the songs as well as the sound. Tunes like "Mood Swing," "Not in This Life," "Trouble Spot," and the sublime "Blind" unfurl sharp, bold melodies over stick-in-your-head ensemble riffs. Ron Spitzer's drums kick and snap, and Stenger's bass lines provide melodic as well as rhythmic backbone. Guitarists Poss, Anne Husick, and Mark Lonergan are also developing a noisier, nastier, but still coherently thematic brand of collective improvisation, showcased in the instrumental rave "Trollbinders Theme." Mayhem and transcendence, sweetness and bite: The thought of what these people might accomplish with a more substantial recording budget is almost frightening.

Acknowledgments

Anthony DeCurtis and Augusta Palmer would like to thank their agent, Sarah Lazin, for her vision, her advice, and her dedication to this project. Without Sarah and her staff, this collection would never have been published. We are both deeply grateful to Jann Wenner for his generosity in allowing us to reprint Robert Palmer's work for *Rolling Stone*. Jann and *Rolling Stone* were crucial to Bob's early development as a critic, his later re-entry into freelance rock criticism in the late 1980s, and now in the preservation of his work. The editors who helped shape Robert Palmer's career are too numerous to list here, but we are very thankful for their belief in his writing and the refinements they made to his published work. We would like to thank David Chiu for his indefatigable work as a research assistant, assembling and retrieving the thousands of articles written by Robert Palmer. Thanks are also due to Scribner editor Brant Rumble and his able assistant Anna DeVries, who deftly guided this book into your hands.

In addition, Anthony DeCurtis would like to thank Augusta Palmer for entrusting him with her father's work. It was a privilege. DeCurtis's love and gratitude go to his wife, Alexandra MacDowell; his daughter Francesca, who was born as this book was taking shape; and his faithful Saint Bernard, Gracie, who shared his office virtually every moment of this book's creation. And deepest thanks to Bob, of course, who remains an inspiration: "Light upon light. Allah guides to his light whom he pleases."

Augusta Palmer would like to thank Anthony DeCurtis for the seriousness and sensitivity he has brought to editing this anthology of her father's work. She is deeply grateful that Anthony has provided the means for her daughter, Laila, and her son, Nicholas, to appreciate their grandfather's work. She would like to thank everyone who contributed funds toward her father's care during the last months of his life. She would like to acknowledge the major contributions of the women in her father's life who helped make this writing possible: JoBeth Briton-Palmer, Debra Rae Cohen, Harriett Tyson, Mary Branton, and Mary Katherine Alden. Martin Cassidy's assistance with reprint permissions was essential to this project's completion. She would like to thank her family—especially her grandmother Marguerite Palmer and her husband, Chris Arnold—for their support during the years it took to create this volume. Finally, she is immensely grateful for the chance to read the work her father left behind, the chance to know him, and the immense gift he gave her when he opened her ears to the world of music that surrounds us.

Permissions

INDEX